Textual Formations
and Reformations

Textual Formations and Reformations

Edited by

Laurie E. Maguire
and Thomas L. Berger

DELAWARE

Newark: University of Delaware Press
London: Associated University Presses

Associated University Presses
440 Forsgate Drive
Cranbury, NJ 08512

Associated University Presses
16 Barter Street
London WC1A 2AH, England

Associated University Presses
P.O. Box 338, Port Credit
Mississauga, Ontario
Canada L5G 4L8

The paper used in this publication meets the requirements of the American National Standard for Permanence of Paper for Printed Library Materials Z39.48-1984.

Library of Congress Cataloging-in-Publication Data

Textual Formations and reformations / edited by Laurie E. Maguire and
Thomas L. Berger.
   p.   cm.
   Includes bibliographical references and index.
   ISBN 0-87413-655-5 (alk. paper)
   1. English literature—Early modern, 1500–1700—Criticism.
Textual. 2. Shakespeare, William, 1564–1616—Criticism, Textual.
3. Transmission of texts—History—16th century. 4. Transmission of
texts—History—17th century. 5. Renaissance—England.
I. Maguire, Laurie E. II. Berger, Thomas L.
PR418.T48T49   1998
820.9'003—dc21
                                        97-38849
                                          CIP

PRINTED IN THE UNITED STATES OF AMERICA

For George Walton Williams

Contents

List of Abbreviations

AEB	*Analytical and Enumerative Bibliography*
DNB	*Dictionary of National Biography*
ELH	*English Literary History*
ELR	*English Literary Renaissance*
HLQ	*Huntington Library Quarterly*
JEGP	*Journal of English and Germanic Philology*
MaRDiE	*Medieval and Renaissance Drama in England*
MLQ	*Modern Language Quarterly*
MLR	*Modern Language Review*
N&Q	*Notes and Queries*
PBA	*Proceedings of the British Academy*
PMLA	*Publications of the Modern Languages Association*
RD	*Renaissance Drama*
RES	*Review of English Studies*
SB	*Studies in Bibliography*
SQ	*Shakespeare Quarterly*
TLN	Through Line Numbering
TLS	*Times Literary Supplement*

Introduction

LAURIE E. MAGUIRE

As part of his process of self-discovery, Lear enters the uninhabited and untamed heath. He moves from the center of the map (the safe and verdant "champains riched" and "wide-skirted meads" represented cartographically on stage in 1.1) to the borders, the areas of the map that traditionally feature cartoons of Aeolian faces blowing unfriendly winds. On the heath Lear encounters the wilds of the map's margins firsthand, addressing the storm in anthropomorphic terms clearly indebted to cartographic iconography: "Blow winds and crack your cheeks. Rage, blow! You cataracts and hurricanoes."[1]

This dialectic between the territorial center and its borders, and the subsequent displacement of the center, encapsulates the history of early modern mapmaking, with its move from a civilized land mass (Jerusalem) at the center of the medieval world map to a wild ocean (the Atlantic) at the center of the Renaissance's. Because the medieval *mappae mundi* depict the world symbolically, Jerusalem is at the center of the world map. The East, the direction of paradise, is at the top; the West consequently appears at the bottom, North at the right, and South at the left.[2] That this representational model is not a given but a convention can be seen from the change of perspective in Renaissance mapmaking. Abraham Ortelius's influential *Theatrum Orbis Terrarum* appeared in 1570. Partly to incorporate the discovery of North America, the center of the Ortelian world map depicts not a land mass but an ocean. Viewers/readers enter the map only to find themselves literally "at sea"; forced to voyage figuratively, the eye and the mind move back and forth, between America on the left and Asia on the right.[3] The Ortelian map is no less a convention than its medieval predecessor, for, as John Gillies reminds us, the positions of America and Asia could easily have been reversed. The significant point, as Gillies observes, is that medieval stasis has been replaced by restlessness, the known by the unknown. In a proleptically postmodern fashion, the center has been displaced. "Localisation" has given way to "open space."[4]

Early modern cartographic history illustrates how definitions of center reflect perspective and preference rather than (immutable) fact. For our purposes it provides a convenient metaphor for the change in perspective of late-twentieth-century Shakespeare scholarship, one that reenacts the cartographic move from center to margin, from local and fixed to open and indeterminate. It is no accident that within the lifetimes of this volume's editors and contributors the political, social, economic, cultural, and ideological maps of the world have been redrawn and reconfigured several times. The critical position is more complex, however, because postmodern Shakespeare criticism involves a paradoxical move, simultaneously centrifugal and centripetal. Shakespeare criticism, in the last twenty years, has both broadened and narrowed its energies, expanding and contracting its boundaries. The many schools that constitute Shakespeare criticism today, and that cover an enormous range of social and political issues, would be foreign territory to the New Critics. There is no area of personal, social, or political history, it seems, that cannot now be brought to bear on Renaissance drama.[5] The paradox is that this move outward has been accompanied by a move inward, for few critics are accomplished in all the new branches of Shakespeare study; consequently one identifies oneself with an approach to the territory (feminist, Marxist) rather than with the territory itself (the author, the period, the genre or subgenre).

Collections of essays have inevitably changed their nature to embrace this paradox of simultaneous expansion and contraction. The proliferation of collections is itself a response to this change of perspective. A new topic or approach requires consolidated support in print. A dozen contributors to one volume will produce a book on the relevant topic more rapidly than can a single author. In the 1980s feminist collections appeared with essays on a wide range of topics: Shakespeare (*Coriolanus*), female autobiography, Elizabeth I's self-presentation, Tuscan nuns, the Italian inquisitions, John Foxe, and the countess of Pembroke.[6] New Historicism adopted a similarly broad model, with collections ranging from *Renaissance Historicism* to *Staging the Renaissance*.[7] In a recent volume on women and race, there seem to be no boundaries of the topic: the essays cover drama, poetry and prose from several centuries, South American and Indian women's history, colonial and postcolonial theory.[8] Thus, Shakespeare criticism is both more and less localized. It is divided into identifiable compartments, but the compartments themselves are more adventurous. They, and the collections of essays to which they give rise, are "extravagant" in the etymologically geographic sense—they travel outside the usual confines. Critical schools and the collections of critical essays that represent them no longer set a bourn how far to be explored. They seek instead "new heaven, new earth."

Bibliography has not yet followed the example of Renaissance cartography or recent scholarly "isms" in decentering, at least where collections of essays are concerned. Eschewing the new expansionist trend in anthologies, textual study adheres safely and conservatively to traditional narrow subjects of organization: the play *(King Lear, Sir Thomas More, Hamlet)*, or the author *(Shakespeare Reshaped)*.[9] This is vexing in that currently some of the most interesting interdisciplinary work revolves around textual study. Not simply about compositor analysis, watermarks, and editing, textual study is also about ideology, politics, feminism, theory, literary criticism, directing. More than mere appendices to textual work, these fields are crucial to textual study, just as textual study is crucial to them. But while critical alliances are forming and performing fruitfully everywhere (Marxist-feminist, lesbian-theatrical), textual study for the most part is still viewed as a self-contained subject. Textual critics have done much to foster this image, and other disciplines have been content to believe the fiction. Like all fledgling powers, political or critical, textual criticism created its identity and defined its territory through a ritual of exclusion, the exclusion of the other. But no discipline is an island, and textual study yields some of its most interesting material when approached from apparently nontextual angles.

With essays dealing with sixteenth- and twentieth-century history, feminism, Shakespeare, the Apocrypha, literary criticism, modern staging, and Renaissance women writers, this volume is more inclusive than usual with anthologies of textual criticism. Such inclusivity sheds new light on traditional topics while implicitly illustrating the territorial insularity of early-twentieth-century textual criticism, a territoriality unchallenged by two world wars. Despite their variety in subject matter, however, the essays are linked by two crucial features: interrogative methodology and readability. Like all good scholarship, the New Bibliography of Pollard, Greg, and McKerrow asked questions. But, as our contributors realize, the answer one receives depends largely upon the question one poses. By reformulating questions this volume tackles textual issues in a new light. The second link among the essays, readability, also stems from a reaction to the New Bibliography. New Bibliographical writing is erratically brilliant and flawed in its contents, but its style is consistent: prosaic and straightforward, it eschews extended metaphor or creative play. One of the most welcome advances in textual criticism in the last twenty years has been its readability. However controversial the metaphors of Gary Taylor (one thinks of his infamous "editors as the pimps of discourse") or the parodic manner of Randall McLeod, the work of these scholars has undeniable literary interest: it is an accessible and enjoyable read.[10] Selected for their stylistic verve as well as for their literary and textual acumen, the thirteen contributions to this volume promise the reader pleasure and profundity.

❀

Part 1 begins by revisiting the New Bibliography. Joseph Loewenstein ("Authentic Reproductions") examines the origin of the New Bibliographical project in the work of Sidney Lee. Moreover, he looks at what else was happening of relevance when the founding New Bibliographers were young: the development of sound recording, the flux in copyright laws, the rise of the rare-book trade. In "Touring and the Construction of Shakespeare Textual Criticism" Paul Werstine exposes with devastating clarity a fundamental anomaly in twentieth-century textual criticism: the equation of putative memorially reconstructed texts with provincial performance. For Pollard and Wilson (originators of the abridged-adapted-provincial-playbook theory)[11] the provincial text was rewritten for publication to bring it into line with the revised London text; thus it is the nonextant text's "badness" that links it to the provinces. When Madeleine Doran subsequently classified *1 Contention* and *The True Tragedy of Richard Duke of York* as "bad quartos" but argued for their theatrical goodness, she, "unwittingly no doubt, destroyed the basis for associating them with provincial performance, or with any performance at all." Nonetheless, as Werstine shows, the association is deeply, if illogically, entrenched in textual criticism.

Greg's *Two Elizabethan Stage Abridgements* is primarily responsible for ossifying "bad quarto" theory into irrefragable truth. Cited approvingly (and apparently unquestioningly) by critics as diverse as H. C. Hart, Kathleen O. Irace, and Brian Vickers,[12] *Two Elizabethan Stage Abridgements* is, as Michael Warren argues, "one of the major monuments of twentieth-century scholarship." Warren's essay, "Greene's *Orlando*: W. W. Greg Furioso," shows how this monument is in need of demolition. Concentrating on one aspect of Greg's approach, his sense of theater, Warren argues for coherent theatrical practice where Greg saw only textual corruption.

Part 2, Interrogatives, broadens the textual picture by reformulating some key questions of twentieth-century textual criticism. In "The Monsters and the Textual Critics" Tom Davis draws on bibliography, forensic science, interpretive criticism, and "real life" to show that textual criticism and literary criticism are identical activities: both are grounded in judgment and interpretation. Acknowledgment of this should prevent the chicane whereby textual criticism is taken as "true" whereas "a literary critical reading is only an interpretation." In a revised version of an essay first published in *Shakespeare Jahrbuch* Barbara Mowat deals with "the problem of Shakespeare texts(s)." Since Rowe's edition of 1709, the textual problem in Shakespeare has been characterized as one of lost manuscripts; inferring the quiddities of the lost MS behind a printed text has been a sine qua non of New Bibliography. Drawing on recent manuscript studies of authors as diverse as Katherine Phillips and John Donne, Mowat shows, surprisingly, that the existence of authorial manuscripts does not make textual work any easier or clearer. "There has been from the beginning an editorial sacralizing of lost manuscripts that has made us frame the problem of Shakespeare's texts incorrectly," Mowat argues, before showing how textual indeterminacy has freed up recent Shakespearean criticism rather than restricting it. We are grateful to *Shakespeare Jahrbuch* for permission to reprint this essay.

A. R. Braunmuller's "How farre is't call'd to Soris? or, Where was Mr. Hobbs when Charles II died?" opens with a stunning example of the confusion of internal and external evidence in editorial work on Dryden before analyzing an analogous conflict in *Macbeth:* editorial treatment of the geographic place name Soris/Forres versus treatment of the personal name Sinel/Finel. Wondering if editorial differences arise "because place-names are more familiar to editors and modern readers than the names of eleventh-century Scottish noblemen," Braunmuller poses a series of stimulating (and frustrated) questions about onomastic criteria, concepts of intelligibility, editorial consistency, and anachronistic commentary. The apocryphal work *The London Prodigal* is the subject of "Shakespeare's Most Neglected Play." Richard Proudfoot's incisive analysis avoids the overemphasized issue of authorship attribution. Proudfoot muses: "There can be few other plays of which it has been seriously proposed that they were written by Ben Jonson, John Marston, Thomas Dekker, Michael Drayton, Thomas Middleton, George Wilkins, and John Fletcher. Either the evidence is more than usually slippery, the attempts at attribution are more than usually lacking in rigor, or the question of authorship is the wrong question to address to this play." Instead Proudfoot focuses on key critical aspects of the play, although it is a tribute to his modesty (or irony) that he manages to answer the one question he professes to ignore.

The contributors to part 3, Contexts, argue for enriched critical understanding through historical relocations of a text. Since its critical recovery by feminist scholars in the 1980s, Elizabeth Cary's *The Tragedy of Mariam* has enjoyed unprecedented attention. Written sometime between 1602 and 1609, the play was first published in 1613. In "Marriage and Divorce in 1613" Jeanne Addison Roberts examines other printed material from 1613, as well as court politics of the time; she illustrates *Mariam*'s relevance to the ongoing debate about matrimony that reached new heights with Frances Howard's notorious separation from her husband, the earl of Essex, and her second marriage to James's favorite, Robert Carr. Valerie Wayne focuses on editorial treatment of the main female character, Jane, in Middleton's *A Trick to Catch the Old One*, in her wide-ranging analysis of "the sexual politics of textual transmission." Jane accuses Walkadine Hoard of rape. "Why has nobody heard her, in all this time?" asks Wayne. "The word and her accusation have never been glossed by any of the fifteen editors of this play. . . . [T]he inattention granted to this concern in the play is far too like the centuries of silence that have greeted women's charges of sexual assault in nonfictional homes and streets and public arenas." Wayne redresses the editorial balance with a detailed legal account of rape and sexual slander in the early modern period. David Scott Kastan also fills in historical background as he looks at the political life and religious beliefs of Falstaff's onomastic original, Sir John Oldcastle. Kastan then analyzes the decision by the Oxford editors to name the fat knight of Shakespeare's *Henry IV* plays "Oldcastle," arguing that, since "Oldcastle" never appears in any of the Shakespeare quartos or folios, the Oxford decision restores a "reading" that was never a "reading" at all.

In part 4, Readings, three critics combine theatrical and textual skills to offer interpretive insights into specific plays. Although he stresses that his is "precriticism," offering building blocks for others, Charles B. Lower's analysis of nomenclature ("Character Identifications in Two Folio Plays, *Coriolanus* and *All's Well:* A Theater Perspective") provides some surprising insights into characters' (and critics') attitudes. What are we to make of the "fact" that the king in *Hamlet* is not given the name "Claudius" anywhere in the dialogue of Q1, Q2, or F? What is our attitude to a count who calls his wife "her" and "she" rather than "Helen," or to a critic who calls this count "Bertram" rather than "Count Rossillion"? What should an editor do to bring a reader's reading experience into line with an audience's auditory experience? In asking such questions Lower highlights an important area of editorial neglect.

Stephen Miller also highlights editorial neglect in "*The Taming of a Shrew* and the Theories," examining the way in which textual critics pay attention primarily to the areas of *A Shrew* that have parallels in *The Shrew*; the strikingly divergent subplot receives scant attention. Miller attributes this neglect to a contradiction in "bad quarto" theory: a "bad quarto" must be different but it must not be too different. Thus the *similar* differences (the taming plot) receive attention whereas the more *different* differences (the subplot) do not. Miller then turns to the subplot in *A Shrew*, arguing for its coherent and deliberate adaptation of *The Shrew*'s complicated Italianate triple-disguise subplot; the adapter responsible for *A Shrew* creates a more conventional rank-obsessed comedy, "the sort of material currently in demand in popular romantic comedies." The derivative *A Shrew* is not "merely" derivative but a conscious critical response to *The Shrew*, as Miller's subtitle explains: "[T]hough this be badness, yet there is method in't." Ralph Cohen also finds structural problems in *The Shrew*'s subplot and recounts how he coped with them when directing the play ("Looking for Cousin Ferdinand"). Turning to the Folio text for help, and eschewing editorial additions from the eighteenth to the twentieth centuries, Cohen describes how the Folio text helped solve problems of clarity, speed, and choreography.

❧

David R. Carlson cast his critical eye over all the essays at an early stage and offered us perceptive textual commentary, sound advice, and much wisdom, as did the anonymous reader for the University of Delaware Press. We are grateful to both. We are in even greater debt to the scholar to whom this volume is dedicated. George Walton Williams was trained by Fredson Bowers at the University of Virginia; his textual interests and expertise range from the drama of the English Renaissance to the poetry of Richard Crashaw, to Episcopalian church history in Colonial America, to the Society for the Propagation of Christian Knowledge, to children's literature. To the editors of this volume, and many of the essayists in it, he has been generous with his time, his energy, his textual expertise, and, most of all, his boundless and unqualified friendship.

NOTES

1. There is a rich and illuminating critical literature on maps. My summary in these paragraphs is heavily indebted to Leo Bagrow, *History of Cartography: Revised and Enlarged by R. A. Skelton* (London: Watts and Co., 1964); Lloyd A. Brown, *The Story of Maps* (London: Cresset Press, 1951); G. R. Crone, *Maps and their Makers: An Introduction to the History of Cartography* (London: Hutchinson's University Library, 1953); John Gillies, *Shakespeare and the Geography of Difference* (Cambridge: Cambridge University Press, 1994); J. B. Harley and David Woodward, *The History of Cartography*, vol. 1 (Chicago and London: University of Chicago Press, 1987); Miriam Moore, "Circumscribing the East: Cartography and the Body in *Othello*," paper presented to the seminar on Shakespeare and Graphic Arts, chaired by John Astington, at the annual meeting of the SAA, 1994; Arthur H. Robinson and Barbara Bartz Retchenik, *The Nature of Maps* (Chicago: University of Chicago Press, 1976); Rodney W. Shirley, *The Mapping of the World: Early Printed World Maps, 1472–1700* (London: Holland Press, 1987). For the point about *King Lear* I am indebted to Jodi Mikalachki (personal communication).

2. These "TO" maps receive their descriptive epithet from the T-shaped bodies of water that trisect the map's O-shaped world. For examples see the woodcut in Isidore of Seville, *Etymologies* (Augsburg, 1472); the Hereford World Map, c. 1280, Hereford Cathedral Library; the "Psalter" map, reproduced in Gillies, *Shakespeare and the Geography of Difference*.

3. See Gillies, *Shakespeare and the Geography of Difference*, 62.

4. The Foucauldian terminology comes from Gillies, *Shakespeare and the Geography of Difference*, 62.

5. In his presidential speech to the Shakespeare Association of America in 1991 Michael Warren spoke only partly in jest when he reminded his audience that Shakespeare studies did not yet have a responsible vegetarian or ecological criticism. Both these areas have since been represented in conference papers.

6. These examples come from Mary Beth Rose's *Women in the Middle Ages and the Renaissance* (Syracuse, N.Y.: Syracuse University Press, 1986), but countless other feminist collections subsequently observed the same broad coverage.

7. *Renaissance Historicism (Essays from ELR)*, ed. Arthur Kinney and Dan Collins (Amherst: University of Massachusetts Press, 1987); *Staging the Renaissance*, ed. David Scott Kastan and Peter Stallybrass (New York and London: Routledge, 1991).

8. *Women, "Race," and Writing in the Early Modern Period*, ed. Margo Hendricks and Patricia Parker (London and New York: Routledge, 1994).

9. See *The Division of the Kingdoms*, ed. Gary Taylor and Michael Warren (Oxford: Oxford University Press, 1983); *Shakespeare and "Sir Thomas More": Essays on the Play and its Shakespearian Interest,* ed. T. H. Howard-Hill (Cambridge: Cambridge University Press, 1989); *The "Hamlet" First Published (Q1 1603),* ed. Thomas Clayton (Newark: University of Delaware Press, 1992).

10. Tom Berger and I are sorry that we were unable to include in this volume articles by these scholars that were already published and readily accessible, and we are happy to take this opportunity to thank Randall McLeod and Gary Taylor for their grace and generosity as we prepared this collection.

11. For use of the term "playbook" instead of the more recent and misleading "promptbook," see William B. Long, *Cooperative Ventures: English Manuscript Playbooks, 1590–1635* (forthcoming).

12. See H. C. Hart, *Stolne and Surreptitious Copies* (Melbourne: Melbourne University Press, 1942); Kathleen O. Irace, *Reforming the "Bad" Quartos: Performance and Provenance of Six Shakespearean First Editions* (Newark: University of Delaware Press, 1994); and Brian Vickers, "*Hamlet* by Dogberry," *TLS,* 24 December 1993, 5–6.

Textual Formations
and Reformations

Part I:
Narratives and the New Bibliography

1

Authentic Reproductions:
The Material Origins of the New Bibliography

JOSEPH F. LOEWENSTEIN

> The time has now come when the English Printer and the English Pub-
> lisher must take their due places in the national estimation. Hitherto the
> Author has had it all his own way.
> —Edward Arber, *A Transcript of the Registers of the
> Company of the Stationers of London, 1554–1640*

Since general reflections on the construction of authorship, Foucauldian in
inspiration, have caught and held the attention of literary critics over the
past decade or so, I hope that an account of the modern (early-twentieth-
century) construction of Shakespeare-in-the-text might hold some interest,
and even might stimulate and guide a reflection on our own postmodern
construction of that authorial textuality. I have a complicated account to
offer—complicated, but not really very subtle—and I should say at the
outset that although avarice, envy, perhaps anti-Semitism, certainly chauvinism, forgery, the hoarding instinct, and sound recording (the usual suspects)
seem to me to have been determining for modern scientific bibliography in
the first decades of this century, the work of its greatest scholars (particularly the work of W. W. Greg) seems to me to have been serious, subtle, and
interesting: it's not a scholarly tradition to which I'd feel comfortable con-
descending. It does seem plausible to consider what this early bibliographical
and editorial revolution might suggest about the motives of our own inno-
vations.

In 1909, the Berne Convention of 1886, providing for international
copyright protection, was revised in Berlin.[1] In order to retain its place in a
growing international marketplace in intellectual property, Britain acceded
to the revision.[2] The British capitulation, confirmed in the Copyright Act of
1911, radically transformed English copyright law. The Berlin revision fixed

the period of copyright protection at the term of the author's life and fifty years after his or her death, thus obviating the regulatory difficulties in copyright systems in which the term of copyright is figured from the date of publication. This was a subtle assault on English ways, since it brought to an end the vehement debate within British law on the appropriate term of copyright, imposing a jurisprudential conclusion from without.

Profuse and incommensurable international laws were not the only stimuli to simplification. The pressure to simplify came from within Britain as well as from without. Thus the unsigned article on copyright in the famous eleventh edition of the *Encyclopedia Britannica* (1910–11) records with obvious perplexity the then current state of legal affairs:

> To sum up the position of artistic copyright in 1909, we find five British acts, three dealing with engraving, one with sculpture, and one with painting, drawing and photography, and between them very little relation. We have three terms of duration of copyright—28 years for engraving, 14 for sculpture, with a second 14 if the artist be alive at the end of the first, life and 7 years for painting, drawing or photography. There are two different relations of the artist to his copyright. . . . The engraver and the sculptor are not required to register; but the author's name, and the date of putting forth or publishing, must appear on his work. The painter cannot protect his copyright without registration, but this registration as it is now required is merely a pitfall for the unwary. Designed to give the public information as to the ownership and duration of copyrights, the uncertainty of its operation results in the prevention of information on these very points.[3]

The issue of what is here called "registration" points to the most obviously revolutionary aspect of the Copyright Act: the etiology of copyright now legally mandated in Berlin. According to the new principles articulated there—in deferential accord with the principles of the Berlin Convention— an author's rights arose from the act of creation itself. This may seem unexceptionable, but in fact it entails a dismissal of very old institutional arrangements in Britain. Up until the Copyright Act of 1911, all suits for infringement of copyright depended upon the procedure mentioned above, registration, which originates in the internal regulatory procedures devised by the Stationers' Company in the sixteenth century. Thus the law, the political structure, of literary property had long been organized around procedures essentially industrial. By canceling the necessity of registration, the Copyright Act, in accordance with the Berlin agreement, broke with tradition and reorganized the legal foundations of copyright.[4]

The Berlin Convention provided the occasion for a wholesale simplification of the British law of intellectual property, and mainly by means of a theoretical bracketing, a willed forgetting, of manufacture and the market.

The reconstituted copyright law protects authorial creativity by offering a statutory hedge against industrial concerns around the author's (somewhat mystified) creative act.[5] The act of 1911 consolidated all the various forms of copyright within a single text and framed those rights in such a way that the complex realities of publishing became, in effect, ancillary to copyright law.[6] The *Encyclopedia Britannica* reviewed the new law with composed relief: "The sensible basis on which the new bill was framed, and the authority it represented, commended it . . ."

With relief, and with sober caution: ". . . commended it, in spite of many controversial points." Radical and simple as it was, the act of 1911 still had the feel of the provisional. And no wonder: during the preceding two decades the marketplace for intellectual property had been an unruly one, partly because of new forms of unfair competition, partly because of pressure on the patent system, but largely because of new developments in what we now call "the media."[7] The proliferation of phonographic recording and the development of the pianola provoked a rethinking of the landscape of intellectual property similar to the rethinking that had attended upon the invention of photography.[8] Such new apparatuses for sound reproduction blurred already contested boundaries between musical text and musical performance, and between artisanal and mechanical production. The legal difficulties presented by the new technology were thrown into relief by a 1908 case brought in America: the plaintiff, a music publisher, alleged infringement of copyright when two songs were transcribed on piano rolls.[9] The more fully consequential problem of phonographic reproduction led to the articulation of the so-called neighboring or mechanical rights. In 1910, the parliamentary committee that was charged with digesting the Berlin revisions in order to draft the 1911 legislation recognized that the new medium of "publication" could not easily be subsumed within existing legal structures. The committee therefore recommended the formation of a Mechanical Copyright Licences Company to protect composers' rights in mechanical reproduction. This was obviously not a simplification, but it did secure, if only temporarily, a remarkable comprehensiveness in the face of burgeoning disseminative technology. Technological innovation had transformed a situation of legal *complexity* into a situation of institutional—in this case, legal—*crisis*. The proliferation of forms of reproduction was one of the motives for attempting to found the law of intellectual property on creative origination rather than on material manufacture.

Perhaps the most important effect of the Berlin revision was that it routed the response to new technology to Parliament and not to the courts; the response was to be by statutory intervention in the law and not by interpretive extension of it. A key feature in the emergence of parliamentary democracy, the displacement of common law by statute, is characteristic of legal developments since the mid-nineteenth century. This displacement effects a partial erasure of the past from the code of law; it secures an enfeebling of memory. The past subsided: as the Parliamentary Committee on Copyright was assimilating the Berne Convention, W. A. Copinger, the greatest authority on Anglo-American copyright law, was dying.

Copinger was not only the author of the standard textbook on copyright, but also the founder, in 1892, of the Bibliographical Society.[10] If the Copyright Act of 1911 made an antiquarian curiosity of the Stationers' Register and thereby quite literally closed a book on the history of literary culture, Copinger's colleagues at the Bibliographical Society were busily leafing through its pages, and had been doing so for nearly a decade. The Bibliographical Society was on a campaign against selective memory. In 1903, with Sidney Lee's 1902 facsimile of the First Folio under review, W. W. Greg pronounced not only on Lee's ignorance of the regulation of the Tudor and Stuart book trade, but on the historiographical amateurishness of virtually all professed literary historians; as if Copinger were setting his historiographical agenda, Greg remarks: "With regard to the old copyright regulations, it should be frankly confessed that we know very little about them."[11] Greg's mentor and student, A. W. Pollard, rose to the challenge of this review in his *Shakespeare Folios and Quartos* (1909) by attempting to specify the various property rights haunting Renaissance dramatic manuscripts, performances, and printed texts.[12] Together, Greg and Pollard made it their larger project to clarify the history of copyright, of stationers' registration, of printing, and of publishing, even as that history was being wiped from the practice of the law.[13] To sum up the conjunctural paradox: in 1909, the Berlin revision of the Berne Convention represented literary culture, for the purposes of law, as a vacuous space with author and a book-buying public at its poles, and with the book as a thin material line of communication between them; in 1909, *Shakespeare Folios and Quartos* represented literary culture as a space thick with books, with scribes and printers, guildhalls and print shops and bookstalls, proclamations and regulations, actors and acting companies, booksellers and book-buyers, a crowded historical field within which one might hope to discern conventions and recurrences and so bring into focus the historically specific lineaments of author and literary work—two starkly different representations of literary culture, but both, I think, responsive to the same conceptual-regulatory crisis, the revolution in reproductive technologies.

It would be easy enough to situate the New Bibliography in a tradition of Shakespearean editing, as McKerrow does in his 1933 British Academy lecture, or in a tradition of nineteenth-century classical editing, as Greg does in his 1945 retrospective for the Bibliographical Society.[14] Indeed, it would be accurate to describe the central project of what we call the New Bibliography as "the disciplined reconstruction of manuscript copy-texts for printed books," a bibliographical project of uncertain Newness. When Greg formulated his "Principles of Emendation in Shakespeare" in 1928, he summarized two decades of practice in the editing of Elizabethan texts and seventy years of classical editing with the simple dictum, "No emendation can or ought to be considered *in vacuo*, but criticism must always proceed in relation to what we know, or what we surmise, respecting the history of the text."[15] It was the crucial work of the great triumvirate—Pollard, McKerrow, and Greg—to tease out the full implications of the phrase "history of the text" by an analytic multiplication of the possible sources of textual variation informed by concentrated attention to the mechanics of printing (McKerrow's specialty) and to the history of the book trade (the centers of interest for Pollard and Greg). It is certainly true that Pollard, who had lived on the same staircase as Housman during his Oxford years, spent the first phase of his scholarly career as an editor of medieval texts (McKerrow, similarly, began with an edition, still reliable, of Thomas Nashe), but Pollard and McKerrow began to distinguish themselves when they shifted their attention to the industrial regularities and regulations that determine the printed text.[16] Shakespeareans understandably locate the New Bibliography in the history of Shakespeare reception at the end of a tradition of enthusiastic, but opportunistic, emendation, but it would be more illuminating to describe the New Bibliography as a research program in industrial history.

But not just any industrial history. I have been suggesting that a new information technology and a legal crisis that that technology exacerbated were somehow determining for twentieth-century bibliographical scholarship, that problems in modern intellectual property somehow motivate research into early modern information technologies and early modern intellectual property. Pollard's *Shakespeare Folios and Quartos* is now remembered as the first work in which the crucial distinction between what we now call the good and bad quartos was proposed, but for Pollard drawing that distinction was merely a stage in a more complex argument that linked textual "purity" with industrial regularity: in his words, "Finding, as we do, that quartos which have good texts and agree with the First Folio are entered regularly in the Stationers' Registers, and that quartos which have bad texts, not agreeing at all with the First Folio, are entered in the Stationers' Register either irregularly or not at all, we are surely justified in

arguing . . . that there is some causal relation at work which connects a good
text with regular entry prior to publication in the Stationers' Register."[17]
The idealized "good" text may be among the least egregious of the lapses
here; *many* aspects of Pollard's argument are wrong. However inaccurate,
Pollard's formulation is the founding myth of the New Bibliography, what
we might call Copinger's dream—that textual integrity and regulated intellectual property are somehow mutually entailed: in this dream the choice
of "best text" and the location of intellectual property rights are identical
labors. The dream was a recurrent one. Confirmed in an historiographic
project that had enveloped all editorial motives, Pollard began his Sandars
Lectures of 1915 with an echo of Greg's 1903 review of Lee: "Legal writers on English copyright have not shown much interest in the steps by
which the conception of literary property was gradually built up." One
year later, the revised lectures, Pollard's reconstructions of the legal history that Parliament had blotted in 1909, were published as *Shakespeare's
Fight with the Pirates and the Problem of the Transmission of his Text.*[18]

I emphasize Pollard's idée fixe in order to remark the attunement of the
New Bibliography to disturbances in contemporary legal culture. But
Pollard's interest in printing *history* and specifically his interest in literary
property must be given a plural etiology: to attend more closely to his professional biography will be to reveal other strata in the archaeology of New
Bibliographical knowledge. When Pollard became secretary of the Bibliographical Society in 1893, a year after it was founded, the society included
a loose coalition of scholars, librarians, and booksellers, but its founding
members were men like Copinger and A. H. Huth.[19] They were collectors:
Huth, the first secretary of the Society, had amassed one of the most important of late-nineteenth-century collections. Acquisition was as important a
context for New Bibliographical practice as was the editorial tradition.[20]
One reason why bibliography was in flux at the turn of this century is that
the market in rare books was changing drastically.

According to John Carter, "the overriding importance attached to chro-
nological priority—first edition, first issue, etc.—as a criterion of the interest of a book . . . is actually of quite modern development, for the average
nineteenth-century collector was as much interested in the finest-looking
or the best-edited edition as in the first."[21] At the turn of the century, however, purely aesthetic criteria were giving way among bibliophile collectors.
This apparently antiquarian turn seems to complement the development of
historiographic editing, but the appearance is misleading. The emphasis on
priority may be best explained in economic terms, as the rationalization of
an older rare-book market in which value had been subject to no calculus
susceptible to simple codification. This is an oddly democratic development, an appreciable, if partial, solvent to the control over market values

exerted by eminent, often aristocratic, collectors. Whatever its scholarly utility, modern scientific bibliography regularizes, and even deliberately enlarges, the bibliophile market. The founding of such institutions as the Browning, Ruskin, Wordsworth, and Shelley societies and the proliferation of enumerative bibliographies of modern authors, both phenomena of the 1870s and '80s, fostered new areas of collecting: the rare-book market expanded, and the bibliographies managed that expansion by establishing degrees of rarity, the essential criteria of value in this market.[22] If, as William Roberts remarked in 1894, "the book market [is] itself a stock exchange in miniature," late-nineteenth-century bibliographers were providing investment profiles.[23]

The evolution of the Bibliographical Society tellingly registers the antiquarian turn in bibliophile practice. Greg's 1945 retrospective shudders over the Society's early interest in what he calls "embellishment," that is, in those sites of aesthetic value—bindings, illustrations, type ornaments—that had been the concern of older collectors.[24] But the Society quickly settled into a decade dominated by incunabular research, that is, into books of irreducible priority.[25] In a 1903 letter to *The Library,* a shrewd and cantankerous borough librarian, J. D. Brown, raised a fuss over the prevailing character of research enshrined in the Bibliographical Society:

> It may be safely said that modern bibliography is exactly the same old egotistical hobby which it was a hundred years ago, when it became a fad for rich collectors. . . . We have elaborate lists of the incunabula arranged in the order of the authors' names; then someone comes along and rearranges these lists under the names of towns, and the names of printers. Not satisfied with this, another group of workers devote themselves to the incunabula contained in particular libraries, and then comes the chronological order crank.[26]

Brown is particularly infuriated by the bibliographical interest in blank leaves: he notes that under the influence of the bibliographer the absence of some key blank leaf ruins a book's market value.[27] Brown is an operophile, not a bibliophile: what offends him is the displacement of value from what literary historians used to mean by "the text." He concludes his intemperate but not implausible diatribe by saying, "In short, the modern bibliographer is a kind of hack for the second-hand bookseller and book collector."[28]

Brown was right, I think, though he had a hard time getting a hearing. There is no doubt that Pollard took the attack seriously—he made sure that his response was published as a companion piece to Brown's, and was a good deal less amiable in his response to Brown's letter than was his wont—nor is there any doubt that he remembered such accusations. In a 1913 address to the Bibliographical Society, near the beginning of a decade and a half of unprecedented inflation in the market value of Elizabethan books, Pollard reflects: "It is sometimes said of this Society that its existence has helped to raise the price of the books about which we write. That is very inconvenient for us individually or for the libraries which we represent."[29] The "we" dissipates some of the archness of "inconvenient": when Pollard made this remark, he had been on the staff of the British Museum Department of Printed Books for thirty years, had been setting purchasing policy for the British Museum library for ten, and was therefore extraordinarily sensitive to trends and fluctuations in bibliophile value. Pollard's sense of convenience had been at issue before. As early as 1894, Falconer Madan took issue with Pollard's decision to close the membership rolls of the Bibliographical Society, suggesting, as would J. D. Brown a few years later, that the decision had been taken in order to inflate the value of the Society's publications.

Pollard's feel for the market in books remained with him to the end of his career, reasserting itself even as his audience changed from a group of wealthy amateurs to a cadre of specialist academics. In his 1933 essay, "New Fields in Bibliography," he recalled that "the Museum itself reaped a rich reward for the publication of the Catalogue"—he is referring to Bullen's catalog of English books in the British Museum published prior to 1640— "for this had considerable sale among antiquarian booksellers, and as, for ten or a dozen years after its issue, the Department of Printed Books still enjoyed the £10,000 a year for purchases secured for it by Panizzi, and American competition was still very slight, the zeal with which the dealers offered it English books printed before 1641 'not in Bullen' met with a ready response, to the great enrichment of the collection."[30] Later in this essay he refers to incunabula as a mine that had finally been exhausted of ore.[31] The phrasing is telling, since it implicates the end of a research project with the end of a half-century of book sales at which the great fin-de-siècle private collections were broken up and, perhaps finally, dispersed to public institutions, the collector's rare book converted to public property and bibliographical datum.

Pollard's involvement in the rare-book market was in large measure responsible for the first analytical triumph of the New Bibliographers, the identification of the true provenance of the Pavier quartos. Experienced bibliographers have this story by heart—how Greg and Pollard together demonstrated that nine Shakespeare quartos, bearing dates ranging from 1600 to 1615, and attributed to various printers and publishers, were in fact printed more or less together, in 1619, by William Jaggard, for Thomas Pavier, a collection no doubt inspired by the 1616 Jonson Folio. Pollard had identified the quartos as a group in 1906, when, in his capacity as chief purchasing officer for the British Library, he was shown, for the second time in three or four years, bound collections of the same nine plays. In 1907, Greg made the technical breakthrough of linking the quartos by layout, typography, and watermark. Pollard, for his part, continued to consult the market, noting in a 1908 review of Slater's *Book-Prices Current* that these particular quartos were relatively easy to come by; they were not at all rare when compared to other Shakespeare quartos, just what one might expect of books issued simultaneously for binding as a collection.[32] But Pollard was not the only member of the Bibliographical Society with his mind on the market. Greg reported, with ill-concealed disdain, on how subscribers to *The Library* reacted to his typographic arguments: "A number of readers, with their heads full of modern book prices, jumped to the conclusion that I must mean that Pavier was endeavouring to obtain higher prices for his books by pretending that they were first editions, and they hastened solemnly to inform me that the desire for first editions was inoperative in the seventeenth century." Greg's own assessment of Pavier's motives will come as no surprise. Writing on the eve of the Berlin revisions to the Berne convention, he proposed that what Pavier "wanted to avoid was the charge of having printed plays, to the copyright of some of which he had no conceivable right."[33] Pollard had his mind on book prices; Greg had his mind on property rights.

The New Bibliographical project was shaped by one more feature of the early-twentieth-century rare-book market, perhaps its most distinctive feature, which is that the market had tilted suddenly westward. When the Britwell, Huth, and Hoe collections were sold off, between 1910 and 1915, the principal buyers were the Henrys Huntington and Folger, but even before those most spectacular purchases—perhaps as early as 1897, when Marsden Perry picked up a sizable chunk of the Halliwell-Phillips collection—British collectors noticed that their American counterparts had begun to dominate the major auctions. I suspect that this trans-Atlantic drift motivated the gentle chauvinism of Pollard's efforts at the Bibliographical Society early in this century. In the Society's June 1900 *News Sheet*, Pollard observed that "so many of the Society's publications have dealt with foreign subjects, that papers on points of English book-lore would be especially welcome."[34] In his 1913 address, in the midst of a major American purchasing frenzy, Pollard described as an "undeniable and very awkward fact" the internationalism of the Bibliographical Society's early work—international because of its orientation to early printing; he called upon his fellow members "to set in order our own English bibliographical house."[35]

To expose how richly Englishness shaped the New Bibliographical project, Sidney Lee is, once again, a name to conjure with. Sole editor of the *DNB* since 1892, Lee had established himself as a great popularizer of Shakespeare a few years later, when he expanded his *DNB* entry on

Shakespeare into an extremely successful book. His 1902 facsimile of the Folio, the book that had so nettled Greg, hardly contributed to his status as a popularizer—the facsimile was produced in a limited edition of 1000—but it did make him seem Shakespeare's great Americanizer. Published on the eve of Lee's year-long lecture tour of the United States, the facsimile seems to have been published with the tour in mind: Lee's introduction appealed to the pride of "English-speaking peoples," but an irate bibliophile, protesting to the London *Standard* that 100 copies had been set aside for the publisher, while 500 copies had been reserved for American subscription sales, winced under the oppression of "Yankee plutocracy."[36]

This is no doubt an extreme response; certainly Pollard's notice in *The Library* was more measured—he neither blames nor praises Lee's introduction. Greg's fuller discussion of the volume, a few months later, is closer in tone to the letter to the *Standard*. "I wish it to be understood that this article is not intended as a review, since I do not propose to make any mention of the many excellences of the volume, but merely to call attention to certain points which must, I think, be excepted from the general praise."[37] Greg excepts these points for nearly thirty pages, and the idiom of scholarly condescension predominates: he refers to "certain obvious errors which cannot escape the attention of any reader familiar with Shakespearian bibliography" and then coolly retrenches, "even the expert is apt to be misled by Mr. Lee's cheerful confidence of assertion."[38] What Greg stigmatizes is the popularizer's ease of assertion and genial disregard for the evidentiary. When Pollard got round to fully digesting Lee's arguments, he was similarly disdainful of Lee's slapdash methods, but his criticism, worked out in full in *Shakespeare Folios and Quartos*, carries a charge nowhere anticipated in Greg's earlier review:

> I find myself opposed to him at almost every point. The [bibliographical] pessimists, of whom Mr. Lee has made himself the champion, seem to me to have piracy on the brain. They depict it as the ruling element in the book-market in Shakespeare's day, Shakespeare and his fellows as submitting to it with what I should account a craven and contemptible helplessness, and the early editions of his plays as so deeply tainted with fraud and carelessness that we can never say where the mischief ends. As for the Elizabethan printers and publishers they are set down as equally stupid and dishonest, and none escape condemnation.

There is much to say about Pollard's disposition to the archival record, but the first, and most obvious thing to say about the project of Pollard's book is that it frames bibliographical research as a character defense. "To me," he writes, "the printers and publishers seem as a rule to have been

honest men." You will appreciate the elegance and economy: the carelessness and dishonesty attributed to Elizabethan book-producers is shifted to
Lee, whose "theory," Pollard tells us, "when extended to cover not an isolated instance but a whole series of depredations, conflicts with . . . common
sense and the English character."[39] So to Greg's hostility to Lee's vulgar
carelessness, Pollard adds indignation over Lee's dearth of patriotism. It is
difficult to resist the suspicion that Lee, whose theories of the transmission
of Shakespearean texts Greg would come cautiously to endorse in the 1950s,
was being positioned in the first decade of this century as a bibliographical
Dreyfus. The editor of the *Dictionary of National Biography*, Sidney Lee,
né Solomon Lazarus, was betraying an English Folio to a Yankee plutocracy, and the honest Elizabethans who had printed the quartos were being
traduced by their most eminent historian. Lee had held aloof from the Bibliographical Society almost from its inception, having joined and then re-
signed from its founding Provisional Committee in the autumn of 1892,
and if Greg's 1903 review of the Clarendon facsimile in *The Library*
sketched lines of institutional opposition, Pollard's 1909 volume on Shakespeare's texts etched them in stone.[40] Long after Lee's death in 1926, his
name is mentioned with opprobrium in the work of the New Bibliographers; even in Greg's compendious 1955 volume entitled *The First Folio*,
where he ends up siding with Lee against Pollard on questions of transmission, he continues to cast aspersions on Lee's learning and scholarly principles.[41]

There are less subterranean reasons, though still not entirely disinterested reasons, for Pollard's attack on Lee. While he was preparing his
facsimile, Lee had sensibly consulted Pollard on the type ornaments and
skeleton. Pollard lets us know that he responded carefully—he *prints* a
transcript of his memo to Lee in *Shakespeare Folios and Quartos*[42]—and
he also lets us know that, in the introduction to his facsimile, Lee had con-
densed the information he had provided and missed its point. Lee suggests
that Jaggard farmed out portions of the printing to other presses, whereas
Pollard's evidence makes it "quite certain that the whole work was printed
in one printing office."[43]

Lee's neglect of Pollard's evidence was more than personal slight; the
conflict of method and conclusions is essential. For Lee, the quarto texts
are almost uniformly unreliable, printed carelessly from surreptitiously
procured bad copies—discarded prompt-books, stenographic transcriptions,
or texts reported by actors—copies long removed from autograph. For Pollard, *some* of the quarto texts *are* reliable, printed with reasonable care
from prompt-books, some autograph, acquired from the acting company,
regularly entered and licensed.[44] For Lee, the Folio copy-texts were no
better than those of the quartos—and were often worse, as when (Lee argues)

a quarto derived from a prompt-book lost in the 1613 Globe fire is replaced by a Folio text derived from an unauthorized transcription, or when the copy-texts *were* the quartos, in which case the Folio text is inevitably more corrupt. For Pollard, the Folio constitutes a substantial improvement, since it prints exclusively from good quartos, corrected good quartos, or from corrected prompt-books. Pollard's Folio is carefully, but efficiently, arranged, while Lee's is the product of haphazard haste. It is no surprise then, that Pollard objected to Lee's suggestion that several shops had been involved in the printing, when Pollard had provided evidence that the book was Jaggard's, start to finish.

Lee's facsimile was highly disseminative, in every poststructuralist sense of the word. The work of the New Bibliographers, on the other hand, confers on the transmission from autograph to playhouse to Stationers' Hall to compositor, pressman, proof corrector and binder, confers on the material mediation of literary imagination a calculus. Though he is not so hardy as to suppose what Shakespeare meant, much less precisely what he *wrote*, Pollard is confident that he can tell good quarto from bad, that he can read textual authority from Arber's *Transcript of the Stationers' Register*. Lee had not only denigrated, but had *mystified*, production; his facsimile sends the Shakespearean text on a book tour into the wilderness.

As I mentioned earlier, Greg ended up siding with Lee, despite the scandal of Lee's lack of method. Pollard, however, became ever more "optimistic" in his textual theories: in his 1915 Sandars lectures and again in his British Academy lecture for 1923 (*The Foundations of Shakespeare's Text*), he undertook to prove that many of the quarto and Folio copy-texts were based on autograph prompt-books. Thus the dense historical field, so richly mapped in the first two decades of this century, comfortably fades as the Folio text recovers its proximity to the author's pen. For Pollard Shakespeare's autograph is distinctive, knowable, known, and his introduction to the essays he collected in 1923 as *Shakespeare's Hand in the Play of Sir Thomas More* therefore grows fervent and tart as he sets Sir E. M. Thompson's work on Shakespeare's handwriting against the assertions of the disseminator: "According to Sir Sidney Lee (preface to 1922 edition of his *Life of William Shakespeare*, p.xiii) Elizabethan handwriting 'runs in a common mould which lacks clearly discernible traces of the writer's individuality.' Cockneys have been heard to say the same of sheep, and yet the shepherd knows each sheep in his flock from every other."[45] By 1934, the year that he gave over editing *The Library*, Pollard advanced the theory that several of the quarto texts were printed from foul papers—effectively, drafts (he had somewhat casually suggested this of some of the Folio texts in the Sandars Lectures)—so that we have texts closer still to some originary authorial moment.

From our own perspective, the friction between Lee and Pollard had as its most enduring effect the genesis of Greg's fruitfully moderate position. He shared Pollard's early commitment to the methodical reconstruction of a regulated past—he had, of course, been instrumental in promulgating the reconstructive method—but from Lee he learned to regard the Shakespearean texts with "anauthorial" (or is the term "unoriginative"?) disenchantment. He eventually developed a bracing vision of a vigorously disseminative textual history: transmission makes meanings. In the prolegomena to *The Editorial Problem in Shakespeare* he wrote, "I feel that a particular edition, and far more a particular manuscript in the case of a medieval work, possesses a certain individuality of its own, which makes it a sort of minor literary creation, whose integrity I am loath to violate."[46] This has a somewhat settled aestheticist feel to it, but his note refers us to a more rambunctious version of the argument, that in his enormously canny 1932 essay, "Bibliography—an Apologia." There, in a gesture of great critical insouciance, Greg devalues the metacritical assumptions underlying the textual criticism of the Vulgate itself:

> An enormous amount of labour has been expended in successive attempts to determine what St. Jerome actually wrote, or what the divine spirit prompted him to write. . . . It would be foolish to depreciate the work which centuries of scholarship have devoted to this unending task.

But he then goes blithely on with the work of depreciation:

> We have in fact to recognize that a text is not a fixed and formal thing, that needs only to be purged of the imperfections of transmission and restored once and for all to its pristine purity,—

This is dangerous ground and he knows it, so he shifts to the mildly anxious rhetoric of sacred history: "a text is not a fixed and formal thing . . . but a living organism which in its descent through the ages. . . ." The pious rhetoric betrays Greg's nervousness as he prepares to inflict a devastating blow on originative authoriality—

> while it departs more and more from the form impressed upon it by its original author, exerts, through its imperfections, as much as through its perfections, its own influence upon its surroundings.

He has hedged, retreated from the representation of authorship as a mere impress of form. The retreat is temporary: once again he will assert the authoriality of transmission itself, the scribal power of inscription, the power of compositors to impose their own "original impression":

> At each stage of its descent a literary work is in some sense a new creation. . . . In some limited sense, each scribe is a subsidiary author, even when he is doing his best to be a faithful copyist, still more when he indulges in emendations and improvements of his own. And this is just what bibliography, with its impartial outlook, recognizes, when it treats each step in the history of the text as potentially of equal importance.[47]

Thus Greg's prolegomenon to the New Cultural History, to Gadamer, and to Jauss. When we casually attribute a monological, idealized, and stipulative attitude to textuality to prepostmodern critics, we should not suppose ourselves to be referring to Greg.

From this distance it will seem odd that a facsimile edition, promising some terminus of textual variation, should have occasioned so complex and, in Pollard's case, so anxious a reaction. But Lee's facsimile constituted a dual assault on Pollard's bibliographical calculus. The first aspect of the assault is obvious: Lee had imagined a bibliographical past full of pirates, a past in which texts proliferate in violation of authorial, censorious, proprietary, or industrial control. But the second violation of the bibliographical calculus has to do with the reproductive technology itself and its disruption of the bibliophile foundations of New Bibliography. Consider one more passage from the eleventh edition of the *Encyclopedia Britannica*, this from Pollard's article entitled "Bibliography and Bibliology." He is discussing "the correction of mis-statements in early books as to their place and *[sic?]* origin":

> A special case of this problem of piracies and spurious imprints is that of the modern photographic or type facsimile forgery of small books possessing a high commercial value. . . . Bad forgeries of this kind can be detected by the tendency of all photographic processes of reproduction to thicken letters and exaggerate every kind of defect, but the best of these imitations when printed on old paper require a specific knowledge of the originals and often cause great trouble. The type-facsimile forgeries are mostly of short pieces by Tennyson, George Eliot and A. C. Swinburne, printed (or supposed to have been printed—for it is doubtful if any of these "forgeries" ever had originals) for circulation among friends. These trifles should never be purchased without a written guarantee.

There is of course no such imposture in the Clarendon facsimile. Yet Lee's collotype facsimile constitutes a strange boundary creature, a manufactured rarity, neither old nor new. Is it live or is it Memorex?

The new reproductive technologies were crucial, of course, to the New Bibliography. Photography had played an essential role in identifying the types and ornaments of the Pavier quartos. The photograph and collotype not only satisfied an expanded bibliophile market, they also made possible what the type facsimiles of the old bibliophile author societies could not: they fostered a cohort of far-flung academic investigators engaged in systematic typographic research and exhaustive investigation of press variants. But as Pollard's article "Bibliography and Bibliology" suggests—and as the article on copyright cited earlier had suggested—the new technology also constituted an assault on authorship as a stabilizing market force. Once again we confront the complex relation between bibliography and the rare-book market.

I have already suggested some aspects of this relation: widening interest in historical bibliography was stimulated by a rare-book market quickened and shaped by single-author enumerative bibliographies. The immediate effect of such enumerative bibliographies was to foster a taste, by which I mean a market, for books in "original condition." If Buxton Forman's *A Shelley Library* (1886) is the landmark single-author bibliography, the new market emphasis on "original condition" was especially encouraged in the bibliographies of modern Victorians produced by T. J. Wise. Book-collecting lawyers will recognize these names as, perhaps, historians will not: Forman and Wise were two of the greatest forgers of all time. What they did was to select individual pieces of poetry or prose from published volumes by the Brownings, Dickens, Eliot, Rossetti, Thackeray, Arnold, Tennyson, Stevenson, Morris, Ruskin, Kipling, and Swinburne, print them as pamphlets, and thus create a first edition.[48] Trained bibliographers, they stayed away from watermarked paper, invented plausible imprints (or omitted them), and imitated the layout of books of the imputed dates. Wise and Forman would then authenticate the pamphlets by describing them in the single-author bibliographies in which they specialized, often with remarks about their interesting provenance and great rarity and with suggestions of appropriate sale prices. The whole episode, with its alliance of scholarship and price-fixing, bibliophilia and bibliography, reached a wonderful conclusion when Wise began to write a column on modern collecting for *The Bookman* in 1893. Or perhaps the crowning glory was when he took over the presidency of the Bibliographical Society in 1922. At any rate, suspicions of some of these pamphlets began to be raised around 1898, and although Wise and Forman had covered their tracks, they did stop the manufacture of these small books before the century ended, at which point Wise began to amuse himself by stealing pages from Restoration plays in the British Museum—about two hundred in all—in order to "perfect" copies of his own. It wasn't until 1903, the year when Lee's collotype came under review from Pollard and Greg, that two bibliographers managed persuasively to discredit two of the Ruskin forgeries by a collation that proved that these Buxton-Wise "originals" had been set up from late editions.

Much later, in 1934, John Carter and Graham Pollard would multiply the bibliographical tests available to discredit the forgeries—type identification, research into the distribution of copies—precisely the tests that Alfred Pollard and Walter Greg had applied in 1907 to the Pavier quartos. Greg had clinched his case with a study of the Pavier watermarks, as Carter and Pollard would clinch theirs with a chemical analysis of the paper used in the Wise-Forman forgeries. What I mean to suggest is that in both instances bibliography was inventing new tests, new ways of mapping the bibliographical past, that scholarship advanced by policing a market in which both authorship and property had been scandalized.[49] Of course this could be reframed from a different perspective: it would be equally fair to say that a forgery is simply bibliography's way of producing a New Bibliography. In each instance the page was held up to the light in such a way that the investigator was relieved of the seductive distractions of the printed word itself. Authorship could only be enforced by looking past its *literal* traces.

It turns out that Wise and Forman posed no threat to A. W. Pollard's arguments for the essential honesty of the English printer, for there is no indication that anyone at the firm of R. Clay and Sons, which had printed the forged pamphlets, had any suspicion of the imposture. In the late 1880s, these printers did a good deal of specialized work for the Browning and Shelley Societies: under the direction of T. J. Wise, they were accustomed to putting out elegant, gently antiqued type facsimiles in limited editions for the members of these societies. The bibliophile type facsimile trained them in the forger's craft as it inured them to its valence: the dyer's hand. Is it a coincidence that the first photolithographed facsimiles of Shakespearean quartos were edited by—and perhaps an inspiration to—that great scholar-forger John Collier?

None of this *quite* reflects on Lee, yet the first suspicions of the Wise-Forman forgeries may help explain why Pollard responded to Lee's facsimile with an animus that would never leave him, an animus that even various tinctures of national pride and anti-Semitism cannot quite explain. His encyclopedia article suggests the connoisseur's proud zeal for the authentic, but even that seems hardly to justify the strength and persistence of Pollard's disapproval. There is no intent to deceive in Lee's facsimile: such intention he exported to a distant and piratical past. But Pollard believed that such a disseminated past was itself an imposture, an intolerable fiction. And Lee's collotype was an accessory after the fact: like the photolithographic facsimiles of his great predecessor, Collier, Lee's collotype was being used, as it were, to authenticate his bibliography, a photograph that generates the truth of its caption.

My meditation on origins might end here, though I think it appropriate to measure just how far the reaction against Lee carried bibliography and how its reactive energy was deflected toward new intellectual production. In the opening of his *magnum opus* on the presswork of the First Folio, Charlton Hinman shrewdly characterized his great predecessor—"Greg's primary concern, in *The Shakespeare First Folio* as in earlier works, is with copy"—and he thus summarizes the retrospective bibliographical calculus of the New Bibliography.[50] The essential preoccupation of both Greg and McKerrow, even when the task at hand was the preparation of a serviceable edition, was with printer's copy; but this retrospection, this seeing back through the printed text, hardly stopped with the assessment of copy. What Greg claims as his goal, in the prolegomena to *The Editorial Problem in Shakespeare*, is "to present the text . . . in the form in which we may suppose that it would have stood in a fair copy, made by the author himself, of the work as he finally intended it." But if this sounds like a Pollardian calculus, it is allowed to veer off toward Lee's disseminative textuality: "In the case of Shakespeare—and the same applies to the Elizabethan drama generally—we cannot hope to achieve a certainly correct text, not so much on account of the uncertainties of transmission—though they are sometimes serious—as because the author may never have produced a definitive text for us to recover."[51] Things fall apart. Of course, textuality is still to be regulated by originative personhood, the same person who, since 1911, had stood at the origin of copyright, though in Greg's account a variable person yields a variant text. Hinman is only a step away, accounting for textual variants by distinguishing individual compositors. But not to designate the compositor, not to name the authorial mood—that is Lee's abyss, and bibliography would not heedlessly stray so far westward again.[52]

The critique I have offered contains observations that cultural historians are accustomed to making and that, in their general form, are not very thrilling—that conceptualization is interested, that intellectual traditions are not internally regulated, and that scholarly projects do not have intrinsic principles of coherence. Of course, others have subjected the projects of the New Bibliography to critique, both local and abstract. My own I would characterize as vulgarly technologist. But, to what end? A sketchy answer, based on the principle that there is nothing like a bit of history to solicit a critique of the present.

My argument that new technologies of reproduction provoked new analyses of intellectual property and authorship and new techniques for *confirming* property and authorship might be expected to have contemporary application. We would expect that the proliferation of new information technologies in our own day might produce a critical renovation of concepts of intellectual property and of creative "pretext," of what Sir Philip Sidney refers to as the "foreconceit" of a work. But such renovation has been sectored, made principally a legislative problem for intellectual property lawyers and a technical problem for software designers and recording engineers. Here in the academy, on the other hand, new information technologies have often propped a cult of the deconstructed text: by and large, inexpensive, portable reproductive technologies have underwritten a "sampled" textual theory, a fetishization of the composite text. During Copinger's information revolution, the Bibliographical Society responded to technology in a fashion that *might* be called reactionary, but I think might more properly be called *critical;* my own sense is that during our own information revolution academic bibliography has partnered technology relatively uncritically. I am troubled by the degree to which such analyses justify and even naturalize the mobile text, give in to what will play in the Peoria of Sidney Lee's America. Postmodern theory often seizes upon our own cultural moment as an age of exorbitant reproduction and sometimes goes on incautiously to endorse such mobile iterability as pluralistic and democratic, thereby forgetting the larger truth that the mass of *this* mass culture is not sui generis, that the dubbing cassette deck may also be described as a *state* apparatus. I wish to resist a wholesale archaizing of the New Bibliography, the archaizing of any attempt to construct a calculus of transmission, and a historical semantics to go with it, on the grounds that any such archaizing would indicate a lapsed faith in agency, in politics, in even a cultural politics.[53] Is it too much to hope that a historicizing of the New Bibliography (even an anecdotal historicizing) might invite us to imagine how our own Newer Bibliography will be historicized, should we end up encumbered with historians of our own?

NOTES

1. The most useful account of the Berne convention, and the most telling reflection of the regulatory "crisis" of the first decade of the twentieth century, is to be found in William Briggs, *The Law of International Copyright* (London: Stevens and Hayes, 1906), 234–42, 264–72, 435–65; and see also Victor Bonham-Carter, *Authors By Profession*, vol. 1 (Los Altos, Calif.: William Kaufman, 1978), 215–16.

2. W. R. Cornish, *Intellectual Property: Patents, Copyright, Trade Marks, and Allied Rights* (London: Sweet and Maxwell, 1981), 299.

3. *The Encyclopedia Britannica*, 11th ed., s.v. "Copyright."

4. In his appendix, "Notes on the History of English Copyright." for the *Oxford Companion to English Literature,* ed. Paul Harvey, 2d ed. (Oxford: Oxford University Press, 1937), Frank MacKinnon points out (883) that publishers continued to register books until the end of 1923 in order to secure copyright in Canada. Canadian statutes of 1921 and 1923 finally obviated this necessity, and use of the Stationers' Register ceased.

5. The statutory nature of this modern form of copyright is itself remarkable. The 1911 act completes a legislative progress that had been initiated in 1709 with the promulgation of the Statute of Anne, the first English copyright statute. The Statute of Anne was by

no means clear, but in the course of the eighteenth century litigation conferred upon it the significance of having radically abridged common law copyright, a common law right that it conceived of retrospectively as a perpetual authorial copyright. One of the few vestiges of this common-law copyright that survived the Statute of Anne was authorial property in unpublished manuscripts, a property that the Copyright Act of 1911 eliminated, reconstituting it as a statutory right. For more on eighteenth-century copyright, see Mark Rose, *Authors and Owners: The Invention of Copyright* (Cambridge: Harvard University Press, 1993).

6. For a description of the Copyright Act of 1911 that foregrounds its simplicity, see Cornish, *Intellectual Property*, 298–300.

7. For new forms of unfair competition, specifically the use of false allegations in comparative advertising, see ibid., 9–11. The pressures on the patent system were not exactly new, though they took new forms. The Patent Law Amendment Act of 1852 had rationalized the British patent system, with the result that patent applications immediately multiplied. A boon for industry, the surge in patenting activity brought with it a rash of unscrupulous application. By 1883, a new patent office was put in place in hopes of subjecting patent applications to more careful formal scrutiny, though the office was not charged to undertake systematic search of prior patents. In 1901 it was demonstrated that at least 40 percent of all new patents duplicated inventions already under patent protection, so that, beginning in 1905, the Patent Office undertook to screen all applications specifically for novelty: thus the beginning of this century saw a considerable expansion of nonjudicial regulation of intellectual property. For more on the evolution of the Patent Office in the aftermath of the Great Exhibition of 1851, see ibid., 80–84.

8. Edison's phonograph dates from 1877; the Pathé and Gramophone phonograph factories began production in 1893; Victor initiated its Red Seal issues in 1902. The problem of photography had been addressed as early as the Fine Arts Copyright Act of 1862, but the solution cobbled together there was so obviously flawed that the original promoters of the act made an effort to stop its passage. Photography remained something of a legal scandal well into this century: the article on copyright from the 1910–11 *Encyclopedia Britannica*, cited above, states flatly that "the great obstacle in the way of securing a really good Artistic Bill has been the introduction into it of photography." But musical copyright was also an obvious problem. The Copyright Act of 1911 established the principles for the formation of the Performance Right Society in 1914, by which Britain imitated French, Italian, and Spanish arrangements for the enforcement of performance rights.

9. *White-Smith Music Publishing Co. v Apollo Co.,* 209 U.S. 1, cited in Lyman Ray Patterson, *Copyright in Historical Perspective* (Nashville, Tenn.: Vanderbilt University Press, 1968), 214–15.

10. And the Malone Society was founded in 1906, largely at the instigation of the then Honorable Secretary of the Bibliographical Society, A. W. Pollard. The history of this instauration in bibliography is set forth in F. P. Wilson, *Shakespeare and the New Bibliography,* revised and edited by Helen Gardner (Oxford: Clarendon Press, 1970), which expands his very long essay of the same title prepared for the 1942 Jubilee celebration of the Bibliographical Society and published in *The Bibliographical Society, 1892–1942: Studies in Retrospect* (London: Bibliographical Society, 1945), 76–135.

11. W. W. Greg, "The Bibliographical History of the First Folio," *The Library*, 2d ser., 4 (1903): 258–85 (267).

12. Like Greg, Pollard was going after Lee, an eminent and sloppy scholar with an easy, anecdotal style, against whom Pollard began to marshal a defensive wall constructed mainly of data culled from the Stationers' Registers. In *Shakespeare Folios and Quartos,* Pollard attempted, contra Lee, to pull the quartos off the rubbish heap: they had been rejected as unfaithful representations of authorial intent and, before Pollard and Greg, that

had simply been that. The New Bibliographers initiated modern bibliography by inquiring into the *medium* of transmission, into the origins and mechanisms of the imputed textual vicissitudes.

13. In Pollard's address to the Bibliographical Society entitled "Our Twenty-First Birthday" (1913), he lays out the New Bibliographical program for historicizing the book: "Between us and the author of any old book stand scribes or printers, publishers, and even binders, and until we have eliminated the errors due to these we cannot reach the true text in which the author has expressed his thought. Now and again we may eliminate these errors by study only of the book itself with which we are concerned, but more often it needs a general knowledge of the ways of the scribes or printers, or publishers or binders of the day to enable us to see what has been done wrongly, and the accumulation of knowledge as to these ways is one important branch of Bibliography." *Transactions of the Bibliographical Society* 13 (1913): 9–27 (25). It is worth noting that Pollard's very first publication was a paper on medieval guilds.

14. And see also Wilson, *Shakespeare and the New Bibliography*, 96–101.

15. W. W. Greg, "Principles of Emendation in Shakespeare," *PBA* 14 (1928): 147–73 (152).

16. Dover Wilson makes a good deal of Pollard's friendship with Housman in his memoir for the British Academy: "Alfred William Pollard," *PBA* 31 (1945): 257–306.

17. A. W. Pollard, *Shakespeare Folios and Quartos* (London: Methuen, 1909), 65.

18. I have cited from the revised second edition (Cambridge: Cambridge University Press, 1920), 1.

19. On the early history of the Society, see F. C. Francis, "The Bibliographical Society: A Sketch of the First Fifty Years," in *The Bibliographical Society, 1892–1942: Studies in Retrospect*, ed. F. C. Francis (London: The Bibliographical Society, 1945), 1–22.

20. See Pollard, "Our Twenty-First Birthday," 10.

21. Carter, *Taste and Technique in Book Collecting: A Study of Recent Developments in Great Britain and the United States,* 4th ed. (New York: Bowker, 1948; reprint, London: Private Libraries Association, 1970), 20.

22. "Just as the stamp album, through the power of irritation exercised by those blank squares, inculcates the desire for completeness, so also does the full-dress author-bibliography" (ibid., 28). That bibliophilia was not only a historical but a market-driven phenomenon may be gauged from the development of reverence for original bindings. A convention arose of preserving collected books in solander cases; Carter remarks, "[T]hat this change in technique was not founded on, and was for some years seldom allied with, any true appreciation of the bibliographical and technical importance of original condition is sufficiently evident from its restriction to books from about 1790 onwards" (29).

23. Cited from *The Fortnightly Review* in ibid., 26.

24. Pollard deftly alludes to the Society's deliberate but incomplete conversion from aestheticism in a passing review of one of the New Bibliographers' most important compendia: "Within the last few days Members have had delivered to them the largest and one of the most noteworthy Illustrated Monographs which it has been the Society's privilege to publish, that on *English Printers' and Publishers' Devices*, by your other Hon. Secretary, Mr. McKerrow. Few of the devices are beautiful, but the book brings us a long step forward to the time when we shall be able to say with approximate certainty at what date any undated and unsigned fragment of English printing was produced and by whom it was printed and published" ("Our Twenty-First Birthday," 20).

25. Had it not been, in fact, for the interests of McKerrow and Greg, interests formed during their days together at Trinity College, Cambridge, the Bibliographical Society might never have become the center for Elizabethan textual studies that it has remained.

26. J. D. Brown, "Practical Bibliography," *The Library*, 2d ser., 4 (1903): 145–46.

27. Ibid., 147.

28. Ibid., 148.

29. Pollard, "Our Twenty-First Birthday," 24; and cf. 10 on bibliographical monographs as investments.

30. Pollard, "New Fields in Bibliography," reprinted in Wilson, "Alfred William Pollard," 185.

31. Ibid., 187.

32. A. W. Pollard, review of *Book Prices Current, The Library*, 2d ser., 9 (1908): 215–16.

33. W. W. Greg, "On Certain False Dates in Shakespearian Quartos," *The Library*, 2d ser., 9 (1908): 381–409 (396–97).

34. Cited by Wilson, "Alfred William Pollard," 284.

35. Pollard, "Our Twenty-First Birthday," 18–19.

36. Sidney Lee, introduction to *Shakespeares Comedies, Histories, & Tragedies, Being a Reproduction in Facsimile of the First Folio Edition, 1623* (Oxford: Clarendon Press, 1902), xi; the letter from "A Mere Englishman" to the *Standard* (London) was dated 1 January 1902 and appeared on 3 January, p. 6. Froude, the Oxford publisher, contested these claims in a letter dated 4 January (published 6 January, p. 37), eliciting the slight concession from "AME" that only sixty copies had been reserved for the publisher (7 January, published 9 January, p. 3); in a letter dated 3 January, J. & E. Bumpus (Ltd.) offered to provide "AME" with a copy, boasting of their "refusal of some tempting offers from American traders" (4 January, p. 2).

37. W. W. Greg, "The Bibliographical History of the First Folio," *The Library*, 2d ser., 4 (1903): 258–85 (258).

38. Ibid., 259, 260.

39. A. W. Pollard, *Shakespeare Folios and Quartos* (London: Methuen, 1909), v, 10.

40. Apparently, A. S. W. Rosenbach pitted the upstart Greg against Lee even before the 1903 review; see Edwin Wolf II, with John F. Fleming, *Rosenbach: A Biography* (Cleveland and New York: World Publishing, 1960), 43.

41. Moreover, character remains an issue for Greg as for Pollard. Thus Greg's defense of the Folio text, in *The Editorial Problem in Shakespeare* (3d ed.), is offered as a vindication of Heminge and Condell: "No one has any longer the right to maintain that Heminge and Condell abused as "stolen and surreptitious copies, maimed and deformed by the frauds and stealths of injurious imposters" the very texts they were themselves reprinting in their edition. Their strictures should be taken to apply only to a specific class of notoriously inferior texts, and these they replaced with good ones. Not only is the essential honesty of Shakespeare's friends and fellows vindicated, but the stigma under which the quartos as a class have laboured is removed" (13). Greg cautiously assents to Lee's position in *The Shakespeare First Folio* (Oxford: Clarendon Press, 1955), 42–43.

42. Pollard, *Shakespeare Folios and Quartos*, 132–33.

43. Ibid., 134.

44. Pollard was so eager to put a good face on the historical record of these texts that he misremembered or misrepresented the circumstances of Pavier's registration of *Henry V* in his discussion of the good and bad quartos, though he had recorded the details accurately elsewhere. In an errata page tipped into *Shakespeare Folios and Quartos*, Pollard responds to advance readings with a correction, admitting that "the discreditable transaction is made a good deal worse than I thought it." In *The Shakespeare First Folio*, Greg points out that by 1923 Pollard was trying to prove that some of the printed texts were from autograph promptbooks (93–96). By 1934, he had moved to claiming that copy was foul papers; see below.

45. A. W. Pollard, *Shakespeare's Hand in the Play of Sir Thomas More* (Cambridge: Cambridge University Press, 1923), 16.

46. W. W. Greg, *The Editorial Problem in Shakespeare,* 2d ed. (Oxford: Clarendon Press, 1951), liv n. 2.

47. W. W. Greg, "Bibliography—an Apologia," *The Library,* 4th ser., 13 (1932): 135.

48. A full account of these forgeries may be found in John Carter and Graham Pollard, *An Enquiry Concerning Certain Nineteenth Century Pamphlets,* 2d ed. (London: Scolar Press, 1983), which is supplemented by Nicholas Barker and John Collins, *A Sequel to An Enquiry Concerning Certain Nineteenth-Century Pamphlets by John Carter and Graham Pollard* (London: Scolar Press, 1983); the progress of these forgeries is narrated in part two ("Reconstruction") of Carter and Pollard's book, 96–152.

49. Barker's comment in the preface to the *Sequel to an Enquiry* indicates the continuing relation between technical analysis and historiography of the book trade (indeed biography of book-men, the study of the biblio-subject) that was the enduring legacy of the New Bibliography: "It gradually became clear . . . that there were a number of unanswered problems that could only be cleared up by typographic analysis of a new kind: it was also clear that the life of Wise, if better documented than that of Forman, needed a parallel chapter if the joint career of the two were to be properly explained. This led in turn to an attempt to reconstruct the course of the crime, during which we came to realize how much evidence of the traffic in forgeries, piracies and other suspect material, particularly in America, remained (and remains) to be found out. . . ." That the research is tied to a sense of scandalized property is indicated by Barker's next sentence: "The distinction between forgery and other forms of fraud became harder to maintain" (12).

50. Charlton Hinman, *The Printing and Proofreading of the First Folio,* vol. 1 (Oxford: Clarendon Press, 1963), 5.

51. Greg, *Editorial Problem in Shakespeare,* x, ix.

52. The most interesting combination of caution and daring at this western brink is Paul Werstine's "The Textual Mystery of *Hamlet,*" *SQ* 39 (1988): 1–26.

53. On the other hand, I have no wish to sustain a cult of "trade," or to promote that overvaluation of small production that has been subjected to such decisive critique in Oskar Negt and Alexander Kluge, *Geschichte und Eigensinn* (Frankfurt: Zeitausendeins, 1981), 175–77.

2

Touring and the Construction of Shakespeare Textual Criticism

PAUL WERSTINE

I

In 1909, Alfred W. Pollard established for this century's editors and textual critics a class of early printed Shakespeare texts he called the "bad quartos."[1] Expressions of strong opinion about the texts so named have accounted for the bulk of Shakespeare textual criticism in this century. At present there is widespread (but, I hope to show, ill-founded) agreement that the so-called bad quartos enjoy a privileged relation to early modern performance. This opinion has a strong impact on the editing of the plays that have come down to us in the forms of both "good" texts and "bad quartos." Many of the "Shakespeare's" now available in bookstores contain stage directions and more than a few dialogue readings drawn from the "bad quartos." When an editor, like Brian Gibbons in his New Arden *Romeo and Juliet*, chooses to omit from an edition a "bad quarto" stage direction, the editor can expect to draw the ire of reviewers defending the stage direction as a valuable indication of performance tradition in Shakespeare's own day.[2] The editorial practice of interpolating bits from "bad quartos" into modern texts has recently been taken to an extreme in the Oxford *Complete Works*, whose editors turn to the "bad quartos" with unprecedented frequency to draw upon these quartos' variant speech heads, stage directions, and dialogue readings. The justification offered by these editors is, however, only the traditional one, namely, the assumption that the "bad quartos" must "represent—however imperfectly—the performance script of a play. . . . Thus the Oxford edition [in its effort to provide the reader with the performing text] takes memorial reconstruction [including "bad quartos"] much more seriously than its predecessors, recognizing the potential value of these texts in preserving corrections and revisions" of other versions of the plays that were printed.[3]

Before following the Oxford practice, Shakespeare editors may wish to subject to critical scrutiny this widespread belief that the "bad quartos" are performance scripts. In attempting to address this question, an editor looks in vain for documentary evidence that would link a "bad quarto" to performance in a special way. All readers of early printed texts are aware that the typical title page for a play advertises the printed text as the one that "hath been often (with great applause) plaid publiquely" or the one that "hath bene sundry times publiquely acted." My first quotation comes from the title page of the 1597 *Romeo and Juliet*, the so-called bad quarto, my second from the title page of the 1599 "good quarto." There is nothing to choose between the title pages in determining which text is to be awarded status as the performance script. And, as yet, no document or record has been unearthed to elevate a "bad quarto" above any other kind of text as a record of what was acted. Without external evidence of the provenance of the "bad quartos," editors and textual critics have had to rely on that most treacherous of commodities—"internal evidence."

In view of the assurance with which the special connection between the "bad quartos" and the stage is asserted, it might seem that the tradition of positing the connection and reading the "bad quartos" in light of it must be coeval with the birth of Shakespeare textual scholarship, with Theobald, Capell, or, at the latest, Malone. Instead, the connection is of very recent origin, having been suggested for the first time in 1919. Like the "bad quartos" themselves, the "performance-text bad quartos" take their being from Alfred W. Pollard, this time aided by J. Dover Wilson. Since the publication of their seminal 1919 *TLS* articles,[4] figuration of "bad quartos" as stage vehicles has undergone many varied transformations. These are the object of study for this essay.

Before turning to these, I want to digress briefly to take up the belief, recently explored by Janette Dillon in a brilliant essay in *Shakespeare Quarterly*, that the special association of "bad quartos" with acting is bound up with the hypothesis that "bad quartos" are memorial reconstructions of plays by actors.[5] The hypothesis that the "bad quartos" were memorially reconstructed by an actor or actors, while now believed by many to be self-evidently true, is also of quite recent origin. It was first advanced *in extenso* by W. W. Greg only in 1910.[6] In an edition of the "bad quarto" of *Merry Wives of Windsor* (1602), Greg sought to identify the actor who played the Host as the one who reproduced the play from memory for an allegedly unscrupulous publisher, John Busby: "[T]he pirate who procured the copy for Busby was none other than the actor of the Host's part."[7] But Greg's supposition of collusion in piracy between publisher and actor-reporter for the purpose of producing a *reading* text of the play in no way required

Greg to postulate the fidelity of the *Merry Wives* quarto to what had been performed. Indeed, Greg explicitly denied any such fidelity:

> One of the hired actors [the one who played the Host] produced, as a result of a week's labour with a not very ready pen, a rough construction of the play, in which, naturally enough, his own part of the Host was the only one rendered throughout with tolerable accuracy.

> It may be, of course, that the actor did not himself write out the copy, but dictated it to some devil in Busby's office.[8]

History then refutes the assumption that the memorial-reconstruction hypothesis for the "bad quartos," in itself, necessarily entails a special relationship between such quartos and scripts for performance. Nevertheless, in defense of this assumption, it may be said that, from its very inception, the hypothesis of "performance-text bad quartos" caught up into itself the memorial-reconstruction hypothesis. The two have since been reproduced together so often that they are now quite indistinguishable from each other.

The first expression of the notion—and it has never been anything more than a mere notion—that the "bad quartos" were, in some sense, actually performed appears in Pollard and Wilson's *TLS* essay entitled "The 'Stolne and Surreptitious' Shakespearian Texts":

> These abridgments [the "bad quartos"] can only have been made for audiences in the provinces, where the conditions of performance and the smaller number of actors, as compared with the fuller London companies, compelled drastic excisions. . . . [S]uch abbreviation would of necessity involve a certain amount of adaptation, since after a rent had been made in the text, it would generally be necessary to stitch the ends together, however roughly.[9]

The grounds for ascribing the "bad quartos" to provincial playing places are slight indeed. Playing in the provinces, Pollard and Wilson tell us, was comparatively rare: "The company for which Shakespeare wrote and . . . also acted did not often go on tour" except, according to Pollard and Wilson, when an especially violent outbreak of plague closed the London playhouses for an extended period, as in 1593–94. Since the provinces had little experience of fine London playing, Pollard and Wilson infer, provincial audiences would have been much less demanding about the quality and duration of performance than their London counterparts: "[T]he groundlings of a London theatre would have had a good deal to say if, after paying for an afternoon's entertainment, they had been fobbed off with anything less," and so "abridgments made for provincial representation . . . would be useless for London performances."[10]

It does not seem too much to say that here Pollard and Wilson anachronistically project upon the late sixteenth century the superiority of London to provincial theater that can be documented only from the eighteenth century.[11] This is not a personal criticism of these scholars; they were limited by the research then available, which was J. T. Murray's spotty, underrepresentative survey of provincial records of dramatic performance.[12] Nevertheless, Pollard and Wilson combine this antiprovincial bias with an antitheatrical bias when they assume that the purely theatrical—rather than authorial—process of cutting must necessarily have been transparently incompetent, producing rough seams in the printed texts of these performance scripts. On top of these binary oppositions between London and the provinces, and between the author and the theater, Pollard and Wilson stack the additional binary opposition generated by Pollard in 1909 between "good quartos" and "bad quartos." It is the very badness of the rent-and-roughly-stitched "bad quartos" that associates them with the provinces, those places of inferior taste and narrow experience, and with the theater, in which dramatic poetry was hacked to accommodate the exigencies of cast and of performance venue.[13] For Pollard and Wilson, the measure of the difference between London author, on the one hand, and provincial acting companies and audiences, on the other, amounts to the difference between the "good quarto" of, say, *Hamlet:*

> To be, or not to be, that is the question,
> Whether tis nobler in the minde to suffer
> The slings and arrowes of outragious fortune,
> Or to take Armes against a sea of troubles,
> And by opposing, end them, to die to sleepe
> No more, and by a sleepe, to say we end
> The hart-ake, and the thousand naturall shocks
> That flesh is heire to; tis a consumation
> Deuoutly to be wisht to die to sleepe,
> To sleepe, perchance to dreame, I there's the rub,

(sig. G2)

and the "bad" one:

> To be, or not to be, I there's the point,
> To Die, to sleepe, is that all? I all:
> No, to sleepe, to dreame, I mary there it goes.

(sig. D4v)

I say "amounts to the difference" because Pollard and Wilson did not believe that any "bad quarto" faithfully represents what was actually performed in the provinces. Instead, they imagined that Shakespeare's company took into the provinces an abridged version of an old play about, say, Hamlet, which Shakespeare had only begun to revise and make his own. Then, when the company returned to London and to Shakespeare, who had in the meantime completed his revision, the company staged the revised version. So great was the company's success in staging the revised and truly Shakespearean version that it was worthwhile for a printer to engage a small-part actor who had performed both in the provinces and in the later London productions to provide the press with a copy of the play. This actor took a transcript of the abridged version performed in the provinces, which was of no further value to the company, and did his best, relying on his imperfect memory, to bring this transcript into line with the truly Shakespearean version. So, for Pollard and Wilson, a "bad quarto" is scarcely the record of actual provincial performance that later editors and critics have taken it to be; indeed, in Pollard and Wilson's wonderfully fanciful narrative, a "bad quarto" remains such a record only to the extent that the rogue actor's memory fails him as he tries to transform the provincial acting version into a purely *reading* text of what Shakespeare finally produced.

Pollard and Wilson's narrative of the genesis of "bad quartos" was, in its highly embroidered complexity, too self-evidently speculative to win complete assent in a scholarly community then dedicated to simplicity as a mark of truth. Among the epigraphs chosen by W. W. Greg for his influential 1922 study *Two Elizabethan Stage Abridgements: The Battle of Alcazar & Orlando Furioso* was Alfred North Whitehead's maxim "Seek simplicity and distrust it." From today's perspective it would seem that Greg, in his transformation of Pollard and Wilson's hypothesis about "performance-text bad quartos" into a much more straightforward account, followed the first half of Whitehead's maxim more assiduously than the second, especially since Greg picked as another of his epigraphs words from *Chu Chin Chow*, "Work can only be done one way." The one way that Greg thought the "bad quartos" of *Orlando* and *Alcazar* could have been produced was the way pointed out by Pollard and Wilson just three years before: provincial touring obliged acting companies to abridge authorial versions that they had staged in London. There is, of course, no document to associate either the *Orlando* or the *Alcazar* quarto with the provinces, nor is there any allusion in the texts that signals provincial provenance. Greg is frank about the absence of anything we might call "evidence" of the printed texts' ultimate origins: "[T]he occasions or circumstances of their production remain largely matter of speculation, and no direct proof of their alleged provincial origin has been attempted in these pages."[14] Greg, however, shares Pollard and Wilson's antiprovincial bias and finds "some plausibility to the provincial hypothesis. It can hardly be without significance that both these plays . . . were first printed [in 1594] just as the companies were returning to London after long wanderings during the years of plague." Like Pollard and Wilson, Greg thought major London companies rarely toured; therefore Greg, like Pollard and Wilson, could assign great weight to the coincidence of one of the few known tours with the printing of *Alcazar* and *Orlando*. Greg's prejudice against the provinces is figured in even stronger terms than Pollard and Wilson's; his contempt for any theater outside London embraces even continental venues. Greg writes of the *Alcazar* quarto:

> [T]here is an intrinsic improbability in supposing any company of standing to have performed on the regular London stage such an eviscerated drama as that presented in the quarto of 1594. The obvious inference is that it belongs to the years of the dispersal, and was prepared for the use of that section of the company which maintained itself by acting in the provinces; possibly even, though less likely, that it formed part of the stock of those members who sought their fortunes abroad.[15]

At the same time Greg's antitheatrical bias also functions strongly in his construction of theatrical practice as being at odds with actual documents that attest incontrovertibly to the nature of that practice. In addition to the printed quartos of *Alcazar* and *Orlando*, Greg had two such documents: a theatrical "plot" of *Alcazar* (i.e. a large sheet, heavily damaged, but listing matters of purely theatrical concern: names of actors assigned to roles, properties, sound calls) and Edward Alleyn's actor's part for the title role in *Orlando*. The theatrical provenance of these documents is established by their being among Alleyn's private papers in the college he founded. The quartos of *Alcazar* and *Orlando*, insofar as they can be compared to these documents, differ enormously from what the "part" and the "plot" demonstrate to have been performed on stage. Granted, there is nothing fixed about performance, and granted, more than one version, indeed many versions, of any play may have been staged; however, in this case, all the available evidence points only to the difference between what was printed and what was staged. Nevertheless, so strong is Greg's antitheatrical bias that he cannot imagine the "wretched old texts"[16] of the quartos to have been produced in any way except through mutation in the theater—that is, as his biases combine, the provincial theater. Greg's prejudice against the theater seems exactly proportional to his identification with the plays' authors. He is dedicated to enhancing Robert Greene's literary reputation by reattributing from the theater to the author what Greg regards as the superior text of *Orlando* preserved in Alleyn's part: "It is by this play, if it could be recovered [in whole, rather than in "part"], and not by Danter's travesty [the quarto] that Greene has a right to be judged."[17]

Greg's narratives about the quartos have proved to be so influential that they require detailed scrutiny. His "critical examination" of the *Alcazar* quarto text represents itself as empirical, as taking its shape in the image of the text itself. Yet the "examination" yields a hypothesis about the quarto text identical to Pollard and Wilson's narrative of rent-and-roughly-stitched texts with which Shakespeare's company allegedly toured in plague time:

> When critically examined the text of *Alcazar* printed in 1594 proves to be a version drastically cut down by the omission and reduction of speeches, by the elimination and doubling of parts, and by the suppression of spectacular shows, for representation in a limited time, by a comparatively small cast, with the minimum of theatrical paraphernalia. . . . All indications point to the adaptation having been deliberately made for a special purpose or occasion, and in what one would on *a priori* grounds suppose to be the normal manner. We may, namely, imagine that the chief omissions were marked in the playhouse copy, that from this a shortened transcript was prepared by a regular scribe, that considerable further alterations and adjustments were made upon the transcript, and that this finally became the copy for the printed text.[18]

What differentiates Greg's position on *Alcazar* from Pollard and Wilson's on the Shakespeare "bad quartos" is Greg's supposition that the "performance text" survives in the printed version intact and unmediated either by further adaptation or by memorial reconstruction. This difference, a difference that identifies the printed text with the performed text, is both innovative and crucial for the development of subsequent narratives of "bad quartos."

Turning to the *Orlando* quarto, Greg reproduces this innovation with a difference, but the difference is his absorption into the *Orlando* narrative of yet other features of Pollard and Wilson's account of the Shakespeare "bad quartos." Here are the familiar elements of (1) the company forced to tour, (2) the cutting of the touring text to reduce its casting requirements, and (3) the sale of the touring company's book upon return to London,[19] but this narrative also re-presents—*purely as a function of performance needs*—all the conjectured activities that, for Pollard and Wilson, served the provision of a printed "literary" text. For Pollard and Wilson, the "bad quartos" were embellished from memory by actors to make the printed texts more like the authorial masterpieces that saw the London stage. But, for Greg, texts are embellished with purely theatrical low comedy to appeal to debased provincial taste, and memorial reconstruction now serves the company's performance need for a so-called prompt-book. The printing of the "bad quarto" is an afterthought, but its incidental supplementarity to the process of the text's construction ensures, in Greg's narrative, that the printed text *is* a performance text.

Greg's hypotheses about *Alcazar* and *Orlando* were at first received rather coolly by experts. Reviewing *Alcazar & Orlando*, E. K. Chambers attacked the foundational assumption of Greg's work, which Greg had borrowed from Pollard and Wilson.[20] Chambers pointed to the absence of any evidence that would associate a shortened text with provincial performance. It did not seem to him self-evident that, in the words of Pollard and Wilson, "abridgments . . . would be useless for London performances"[21] and so must originate with provincial tours. Chambers wrote: "I do not think that there is anything which shows that the conditions of provincial performance or the tastes of provincial audiences entailed shorter plays than were customary in London" (246). Evaluating Greg's elaborate and speculative theory about *Orlando*, Chambers modified the Pythagorean Theorem to observe that "the probability of such an hypothesis is in inverse ratio to the square of the number of separate conjectures which it contains. . . . I am . . . sceptical as to the possibility of reconstructing forgotten episodes of stage history, without more evidence than 'critical bibliography' by itself supplies" (248). The slipperiness of Greg's "critical bibliography" presents itself in his demonstration that the *Orlando* quarto is a provincial performance text because it can be staged by a cast of seven men and two boys. When the quarto requires the presence of "twelue peeres," Greg denies that it can be, in this regard, actually the performance text and discounts the literal text for making "impossible demands on the cast," that is, on his conjectural cast.[22]

In spite of Chambers's laudable skepticism, such is human credulity that Greg's theory about *Orlando* proved attractive to many because it was simplicity itself in comparison to what Pollard and Wilson had proposed as the origins of "bad quartos." By 1923 R. Crompton Rhodes had appropriated (and adapted) it for the Shakespeare "bad quartos," ignoring even Greg's statement that "we should look with suspicion on any theory that claims to be universally applicable."[23] In taking over Greg's work, Rhodes postulated as the source of a "bad quarto" the memory of only a single actor, rather than the collective memory of the whole company. In a second simplification Rhodes discounted deliberate abridgment of the text for alleged provincial presentation, but attributed the shortness of the "bad quartos" to the failure of the memories of those who reconstructed them.[24]

Rhodes was soon joined by others. In what was then received as an empirical study of *The Contention* and *The True Tragedy* (the earliest printed versions and the "bad quartos" of *2* and *3 Henry VI*), Madeleine Doran arrived in 1928 at conclusions that are virtually identical to those of Greg about *Orlando* six years earlier.[25] Doran does not remark on the identity of her findings and Greg's because hers, like his, are represented as arising self-evidently from different texts:

They appear to be shortened acting versions that have attained their present form through reporting and rewriting. Suppose that in 1592–93 a division of the "large London Company" . . . was made and that some went travelling. . . . Some of them had acted in the Henry VI plays. They produced the plays in the country with the necessary abridgement. The prompt-book would probably have been left with the company in London; its absence would allow occasional omissions of necessary material to be made and . . . effect permanent alterations. If only a few actors knew the plays they might make up a new prompt-book. . . . In the course of their performance they would pick up comic bits put in extemporaneously or suggested by the acting director, and ineffectual Latin lines would fall out. The company returns to London in the fall, is forced by hard circumstances to scrape together whatever it can by selling its properties and what plays it may have. They are legitimately the company's by right of acting. If the actors have made up a prompt-book in the country they can turn it over directly to . . . the publisher.[26]

In one important respect, however, Doran departs from Greg. While, for Greg, the "bad quartos" of *Alcazar* and *Orlando* are "wretched old texts" and "editors have complained of the badness of the texts in early prints," in Doran's view "it cannot be overemphasized that the Quartos [*The Contention* and *The True Tragedy*] are good acting versions [in] their accretion of comic matter, and the absence from them of a great deal of elaborate metaphor that has fallen out with the non-dramatic material [when] they have been acted, probably in the country, in some form similar to the one in which we have them."[27] It appears from this statement that by 1928, the date of Doran's writing, the origin of the "bad quartos" in provincial playing had already come to be regarded as a fact. It had already been forgotten that this fact had only nine years before been the innovative construction of Pollard and Wilson, a construction that depended wholly upon the allegedly self-evident badness of "bad quartos," a badness that could be matched with Pollard and Wilson's construction of provincial taste as bad. By reevaluating the "bad quartos" as in any sense "good," Doran, unwittingly no doubt, destroyed the basis for associating them with provincial performance, or with any performance at all, since provincial performance was the only kind of performance to which she or her predecessors linked "bad quartos." As soon as "bad quartos" are thought somehow "good," if only as "acting versions," there is no reason any longer to dissociate them, in Pollard and Wilson's terms, from the London theater or from London playwrights, both supposed to be "good." Yet, if the "bad quartos" in their newfound goodness are to acquire such associations, there is nothing to separate them from the "good quartos" and Folio-only plays, which enjoy the same associations, and therefore nothing with which to secure any privileged link to the theater for the "bad quartos."

By the thirties, Greg's speculations were so entrenched in Shakespeare textual criticism that, paradoxically, even those rebelling against them continued to embrace the greater part of them. The rebel was W. J. Lawrence, out to dissociate himself from the views of "eminent scholars who ought really to have known better that certain of these shortened versions were made by the players possessing the full texts for their own particular use while travelling about the country. There is not, however, a scintilla of evidence in favor of this assumption."[28] Yet the assumption that Lawrence seeks to establish in place of Greg's differs only slightly from Greg's, and there is not a scintilla of evidence in favor of it either. According to Lawrence, the "bad quartos" of *The Contention, The True Tragedy, Orlando, Romeo and Juliet, Merry Wives, Henry V,* and *Hamlet* all take their origin with a member of a small provincial company of actors with access to the playhouse manuscripts of the London company. This character of Lawrence's invention adapted and retranscribed these manuscripts to meet the needs of provincial playing that Pollard, Wilson, and Greg had by now established as facts: first, shorter performance time that required "long reflective soliloquies [be] cut to the bone,"[29] and, second, a smaller cast.

Entrenchment of Greg's theory is also evident in the way in which scholars who adopt it as the groundwork of their investigation can afford to profess skepticism about the unsubstantiated details that constitute the theory without thereby calling the theory into question. So D. L. Patrick, whose narrative about the origin of the "bad quarto" of *Richard III* is wholly indebted to Greg's paradigm, can remain loftily indifferent to such a crucial juncture in his story as the precise circumstances under which the rusticating actors of Shakespeare's company reproduced from memory their book of *Richard III* without Patrick apparently having to risk the collapse of his narrative:

> It is unnecessary to assume that the original copy was lost, stolen, missing, or left behind in order to believe that the company caused a new copy to be made, and set down in this new copy the lines and words that they were speaking upon the stage when they presented the play.[30]

The most substantial tribute to Greg's work on *Orlando* and *Alcazar* can be found in the great tome compiled by Alfred Hart in 1942 entitled *Stolne and Surreptitious Copies: A Comparative Study of Shakespeare's Bad Quartos.*[31] The standard for comparison employed by Hart was *Orlando.* Hart believed that he could prove the origin of the Shakespeare "bad quartos" by constructing categories of quantifiable data to show that these quartos differ from the "good" texts in the way that the *Orlando* quarto differs from the manuscript part for the lead role. And what he believed he could prove is that the Shakespeare "bad quartos" have precisely the same genesis as the one that Greg conjectured for the *Orlando* quarto. Hart's endorsement of Greg's achievement is a masterpiece of positivistic overstatement at the furthest remove from the skepticism with which Chambers greeted Greg's narrative:

> Dr. W. W. Greg's *Two Elizabethan Abridgments* (1923) is a model handbook of the principles and practice of investigating play-pathology. It represented a long-overdue revolt against the sterile warfare of theory-mongers, and cleared the air with an invigorating breeze of good sense. He kept to the narrow path of the scientific method, and obtained all his results concerning the genesis of *Orlando Furioso* Q1 from his closely reasoned analysis of the materials in that play and in the Dulwich MS. of Orlando's part. His deductions are such and so many as the facts will support. Up to the present no one has questioned his facts, methods or conclusions; he has definitely proved that all the forms assumed by corruption in this play were beyond question the work of actors and reporters.[32]

Hart's tone can still be heard today in the work of Brian Vickers, for whom Hart "irrefutably [has] confirmed" the nature of the *Hamlet* "bad quarto" as, so to speak, "*Hamlet* by Dogberry."[33]

Nowadays, Vickers is in the minority in echoing Greg and Hart's denigration of the "bad quartos." Doran's version of the story, rather than Greg's, has, in the last couple of decades, become the more powerful narrative because of the rise of a performance criticism that has valued the stage over the page. Such criticism still employs Pollard and Wilson's purely arbitrary linking of "bad quartos" with performances outside London but employs it to elevate the formerly "bad quartos" to a status equal to that accorded to the "good" texts. Ritualizing this newfound equality in what he calls a "marriage of good and bad quartos" of *Romeo and Juliet*, Random Cloud authorizes his Blakeian ceremony by giving the "good" and the "bad" equally respectable genealogies—the "good quarto" of *Romeo and Juliet* is the play as Shakespeare wrote it and the "bad" one is "held to reflect an actual production."[34]

II

Recent scholarship has done much to call into question Greg's narrative of "bad quartos" as provincial playing texts and, therefore, to call into question all that has issued from it in the last seventy years. Yet no one has drawn together this scholarship and brought its weight to bear on the "performance-text bad quarto" story. Paradoxically, therefore, the very scholar,

David Bradley, who has done most to undermine Greg's *Alcazar & Orlando* still regards "bad quartos" as provincial playtexts.[35]

Take, for example, Greg's assumption, which he shared with Pollard and Wilson, that provincial theatrical taste was inferior to London's, for the London companies rarely toured, doing so only when extended and serious plague inhibited them from playing in London or when their fortunes failed and drove them out of the city. Sally-Beth MacLean, executive editor of the Records of Early English Drama, has drawn upon the records of performance being amassed by that team of scholars to show that, far from "wandering" (to use Greg's term) in the country when they were dispersed from the London theaters, players followed traditional "tour routes . . . across England to towns and households with an established taste—and even need—for public and private entertainment." And, she points out, "it is worth emphasizing that [the Chamberlain's Men] did travel outside periods of inhibition in London."[36] MacLean and Somerset both indicate that in the years 1594–1603, in spite of gaps in the surviving records, the Lord Chamberlain's Men can be demonstrated to have toured four times. Their most extensive tour, according to Somerset, took place not in the early nineties, as Pollard and Wilson thought, but in 1597. Ingram calls attention to the considerable costs that a company would have to bear in touring, costs that would have prevented any company as destitute as, in his *Orlando* narrative, the Queen's Men were supposed by Greg to have been when they set out for the provinces.[37] Indeed, according to surviving records examined by Somerset, the King's Men became more active in the provinces only when they had achieved their status, and with it their wealth, as the preeminent London company.

Then there is the assumption, invented by Greg, that traveling troupes could expect to be granted permission from officials of provincial towns and cities to stage plays for which the companies had no "books," that is, texts of the plays containing authorization by the Master of Revels for their performance. In his *Orlando* narrative and in the Shakespeare "bad quarto" narratives that depend on it, the traveling companies are represented as performing with no book or with an unauthorized book that they have memorially reconstructed. Yet there are records, extant and already in print in Greg's time, that show concern by provincial officials for documentary evidence of the Master of Revels' approval of the plays in the touring companies' repertories. In the Hall Book at Leicester is inscribed on 3 March 1583/84 "Nota. No play is to bee played, but such as is allowed by the sayd Edmund [i.e., Edmund Tilney, Master of Revels], & his hand at the latter end of the said booke they doe play." There is also a warrant signed by the Lord Chamberlain on 20 November 1622 ordering mayors and other officials to "forbid & supresse all such playes shewes motions feates of actiuity sights & eury of them vntill they shalbe approved lycensed & authorized by the said Sr John Astley [Master of Revels] or his said Deputy."[38] These documents can, of course, be invoked to demonstrate that civic officials were lax in reviewing traveling players' documentation as well as to indicate that they were officious. It seems likely, since history is histories, that they were both, and therefore Greg's presumption of laxity cannot stand.[39]

Another Greg datum was that a traveling troupe would constitute only a fraction of the London company. Here Greg may well have been right, although there is extant only one documented instance of the size of a traveling troupe relative to the London company from which it was drawn, and even in this case the counts are a half-dozen years apart. In 1624–25 the King's Men's London company was thirty-five strong; in 1619, a touring troupe from the company comprised fourteen men.[40] This case, if it can be trusted at all, indicates, as a rule of thumb, that a touring company was less than half the size of its London parent.[41] At the same time, one must take into consideration that London companies grew enormously from the 1590s and early 1600s, when the "bad quartos" under consideration here were printed, to 1624–25. Bentley estimated that in the early period the Lord Chamberlain's did not exceed sixteen.[42] According to the rule of thumb (for what it's worth), a traveling troupe from the Lord Chamberlain's may not have been greater than seven in the 1590s, a number exactly equal to a recorded count for one Chamberlain's touring company in 1593. Indeed, none of the recorded counts of traveling troupes before 1600 exceeds ten.[43]

In applying to the Shakespeare "bad quartos" Greg's fairly well grounded assumption that only greatly reduced numbers toured, Shakespeareans have been at pains to "prove" (in Hart's parlance) that these quartos could be staged by small companies. For a long time, Shakespeareans were satisfied with the "proof" that particular "bad quarto" stage directions called for fewer actors than did directions in the "good" texts, while ignoring or discounting other stage directions in the "bad quartos" that called for more actors.[44] Such scholarly practice has been called seriously into question by Scott McMillin, who has argued that the "bad quarto" of *Hamlet*, in spite of its calling for many fewer roles than the "good quarto," would have required just as large a cast of speaking actors (eleven) as the "good quarto."[45] To make this argument, McMillin constructed the doubling patterns or casting charts for the "good" and "bad" quartos, using the rules for doing so that Greg had outlined in *Alcazar & Orlando*.[46]

There is no necessary connection between actual theater practice in the sixteenth and seventeenth centuries and Greg's rules, of course, but the results of their recent (re)applications not only to the Shakespeare "bad quartos" but also to the *Alcazar* and *Orlando* quartos may be of interest. According to Greg, the *Alcazar* quarto could be staged by twelve men (and four boys)—somewhat more than are to be found in touring troupes of the 1590s. But Bradley, who has applied Greg's own rules to the quarto, disputes Greg's calculation and insists that no fewer than fifteen men—and perhaps as many as eighteen—are needed.[47] For Greg, seven men (and two boys) could put on the *Orlando* quarto—just the number in a 1590s touring company; but Bradley's count is sixteen men and three to five boys—a full London company. According to Bradley, the "bad quartos" of *2* and *3 Henry VI*, touring texts in Doran's narrative, require "casts of over twenty-four, well in excess of the casts of the Folio texts, although they, too, are abnormally large."[48] Several scholars have recently used Greg's rules to devise casting charts for other Shakespeare "bad quartos"—*Romeo and Juliet, Henry V, Hamlet*, and *Merry Wives*. None requires fewer than twelve men (boys not included); one is thought to need as many as twenty men.[49] While the results are various and the method at least somewhat dubious, there remains a wide gap between the results and the recorded sizes of touring troupes around 1600. The gap does not prove that the "bad quartos" cannot be touring texts, but it does prove that the "bad quartos" cannot be *shown to be* touring texts.

Perhaps the discovery that has most dramatically turned over Greg's entire project in *Alcazar & Orlando* is Bradley's discovery of Peele's English source for *Alcazar* and Bradley's comparison of the source with the quarto. Bradley shows that, rather than being a cut theatrical text, as Greg argued, the quarto is far more probably a version of the playwright's own composition. Bradley writes, "[I]n every case where Greg suspects some large excision, Peele is most often following his sources with fidelity and has used all the available material. On the occasions when we can see that there is more in the sources that might have been used, there are reasons of casting that can be advanced to show why it was not. It would, indeed, be astonishing, if a play that had originally contained a good deal of incidental matter, had been cut down, in all relevant sections, in a way that accidentally brought it into such close and literal conformity with its sources as is the case with *Alcazar*."[50] Since Greg evidently mistook the authorial for the theatrical with *Alcazar*, there is no reason to trust his parallel construction of the *Orlando* quarto as a provincial theatrical text. After Greg, every representation of a Shakespeare "bad quarto" as a provincial theatrical text is by analogy with Greg's *Alcazar & Orlando*. What is perhaps most remarkable about Bradley's study is that he continues to reproduce the narrative that the Shakespeare "bad quartos" are touring and therefore also performance texts *after* he has removed the ground on which this narrative has been raised.[51]

III

The narrative of the "bad quartos'" origin in performance has been reproduced so often this century that now some scholars choose to forgo any
gesture towards this narrative and suggest that the "bad quartos" are self-
evidently performance texts. For example, Graham Holderness and Brian
Loughrey introduce the "bad quarto" of *Hamlet* by announcing its "intrinsic theatrical capacities."[52] Holderness and Loughrey construct an opposition between editors, with their concern about "literary" deficiencies of the
"bad quarto" *Hamlet*, and theater practitioners, with their appreciation of
these "intrinsic theatrical capacities." The implication is that theatrical practitioners have access to the "bad quarto" that is unmediated by the history
of its scholarly reception; these practitioners can therefore be depended
upon to discover in their performance of the text the true nature of its origin. Perhaps one might reply with the rather obvious generality that there
can now be no unmediated access to a sixteenth-century text, or one might
cite Nietzsche on the confusion between the use to which something may
be put and the purpose for which it may originally have been constructed:

> There is no set of maxims more important for an historian than this: that the
> actual causes of a thing's origin and its eventual uses, the manner of its
> incorporation into a system of purposes, are worlds apart; that everything
> that exists, no matter what its origin, is periodically reinterpreted . . . in
> terms of fresh intentions.[53]

But there is no need to limit the argument to such general terms. A
brief look at the discourse surrounding the earliest and the most recent
productions of the *Hamlet* "bad quarto" indicates how strong the influence
of scholarly opinion has been upon those who have directed, performed in,
and reviewed these productions. William Poel directed and starred in the
earliest production of 1881, an academic (rather than professional) undertaking whose staging and reception have recently been studied by Marvin
Rosenberg.[54] Poel approached what has come to be called the "bad quarto"
from quite a different angle from the one discussed in this paper. Instead of
reading the "bad quarto" as if it were a text that had once been performed,
Poel read it as thoroughly mediated by the complex mechanics of its genesis
and publication as these were understood in Poel's day. According to Poel:

> [T]he actor cannot help recognizing that the Editor [of the "bad quarto"] has
> endeavoured to reproduce the play as he saw it represented. . . . [I]f the
> printer's blunders could be corrected, a performance of the Quarto might be
> of some interest to students.[55]

Poel's words indicate his subjection to the narrative widely employed in the late nineteenth century to explain how some quarto texts came to be so garbled: a reporter (here called the "Editor") in the audience took down notes on the performance, perhaps with the aid of shorthand; these notes, supplemented by the contributions of a so-called hack poet, became printer's copy for a quarto like *Hamlet* Q1, whose text suffered further damage in the typesetting.[56] Poel's representation of the *Hamlet* Q1 on stage was powerfully influenced by this narrative; he depended on the quarto's larger features—the "arrangement of the scenes, the stage directions, the omissions, and the alterations"—"to guide and instruct" a director.[57] But in none of his productions did he have much confidence in its actual wording; his 1900 production was evidently criticized for its departures from the dialogue of the First Quarto. He replied in the *Athenaeum:*

> With reference to the recent performance by the Elizabethan Stage Society of the First Quarto "Hamlet," some of the press have objected that the text of the Quarto was not given as it was written. Perhaps, as many students may not be acquainted with the text of this quarto, space may be allowed me . . . to state that the language as it stands cannot be spoken on the stage, the sentences being unconnected to each other, and not even completed. Revision [by Poel, that is, not Shakespeare], therefore, was essential, and the plan adopted was that of replacing the imperfect lines by those of the First Folio. [58]

Poel's reviewers also judged his productions through the medium of contemporary scholarly theory about the First Quarto's origins. So the *Era* reviewer indicated that Shakespeareans "will doubtless be disposed to think that a 'stupid stage hack' had been at work on this ["botcher's text, the barbarously mutilated and imperfect version of the piratical printer"], and certainly will be indisposed to debase their idol [Shakespeare] by believing that he could ever have penned some of the rubbish for which this first quarto would make him responsible."[59] This reviewer could confidently predict the response of Shakespeareans who would see the production by reproducing what Shakespeareans had already written about the text before it was ever produced.

When Christopher McCollough, now a lecturer in drama at Exeter University, played Hamlet in a production of the "bad quarto" at Swansea in 1982 and when Sam Walters, artistic director of the Orange Tree Theatre in Richmond, directed the "bad quarto" *Hamlet* in 1985, scholarly opinion, as this paper has been at pains to demonstrate, had changed. Its change is registered in the discourse surrounding these productions, which is informed by an array of scholarship on the "bad quartos." Approaching the "bad quarto" *Hamlet* after a half-century of textual criticism written under the influence of Greg and Doran, with their insistence that "bad quartos" were actually performed, Walters was able to direct the "bad quarto" in the confidence that "It gives us a very clear idea . . . of what the Elizabethans regarded as the theatrical qualities of the play."[60] Or, in McCollough's words, "The First Quarto speaks to us of what might have been happening on the Elizabethan stage. . . . There are all sorts of clues in the play about how actors were working."[61] Walters had thoroughly assimilated scholarly opinion about just how the "bad quarto" embodied "theatrical qualities": "there were . . . ways in which the First Quarto probably reflects the practices of a touring company."[62] True to this opinion, Walters did not modify the "bad quarto" dialogue to make it more intelligible, as Poel had; instead, Walters, in his words, "did it in a rather purist way."[63] Reviewers of the Orange Tree production, who behaved themselves as responsible members of the community and, like Walters, researched prevailing scholarly theories to equip themselves for their task, were, as a consequence, much kinder than their nineteenth-century predecessors who attacked Poel so harshly. Nicholas Shrimpton found the production attractive in part because he had been taught by twentieth-century scholarship to imagine the original production of the "bad quarto" as staged, like the Orange Tree production, outside of the big London playhouses by a small company. So he found the "bad quarto" and the Orange Tree a perfect match: "The brevity of [the "bad quarto"] text proved ideally suited to the kind of small-scale performance for which it was, very probably, originally intended. Regional repertory companies who shrink from the cost of a conventional *Hamlet* might well consider this alternative."[64] Other reviewers reproduced the division that has marked scholarly writing since Doran, with her emphasis on how "bad quartos" sacrifice the literary text in the service of "good" theater: "Never mind lines like 'To be, or not to be, I there's the point' . . . the 1603 edition of *Hamlet* is a brisk, exciting play that lacks only the best qualities of subtlety and poetry in the second, authentic quarto"; "Great lines may be missing from this version but the vitality . . . means that we never feel the loss."[65] The more enthusiastic reception of the 1985 production of the *Hamlet* "bad quarto" cannot logically be reduced to a confirmation of the reigning scholarly belief that the quarto is a performing text; it would be more accurate to suggest that the reception has been produced by the belief it is supposed to have confirmed.

Such pre-post-erousness is produced by the power of academic narrative, in this case the power of Greg's "provincial performance-text bad quarto" narrative. As this paper has tried to show, it does not seem enough to oppose Greg's narrative, for those who have staged themselves as its opponents, like Lawrence, end up reproducing what they oppose. It may not even be enough to have undone the narrative, as this essay has tried to do, to show how Greg's assumptions are groundless. After all, there never was any evidence to support the claim that the "bad quartos" were performance texts either for the provinces or elsewhere, and Chambers, for one, knew and said there was none. To say the same thing again today, no matter at what length and in what detail, may do little to diminish the influence of this narrative, which seems to have acquired a life of its own in the repetition of readerly desire to receive it as true.[66]

NOTES

1. A. W. Pollard, *Shakespeare Folios and Quartos* (London: Methuen, 1909). Pollard put five texts into his category: *Romeo and Juliet* (1597), *Hamlet* (1603), *Henry V* (1600), *Merry Wives of Windsor* (1602), and *Pericles* (1609)—the only early printing of this play. Since 1909 various critics have sought to expand the category of "Shakespeare bad quartos" to include such diverse texts as *The Taming of a Shrew* (1594), *Richard III* (1597), both parts of *The Troublesome Reign of King John* (1591), *King Lear* (1608), *The First Part of the Contention* (1594, supposed to be a "bad quarto" of *2 Henry VI*), and *The True Tragedy of Richard Duke of York* (1595, supposed to be a "bad quarto" of *3 Henry VI*). The category has been still further extended to include a large number of other printed texts (and even one manuscript text) that have no relation to "Shakespeare." There has never been any enduring consensus, however, about how many and which texts are to be called "bad quartos," even though it has been very much in the interests of some members of the editorial community to represent such a consensus as existing, or, usually, as having until recently existed and being about to exist again, just as soon as detractors of the category are silenced. Some editors and textual critics use metonymy to refer to the "bad quartos" as "memorial reconstructions," thereby reifying their preferred theory of these texts' origin.

2. Brian Gibbons, ed., *Romeo and Juliet* (London: Methuen, 1980). Arguing that "the First, 'Bad' Quarto of *Romeo and Juliet* (1597) . . . obviously derives from a performance," Alan Brissenden castigates Gibbons for omitting the Q1 stage direction "*He offers to stab himselfe, and the Nurse snatches the dagger away*" (Brissenden, "*Romeo and Juliet*, III.iii.108: The Nurse and the Dagger," *N&Q*, n.s., 28 [1981]: 126–27). My own ox has similarly been gored; in an otherwise much-appreciated favorable review of the first eight volumes of the New Folger Shakespeare (ed. Barbara A. Mowat and Paul Werstine [New York: Simon and Schuster, 1992–])—an edition that eschews the "bad quarto" stage directions on grounds that will become clear as this essay proceeds—David M. Bevington remarks, with reference again to *Romeo and Juliet*, that "the editors thereby lose, if nothing else, valuable visual information in Q1's . . . [stage direction] Juliet *'goeth down from the window'* at 3.5.68" (review of the New Folger Shakespeare, *Archiv*, 1994).

3. See Stanley Wells et al., eds., *William Shakespeare: The Complete Works* (Oxford: Clarendon Press, 1986 [Modern Spelling]; 1988 ["Original" Spelling]), and Stanley Wells et al., *William Shakespeare: A Textual Companion* (Oxford: Clarendon Press, 1988), 28.

4. A. W. Pollard and J. Dover Wilson, "The 'Stolne and Surreptitious' Shakespearian Texts," *TLS*, 9 and 16 January 1919, 18, 30.

5. See Janette Dillon, "Is there a Performance in this Text?" *SQ* 45 (1994): 74–86. Section 3 of this essay was inspired by her paper.

6. W. W. Greg, ed., *Shakespeare's Merry Wives of Windsor, 1602* (Oxford: Clarendon Press, 1910). It is not possible to trace the theory very far back before Greg. Although G. I. Duthie (*The "Bad" Quarto of Hamlet: A Critical Study* [Cambridge: Cambridge University

Press, 1941], 41) has credited Tycho Mommsen (1857) with first advocating memorial reconstruction by an actor, William Bracy (*The Merry Wives of Windsor: The History and Transmission of Shakespeare's Text*, University of Missouri Studies 25, no. 1. [Columbia: Curators of the University of Missouri, 1952], 33–35) has demonstrated that it was first articulated, however briefly, in 1881 by Richard Grant White in connection with *Hamlet* Q1.

7. Greg, ed., *Shakespeare's Merry Wives of Windsor*, xl. It has sometimes been claimed by later editors and textual critics that Greg "proved" that the actor who played the Host was responsible for the quarto version, but Greg himself, far from sharing this view, later expressed profound doubts about his hypothesis and no sympathy for attempts to extend it to some other "bad quartos" (see his review of Harry Hoppe, *The Bad Quarto of Romeo and Juliet*, *RES*, n.s., 1 [1950]: 64–66. See also Paul Werstine, "Narratives About Printed Shakespearean Texts: 'Foul Papers' and 'Bad' Quartos," *SQ* 41 [1990]: 65–86, especially 77).

8. Greg, *Shakespeare's Merry Wives of Windsor*, xliii, xli.

9. Pollard and Wilson, "Stolne and Surreptitious," 18, 30.

10. Ibid.

11. Alan Somerset surveys and dismisses the literary "evidence" that has been cited for the projection of London's later theatrical superiority back into the sixteenth century; Somerset finds it wanting. He also counters Bentley's assertion that "there is little evidence that the local authorities received the travellers with enthusiasm" (G. E. Bentley, *The Profession of Player in Shakespeare's Time, 1590–1642* [Princeton: Princeton University Press, 1984], 84) with the information that in 95 percent of the recorded cases from Shakespeare's lifetime, touring companies were welcomed, rather than resisted, when they came to play. See Somerset, "'How chances it they travel?': Provincial Touring, Playing Places, and the King's Men," *Shakespeare Survey* 47 (1994): 45–60.

12. J. T. Murray, *English Dramatic Companies, 1558–1622*, 2 vols. (London: Constable, 1910).

13. The antiprovincial bias is still writ large in the research upon which the Oxford Shakespeare is based. According to Gary Taylor, the "bad quarto" of *Henry V* "was *undoubtedly intended*, not for the sophisticates of London, but for provincial audiences, whose tastes and expectations would be by comparison relatively old-fashioned" (Stanley Wells and Gary Taylor, *Modernizing Shakespeare's Spelling [with Three Studies in the Text of "Henry V"]* [Oxford: Clarendon Press, 1979], 77).

14. W. W. Greg, *Two Elizabethan Stage Abridgements: The Battle of Alcazar & Orlando Furioso* (Oxford: Frederick Hall, 1922), 5.

15. Ibid., 14.

16. Ibid., 2.

17. Ibid., 310.

18. Ibid., 15.

19. Ibid., 351–57.

20. E. K. Chambers, "Abridged Play-Texts." Review of *Two Elizabethan Stage Abridgements*, by W. W. Greg, *The Library*, 4th ser., 4 (1923–24): 242–48.

21. Pollard and Wilson, "Stolne and Surreptitious," 30.

22. Greg, *Two Elizabethan Stage Abridgements*, 248, 288.

23. Ibid., 5.

24. R. Crompton Rhodes, *Shakespeare's First Folio* (Oxford: Blackwell, 1923). Rhodes also allowed for the possibility that the player might have kept his own part (contrary to Greg, who thought that any company that owned the book of a play would secure all the parts as well). This might account for the (nearly) word-perfect reproduction in *Hamlet* Q1 of the Q2 versions of the single speeches attributed to the characters Voltemand and Lucianus

(the latter appearing only in the Mousetrap), but Rhodes was overextending this possibility in applying it to all the Shakespeare "bad quartos." His argument may have swerved in this direction in an effort to identify whatever practices were used to create the Shakespeare "bad quartos" with eighteenth-century practices with Sheridan's text about which Rhodes himself had discovered documentary evidence. For example, a manager of a provincial theater, one Hughes of Exeter, wanted *The School for Scandal* for his company. He was able to persuade an actor from one of the companies that had performed the play to help him. This actor, John Bernard, collected *the written parts* for eight roles: "With these materials for a groundwork, my general knowledge of the play collected in rehearsing and performing in it above forty times, enabled me in a week to construct a comedy in five acts" (quoted in Peter Alexander, *Shakespeare's Henry VI and Richard III* [Cambridge: Cambridge University Press, 1929], 70–71).

25. Madeleine Doran, *Henry VI, Parts II and III: Their Relation to "The Contention" and the "True Tragedy,"* University of Iowa Humanistic Studies 4, no. 4 (Iowa City: University of Iowa Press, 1928).

26. Ibid., 81–82. Doran also allows for the possibility that the company performs the play only from memory in the country, and that they reconstruct what they played only in order to sell to a printer (82). Even in this scenario, however, Doran identifies the printed text wholly with the performed text.

27. Greg, *Two Elizabethan Stage Abridgements*, 1–2; Doran, *Henry VI*, 76.

28. W. J. Lawrence, *Those Nut-Cracking Elizabethans* (London: Argonaut, 1935), 156.

29. Ibid., 159.

30. D. L. Patrick, *The Textual History of "Richard III,"* Stanford University Publications, Language and Literature, 6, no. 1. Stanford, Calif.: Stanford University Press, 1936), 147–48.

31. Alfred Hart, *Stolne and Surreptitious Copies* (Melbourne: Melbourne University Press, 1942).

32. Ibid., vii.

33. Brian Vickers, "*Hamlet* by Dogberry," *TLS,* 24 December 1993, 5–6 (5). Compare Kathleen O. Irace, *Reforming the Bad Quartos* (Newark: University of Delaware Press, 1994), which accepts Greg's conclusions regarding *Orlando.* Contrast the skepticism of Kristian Smidt, who has studied the relevant literature, with the enthusiasm of Hart and Vickers for Greg's work: "When a sufficient number of people adhere to a theory it assumes a specious authority. Unfortunately the provincial theory is only guesswork" (Kristian Smidt, *Iniurious Impostors and "Richard III"* [New York: Humanities Press, 1964], 27).

34. Randall McLeod (alias Random Cloud), "The Marriage of Good and Bad Quartos," *SQ* 33 (1982): 421–31 (426).

35. David Bradley, *From Text to Performance in the Elizabethan Theatre* (Cambridge: Cambridge University Press, 1992).

36. Sally-Beth MacLean, "Tour Routes: 'Provincial Wanderings' or Traditional Circuits?" *MaRDiE* 6 (1993): 1–14 (9, 10).

37. William Ingram, "The Costs of Touring," *MaRDiE* 6 (1993): 57–62.

38. J. T. Murray, *English Dramatic Companies, 1558–1642*, vol. 2 (London: Constable, 1910), 320, 352.

39. Cf. Bradley: "That [traveling companies] could have taken very great liberties with their [licensed] texts, however, seems to me against the balance of probability and involves the assumption that the Mayors and Headboroughs of towns who attended the performances were as naive and low-class as it sometimes suited Sir Walter Greg to represent them" (*From Text to Performance,* 73).

40. Bentley, *Profession of Player*, 186–87.

41. Alwin Thaler ("The Traveling Players in Shakspere's England," *Modern Philol-*

ogy 17 [1920]: 129–46) lists the following counts for traveling troupes (all taken, he says, from Murray's book, although he fails to give accurate references for some of them):

6   [no accurate reference—also the case with the rest that are not marked]
6   (Sussex's 1570)
7   (Chamberlain's 1593; Thaler says this list is incomplete)
8
10   (Worcester's 1583)
10
13   (Ellis Guest's, 1628)
15   (Queen's Men 1619)
16   (1640)
18
20   (Lady Elizabeth's 1618)

While it makes no sense to take an average of such different companies on such widely different dates, Thaler takes the average and calls it 10–12, making it the average size of a touring troupe. Bentley has higher numbers on the whole: 20 (1624), 15 (1634), 14 (1611), 13 (1612), 16 (1612), 15 (1619—as above), 14 (1619/20), 20 (1618/19—as above), 11 (1636), 28 (1634/35—Bentley thinks two companies are listed together here), 2 men, 14 boys and 5 horses (1615) (*Profession of Player*, 184–86). Such numbers would push the "average" much higher to 14.5, but again it is hard to see how an average would be meaningful.

Bradley thinks that "the whole company travelled" (*From Text to Performance*, 64). To support this contention he must adjust recorded figures upward, by, for example, inflating the count of Worcester's Men on tour at Norwich in 1583 from the recorded number of 10 to 14 by supposing that only the number of sharers is recorded and that the sharers must have been accompanied by hired men.

42. G. E. Bentley, *Shakespeare: A Biographical Handbook* (New Haven: Yale University Press, 1961), 123.

43. See note 40.

44. See, for example, Harry R. Hoppe, *The Bad Quarto of Romeo and Juliet* (Ithaca: Cornell University Press, 1948), 95–99; cf. Robert Burkhart, *Shakespeare's Bad Quartos: Deliberate Abridgments Designed for Performance by a Reduced Cast* (The Hague: Mouton, 1975), 55–65.

45. Scott McMillin, "Casting the *Hamlet* Quartos: The Limit of Eleven" in *The "Hamlet" First Published (Q1, 1603): Origins, Form, Intertextualities,* ed. Thomas Clayton (Newark: University of Delaware Press, 1992): 179–94.

46. Greg's rules presume no role splitting and no back-to-back doubling, but there is documentary evidence of both practices. As David M. Bevington has observed (*From "Mankind" to Marlowe* [Cambridge: Harvard University Press, 1962]) doubling patterns printed together with five early Elizabethan plays occasionally demand back-to-back doubling. The latest of these plays appeared in print in 1579. Similar doubts apply to the discounting of role splitting. There is little evidence of role splitting after the 1570s, but any security in the assumption that we can eliminate this possibility is challenged by the playbook of Massinger's *Believe as You List* (1631), which contains two exceptions. Of course, if one does not follow Greg' rules, one is unable to indulge the desire to construct doubling patterns at all.

47. Bradley, *From Text to Performance*, 127.

48. Ibid., 51. These figures of Bradley's are supported by T. J. King's independent counts of 24 men and 5 boys for *2 Henry VI* and 22 men and 5 boys for *3 Henry VI* (*Casting Shakespeare's Plays: London Actors and their Roles, 1590–1642* [Cambridge: Cambridge University Press, 1992], 78–79). Minor discrepancies between different scholars' counts are to be expected in light of the frequent indefiniteness and/or ambiguity of stage directions

and speech prefixes in early printed texts, as well as in view of the slightly different assumptions that different scholars entertain about theatrical practice, and the possibility of its representation in printed texts—matters on which there is much uncertainty.

49. Johnson: *Merry Wives:* 14, and 4 boys in the last scene (Gerald Johnson, "*The Merry Wives of Windsor,* Q1: Provincial Touring and Adapted Texts," *SQ* 38 [1987]: 154–65); Taylor: *Henry V:* 11 *(Modernizing)* (corrected to 12–13 in my "McKerrow's 'Suggestion' and Twentieth-Century Shakespeare Textual Criticism," *RD* 19 [1989]: 149–73 [164–65]); Bradley: *Romeo:* 12, with 6 or 8 boys (*From Text to Performance,* 234); *Henry V:* 16, with 3 to 5 boys (ibid., 235); *Hamlet:* 12, with 3 boys (ibid., 236); *Merry Wives:* 16, with 7 boys (ibid., 235); King: *Romeo:* 16, with 5 boys (*Casting Shakespeare's Plays,* 82); *Henry V:* 20, with 4 boys (86–87); *Hamlet:* 15, with 3 boys (ibid., 88); *Merry Wives:* 13, with 8 boys (ibid., 89).

50. Bradley, *From Text to Performance,* 170.

51. Ibid., 9.

52. Graham Holderness and Bryan Loughrey, eds., *The Tragicall Historie of Hamlet* (Lanham, Md.: Barnes and Noble, 1992), 19.

53. F. Nietzsche, *The Birth of Tragedy and The Genealogy of Morals,* trans. Francis Goffing (Garden City, N.Y.: Anchor, 1956), 209.

54. Marvin Rosenberg, "The First Modern English Staging of *Hamlet* Q1," in Clayton, ed., *"Hamlet" First Published,* 241–48.

55. Marion O'Connor, *William Poel and the Elizabethan Stage Society* (London: Chadwick-Healey and the Consortium for Drama and Media in Higher Education, 1987), 21.

56. Cf. A. W. Ward and A. R. Waller, eds., *Cambridge History of English Literature,* vol. 5 (Cambridge: Cambridge University Press, 1918), 263. Holderness and Loughrey are mistaken in identifying Poel as subscribing to a theory of memorial reconstruction (eds., *The Tragicall Historie,* 18). No such theory was yet available to Poel in 1881, since it was not until that year that Grant White first even hinted at the possibility that memory might have played a role in the creation of *Hamlet* Q1. It was many years later that Greg developed a *theory* of memorial reconstruction.

57. O'Connor, *William Poel,* 21.

58. William Poel, "The First Quarto 'Hamlet,'" *Athenaeum* 3776 (10 March 1900): 316.

59. Quoted by Rosenberg, "The First Modern English Staging," 243.

60. Bryan Loughrey, "Q1 in Recent Performance: An Interview," in Clayton, ed., *"Hamlet" First Published,* 125–36.

61. Ibid., 124–25.

62. Ibid., 127.

63. Ibid., 125. But not altogether in a "purist way," as Nicholas Shrimpton noted in his review, because "Walters had, reasonably enough, made absolute fidelity subordinate to the needs of performance and tidied up a few of the more ludicrous and confusing variants" (Shrimpton, "Shakespeare Performances in London and Stratford-Upon-Avon, 1984–85," *Shakespeare Survey* 39 [1985]: 191–98 [194–95]). Championing every word in the "bad quarto," Holderness and Loughrey dispute that Walters made the changes heard by Shrimpton (eds., *Tragicall Historie,* 28–29).

64. Shrimpton, "Shakespeare Performances," 195.

65. B. A. Young *Financial Times,* 5 March 1985, and Desmond Christy, *Guardian,* April 1985, quoted in Holderness and Loughrey, eds., *Tragicall Historie,* 19.

66. My thanks to Barbara A. Mowat and Eric Rasmussen for much valued help during the composition of this paper.

3

Greene's *Orlando:*
W. W. Greg Furioso

MICHAEL WARREN

The primary object of this essay [is] to prove from actual documents
the existence of a class of shortened adaptations of Elizabethan plays.

It will, I think, be admitted that the evidence available concerning the
history of the text is not only very complicated, but on the face of it
contradictory.

[John Dover Wilson's] theory is clearly suggested by the wish to find a
common explanation for all the cases under consideration. This is a
very natural and proper desire, but it is not a ground of argument.

It only remains to state my theory of the origin of Q, in other words to
construct a narrative of events that shall embody the external evidence
and at the same time explain the observed peculiarities of the text.
—W. W. Greg, *Two Elizabethan Stage Abridgements*

I

*Two Elizabethan Stage Abridgements: The Battle of Alcazar & Orlando
Furioso* is one of the major monuments of twentieth-century scholarship
concerning the early modern English drama; it is devoted to the exhaustive
examination of the relations between four important documents: two manuscripts without any authorial or scribal identification, namely, "The Plott of
the Battell of Alcazar" and the part of Orlando; and two printed quarto
texts, also without authorial ascription on their title pages, namely, *The
Battell of Alcazar* (1594) and *The Historie of Orlando Furioso* (1594). *Two
Elizabethan Stage Abridgements* itself also lacks any author's name on the
title page, a characteristic of many volumes in the Malone Society Reprint
series at that time;[1] the title page announces it as "The Malone Society /

Extra Volume / 1922," and the facing page indicates that it was "Printed for the Malone Society by / Frederick Hall M. A., at the / Oxford University / Press / 1922." All of this material is in the Society's characteristic lapidary upper-case. Meanwhile, the verso of the title page bears the following statement in the conventional mixture of upper- and lowercase: "The present essay in critical bibliography is presented to members of the Malone Society by the author, W. W. Greg"; it is signed *"Gen. Ed."* and is dated *"Apr.* 1923." The *"Gen. Ed."* was (as Greg himself would write), of course, W. W. Greg.

It is fitting that an essay that focuses on Greg's interpretation of two unique material documents of the early 1590s should begin by drawing attention to the absence of the author's name from the title page and to the anomaly of two apparently contradictory statements relating to the date of publication.[2] An "extra volume," *Two Elizabethan Stage Abridgements* was the first book of independent criticism that the Society had published; everything prior to that had been "reprints" of rare plays or else "Collections" of documents relating to the theater, as has everything published since then. Provided at no extra cost to the members, it was Greg's unsolicited gift to the world of scholarship, a study of two documents and two texts on a scale that had not been performed before. For Greg, it was the natural development of his work for the Society and in general: editor of the first six volumes in the Reprints series, he had issued texts of *Alcazar* and *Orlando* as the first two publications, both dated 1907 on the title page and with a general editor's note signed *"Dec.* 1906" on the reverse. Given Greg's role in the Society and in the world of bibliographical scholarship, the anonymity of the title page suggests a magisterial modesty.

The book itself, despite its formal opening, is far from impersonal; Greg presents himself immediately as a scholar among scholars, a personal voice recording his thoughts and insights and discoveries in first-person observations. After a dedication to Alfred William Pollard and John Dover Wilson, his "Forewords" describes how the plot and the part aroused his interest as he prepared his 1907 edition of the *Henslowe Papers* (in which they appear as an appendix) and how "with a view to instituting a critical comparison [he] persuaded the Malone Society to include reprints of the original editions of *Alcazar* and *Orlando* among its first year's publications"; more than fifteen years later he "take[s] up the problem anew with a definite object and I trust a better chance of success."[3] The objective as stated in the first paragraph of the "Forewords" is at least to establish the existence of a class of "shortened texts of Elizabethan plays in general" (1). But in the case of *Orlando Furioso* he had a further aim: the consolidation of the case for the existence of reported texts, texts produced with the help of nonauthorial memory. He had first advanced his conception of memorial reconstruction in his type-facsimile edition of the 1602 quarto of

The Merry Wives of Windsor in 1910,[4] but *Orlando Furioso* gave him a special advantage since its 1594 quarto could be compared against not a later printed version but a contemporary manuscript: Alleyn's part of Orlando, the only surviving professional actor's part from the period and a document presumably close to an authorial original.[5] Greg's extensive examination proved for him the inevitability of the hypothesis and established powerfully in scholarly discourse this category for the discrimination of early printed texts; it also incidentally provided a foundation for a number of other conventional ideas, such as the smaller company for provincial touring, the debased taste of the provinces, the touring company without a prompt-book, and so forth. Greg's essay has occupied a position of eminence since its publication; the theory has flourished and has been until recently a widely accepted and rarely challenged principle in editorial theory and practice.

Until recently the Greg volume has also gone largely unchallenged. At its first publication it received a fraternal interrogation by E. K. Chambers in a review article[6] that begins by describing it as an "intricate investigation, pursued through a substantial quarto volume, with all his remarkable powers of subtle analysis and remorseless patience," and that later states that "It would be of high value, as a model of textual treatment, quite apart from the direct end which it subserves."[7] After documenting his disagreements over the interpretation of some of the historical data, he records his view that Greg's concluding hypothesis concerning the origins of Q *Orlando Furioso* "accounts with remarkable ingenuity for all the peculiarities of the quarto text"; he then adds, however, that "Some of the fundamental features seem to me . . . individually hard to accept."[8] After a series of queries about Greg's positions, he concludes by saying that he "must frankly confess that [he has] no alternative reconstruction of the facts to oppose to Dr Greg's."[9] For the next seventy years most critics found themselves in the same position, though rarely advancing doubts as Chambers had done. B. A. P. van Dam is the sole conspicuous skeptic of the early period. He challenged Greg's work in 1929, arguing for greater error in the transcription of the Orlando part than Greg allowed, and assuming stenography as the method of reporting of the quarto text.[10]

Later textual studies by Sujit Kumar Mukherjee (1965) and Tatsumaro Hayashi (1973) add nothing to knowledge.[11] In a "Recent Studies" article on Robert Greene in 1990 Kevin J. Donovan reports no new work.[12] Critical essays on the play have not been plentiful. Of those articles published in the last twenty-five years, the essays of Gelber (1969) and Babula (1972) both quote from Greg's Malone Society reprint but ignore the problems of the text.[13] In his book on Greene, Charles W. Crupi acknowledges the issues that *Two Elizabethan Stage Abridgements* raises, but is not concerned with them beyond commenting that "the text [of *Orlando*] as we have it is obviously corrupt"; he quotes throughout from the Collins edition of the play.[14] In 1979 Gary Taylor attacked the circularity of Greg's argument concerning *Alcazar*, but he did not challenge his approach to *Orlando*.[15] In 1992 David Bradley produced a complete reexamination of Greg's discussion of *Alcazar* and its plot, presenting a new hypothesis that a plot "served . . . two essential functions: first, as a means of making out the actors' scrolls correctly, and second, as a skeleton or ground plan of the action." In the course of his examination of plots he alludes to Greg's arguments about *Orlando Furioso* and briefly challenges Greg's judgment: "One may take issue at every point with the readings that Greg judges on bibliographical grounds to be 'superior' in the scroll."[16] Since then Laurie Maguire has raised major questions about the arguments of the volume in her study of memorial reconstruction: she points to a number of anomalies and inconsistencies that arise from Greg's treatment of the evidence, especially concerning *Orlando Furioso*. She argues cogently that "Greg's method of identifying memory in Q *Orlando* is characterized by a lack of rigour."[17]

The reasons for the absence of further critical examination of Greg's work or reexamination of the material evidence are not hard to find. In a textual climate devoted primarily to the complex issues of the Shakespeare texts and especially to the discrimination of copy behind the quartos ("bad" and "good") and the Folio there appeared no reason to return to complex issues that Greg was judged to have explored thoroughly and satisfactorily; with memorial reconstruction a proved hypothesis, there was no need to revisit the sites of origin. I believe a more important reason lies, however, in Greg's book itself, which must be one of the most intimidating works of scholarship in the field. What Chambers called "his substantial quarto volume" is formidable in its appearance, in the density of its material, in the formats of its parallel texts, in its charts, in its confident justification of its hypotheses, in its persistent cross-referencing of evidence, and in the organization of its argument. Although the study of *Orlando Furioso*, with which I shall be chiefly concerned, may be read separately, many of its principles derive from the prior discussion of *Alcazar*. The layout of sections concerning *Orlando* is apparently systematic and informative, and gives an impression of clarity: introduction and summary; parallel texts of the part of Orlando (designated A) and the 1594 quarto (designated Q); a textual commentary on the parallel texts (which incorporates commentary on all of the quarto text, and so necessitates immediate access to a copy of the 1907 reprint), and then five separate sections that constitute a further comprehensive review of the features of the Q text. Although this arrangement appears to be a disciplined systematization of a daunting body of complex perceptions, and may indeed be the best possible organization for a difficult task, the experience of the text and commentaries is, even for the dedicated scholar, uncomfortable and exhausting. Textual scholarship is never mistaken for light reading, but Greg's presentation taxes the mind unusually, as one is obliged to move backward and forward in the work to read its arguments: "Q 33. The repetition from 1.27 may be original, but it is suspicious, especially in view of 1. 106" (204) (a reference to material outside the immediate book, but relatively easy to check since it does not require one to locate other places simultaneously in the primary book); "1168–75. The curious reconstruction of these lines, with the insertion of replies by Argalio, is discussed at p. 304 (for the subsequent omission in Q cf. p. 294)" (233); "1174. This illuminating corruption is discussed at pp. 299, 338" (233); "Q 1517. Like 1.1517, and part of 1.1521, this is evidently of the nature of gag (cf. pp. 304, 347)" (245); "Q 557. *No.* Again an insertion which the line will not bear (cf. p. 317). But it is required by the previous, very fatuous remark, which is thus further proved unoriginal. *For* may also belong to the reconstruction" (212).

As these quotations suggest, to understand the commentary one needs to read the later material simultaneously. And the later material is hardly friendly to the reader, as the following passage from the subsection entitled "Metrical Characteristics" indicates: "The curiously reconstructed passage, Q 667–9, is metrical, the additional line being particularly smooth. Nor do the inserted lines of Q in general stand out as metrically faulty: Q 1256, 1297–8 (possibly original), and 1407 are perfectly regular; so is Q 1540, though the following line is shaky; Q 1578 is only a foot short. Observe likewise that several of the more extensively reconstructed lines, such as Q 1176, 1287–8, 1360, 1485, 1490, 1586–9, in nowise [*sic*] betray their character through any irregularity in the verse" (328). It is not a matter of foolishly expecting complex material to be simplified so that it may be grasped at one sitting in a single linear reading. Rather, the brief summary of "conclusions to which the subsequent chapters of this study lead" on 133–34, prior to the parallel texts, is not adequate to support or enable a reading with any critical insight of the succeeding pages of textual commentary, which themselves constantly point to future cumulative arguments in the subsequent sections; and rereading is far harder than in most books. The verbal rhetoric protests that the book is designed to clarify a set of issues, but the experience of the book is of the accumulation of masses of data that are prejudged for the reader on principles that are not explained or justified. Indeed, one is expected to read in a state of suspended or partial knowledge throughout, accepting assumptions that are parts of hypotheses presented as facts: for instance, "Q 1027–42. This passage is necessarily absent from A, since it contains no speeches of Orlando, but it is related to the subsequent reconstruction of Q 1058–63, which *is known* to be unoriginal. It is *in fact* an insertion of Q. On this and the omission of A 179 see p. 305 (cf. p. 301)" (229; emphasis mine). Moreover, after such elaborate annotations of the text with their constant directions to future acts of clarification at later points in the book, there appears in the last section a fulfillment of this rhetoric of suspense: the "Critical Conclusions" are presented in a mode that suggests that they are the climax of a narrative in which the reader has been led through a mystery and now, Doctor Watson-like, will enjoy the presentation of the full picture. "It will, I think, be admitted that the evidence available concerning the history of the text is not only very complicated, but on the face of it contradictory" (349); "To reconcile these contradictions will be to solve the riddle of the quarto text" (350); "I now propose to bring forward one last piece of evidence which will, I believe, set us on the right track towards our goal" (350) . But that evidence (which concerns the two roundelays and has been discussed already on 218–19 and 302–3) is now introduced as if it were a fresh consideration, and in a mode of confident tentativeness. "The absence of these poems from A deprives us of any external criterion for the state of Q, but in the course of a minute study of the parallel texts the conviction has grown upon me that these lines are word-perfect and that they are of a sort that the reporter would almost inevitably have mangled. . . . The significance of this is obvious since it allows us to assert with some confidence that Q was prepared in the playhouse itself by a company which possessed the properties used in representation but was yet unable to avail itself either of the prompt-copy or of the individual actor's [*sic*] parts" (350–51).

This is not sound argument. No matter how much the conviction has grown upon one, one cannot claim responsibly either that lines are "word-perfect" in the absence of any secondary evidence, especially in a text otherwise condemned for its "corruption," or "that they are of a sort that the reporter would *almost inevitably* have mangled" (emphasis mine). Greg begins this transition to his "theory which at least takes cognizance of all the facts and may claim to be judged on its own merits" (351) by immediately anticipating and defending himself against charges of bad judgment: "I wish to avoid overstressing this evidence because I am aware that readers may be inclined to regard it as a figment of my imagination" (351). But that is what it is, and it certainly is not what would commonly be called evidence, even though he uses the word twice about it. This rhetorical pose of impartial objectivity coupled with preternatural percipience leads into Greg's final narrative, presented as the whole story finally achieved or revealed. But everything that has occurred so far has already been expressed in terms of this revelation; it underlies all the prior sweeping observations about Q. One is not persuaded by argument and evidence; rather one is bludgeoned into submission by confident repetition and a bewildering density of reference.[18]

But to assert that the organization and the method of argument of a work is unsatisfactory or misleading is not to disprove the hypothesis. A reassessment of the relation between A and Q is needed, and that can only be achieved by passing through Greg. As a contribution to this major undertaking I propose to conduct an investigation of certain passages in the two texts that are crucial to Greg's arguments. I wish to challenge certain assumptions that he makes so that further discussion may be conducted that may lead either to a new formulation of the relation between A and Q, or to a confirmation of Greg's views based on a new analysis of the evidence. In this I see myself continuing the work of David Bradley and Laurie Maguire; but where Maguire has been primarily interested in the idea of memory, I shall concern myself mostly with matters in which Greg makes assumptions about theater practice. I shall begin by summarizing Greg's relation of the documents and then proceed to focus first on issues that relate specifically to A, and then to some that relate to Q.

II

At an early stage of the formal argument that occurs after his general introduction to *Orlando*, the parallel texts, and the textual commentary, Greg sets out to articulate the relation between A and Q. He quickly asserts the authority of A: "Since A is an actor's part we may reasonably assume it to have been transcribed directly from a prompt-copy" (261). Having confidently described A as supplying "us with the most authoritative text possible of the play," he immediately, and not inappropriately, multiplies the possibilities of origin for Q, beginning from the reasonable proposition that "There is no abstract necessity why Q should go back to that prompt-copy" (261). He soon concludes, however, that Q is a "derivative" version of the play represented by A: Q is "demonstrably an incomplete" text, and Q-only passages "mostly differ in style" from the rest of Q (262). His key point in this argument, however, is that "common errors in A and Q prove that they depend ultimately upon a common original which we call X," and that X may be identified "with the prompt-copy from which A was directly transcribed" (262). Later X is described as a "playhouse manuscript" that "was a fair-copy made by a scribe from the rough sheets of Greene's original draft [that] had been worked over and altered, possibly by the author, to an extent that rendered it in parts not a little obscure, previous to its use by the scribe of A" (267). Of this hypothetical manuscript A is, in Greg's assessment, "an essentially faithful transcript" (266), and for all its problems A carries authority for Greg. The relation of A and Q is established from the earliest stage as a contrast of unequals, the assumption being that A is a "good" text and Q a "bad" text, with the absent authorial original serving as the ultimate source of value.

In setting up this duality, however, Greg makes some curious assessments of A's goodness. A is damaged and fragmentary, and Greg's reconstruction of its original physical form and dimensions is a fascinating study in redemption. Nevertheless, one may not be as persuaded as Greg is of the goodness of the text of A. Indeed, contrary to Greg's view, I would posit that A is not a particularly good text. On 263–67 he surveys the thirty-five passages "in which the reading of A is challenged" (265), and concludes on a note of optimism, beginning with the statement that "It seems on the whole probable that when criticism has done its worst there are hardly a score of instances in which A can be convicted of any serious departure from its original" and ending with the observation that "Considering the severity of the test which comparison with Q enables us to apply, I think that this result is rather remarkable, and that we can without much risk of error accept A as an essentially faithful transcript from the original prompt-copy" (266). It is tempting to fall into the trap of overstatement when responding to such a piece of rhetorical pleading, with its co-opting use of the "us" sliding into the modesty of "I think . . . rather remarkable," only to emerge once more in the reassuring statement that "we" can safely grant credibility to the A text. But Greg's own analysis raises questions about the nature of A as a part. I would like to consider it as a working part for an actor before considering its relation to Q or any hypothetical X.

It may be, as Greg says, that the scribe of A "was frequently unable to read his copy" (266) for some reason, and so produced a part that presents problems for a later reader. But a reader having problems is different from an actor having problems: readers can simply suspect error, be disconcerted, and move on to the next passage, but actors have to stand in public and speak and do things; they expect and are expected to make sense for others. In this respect some of those small "slips" that Greg uses Q to correct are the sort of routine errors that give little trouble: one does not need Q to interpret "maskine" (A 42) as "masking," or "lighneth" (A 314) as "lightneth." Odd verbal dissonances, such as "may" (A 217) where "must" seems to be required, or "speakes" (A 280) where one might expect "speak'st," or "welcome" (A 515) where a past tense could be anticipated, are such as any actor could endure and edit for himself.[19] In such cases, and others that Greg reviews on 263-64, his statement that "there is something, however slight, inherently objectionable" (265) in some readings independent of any comparison with Q is unexceptionable, however strained the oxymoron. But elsewhere the part would present problems. There are numerous places in which the text of A is obscure to the point of unintelligibility, and the commentary is trenchant:

> hir name hir writing, foolishe and vnkind
> no name of hirs, vnlesse the brokes relent
> to hear her name, and Rhodanus vouchsafe
> to rayse his moystened lockes, from out the Reedes
> and flowe with calme, along his turning bownds
>
> (A 25–29)

Greg: "This passage, as it stands in A, is certainly involved and, strictly speaking, senseless" (216).

> that woundring you proue poor Orlandos foes
>
> (A 81)

Greg: "There is something wrong here. As it stands neither text seems to make any sense" (221).

> wher both the lillye, and the blusshing rose
> syttes equally suted, with a natyue redd
>
> (A 195-96)

Greg: "The conceit in A is hard to follow and the text is not above suspicion" (231).

> Thankes Angelica for her
>
> (A 509)

Greg: "This is not intelligible, and may be corrupt" (248).

While I may disagree with the precise terms of each of Greg's formulations, in general I accept that all these passages in A are problematic and presume that they were not intelligible to the actor who was to play the role. Elsewhere there is evidence of serious uncertainty. One of the notable features of the part is the number of times that either a corrector or Edward Alleyn himself was obliged to modify the work of the scribe. For instance, at A 208, a passage for which there is no Q equivalent, the corrector entered a complete line, "inconstant base iniurius & vntrue," where the scribe had apparently left a blank space; he intervened similarly at A 239 "when *crimson* Daphne ran away for loue," and at A 243 "Clyme vp the clowdes to *Galaxsia* straight" (italic marks the additions). But what remains striking

is not that the scribe left gaps within the part to be filled in later, perhaps by
him, perhaps by others, but that some gaps were not filled. In at least three
places the blank space remains empty:

> dare Medor court my venus, can hir eyes
> bayte any lookes, but such as must admyre
> what may Orlando deme
>
> (A 48–50)

> the pretious shrubbes, the   & mirh
>
> (A 521)

> more braue, then wer t<hos   >keles
>
> (A 531)

In each case Greg's comment is apt. Of A 48-50 he writes: "At this point Q
omits a line and a half preserved in A. This is perhaps not surprising considering their obscurity. . . . There is reason to suppose corruption" (219–
20). Of A 521: "The missing word is presumably *frankincense*: the scribe
habitually leaves too little room" (248). And of A 531, the last line of the
part, Greg writes in a note on Q 1592, its corresponding line: "It is mutilated towards the end, but it is almost certain that where the tear occurs the
scribe had left a blank. The space is quite inadequate to the four syllables
required, and there is no reason to suppose that Q's reading *gallant Grecian* is not original" (248). From the fact that "In eighteen passages the
scribe left blanks where he was unable to decipher his copy or suspected its
accuracy," Greg infers that while "These are undoubtedly defects in his
transcript, . . . they argue conscientious care on his part" (272). Greg emphasizes that considerable efforts were made to correct the part: to him the
fact that "In ten cases a corrector . . . made more or less substantial additions or alterations therein . . . [and that] There are also perhaps two dozen
small corrections made either by the scribe himself . . . or by the reviser . . .
shows that some care was taken to bring the transcript into agreement with
the original, but it does not suggest any very serious degree of inaccuracy"
(272). That is possible, but I believe that the evidence is susceptible of
another interpretation.

This accumulation of data leads me to hypothesize not that A may be
"an essentially faithful transcript from the original prompt-copy" (266),
but that it may have been an inadequate document to serve an actor who
had to perform a role. The uniqueness of the Orlando part, its association
with Alleyn, its latent value as an isolated point of comparison with a printed
text—all these features encourage a great investment in the document, and
the assumption has been (and Greg's work has served to reinforce this gen-

eral conviction) that this is a serviceable part, such a part as an Elizabethan actor would expect to use in his profession.[20] But I wish to propose a suspicion that should be entertained. As a category of one this part provides no secure basis for generalization; what if the part were regarded not just as damaged by use and time but also as originally unfinished and imperfect, for some reason unused or rejected? For all its assumed value for scholars, it is not clear that as it stands it is a "good part." What actor wants to play a gap or a confusion? If it is Alleyn's part, revised by him, why is the word "frankincense" not inserted, or the words "gallant Grecian," especially if, as I am ready to accept, they are the probable readings? Greg's confidence in the accuracy of the part may be misplaced; it may be less reliable than he thought.

Having cast doubt on the reliability of A in general, I wish now to turn to a passage that plays a crucial role in Greg's hypotheses, and to argue that at this point the A text is actually quite adequate as it stands and needs no help from Q to be intelligible and playable. One of the cruxes for Greg or for anyone approaching these texts is the place where Q prints the roundelays that Orlando reads. Q reads as follows:

> Orlando reades this roundelay
> Angelica is Ladie of his hart,
> Angelica is substance of his ioy,
> Angelica is medcine of his smart,
> Angelica hath healed his annoy.
> Orl: Ah false Angelica. What haue we more?
> Another.
> Let groues, let rockes, let woods, let watrie springs,
> The Cedar, Cypresse, Laurell, and the Pine,
> Ioy in the notes of loue that Medor sings,
> Of those sweet lookes Angelica of thine.
> Then Medor in Angelica take delight,
> Early, at morne, at noone, at euen and night.
> Orl: What dares Medor court my Venus?

(Q 647–60)

The equivalent passage in A reads:

> what ~~Italiano per dio~~
> dare Medor court my venus, can hir eyes
> bayte any lookes, but suche as must admyre

(A 47–49)

Greg approaches this crux on three separate occasions (218–19, 302–3, and 350–51). The material proves difficult for him to work with: A lacks poems that in his opinion the play requires, and a phrase in A, "Italiano per dio," has been written and crossed out; Q has the stage directions "Orlando reades this roundelay" at Q 647 and "Another" at Q 653, prints the two poems, and gives Orlando a new speech prefix after each poem; A has a line and a half of text after "dare Medor court my venus" that Q lacks. Two questions are urgent for Greg in the context of his assumptions about the origins of the texts. How did the actor of A speak the poems if they were not in his part? How did the poems come to be differentiated in the printing of Q if a reporter would know them merely as part of the spoken text of the play?

Greg's solutions are ingenious, although, as I hope to show, not necessarily correct. In the first instance he argues: "The absence of the roundelays from A is most instructive, since it shows that they were not learned as portions of the part but read by the actor from the actual scrolls hung up on the stage. . . . This deprives us of the means of checking the text offered by Q, but careful consideration suggests that it is quite unusually accurate" (218). This unfounded assumption of Q's unusual accuracy allows Greg to resolve his second problem with the aid of other presumptions based on the presence of the medial stage directions and new speech prefixes: "Thus the inference both from typographical and textual evidence is that the source of these ten lines is different from that of the surrounding text, in other words that the reporter was able to transcribe the actual scrolls used in performance" (351). I have already quoted Greg's anxious anticipation of criticism of this passage ("I wish to avoid overstressing this evidence because I am aware that readers may be inclined to regard it as a figment of my imagination"), with its claim that even if wrong it points to a comprehensive theory of the texts. But it is not evidence with which this theory is concerned, but the justification of the theory. Alternative and simpler explanations of these particular data are available.

First, there is no reason to assume from A that the actor playing Orlando from that part was expected to speak two roundelays aloud onstage. Read without a prejudicial awareness of the Q text, A makes theatrical sense: Orlando spies the poems on the trees, reads them in silence, and then says "what / dare Medor court my venus, can hir eyes / bayte any lookes, but suche as must admyre. . . ." There is no need for him to do more. What of the canceled "Italiano per dio"? The origin and the cause of the deletion of this phrase can only be a matter of speculation, but it is useful to inquire how the phrase might have functioned if it had been played. It would be Orlando's exclamation upon seeing the poems, an exclamation that might explain why they were not to be read aloud, as being incomprehensible to the audience. The audience does not need to know the verbal content of the poems, since everything in the plot has made it evident already; Q's roundelays merely present the illustration of what has already been anticipated, and Orlando's subsequent behavior does the rest. It may be that "Italiano per dio" was crossed out because it was judged unnecessary to the role. Second, Greg's assumption that the actor did not learn the poems with the rest of his part but rather read them from the actual scrolls is an extraordinary idea that has, to my knowledge, no foundation in theatrical practice. On 302, after again insisting without any evidence that "these verses, or at least some equivalent, must always have formed part of the text" and that their absence from A "proves" their presence as properties, he justifies this invention by stating that "No doubt in a playhouse which was what we should call a repertory theatre, where 'runs' were unknown and a dozen representations constituted a tolerable success, it was desirable so far as possible to lessen the burden on the actors' memories, and we may presume that such devices as this were frequent" (302–3). This is an extraordinary act of supposition, even for Greg. He is unreasonable in assuming that ten lines of verse would make any difference to an actor of a major part of at least five hundred lines, especially ten lines of verse of which four are of a simplicity that makes memorization easy.[21] Moreover, no actor will normally rely on props rather than memory: props are fragile, are subject to provision by others, and get damaged or lost.

Greg's solution to his second problem, the paratext surrounding the roundelays in Q, depends absolutely on his theory of their being written on the scrolls and on the further supposition that the scrolls were available to the preparer of Q, who copied them rather than relying on some memorial agent. But if Q is not a reported text in the form that Greg desires, there is no need to perceive the presentation of these roundelays as in any way special. Moreover, nothing in their typography gives evidence upon which to build a theory of origins; as Greg's own discussion on 218 makes clear, the variant practices in relation to letters appearing in printed plays present a record of inconsistency from which no principle can be derived.[22] However, it is notable that when Greg comes to his final discussion of the passage as "one last piece of evidence which will, I believe, set us in the right track towards our goal" (350), the two stage directions coupled with his "conviction" that the poems are "word-perfect" enable him to infer that the poems were transcribed from "the actual scrolls used in the performance," and that inference allows him to draw the conclusion noted at the start of my discussion, that "Q was prepared in the playhouse itself by a company which possessed the properties used in representation but was yet unable to avail itself either of the prompt-copy or of the individual actor's [*sic*] parts" (351). The totality is a fantasy that has no foundation in any evidence that Greg presents concerning Elizabethan theatrical practice.

Similar problems occur with Greg's treatment of the Q-only speech in which Orlando virulently condemns womankind for treachery and cruelty; the speech begins:

Foemineum seruile genus, crudele, superbum:
Discurteous women, Natures fairest ill,
The woe of man, that first created cursse;
Base female sex, sprung from blacke Ates loynes,
Proud, disdainfull, cruell and vniust. . . .

(Q 718–22)

Greg asserts that "These fourteen lines are certainly original, and the most likely explanation of their absence from A is that they were deliberately cut for reasons considered at p. 303. They certainly duplicate to some extent the Italian verses that follow" (222). On 303 the passage "seems unquestionably original," and its absence from A is attributed to cutting by Alleyn, "who would not wish the effect of his swank Italian tirade to be impaired by a preceding paraphrase." This observation is notable for the crudity with which an unjustified attribution of vanity to an actor is passed off as responsible argument, but what is more interesting is that the idea involves yet another layer of thinking about the text, because it presumes that Alleyn had access to the hypothetical prompt-book in advance of the preparation of his part and was able to arrange that the preparer of the part not write out that speech. Further, as Greg moves into considering the function of the speech, his confident assertion is undone by his own footnotes. He remarks of the speech, "No doubt this was in the first instance intended for the benefit of an audience unable to appreciate Ariosto in his own tongue." Even before one reads on into the next sentence, which introduces the idea of "at least one line elsewhere in Q [that] would seem to have been *accidentally* omitted by the scribe of A" (emphasis mine), one is drawn to the footnote in which he concedes that a nearby Q "omission" of two lines in A "suggests that there may be alternative versions here." The next sentence in the footnote opens whole worlds of possibility: "Assuming A 89–91 to be authentic, of which we cannot be quite certain, it is not impossible that Greene, if the manuscript ever found its way back into his hands, may have made the substitution in one direction or the other" (303 n. 2). The ideas in this amazing sentence, which entertains the possibility both of "unauthentic" material in A (beyond errors of transcription) and of authorial revision in the prompt-book behind A and Q, are never developed, however. But the weakness of the structure of the argument is made transparent by such asides.

III

The greater part of the argument concerning *Orlando Furioso* in *Two Elizabethan Stage Abridgements* is devoted to the defects of Q as discerned by

comparing it with A; since Greg exalts A as a reliable source of information about the desired original from which Q has declined, features of difference tend to be constructed negatively as omissions, inferior additions,
or corruptions in Q. Greg's management and classification of large numbers of examples are remarkable here, and his observation is often acute,
especially in his examination of the possible presence of "actors' gag,"
amplifications of the text through actors' contributions, and in his attention
to questions of meter. For instance, he discusses two passages where the
meter appears to be disrupted by unnecessary phrases. At Q 1099–1102[23]
the following exchange occurs:

> Mar: His Court is his campe, the Prince is now
> in armes.
> Turpin: In armes? Whats he that dares annoy so
> great a King.

Greg is right to suspect that Turpin's words "In armes?" are superfluous to
the presumed blank verse pattern (304). And at Q 1521–25 the text reads:

> Orl: Heare you sir: You that so peremptorily
> bad him fight,
> Prepare your weapons for your turne is next,
> Tis not one Champion that can discourage me,
> Come are yee ready.

The A-text contains lines to which these may be compared:

> You that so proudly bid him fight
> out with your blade, for why your turne is next,
> tis not this champion can discorage me
>
> (A 442–44)

The comparison confirms that if Q derives from some document related to
A, Q has expanded the text to include "Heare you sir" and "Come are yee
ready." But in this context it is important to draw attention to Greg's recognition that the first line in A is only eight syllables; in the textual commentary he addresses the issue: "I suspect that *peremptorily* is correct since it
gives both better sense and better metre than A's *proudly*" (245). He is
obliged here to acknowledge the contradictoriness of the evidence, even as
in his persistent criticism of repetitions of individual words in adjacent or
proximate lines he must admit his preference for Q's readings over A's in
the following passages:

for I thou seest / I am mighty Hercules
see whers my massy clubb vpon my neck

(A 105–6)

Thou seest I now am mightie Hercules:
Looke wheres my massie club vpon my necke.

(Q 760–61)

Instead of pursuing the complexities and contradictions of Greg's perceptions of variation between the texts, I wish to return to the earliest part of Greg's analysis of the Q text and to address aspects of his argument concerning the playhouse. Once more the point of entry will be Greg's theatrical judgment.

Greg's scenario for the nature of Q involves the perception that it is a reduced version of the original from which A derives. He notes that A records 467 lines of Orlando's part, but only "approximately 277 reappear in Q"; assuming a proportional level of omission in Q of material that appeared elsewhere in the original, and taking into account the number of lines that he classes as nonauthorial additions to Q, he calculates that the Q text of 1465 lines (represented by 1613 lines of type) probably derived from an original "full text" that "contained perhaps 2400 or even 2500 lines" (310). For Greg Q is very much cut, and it is in this context that he reads the Q text. Although the mathematics is interesting and the argument plausible, the evidence he adduces to prove the badness of the state of Q is open to challenge. In section 10, "General Features of the Quarto Text, together with Minimum Cast" he expresses his dissatisfaction with the dramaturgy of the early scenes and shows a desire that the action should proceed with at least a Shakespearean amplitude, if not an Ibsen-like meticulousness. On page 278 he performs his reconstruction:

> I would quite tentatively suggest that the original arrangement of the opening scenes was somewhat as follows: (i) the assembly and quarrel, Q 1–247; (ii) Orlando, Angelica, and Marsilius; Orlando plans an attack on Rodomont; Marsilius determines to approach Sacrapant; (iii) Sacrapant's ambition and Argalio's invitation, Q 248–377; (iv) the attack on the castle, Q 378–452; (v) Orlando and Angelica; Marsilius' "league" with Sacrapant; (vi) interview of Medor and Angelica, now only Q 453–66; (vii) Sacrapant meets Angelica coming from the grove and plans his treason, Q 467–571; (viii) an unidentified scene; (ix) Orlando's madding, Q 572, &c.

This structure is the conclusion of a sequence of discussions of individual scenes that Greg finds unsatisfactory in their presumed abbreviated states. Although he may indeed be correct that the text is cut from the original, the forms that his dissatisfaction takes do not justify the conclusion at which he seeks to arrive. As with the actor's part, he is not sensitive to theater conditions; he is strictly concerned with literary and narrative values and not with performance.[24] To suggest that the Q text is not as "bad" as he believes it to be, I would like to examine two passages on which he focuses.

At the end of the first major scene of Q, three of the four rejected suitors—Rodamant, Mandrecard, and Brandemart (but not the Soldan of Egypt)—angry at Angelica's choice of Orlando, vow to attack her father Marsillus for his affront in approving her choice; the scene closes as follows:[25]

> Bran: Tush my Lords why stand you vpon termes
> Let vs to our Skonce, and you my Lord to Mexico.
>   Exeunt Kings.
> Orl: I sirs, inskonce ye how you can, see what
> And thereon set your rest.   (we dare,
>   Exeunt omnes.
>   Manent Sacrepant and his man.
>
>   (Q 242–48)

Of these lines Greg remarks in his notes: "At this point the text breaks down. The lines which summarily wind up the episode are little more than the remnants of verse. It would seem that an adapter has cut the concluding speeches" (208). It would be useless to engage in an argument for the excellence of the quoted lines: after the first two hundred lines or so of fairly regular blank verse, they are not of the quality of what has gone before. It is not clear whether Greg is stating that these are the surviving pieces of two speeches from which material has been excised, or whether speeches other than these that survive in rudimentary form have been excised completely. But this idea of excision is important because of Greg's view of what follows. Sacrepant remains onstage with his man, and utters a vaunting speech in which he sees that the imminent war will bring such chaos that he will triumph, gaining both Marsillus's crown and Angelica:

> Boast not too much Marsillus in thy selfe,
> Nor of contentment in Angelica;
> For Sacrepant must haue Angelica,
> And with her Sacrepant must haue the Crowne:
> By hooke or crooke I must and will haue both.
>
>   (Q 249–53)

Within thirty-five lines, however, Sacrepant is clearly talking to his man in a circumstance—"these mutinies"—where there is military action afoot:

Sirra, what thinkes the Emperor of my colours,
Because in field I weare both blue and red at once?
Man. They deeme my Lord, your Honor liues
        at peace,
As one that's newter in these mutinies,
And couets to rest equall frends to both. . . .

(Q 282–87)

For Greg this is one of many instances of the "cutting down" of the original: "We hardly need comparison with the manuscript to show that this is indeed the case. The very first scene affords clear evidence. . . . It is evident . . . that some considerable time has elapsed since the quarrel and that hostilities have actually begun. In other words two separate scenes have been brought together by the excision of intervening matter and have coalesced on the stage" (275–76). I wish to resist Greg's hypothesis, which is nevertheless quite reasonable given the peculiar lines that precede this passage, and propose instead that the stage action of Sacrepant's speech may not be as Greg interprets it.

Passage of time on the stage of this period is far from realistic; in the context of a scene that lasts a whole night, Iago's "By the mass, 'tis morning; / Pleasure and action make the hours seem short" (*Othello* 2.3.378–79) can be read as a metatheatrical comment.[26] In this scene Greg reads the first speech as a commentary by Sacrepant at some time later than the lords' wooing scene; he is reading back from line 283. But in the theatrical sequence there is no sense of lapse between the "Exeunt Omnes" and Sacrepant's prompt reflections on Marsillus's vulnerability; indeed, the speech appears to respond immediately to what Marsillus has just said and done before leaving the stage. Greg assumes a passage of time occurring *in* line 248, "Manent Sacrepant and his man." I would argue that Greg is seeking literary time or narrative time, not dramatic or theatrical time, and I would advance in justification of this distinction a similar passage from a text whose "goodness" is unchallenged: *Richard II* in any of its quarto or folio manifestations.

In 1.4. Aumerle reports that he "brought high Herford . . . / But to the next high way, and there I left him" (1.4.3–4); at line 54 Bushy announces Gaunt's imminent death. In 2.1 Gaunt speaks with York, the king arrives, is reproved by Gaunt, and after Gaunt's death offstage confiscates his property. At his exit, Northumberland, Willoughby, and Ross discuss the grievous condition of England under the king's abusive government, and within sixty lines Northumberland is announcing that Bolingbroke and a body of dissidents have an invasion fleet on the sea heading for England, and that they have been delayed only because they were waiting for the king to leave for Ireland. This dialogue is some seventy-seven lines long (2.1.223–300). It contains a literary-narrative problem: the events displayed do not correspond to any realistic temporal sequence so far evidenced in the play—Bolingbroke has been gone only a few hours. But no one ever argues for a missing scene or for the indication of a passage of time between the king's exit and Northumberland's speech.[27] In this respect the seventy-seven-line scene is analogous to the situation in *Orlando Furioso:* the initial exchanges of the dialogue in *Richard II* connect with what has just occurred, but the subsequent exchanges move the plot into its next phase—time passes before our eyes, while we concentrate on the significance of events and actions. The scene ends at a much later time than when it began. This, I believe, is what happens in Sacrepant's scene in Q, a conventional theatrical move that Greg examines in terms of realistic narrative values. Although the context that surrounds the passage in *Richard II* inspires more confidence, it is important when looking at problematic texts not to exaggerate the problems, and that is what Greg does in this instance.[28]

The discussion of the second passage also requires reference to the dramaturgy of the scene from *Richard II*.[29] When the king and queen enter to Gaunt in 2.1, the Folio indicates that "*Aumerle, Bushy, Greene, / Bagot, Ros, and Willoughby*" (TLN 710–11) also make their entrance then, and that on the king's departure "*Manet North. Willoughby, & Ross*" (TLN 872). The quarto stage direction for the entrance does not indicate who accompanies them, "*Enter king and Queene, &c*" (sig. C4). To their exit it simply adds "*Manet North.*" (sig. D2) and maintains its silence about the others, who immediately engage in conversation with Northumberland; although a reader, actor, or director of the quarto text will probably assume that Ross and Willoughby are designated by the "*&c,*" they could be conceived as entering as the king exits. The quarto text with its less specific stage directions and absence of scene division does not limit us as the Folio can, or as a modern edition will. In either text, however, it is possible to conceive the scene's conclusion as taking place somewhere other, as well as sometime other, than its place and time of origin.[30]

I wish to apply this principle of interpretation to a scene in which Greg detects cutting. At Q 544ff. Sacrepant tells his man about his plan to enflame Orlando with jealousy:

> Hard by for solace in a secret Groue,
> The Countie once a day failes not to walke:
> There solemnly he ruminates his loue.
> Vpon those shrubs that compasse in the spring,
> And on those trees that border in those walkes,
> Ile slily haue engravn on everie barke

The names of Medor and Angelica.
Hard by Ile haue some roundelayes hung vp.

(Q 544–51)

After giving his man instructions to dress as a shepherd, he says, "And marke thou how I play the caruer," the man exits, and the stage direction reads "Sacrepant hangs vp the Roundelayes on the / trees, and then goes out, and his man enters / like a shepheard" (Q 569, 572–74). Concerning this passage Greg aptly dismisses the anxieties of Greene's past editors, who "have been troubled by the fact that in all this Sacrapant [*sic*] never carves the names at all," and dismisses Dyce's introduction of a stage direction in which Sacrepant carves. He continues:

> This [the carving], however, would be an insufferably tedious piece of business, and, moreover, Sacrapant is not at the time in the "secret Groue." No doubt the stage-direction marks the beginning of what was originally a new scene. Sacrapant is discovered in the grove, having already carved the names as the audience may see, and now engaged in hanging up the roundelays. And we may conjecture that he did not leave the stage without speaking. Again intervening matter has been cut out and two originally distinct scenes have coalesced. (276)

This seems again to be a piece of criticism insensitive to theatrical practice. One must begin by asking how Dyce (and Greg) expected Sacrepant to carve the names, and what Greg assumed that the audience saw onstage when Orlando recognizes the names of Angelica and Medor carved together (Q 618–39). I do not know the answer to these questions, but presume that perhaps nothing was there, and that on the line "And marke thou how I play the caruer" Sacrepant established visually onstage that the names were "engravn on everie barke" by performing some perfunctory theatrical code for carving or by pointing to some location where the imaginary carvings were to be conceived as being, after which he hung up the roundelays, in whatever form they were represented, presumably the form used a few years later for another Orlando to hang verses on trees. The action of this sequence presents no problem except to the realist approach. There is no need for the presumption of a missing scene; Greg assumes it is an interview between Angelica and Medor in the "secret Groue" that exists in Q as "a fragment" at Q 453–66 (277), during which time Sacrepant prepares his carvings and his roundelays. But Q is a theatrical narrative, and does not follow the conventions of realism.

I do not mean to argue from this the excellence of Q's dramaturgy or its authorial origin; I am concerned merely to challenge a mode of thinking that gives false grounds for disparaging Q. Lest the example of *Richard II* appear isolated and open to debate, I would like to consider a second Shakespearean passage where stage location is fluid, and where attachment to realistic criteria produces interpretive problems of the very kind that Greg is creating for himself here. Q *Othello* has no scene divisions in the fourth act; F does, and all modern editions follow F in including them. In 4.2, Othello's conversation with Desdemona is conducted somewhere apparently private: he tells Emilia to shut the door (4.2.28) and behaves as if he were in a brothel. At his departure Emilia leaves the stage to bring in Iago; after their conversation the women go in when "these instruments summon to supper" (4.2.169). When they leave the stage Roderigo enters to Iago: where does their ensuing conversation take place? Some explanation could be made for Roderigo's presence in what seems to be the general's private quarters, but that seems implausible.[31] Rather it seems that Iago has stayed onstage, and the location has altered. No critic that I know of has ever suggested that a scene is missing between the exit of Desdemona and Emilia and the entrance of Roderigo. Fluidity of location operates successfully here, as it does in Q *Orlando Furioso.*

IV

At the beginning of *Two Elizabethan Stage Abridgements,* beneath the dedications to Pollard and Dover Wilson, appear three epigraphs. The last is Alfred North Whitehead's famous dictum, "Seek simplicity and distrust it." Greg's work seems to follow that injunction, but perversely: it creates a labyrinth in fulfilling a simple desire. On page 256, Greg begins his analysis of the phenomenon of "reporting," one of three "relational possibilities" between texts that he proposes, the others being literary revision and stage adaptation. After reviewing "certain hypothetical cases of reporting" (256) in a single paragraph two pages long, he begins the next by suddenly announcing: "Reporting, then, is an exceedingly important and widespread bibliographical phenomenon" (258). Nowhere in those two pages is there any evidence adduced to support this statement; it merely springs out of a context that has encouraged a sense of probability and has rendered the reader receptive to the idea upon which the previous hundred pages have been constructed. It is actually just Greg's assertion of his own desire.

That desire for a fact called "reporting" or "memorial reconstruction" pervades all the data in the essay on *Orlando Furioso.* As Laurie Maguire has pointed out, however, Greg establishes no criteria by which to test the validity of his selection of features in a text that might indicate memorial origins. Rather, he assumes that the quarto is a case of reporting, identifies (with the aid of A as a control) some features in it that may be assumed to be consequent upon reporting, and proves to his satisfaction that the text is reported.[32] Such a process of advancing a hypothesis, presenting the evidence, and concluding the hypothesis proved is not in itself faulty; the faultiness here lies in the failure of the argument concerning the evidence to convince, for neither A nor Q is quite as Greg describes it.[33] And, as Greg himself acknowledges, the evidence in the relation of A and Q is often contradictory.

No one who considers these documents and who works on Greg's analysis of them can fail to be awed by his ability to marshal great quantities of data and to construct a narrative to account for them. At the close of the book (352–57) he presents his final scenario, one that relates the documents to the cloudy history of the theater companies with which they have been associated. He imagines that soon after 26 December 1591 (Greg's probable date for the performance of *Orlando Furioso* at court), the Queen's Men, who owned Greene's play, were "in very low water . . . and they disappeared from London shortly afterwards . . . part[ing] with several of their plays" (352–53). The manuscript of *Orlando* then came to Alleyn, who was acting with Lord Strange's company. Greg presumes that the touring company continued to perform the play in the provinces without a prompt-book, and that the play underwent a slow mutation as it was adapted to new audiences, and as new actors learned their parts "by ear in the course of rehearsal" (354) rather than from conventional parts. At some date there was a need for a prompt-book, and that was created by a group reconstruction: "All the members who had a working knowledge of the play met together and, having secured the services of a ready writer, proceeded in turn to dictate their parts as well as their memories would allow" (354). Greg works from the knowledge that they performed at court on Sunday, 6 January 1594; he uses Henslowe's report that on 8 May "they broke & went into the contrey to playe"[34] to surmise that they sold their manuscript to John Danter, who printed it—but not before he had had the Latin checked and the classical names rendered with some correctness, and had "transferred his rights and to some extent his responsibility in the matter to Cuthbert Burby," who became the publisher of what Greg calls in his prejudicial penultimate sentence, "the strange abortion" (357).

This elaborate and inventive reconstruction of possible events is a maze whose complexities are such as only the experience of daily life or university administration can rival; that being so, it has a certain plausibility, although like all such constructions it is, as Greg says, only a theory, and "The value of such a theory, that is the likelihood of the narrative being true, must be judged by its antecedent plausibility—that is its consonance with experience—and the completeness and economy with which it accounts for the facts" (352). Unfortunately, the experience with which it needs to be consonant is that of the theater of the 1590s, and there does not exist the evidence by which such plausibility might be judged. Nevertheless, like E. K. Chambers in the penultimate sentence of his review in *The Library*, I too "must frankly confess that I have no alternative reconstruction of the facts to oppose to Dr Greg's."[35] At the same time, however, I hope that I have shown that although his narrative could conceivably be true, many aspects of the argument and of the use of the evidence are dubious.[36]

NOTES

1. *The Battle of Alcazar* and *Orlando Furioso*, for instance; in both cases the title page of the original bears no author's name. The treatment of books where the author's name is on the title page appears inconsistent from as early as volumes 12 and 13 (both dated 1909). Two reprints dated 1921 and 1925 frame the Greg volume and illustrate the inconsistency: vol. 45 (1921), *James the Fourth*, does not have Greene's name on the title page, while vol. 51 (1925), *Edward the Second*, prints Marlowe's. However, the identity of the preparer/editor of any text is always recorded in a general editor's note on the verso of the title page.

2. There is a third incongruity that should be noted: while the book's title is clearly *Two Elizabethan Stage Abridgements*, the spine reads *Alcazar & Orlando*.

3. W. W. Greg, *Two Elizabethan Stage Abridgements: The Battle of Alcazar & Orlando Furioso* (London: Malone Society, 1922), 3. Wherever possible, references to this volume are included directly in the text.

4. W. W. Greg, ed., *Shakespeare's Merry Wives of Windsor 1602* (Oxford: Clarendon Press, 1910).

5. The title page of the quarto reads: "THE / HISTORIE OF / Orlando Furioso / One of the twelue Pieres of / France. / As it was plaid before the Queenes Maiestie. / LONDON, / Printed by Iohn Danter for Cuthbert Burbie, and are to be / sold at his shop nere the Royall Exchange. / 1594." All quotations are drawn from W. W. Greg, ed., *The History of Orlando Furioso, 1594* (London: Malone Society, 1907). The manuscript of the part of Orlando is Dulwich College MS I, fols. 161–71; it is reproduced in collotype facsimile and transcribed in W. W. Greg, ed., *Dramatic Documents from the Elizabethan Playhouses. Stage Plots: Actors' Parts: Prompt Books. Reproductions and Transcripts* (Oxford: Clarendon Press, 1931). All quotations in the text are from Greg's transcription in *Two Elizabethan Stage Abridgements*; I have expanded scribal contractions silently.

6. E. K. Chambers, "Abridged Play-texts," *The Library*, 4th ser., 4 (1923–24): 242–48.

7. Ibid., 242, 244.

8. Ibid., 247–48.

9. Ibid., 248.

10. B. A. P. van Dam, "Alleyn's Player's Part of Greene's *Orlando Furioso*, and the Text of Q of 1594," *English Studies* 11 (1929): 182–203, 209–20.

11. Sujit Kumar Mukherjee, "The Text of Greene's *Orlando Furioso*," *Indian Journal of English Studies* 6 (1965): 102–7; Tatsumaro Hayashi, *A Textual Study of Robert Greene's "Orlando Furioso" with an Elizabethan Text*, Ball State Monographs 21, Publications in English 15 (Muncie, Ind.: Ball State University Press, 1973).

12. Kevin J. Donovan, "Recent Studies in Robert Greene (1968–1988)," *ELR* 20 (1990): 163–75.

13. Norman Gelber, "Robert Greene's 'Orlando Furioso': A Study of Thematic Ambiguity," *MLR* 64 (1969): 264–66; William Babula, "Fortune or Fate: Ambiguity in Robert Greene's 'Orlando Furioso,'" *MLR* 67 (1972): 482–85.

14. Charles W. Crupi, *Robert Greene* (Boston: Twayne, 1986), 108; J. Churton Collins, ed., *The Plays and Poems of Robert Greene*. 2 vols. (Oxford: Clarendon Press, 1905). Greg had no respect for Collins's edition; see his review in *MLR* 1 (1905–6): 238–51, or, for example, *Abridgements*, 207, note on Q 131: "*Durandell*. Collins has one of his thoroughly misleading notes."

15. Gary Taylor, "Three Studies in the Text of *Henry V*," in Stanley Wells and Gary Taylor, *Modernizing Shakespeare's Spelling with Three Studies in the Text of "Henry V"* (Oxford: Clarendon Press, 1979), 120–23.

16. David Bradley, *From Text to Performance in the Elizabethan Theatre* (Cambridge: Cambridge University Press, 1992), 88, 67.

17. Laurie E. Maguire, *Shakespearean Suspect Texts: The "Bad" Quartos and their Contexts* (Cambridge: Cambridge University Press, 1996), 83.

18. I referred in passing on p. 68 to Greg's use of "of course." The frequency of his use in the "Textual Commentary" of words and phrases that preclude debate is notable. The following list is not exhaustive. "Of course": Q 315–22; Q 438; Q 445–47; 608; Q 998–1000; A 238; 1266; Q 1311–12; A 365; Q 1560–62; Q 1601; Q 1611. "Doubtless": Q 302; Q 498–505. "No doubt": 642; 1407. "Clearly": 1048; 1182–83. "It is clear that": Q 315–22; 471–72; Q 1129. "There is no question that": Q 323. "is evident": Q 983–1009. "Evidently": 1015–16. "Certainly": Q 94. "Manifestly": Q 412–18. "Obviously": Q 442; 1182–83; 1268. "Almost certainly": 1297–98. "Can hardly be": Q 1138–39. "Must belong": 1303–14. "It is in fact": Q 1027–42. Similar uses appear in the narrative commentary as well.

19. Cf. Tom Davis's essay, "The Monsters and the Textual Critics," in this volume.

20. The publication of "The Part of Poore," prepared by David Carnegie, in *Collections XV* (London: Malone Society, 1993), 111–69, makes available another actor's part of the period, but it is from an amateur performance at Christ Church, Oxford, and no other evidence exists for the play from which it derives. This part and the three others that appear with it in the same manuscript book are discussed in David Carnegie, "Actors' Parts and the 'Play of Poore,'" *Harvard Library Bulletin* 30 (1982): 5–24.

21. I have never seen this idea entertained in relation to the poems of Orlando that Rosalind and Celia read in the third act of *As You Like It*.

22. Greg's discussion of the inconclusive evidence concerning the printing of "letters" in editions of Shakespeare and Jonson shows his desire and his inability to make a sound case for his speculation but his persistence with it nevertheless. To the evidence that he cites I would like to add the treatment of Edgar's reading of the letter in the fourth act of *King Lear*. In Q1 there is no introduction of the letter in the uncorrected state of sig. K1r, but the corrected state prints "*A letter.*" at the end of the line above; there is a new speech prefix afterward in both cases. In Q2 "*A letter.*" appears medially in the line before the letter, and there is a new speech prefix afterward. In F "*Reads the letter.*" appears medially in the line before the letter, and there is no new speech prefix afterward.

23. Greg numbers by lines of type, not lines of verse.

24. See Gary Taylor's discussion of Greg's study of *Alcazar*: "Greg's analysis is also repeatedly hampered by a rather poor sense of the theatre, a quality surely of paramount importance in any discussion of theatrical adaptation" (*Three Studies in the Text of "Henry V,"* 122).

25. In discussing passages from Q I follow its spellings of the characters' names. Throughout his study Greg uses spellings derived from A because "where the names of the characters vary in A and Q it is A that agrees with the source" (262).

26. All modern spelling quotations from Shakespeare are from G. Blakemore Evans, ed., *The Riverside Shakespeare* (Boston: Houghton Mifflin, 1974).

27. David Bradley also discusses this scene and its "telescoped time-scheme" to illustrate the nature of theatrical time in *From Text to Performance*, 29.

28. The reference at Q 283 to Sacrepant's wearing "blue and red at once" suggests a change of clothes somewhere after Q 248. I see no reason why such a change (the putting on of a cloak?) should not take place onstage.

29. Quotations from the Folio are from *The Norton Facsimile: The First Folio of Shakespeare*, prepared by Charlton Hinman (New York: W. W. Norton, 1968). Quotations from the quarto of *Richard II* are from *Richard II 1597*, ed. Charlton Hinman, Shakespeare Quarto Facsimiles No. 13 (Oxford: Clarendon Press, 1966).

30. David Bradley discusses the aspect of location in this scene in his exposition of "the place-logic of entrances" in *From Text to Performance*, 32–33.

31. In the Shakespeare Santa Cruz production of 1990 the conversation between Iago and Roderigo took place in a stage space that was dominated by Desdemona's bed; Roderigo's curiosity was emphasized, as was Iago's audacity in bringing him into such a private space. Interesting justifications for this location abounded; I found the situation always implausible.

32. Maguire, *Shakespearean Suspect Texts*, 83–84.

33. For a discussion of the relation of rhetoric and proof in textual criticism, see Gary Taylor, "The Rhetoric of Textual Criticism," *TEXT* 4 (1988): 39–57.

34. Greg, *Two Elizabethan Stage Abridgements*, 356; for the complete entry, see *Henslowe's Diary,* ed. R. A. Foakes and R. T. Rickert (Cambridge: Cambridge University Press, 1961), 7.

35. Chambers, "Abridged Play-texts," 248. He concluded the review with a salutary comment: "Perhaps I am temperamentally sceptical as to the possibility of reconstructing forgotten episodes of stage history, without more evidence than 'critical bibliography' by itself supplies."

36. I wish to thank A. R. Braunmuller, Laurie Maguire, Lee Rappold, and Paul Werstine for their help and advice in the preparation of this paper.

Part II:
Interrogatives

4

The Monsters and the Textual Critics

TOM DAVIS

Imre Lakatos, in his brilliant deconstruction of the practice of mathematics, suggested that one of the ways that mathematicians cope with exceptions to a theorem is by a strategy that he called "monster-barring."[1] You simply label the exception as so bizarre as not to qualify as a true refutation, and then can behave is if it did not exist: as the Lacanians would say, it becomes part of the Other. This strategy, however, as both Lakatos and Lacan knew well, does not work. A problem is a problem, and does not cease to exist by a simple relabeling. The theory of textual criticism, in my view, is beset by these monsters, in the form of paradoxes, impossibilities, deceits. This paper is an attempt to let the monsters speak, and to see if thereby they can be accommodated.

I would like to offer three propositions:

1. Textual criticism is necessary.
2. Textual criticism is impossible.
3. Textual criticism is universal.

In other words, we must go on, we can't go on, we go on. For Beckett this seems to have been agonizing, and for textual critics too, life sometimes seems a little insoluble: beset, in fact, by monsters of every kind. But for the rest of us, this is how life is lived, from compromise to compromise: something we do constantly, without too much trouble.

In order to demonstrate this I will begin with a classic textual crux from *Othello* that is intended to demonstrate the impossibility of textual criticism. I will then discuss how textual criticism is something we do all the time, and offer a description of this real-life textual criticism. Next I intend to compare and contrast this with textual criticism proper, and show (I hope) how much of the theoretical argument inspired by the latter arises

from a process of mystification that obscures the essential identity of the
two processes, specifically with regard to two traditional causes of dispute:
the science/art distinction in textual criticism and the problems around
author's intention. I end with a personal reminiscence, a cheerful conclusion, and the answer to a riddle proposed by A. E. Housman.

When I was an undergraduate, in a more heroic age of literary criticism, there seemed to be two views available of the play *Othello*. One of
them, which one could call the Tom Brown view, was associated with the
Victorian critic Bradley, and depicted the hero of the play as an essentially
decent chap who had been led astray in an inadvertent moment. The Tom
Brown view went with the Flashman view of Iago, naturally. The critic F.
R. Leavis, on the other hand, who had spent the First World War in a Quaker
ambulance unit, was understandably less enthusiastic about generals, and
reread Othello as the villain of the play: a superficial individual, the leading astray of whom was no problem at all. This view naturally went with
the demotion of Iago to a narrative convenience. One of the arguments in
favor of Leavis's view, which I remember finding particularly plausible,
centered on Othello's final soliloquy; a damaging blow to the Tom Brown
theory was that Othello, having transgressed rather seriously even by the
more relaxed ethical conventions of Jacobean tragedy, doesn't appear to be
particularly apologetic. In later years, as the result of my metamorphosis
from Leavisite to textual bibliographer, I discovered that that really rather
depended on which text you read.

For instance, if, like a large proportion of the undergraduate popula-
tion you happened to consult the New Arden Shakespeare, you would read
a text based in a crucial place on the quarto of 1622, the original of which
reads as follows:

> When you shall these vnlucky deedes relate,
> Speake of them as they are, nothing extenuate,
> Nor set downe ought in malice; then must you speake,
> Of one that lou'd not wisely, but too well:
> Of one not easily iealous, but being wrought,
> Perplext in the extreame; of one whose hand,
> Like the base Indian, threw a pearle away,
> Richer then all his Tribe.[2]

Here Othello is comparing himself to an Indian, who would not understand
the value of what he has just thrown away, however precious to others; his
act in so doing could therefore not be blamed. The primary signification of
"base" would therefore have to be, not moral, but social: low in the scheme
of things. Since what he is talking about is the brutal murder of his own
wife, it is hard not to see this, as Leavis would say, as self-justification.

If however you happened to buy the cheap Signet edition, which believes (following Greg) that the Folio is right wherever it is not obviously wrong, then the text you would read would derive from this:

> When you shall these vnluckie deeds relate,
> Speake of me, as I am. Nothing extenuate,
> Nor set downe ought in malice.
> Then must you speake,
> Of one that lou'd not wisely, but too well:
> Of one, not easily Iealious, but being wrought,
> Perplexed in the extreame: Of one, whose hand
> (Like the base Iudean) threw a Pearle away
> Richer then all his Tribe[3]

Here, in the Folio version, the situation is quite different. Opinions have varied slightly as to who this Judean might be, but a solid majority feels that Othello is actually comparing himself to Judas, the supreme betrayer, whose remorse was so great at the realization of what he had done, and lost, that he, as Othello is about to do, committed suicide. In that case "base" now implies a very heavy self-condemnation—the heaviest possible, in fact—and Leavis's unrepentant Othello vanishes into thin air.

What are we to do with this situation? Or, rather, what are literary critics to do? The first thing that we can observe is how important textual criticism is to literary criticism: how completely and utterly literary critics are at the mercy of the vagaries of textual transmission, and, in the case of Leavis (notoriously) but of many others too, how little they seem to be aware of this. Here we have two famous and seminal interpretations, that affected the reading practice of generations, almost entirely dependent (it is not too strong to say) on variation of one letter in one word; and each critic is completely unconscious of this fact. It is a distinguishing characteristic of the way that literary texts are read that immense importance can suddenly be invested in a single word, letter, or even comma, out of any that compose it unpredictably. Other texts—computer programs, for instance, or bank statements—may similarly have momentous consequences attached to tiny items, but this significance is predictable. With literary texts, as Morse Peckham has pointed out,[4] you can never tell which word may be seized upon and installed as the core of an argument.

The second piece of information that we can derive from our reading of the readings in *Othello* is that there is absolutely no way of knowing with any degree of certainty at all which of the two readings to choose as the basis of our interpretation of the play. Let us look at what a textual editor might do with this problem.

Essentially there are two ways of doing textual editing, which correspond to what used to be called the art and the science of textual criticism. The science approach in this case will begin, perhaps, with the insights of analytical bibliography, which hopes to be able to tell us which compositor set which bit of text, what the relation is between the Folio and the quarto (though in this latter instance I suspect the bibliographer would have to use the techniques of the traditional textual critic, collation and recension) and so on. To make a long story short, there is no agreement of any significance between textual editors that will help us at all with the Indian/Judean problem: neither of the two witnesses has preponderant authority for any instance of variance. Greg's view as to the supremacy of the Folio, in spite of the respect which his opinion properly attracts, is not widely accepted, but no alternative view seems to have clearly emerged.

All that science can tell us is that the problem is probably paleographic in origin. In other words, somewhere behind one or other version there may well have been a bit of handwriting in which it was possible to mistake the u for the n or vice versa. This doesn't help much, except in one important respect: if it is true, it makes it unlikely that Shakespeare wrote both words, one as a revision of the other.

But apart from this there is nothing that we can do except use art: or, as it is commonly called, literary judgment. We must look at the context of the whole play, and of Shakespeare's plays, and of what we know about literature, to find the answer. In this activity the textual critic and the literary critic are effectively one and the same.

The arguments between those who favored art and adherents of the supremacy of the science approach are now, mercifully, part of the interesting history of mid-twentieth-century bibliography, and there is a general air of comfortable agreement that when science won't help you, art will have to do, unreliable and disputatious though it may be. Or, to put it in the normal and more respectful and optimistic terms, the textual editor will, when other methods are not useful, resort to literary judgment; he or she will operate as a literary critic. However, this is to some extent a cover-up, as every textual critic faced with the daily insolubility of textual cruces knows very well.

This, I would suggest, is because there are two essential differences between literary and textual criticism, which are disguised by the reverence attaching to the concept of "literary judgment." The first difference is this. The readings produced by textual critics, once produced, are taken as true; the person who produced them, and his or her labors, become immediately invisible. The edited text is what people read, not the lemmata or even, much, the textual introductions; and they expect this text to be correct. I would suspect that Leavis's un(textual)critical approach to *Othello*, after nearly half a century of sustained propaganda about the importance of textual criticism, is still the norm rather than the exception. However influential the readings of a literary critic, no one treats them with the same—quite extraordinary, when one thinks of it—faith that is commonly applied to the labors of textual criticism: these are taken for granted as being the true, correct, and only readings, whereas everyone knows that a literary critical reading is only an interpretation, which can be readily superseded by a more plausible one, and no doubt will be, as fashions change.

Secondly, even if this misapplied faith were not applied, and the reading public, having learned the tedious mysteries of textual critical analysis, knew just how provisional the apparent solidity of the edited text often is—even then the textual critic's position would not be much improved: there is another, and much more painful, distinction between textual and literary criticism. Literary critics make an entire profession out of not agreeing with each other: interpretations must be individual, or they are worthless. But textual critical judgments aren't like that: their job is not to be interesting, but (in some sense) to be "true." So, not surprisingly, there is definitely no settled literary critical opinion as to the meaning of *Othello*; how is a textual critic to operate? Telling him or her to behave like a literary critic doesn't really help matters, I would suggest; in fact, the reverse.

In practice, as a reading of the textual notes attached to this particular crux in various editions of *Othello* makes clear, this literary-critical technique has not produced anything like a single view, or a solution to the problem. For instance (taken more or less at random):

> Othello is lamenting his ignorance, stupidity, gullibility and descent to savagery, none of which is applicable to Judas. The kiss Othello gives Desdemona is hardly a sign of betrayal so much as an instinctive sexual response at odds with his mental conviction of her guilt.[5]

> Judas did not betray through ignorance of the value of his victim, nor did he throw his "pearl" away, but received thirty pieces of silver. Nor did Othello betray Desdemona in intention, but only in fact.[6]

> F. "Iudean," which some prefer and take as referring to Judas. But he was the archetype of treachery, of which Othello, an "honourable murderer," never accuses himself.[7]

And so on. What is remarkable, apart from the air of weighty certainty of these insubstantial suppositions, is the fact that while the textual critics are dutifully behaving like literary critics, they seem to be completely unaware of the rather famous critical debate about this play, which Leavis initiated (for nonreaders of *Scrutiny*) in 1952; as unaware, in fact, of Leavis's existence as he seems to be of theirs.

Nonetheless what the textual critics are doing is what textual critics do do: they pretend to be literary critics and behave with some confidence, as if they know the answer and how to argue a case for it. This seems natural; after all, both editors and readers of edited texts have been trained in undergraduate literary courses to behave in just this way. But as I have said, there is a clear distinction between the kind of truth content attaching to literary interpretation and that which is appropriate to textual criticism, and to confuse one with the other, and use rhetoric to reinforce it, only serves to conceal what I think should be clear from the *Othello* crux: the answer is impossible. We cannot know. The degree of knowledge attainable by textual critics, at those points—the cruces—where their art or science is truly tested, is not commensurate to the importance placed by literary critics on its results. In that sense, it seems to me, textual criticism cannot be done.

In spite of all this, it is still true that textual criticism, in the widest sense of the words, is some thing that we all do; it is a natural and instinctive activity. We all edit the world we perceive; otherwise we could not make sense of it. If the world is a book, then in order to read it we have no choice but to be editors. In a slightly narrower sense—that is, with regard to all of the many linguistic texts that we meet in everyday life, both written and spoken, we expect, as part of the normal course of nature, a certain amount of corruption, and make our ad hoc emendations as often as we find it necessary without giving the matter too much thought. In speech, if we mishear, or hear what we take to be a slip of the tongue, we can either silently edit to what we believe is a more acceptable version, or we can ask the speaker if that was what he or she meant to say. In my daily paper I expect a misprint or two, and emend as necessary; if I can't work out the true reading there is perhaps a minor irritation, but no more; it is not worth spending the time, over breakfast. If I really need to know what the author meant, say in the case of a mail-order advertisement for something that I might wish to buy, I can phone, or write, or go ahead and test my conjectural emendation by acting upon it and seeing what happens. Our inevitable response to the inevitable muddle is that we negotiate, compromise, and muddle through; specifically, we try quite hard to negotiate a balance between the amount of effort spent in editorial activity and the value that results from it. Were it not for this universal balancing my daily newspaper would be deluged with phone calls and letters, and breakfast would stretch into the middle of the afternoon.

Indeed, perfect accuracy is not something we particularly like: it seems soulless and stupid. My word processor is perfect. It responds with idiotic perfection to every keystroke I make, right or wrong: it doesn't edit the world in any way whatsoever. All of the errors that I make, since (unlike it) I happen to be human, find their way into the process of typing and are reproduced with complete fidelity. It behaves, in fact, like that impossible ideal of the classical textual critic, the scribe who is an accurate moron. This fidelity, this lack of a textual critical function, is so counterintuitive that one of the first add-ons developed for the basic word-processing program was a crude textual editor in the form of a spelling checker.

Before I acquired the word processor I would write in my not very legible longhand, and give the result to the departmental secretary, who, because she is also a human being, is a textual editor, and would correct my spelling mistakes, using, as humans do, whatever seemed to her to be an appropriate amount of effort to make sense of the bit of the universe at hand—in this case, my illegible longhand. And, being human, she would also make mistakes, which I would then edit. Corruption is universal; textual criticism is natural to humans. We don't give the matter much thought.

Perhaps for this reason it is important to think about it. What do we do, when we do textual criticism? In doing this universal human activity we operate, I would suggest a very simple, but for its purpose quite adequate, communications model. Something like this: A message originates (by some occult means) in someone's mind. In order to communicate it he or she encodes it in one or more of a wide range of physical forms (paper, sound waves, electronic impulses) by which means it is transmitted to the recipient. Unfortunately the process of rendering this rather insubstantial object substantial also tends to introduce what information-theory people call "noise," and what textual critics, with their characteristic leaning towards theology, call "corruption." The recipient has to decode the immaterial message from the material vehicle, and this process will often involve a certain amount of editing out of this "noise" so that the message is received in a form as free from it as is thought necessary for adequate comprehension.

Now, this model is useful, but it is only useful for the purposes to which it is normally put: that is, everyday commonsense textual criticism. It is however a powerfully persuasive explanation of what goes on, and therefore has been roped in to account for what goes on in a much more complicated task: the textual criticism of literary artifacts. How, in practice, does this everyday model work?

I will offer as an example the address of a letter sent to me once:

Mr T. R. Davis
Lecturer in Didliography and Paleography
Department of English
University of Birmingham

I would suggest that when we are confronted with a message like this, the following process, or something like it, takes place:

1. Something is wrong.

The message doesn't fit with our (lexical and encyclopedic) expectations of what it should be like. In this instance, I noticed immediately, having studied many envelopes addressed to myself, that this was deviant, and my lexical/encyclopedic knowledge told me that (wishful thinking aside) "didliography" is not the normal term for the study of the history of printing and allied matters.

2. What is the "true reading"?

Almost at the same time as stage (1) notices the deviance, the answer suggests itself: the "error" evokes the norm in the act of identifying it as deviant.

3. How did the "error" come about?

This part of the process is optional, and often feels supernumerary or not worth the trouble. If I conjecture that a typist somewhere must have made a mistake from dictation, on the basis of my knowledge that (a) typists are often dictated to, and (b) the sounds associated with the graphemes *b* and *d* are heard as resembling each other in English, then this feels like a different kind of process from (1) and (2). Firstly, it is conscious and worked out, while the other steps are intuitive and rather fast. Secondly, in this case it is unnecessary, because the range of solutions to the problem is highly limited and easily available: the answer is obvious, and all stage (3) can do is to confirm it, or to satisfy intellectual curiosity.

But if the answer is less obvious, then (3) can sometimes come into its own. Here is another (again genuine) address:

> Mr T. R. Davis
> A.V.I.S.
> Department of English
> University of Birmingham

My internal encyclopedia tells me that this message is quite abnormal, since it refuses to allow a connection between the institution I work in and the well-known car-rental firm. But stage (2) springs less readily to mind. Why this mysterious acronym? Maybe it's important, and I should know about it? Stage (2) is not helpful, because the immediate linguistic and encyclopedic norms don't suggest a valid reason for the acronym to be there. Therefore I move to stage (3), and, after a reasonably short period of intense thought, the answer springs to mind: knowledge of the process of transmission points out to me that (a) this message, like the last one, may have been derived from dictation, (b) there are two possible spellings of my surname that dictators need to distinguish, and (c) typists often have better things to think about than typing yet another tedious address. Thus stage (3) gives us the answer to stage (2).

But, as readers will have noticed, this rather satisfactory solution to the problem is unusual. Mostly stage (3) is of no help whatsoever and we are driven back to stages (1) and (2): into the empty slot in the context vacated by what we have spotted as odd, for whatever reason, we try to fit some new item that we feel might make more sense.

It is, I hope, quite clear that this process is in important respects identical with that of traditional textual criticism. Stages (1) and (2) are art, and stage (3) is science. Stage (1) contains in itself the process of collation, here done in memory against all of the other envelopes addressed to myself that I have seen. Stage (2) is the intuitive reference to whatever norms are appropriate and available (in the case of textual critics, these are usually not only the normal linguistic models, but also specifically literary or theological ones, or sometimes both). And stage (3), of course, is the domain of bibliography, and stemmatics, and paleography, and all the rest of the repertoire that the textual critic uses when the problem can't easily be solved by simple common sense.

All of these stages, in traditional textual criticism, have however been somewhat disguised by a process that one can only call mystification. Stage (2) is, as we have seen, normally called "literary judgment," with consequent confusion; stage (3) is often given the equally mystifying title "scientific," a term that has attracted an equivalent, but quite opposed, privileging process in this society. Here are the first two monsters that beset textual criticism; these, I hope, can fairly readily be identified as nonentities.

If we look at the processes of "literary judgment" and "bibliographical analysis" in the light of the three-stage process identified above, we can see that they are in fact rather similar: they both attempt to resolve a perceived anomaly by reference to supposed norms. In the first case what we look at is a range of similar linguistic circumstances, and in the second, we summon up and relate a set of constructed normal circumstances surrounding production and dissemination of documents or other texts. Stage (1) feels intuitive because its medium is language, whether literary, theological, or normal speech, and we are able to access and select huge amounts of normative linguistic material of whatever kind very quickly indeed; it is part of usual (and utterly remarkable) language use. But the process is so quick that in applying it to problems of the textual critical kind it feels like a kind of magic flash, wonderfully useful but somewhat occult and therefore unreliable; as indeed it is, because there is no way that we can subject the process to a conscious process of validation. Contrast this with the bibliographically based insights of even a giant like Greg, which are on the whole accessible, and can be checked and subjected to falsification processes. But I only have conscious access to a tiny fraction of all of the contexts that provide the meanings for the words that I myself use, let alone those of other people's meanings. It comes down to a matter of intuition, which is often undistinguishable from blind faith; and this, I suggest, is why textual critics traditionally have such violent arguments.

I can here offer an example that shows this intuitive process, and its mystification, in a somewhat dramatic light. The passage is from A. E. Housman, who, of all textual critics, made rudeness to his colleagues, and indeed (in the following passage) to everyone else, into a high art:

> The following stanza of Mr de la Mare's "Fare well" first met my eyes, thus printed, in a newspaper review.
>
> > Oh, when this my dust surrenders
> > Hand, foot, lip, to dust again,
> > May these loved and loving faces
> > Please other men!
> > May the rustling harvest hedgerow
> > Still the Traveller's Joy entwine.
> > And as happy children gather
> > Posies once mine.
>
> I knew in a moment that Mr de la Mare had not written rustling, and in another moment I had found the true word. But if the book of poems had perished and the verse survived only in the review, who would have believed me rather than the compositor? The bulk of the reading public would have been perfectly content with rustling, nay they would sincerely have preferred it to the epithet which the poet chose. If I had been so ill-advised as to publish my emendation, I should have been told that rustling was exquisitely apt and poetical, because hedgerows do rustle, especially in autumn, when the leaves are dry, and when straws and ears from the passing harvest-wain (to which "harvest" is so plain an allusion that only a pedant like me could miss it) are hanging caught in the twigs; and I should have been recommended to quit my dusty (or musty) books and make a belated acquaintance with the sights and sounds of the English countryside. And the only possible answer would have been ugh![8]

Clearly Housman is making the point that he has magical powers, a position that he reinforces by the brilliant maneuver of not telling the reader what the answer is. Anticipating in his practice the theoretical work of

Stanley Fish by half a century, he leaves the reader gasping at his or her own inability to solve the conundrum: surprised, as it were, by sin.

Or this reader, at any rate; to such an extent that (with profound feelings of inadequacy at ever having pretended to be a textual critic) I went over to the library and looked up the answer in de la Mare's works. The answer to Housman's riddle is . . . not too phonetically/graphemically dissimilar from the compositor's error. But stage (3) is of no use whatsoever: what one has to do is to conjure up the legal English words that have a sufficient-seeming phonetic/graphemic resemblance to "rustling," try them out, and see if they fit into the context. And "fitness" here means (a) producing valid meanings, and (b) producing the sort of valid meanings that we associate with the body of texts known as "de la Mare's works." To do all of this "in a moment," as Housman did (assuming that he wasn't lying, an assumption to which I am not completely committed) means only (only!) that you can access a lot of comparison material rather fast; what is truly remarkable is that Housman claims to have spotted the apparently inoffensive "rustling" as being deviant, by a rather highly developed stage (1) process of comparison and contrast, of normality and deviance.

But not by any magical process. Even if we take this anecdote as being fictional, it is still instructive: what the fiction is concerned to instill is precisely mystification of the kind that I have described: as if "literary judgment" were somehow different from the normal process of language use. At base, it is not. The fictional (or not) hero of Housman's narrative knew a lot of contexts; that's all.

We can now turn to the main target of my analysis: the author's intention. Alert readers cannot fail to have noticed (the rest will be surprised by sin yet again, presumably) that I managed the above description of the textual critical process without any reference whatsoever to the intention of the author of any of the documents I mentioned. That this was quite difficult, and that the description may seem odd or labored in places, not to mention beset with quotation marks, is because the commonsense language that we use to talk about textual criticism is deeply imbrued with intentionalism; it is based, as I said earlier, on an excessively simple communications model. What I have described is what we actually do, when we do textual criticism; and this doing has (normally) no reference at all to authors or intentions. Not, at any rate, when we deal with written language. And this is the crucial point. So strong is the speech model that we use it in places where it is inappropriate and misleading, and the result is confusion. And particularly the confusion of intentionalism.

Let us look into this model a little more closely. If someone makes a mistake in talking to you, you might well ask them what he or she meant. We want (following our simple communications model) to know what the sender intended to encode and transmit, but was prevented by whatever vagary in the system. Intended meaning, in the shape of a pure version of the message, uncontaminated by any corruption, to which the sender (and only the sender) has access and can refer without trouble, is a vital part, perhaps the most vital part, of the commonsense model of textual criticism. It is the truth, the essence, the original pure message, which (we think) needs absolutely to exist in order that we can decide that that which is not it is false. All of this seems very true; unfortunately, as far as textual criticism is concerned, it is defective.

The problem is, at its root, that the model works reasonably well for speech, but not well for written language; and textual criticism is only done on written language. The model's defect is that it makes no distinction at all between written and spoken language, and since this distinction is lacking, there is confusion, of a quite complicated nature, because our image of written language is influenced by the spoken variety, and of the spoken, on the other hand, by the written.

Firstly, most of the messages which we encounter, and which most humans have encountered since language came into existence, are spoken: straightforward, pitched at the comprehension of the hearer, face-to-face, and short. Since they are spoken, there is normally easy access to a speaker, who can inform us of his or her intended meaning. In these cases the model works well; so well, in fact, that we export it instinctively to situations for which it is not appropriate. It is one thing to apply an intention model when someone says "pass the salt"; quite another if the text at hand is *Middlemarch*. Nonetheless, it seems that since, however literate we may be, speech comes first, it is taken as the norm of communication, with, in Derrida's now famous formulation, its "metaphysic of presence."

The situation, however, is more complicated than that. Speech may be primary, but we do live in a highly literate culture—where, for instance, spelling (irrationally) influences pronunciation, and not the other way round—and so our view of face-to-face spoken interaction is that it is something like the kind of conversations that people have in novels, where people do indeed seem to pass messages, in the form of coherent packages of words, to each other, as in our simple communications model. We could call this (following Popper) the bucket theory of communication: the contents of one bucket are poured, unproblematically, into another, as meaning is transferred. This depends, in its turn, on a bucket theory of mind: a receptacle in which things can be contained and preserved, steadily and intact.

But actual conversation, and actual minds, are not at all like that. For one thing, as well as the words spoken there is a great deal of use of gesture, intonation, facial expression, pausing, eye contact, and much, much else. What we need this rich repertoire for is the negotiation of meaning. Whether the dialogue is between strangers or lovers, in and around the words spoken is a complex tissue of questions and answers: Am I being rude, respectful, too subservient? Am I invading your space or breaking your rules? Or, alternatively, am I winning? And so on.[9] But the principal question, over, above, and within the variety of social codes, is: Do you understand what I mean to say? Now, the important point is that this question is normally negotiated moment by moment. Intentions in speech, like messages in speech, are not as written discourses seem to be, somehow wholly intended and delivered en bloc; they are part of the normal give-and-take of conversation. The mind is not a bucket: it operates in time, not spatially, so that it finds it very difficult (without years of training) to hold large structures at once; normally the mind is wayward and hard to control, with thoughts, intentions, and impulses passing into and out of existence, like dust floating in sunlight. Once said, the words and their intentions fade quickly in comparison to that moment, and the words to come are vague, provisional, and highly dependent on information that has not yet arrived. To reuse Saussure's illuminating analogy, conversation is like chess: what tends to matter most is the current position, not how we got there.

Since intentions are so evanescent, I would suggest that only in this highly interactive situation, this plenitude, is the concept of intention at all meaningful. It is a truism of grammatology to say that in written discourse the speaker is absent, in time and in space: this, indeed, was one reason why writing was invented. The other reason was that writing captures and preserves in time the momentary existence of spoken words, which was found to be very useful for the invention of (for instance) novels, among many other items. In speech the speaker is present and the text is (outside the moment of speaking) absent; in writing the author is absent and the text is (seems) present, all of it: an object we hold in our hands. In our model of communication we (naturally) take the best of both worlds—the comforting presence of the author and the comforting solidity of the text—and suppose that we can somehow obtain from this author (who is, perhaps, not just absent, but dead) a coherent, sustained, and solid set of intentions and meanings for all of the words in the whole of this supposedly solid text.

It is of course possible to deconstruct both author and text even further. We can deconstruct the author, for instance, by following Derrida and Lacan, who question the presence and the existence (respectively) of an intending subject even in spoken interaction. So for a (perhaps predominant) group of current literary theorists the preferred model of spoken discourse would be altogether more vertiginous than the discourse-analysis model that I have offered: what is being negotiated, they would suggest, is not only meanings but the illusion of a meaning subject.

There is another useful way to refine our model of what goes on in the act of reading and writing: we can deconstruct the seeming solidity of the text, the presence of the book in our hand as we read. Take *Middlemarch*. What is it? Of course it is a *book*, so many pages, so many words. So solid is the presence of this printed object that it is very hard to think of *Middlemarch* without referring to some aspect of its writtenness, its physical form. But the meaning of *Middlemarch* only happens when someone is reading, writing, remembering, or anticipating it.

This meaning, therefore, is never anything but the mental construct of a reader or writer. In the course of reading, the book exists only as the result of a negotiation, constantly changing as we read on, between selective memory and a pattern of anticipations, together with a small area on which the consciousness is currently focused. Just like in conversation, meaning is negotiated, but the difference is that the words to come are fixed, and what we negotiate with is the text itself: the words written on the page. It is comforting and customary to feel that someone is present in the text and addressing us, but in fact there is no one there: the words and the reader are all there is. Similarly it is a normal illusion to suppose that when we read or think or talk or write about an extensive—say, a literary—text we are in possession of the whole thing, as solid and present as the book we read it in; but this is not true either: like everything else we perceive or know, it is only made up of memory, anticipation, and the fleeting moment of awareness.

In the act of writing, too, the book exists only as a pattern of anticipation and memory; here, as in conversation, the words to come are negotiable, but again the negotiation is not with a hearer, but the text itself. It is as impossible for a writer as for a reader to hold the whole text constantly in mind, like a deity for whom his or her creation is eternally present; if we discuss *Middlemarch* then you and I are comparing our selective and unique recollections of the text, which will be constructed on the basis of various theories that we have about it. And this would be true if we were to discuss it with George Eliot too: even for a short document I cannot possibly recall the complex patterns of impulse and desire, of negotiation and selective memory and anticipation, that went through my head as I produced it, and (I assume) neither could she; precisely because we are constructed by a culture that enables me to create written documents, the art of memory and the training of concentration are not much taught, but even if they were, the task would be impossible.

Since this is so, if I am offered someone else's reading of a passage I have written, I will probably respond to it as just another reader; in any case, I know well that what the words will mean, however I may have intended them, is what a significant proportion of readers will read them as meaning, and once they are written and promulgated I do not have much control over that. This is of course a truism of current literary theory; but it is also true that if I am asked my opinion as to the wording of a passage I have written I will respond principally as just another textual critic and normalize to whatever I expect the passage to be.[10]

For this is what we do, in fact, in our daily textual criticisms. If a passage looks odd for some reason, or if we see two or more texts that are assumed to be versions of the same, but which differ, we make the situation make sense by normalizing the offending irregularity against expectations derived from the text and other texts, and from a large number of other sources, just as we do when we read or, for that matter, when we perceive the world in any way whatsoever. In the case of reading and textual criticism (and for some people, of course, in perceiving the world) it is comforting to think that we are thereby getting in touch with the intentions of an author, an author who is in charge, in control, and has the whole text in his or her head. This is not so.

I think it may be helpful at this point to offer a piece of personal experience that I have found extremely helpful in thinking about this problem. Some years ago I found that my training in bibliography and paleography was quite applicable to the solution of problems in forensic document analysis, as we call it: the detection of forgery, in other words. I have now been operating as what lawyers call a handwriting expert for some time, and it is my primary research interest. Readers who notice a certain detachment from the rather exquisite agonies of textual bibliographers will now know why.

I found, as I say, my training very useful, and entirely appropriate; in some ways more so than that of my colleagues in this field, who all received their initial training in the "hard" sciences of physics and chemistry. In one important respect, however, I was at a disadvantage. I found that I regarded the mysteries that are given to me every day as personal challenges, and any degree of insolubility in them as a personal affront. They were monsters, to be defeated with my very own sword. This is not entirely bad: it gave a certain energy to my work, and to my defense of it in court, but what went with it was a very marked temptation to use rhetoric to make the evidence give up more than it had to offer. This, as is well known, is a notorious characteristic of bibliographers and textual critics, and a fairly harmless part of life's rich comedy. Forensic science is, however, a more serious business even than cruces in *Othello:* it puts people in prison, and takes away their money, their livelihood, their reputation—or saves them from these fates. It is not to be trifled with. Such trifling had been beaten out of my colleagues the scientists at a very early age: if the evidence won't play ball, then you don't help it along. This is fundamental; it is the scientist's concept of sin.

The distinction crystallized for me in a conversation with a lawyer; we agreed that the essential difference between us was that his job was to make a case, and mine was not; the scientists' role is to let the evidence speak through their knowledge, skill, and theoretical framework; but it can say only what it has to say, not what they want from it. This may be hard for the defendant or (more normally) the prosecution, but that is the way the real, as opposed to the fictional, world happens to be constructed. Scientists run up all the time against the intransigence of nature, which will not easily conform to human expectations and desires; it is part of the job, taken for granted: expected, in fact. Textual critics, who deal in fiction all their working lives, are locked into the messy and rather corrupt obfuscations of ideology, which creates monsters that are not theirs. If the evidence will not deliver what the literary criticism needs, either because it is intransigent or absent, or because the needs are incompatible with the way the world is, then it is not for the textual critics to do any thing other than point this out. They must offer a solution, since the job description (dictated by literary critics) demands one, but they should make absolutely clear the degree of unlikelihood, or impossibility, that that solution represents. Modesty, and a sense of humor, are the answer—not reverent appeals to literary judgment, or to a nonscientist's version of science, or, most of all, to the reification of the text, the author, and his or her intentions. If we can do this, and can simply accept, like any scientist, the intransigence of nature, its stubborn refusal to open up secrets to even the most dedicated inquirer, then the monsters, I suggest, vanish. Textual criticism is then a perfectly possible and satisfactory activity: after all, we do it every day.

What de la Mare seems to have written, incidentally, is "rusting."

NOTES

1. Imre Lakatos, *Proofs and Refutations, the Logic of Mathematical Discovery*, ed. John Worrall and Elie Zahar (Cambridge: Cambridge University Press, 1976).

2. From the facsimile in *Shakespeare's Plays in Quarto*, ed. Michael J. B. Allen and Kenneth Muir (Berkeley: University of California Press, 1981), 834.

3. First Folio, V.ii, from the *Norton Facsimile*, prepared by Charlton Hinman (New York: W. W. Norton, 1968), TLN 3652–59.

4. Morse Peckham, "Reflections on the Foundations of Modern Textual Editing," *Proof* 1 (1971): 122–55.

5. *Othello*, ed. Norman Sanders (Cambridge: Cambridge University Press, 1984), 192.

6. *Othello*, ed. E. C. Horwood and R. E. C. Houghton (Oxford: Clarendon Press, 1968), 231.

7. *Othello*, ed. Alice Walker and John Dover Wilson (Cambridge: Cambridge University Press, 1957), 218.

8. A. E. Housman, *Selected Prose*, ed. John Carter (Cambridge: Cambridge University Press, 1961).

9. It is interesting, and relevant, that in the electronic chat of the Internet, which stands in a hyperspace somewhere between conversation and letter writing, a whole repertoire of codes has evolved to make up for the deficiencies of ASCII in conveying just these negotiations and nuances. If you make a joke, you signal it, so that the receiver receives your intention: (vbg) for Very Big Grin. And so on.

10. As an author I am, however, conventionally allowed control over meaning and wording in one way; I can revise. If economic circumstances allow, I can enter the text with a whole new complex of impulses, memories, anticipations, and interactions, and tinker with it, to a greater or lesser extent. Then in normal circumstances people will pay attention to the new document that I have created and act appropriately; human beings are expected to change their minds a little, however inconvenient this may be.

5

How farre is't called to Soris? or,
Where was Mr. Hobbs when Charles II died?

A. R. BRAUNMULLER

And besides, Jack is a notorious domesticity for John.
—Oscar Wilde, *The Importance of Being Earnest*

The world of the imagination is a replica of the world of experience, and the proper names of the former belong to much the same classes as those of the latter.
—Alan Gardiner, *The Theory of Proper Names*

Will the formalist, structuralist, or exegetical successes eliminate the raw force of reference? In other words, will the system govern the circulation of objects? Will it regulate the effects of meaning that result from that circulation?
—Ora Avni, *The Resistance of Reference*

For the reader who likes such things, this chapter concerns editorial principles and editorial practices; for those readers who do not, it is also a chapter about a real town (not Marianne Moore's toad) in an imaginary landscape, about imaginary, or perhaps real, persons in imagined actions, about the readerly construction or constitution of a text, and human error.

Working backward, I start with Charles II's death. In March 1685, Jacob Tonson published two quarto editions of *Threnodia Augustalis*, John Dryden's "Funeral-Pindarique" on the death of Charles II. Both quartos remark the royal doctors' failure to save the king:

> The vain *Insurancers* of life,
> And He who most perform'd and promis'd less,
> Even *Short* himself forsook th' unequal strife.[1]

Tonson reprinted the poem in the first, posthumous, collected edition of Dryden's works, a folio of 1701, but now there is an erratum change of

"He" (in the second quoted line) to "They," and the third line reads "Even *Short* and *Hobbs* forsook th' unequal strife":

> The vain *Insurancers* of life,
> And They who most perform'd and promis'd less,
> Even *Short* and *Hobbs* forsook th' unequal strife.

Vinton A. Dearing, responsible for the text in the standard modern edition, records this "interesting variation," but banishes it to the textual notes and does not collate the 1701 printing because that folio "seems not to have been revised by" Dryden.[2] Fair enough (or fair enough for now), but setting aside *who* made the change, one wonders *why* the change was made, and various proposals (usually assuming that Tonson was the source, complimenting Hobbs the purpose) have been put forward.[3] Since Dearing's editorial effort, research by G. C. R. Morris has shown that Thomas Hobbs (not Hobbes the author of *Leviathan*) as well as Thomas Short attended the king in his final days; they were among no less than sixteen (or now, seventeen) "Sons of Art" who did so.[4] Once Hobbs appears (or once later scholars know he appeared) at Charles's bedside, the 1701 folio reading begins to look more authorial and less Tonsonian, especially since Hobbs also ministered to Dryden himself in 1697.[5] When the third volume of the California edition of Dryden's *Works* was in preparation, an effort to identify *"Hobbs"* as one of Charles's medicine men failed, and (here's the important point for my argument) the textual editor *accordingly* did not accept the posthumous folio's reading but retained the first quarto's reading.

The sequence signifies: although known as a surgeon (later physician) in the period, known indeed as one who later treated Dryden, Thomas Hobbs was not known (in 1969, the California edition's date) to have treated Charles II, and the 1701 line was thus categorized as nonauthorial; once scholars established (in 1975) the line's accuracy as historical record, not only the line but the text in which it appears assumed a quite different authorial (or quasi-authorial) status.[6]

That is, had proof been available that Thomas Hobbs (or any *Hobbs*) treated Charles II, a reading from a posthumously published text of questionable, or at least unproven, authority would have been accorded much more attention . . . not because the fact of Hobbs's presence made the reading necessarily more likely to be Dryden's (Tonson or someone else could still be the source of the change),[7] but because the folio reading accorded with, and the quarto reading violated, the newly established fact that Short and Hobbs, not Short alone, attended the king.

This example confuses the sometimes clear distinction between internal and external evidence, because in the history of criticism and textual scholarship Hobbs at first did not minister to Charles II (or was not known to have done so) and at a later time did (or was found to have done so). The more-or-less immutable "fact" of Hobbs's presence, once known, changed the narrative scholars told about the textual history of the 1701 folio.[8]

⁂

Consider two related but slightly different examples from William Shakespeare's and Thomas Middleton's *Macbeth*, first printed in the Shakespeare folio of 1623 (F1). After the three sisters' appearance at the start of act 1, scene 3, two characters walk (or possibly ride) onstage, one commenting on the fairness and foulness of the day, the other wondering how soon they are likely to reach where they are going: "How farre is't call'd to Soris?" (TLN 138).[9] Perhaps because of editorial principle or because English compositors and English editors are ignorant of Scottish geography or for some other cause, "Soris" makes its way through the anonymous 1673 quarto of *Macbeth*, the 1674 quarto of Davenant's adaptation, and all four seventeenth-century folios of Shakespeare's plays and Nicholas Rowe's two or three early-eighteenth-century editions. Alexander Pope, cleaning up and throwing out text, set it right: Soris is, of course, "Foris" (Pope, 1723) or "Fores" (1773 Variorum edition) or "Forres" (Harry Rowe, 1797, and almost everyone else). By the mid-nineteenth century, a superior school edition, the Clarendon, could change the text without comment and offer this indisputable note: "Forres is near the Moray Frith, about halfway between Elgin and Nairn."[10] So Forres is, or was a few summers ago when I visited it, but are this reading and this note to the point? If I were an ignorant reader, and I am, I would want to know where or what "Soris" was or is, or what it meant, not what or where Forres was or is. Later in the same scene, Macbeth reflects on the sisters' words, and he remarks: "By *Sinells* death, I know I am *Thane* of Glamis" (TLN 171). The obvious inference is that Macbeth inherited the title from one Sinell, and it seems patriarchally plausible that Sinell was, as Pope notes, "The father of Macbeth." Early and late, the printed tradition—seventeenth-century quartos and folios, Rowe and the later named editors—agrees to the jot and tittle that *Sinells* (usually modernized to "Sinel's" or some variant) should stand in the text, and the old New Variorum edition edited by H. H. Furness Jr. (1873) does not even collate the reading.

Elementary knowledge of early modern English handwriting explains the seeming "mistake." The same error produced Soris and Sinells: the misreading of a manuscript *f* as *ſ*, the secretary "long" ess. Foris and Finells in manuscript become Soris and Sinells in print. The errors occurred at two different points in the transmission of information to Shakespeare and from him. Holinshed quite frequently prints "Fores," and Shakespeare (dyslexic, or misreading his notes, or forgetting his reading) or Compositor A (misunderstanding his copy)[11] or someone elsewhere in the manuscript stem evidently misread the handwritten *f* as *ſ;* Holinshed does, however, write of "Sinell the thane of Glammis" and father of "Makbeth,"[12] although we all know, along with the omniscient Geoffrey Bullough, that Makbeth/Macbeth's father was "Finele" or "Finley" or "Findlaech."[13]

❧

At the microeditorial level, the issue seems clear: If Soris becomes Forres, why should *Sinnels*/Sinel's not become Finel's? Yet "Soris" has almost universally been emended in editions of *Macbeth* since Pope's, while "Sinells" in some form persists.[14] Here follows an obvious question. Do the editorial differences arise because place-names are more familiar to editors and modern readers than the names of eleventh-century Scottish noblemen and/or because changes (or "errors") in place-names are therefore more likely to produce complaints of editorial ignorance or bad reviews? Is it because Forres may still be visited, but Raphael Holinshed and his sources are all generally unreliable books or manuscripts and much of his and their purported history is legendary or uncheckable? If we could (and I suppose a historian of medieval Scotland might) discover Finele/Finley/Findlaech father-of-Macbeth in, for example, eleventh-century legal documents or in his grave, do we then change the text, as the discovery of Mr. Hobbs at Charles II's bedside would lead Dryden's editor to rewrite line 188 of *Threnodia Augustalis*?[15]

Another approach to the problem of authorial error explicitly or implicitly appeals to authorial intention. Decades ago, W. W. Greg's "Rule 1" for editors asserted, and the editorial instructions for the Oxford English Text edition of Shakespeare's works now in progress echo him, that the editor

> may be allowed to rectify any blunder which it is certain that the author [e.g., William Shakespeare] would have rectified as such had it been pointed out to him, provided that neither the nature of the blunder nor the form of the correction is open to doubt.

Greg then almost recognizes the inconsistencies of his rule by prohibiting "the removal of inconsistencies that the author overlooked and may indeed have regarded as permissible or insignificant."[16] We quickly recognize that Greg's "rule" reifies the editor's opinion, however well informed, as the author's intention. Only the editor decides whether (in this instance)

Shakespeare would have corrected the error "had it been pointed out to him" and only the editor decides whether "the nature of the blunder" or "the form of the correction" cannot be doubted. Greg's halfhearted qualification about what the author might have "overlooked" or regarded "as permissible or insignificant" error merely instantiates editorial clairvoyance. If an editor can know, or imagine, or guess Shakespeare's reaction when a blunder is pointed out, the editor can certainly know, imagine, or guess what Shakespeare would regard as permissible or insignificant. Who else might conceivably share in the decision?

Greg possessed at least the overvalued quality of consistency: Folio print and late Tudor manuscript he treated the same. Nearly a half-century earlier, describing how one should edit Philip Henslowe's manuscripts, Greg observed how difficult he found Henslowe's handwriting and added what sounds like a self-satisfied coda:

> It is at times far from easy to tell exactly what he [Henslowe] has written, so that I have been constantly forced to print a compromise between what he apparently intended to write and what can actually be read. I am inclined to insist on this point since it applies, I fancy, to many more texts based on MSS. than their editors seem willing to allow.[17]

The confident knowledge of what Henslowe "apparently intended to write" is breathtaking, especially if Greg perceives "what can actually be read," however nonsensical it may have seemed to a young and still-inexperienced scholar, or any trained reader. More astonishing is Greg's refusal to define the "compromise" his transcript represents. What are the criteria for compromise? Perhaps my surprise is exaggerated or naïve. After all, Greg's transcript confidently redates Henslowe's entries referring to Sunday performances because Greg thought Sunday performances nonexistent in the late sixteenth and early seventeenth centuries. He was, it seems, wrong.[18]

Yet Greg's warning is an honest one, one any manuscript transcriber could echo and document, but Greg fails to consider an obvious "compromise" that is truly no compromise: print "what can actually be read" and let others—perhaps Greg himself, now editor or annotator, not transcriber—reexamine the manuscripts and (re)interpret the evidence.[19] The transcriber's task ends with decipherment; the editor's and critic's task begins there. Difficult as it may be, the distinction must be maintained and should be seen to be maintained.

A third, widely employed solution to the problem of error is the attempt to draw a distinction between a "document" and a "text" or "work." The former category includes such items as governmental paperwork and an author's drafts; the latter category includes collections of words represented as imaginative, fictional, and/or intended to be of interest many years after their creation. Editors, it is said, should resist the temptation to correct (indeed, to edit) the former group of writings, whereas—in the interest of a transhistorical and transcendental collection of marks on paper—they should at least consider correcting the latter.[20] The distinction between historical document and literary text fails as quickly and for the same reasons as the attempt to differentiate between "literary" uses of language and all other uses. Metaphor and metonymy are pervasive linguistic properties and will not serve to distinguish the subpoena from the lyric, the contract from the epic, and distinctions among their hypothesized authors and their intentions will survive scrutiny no longer.

Reflection on proper names in Shakespearean texts and their editorial treatment has produced some interesting arguments and some new names.[21] One discussion concerns the dramatis personae of *Macbeth:*

> The names of characters in *Macbeth* are very consistent, and need no altering from the usage of the first Folio to make them intelligible; but editors have normally altered some names, in the interest of modernity, or historical accuracy.[22]

I do not understand the criterion of intelligibility. What is an *un*intelligible personal name?[23] Do persons who pronounce every apparent syllable in "Gloucester" have ipso facto an inferior understanding or appreciation of *King Lear* to those who do not? Does a reader's simple or sophisticated understanding of *Richard II* depend upon knowing how many syllables there are, or were once, in "Aumerle"? What follows from our learning that the graphic symbols spelling "Leveson" are pronounced (or were pronounced) "Lewson," "Mainwaring" pronounced "Mannering," "Brougham," "Broom"? Closer to our examples, what follows from knowing (or indeed learning) that "Moray" and "Elgin" in the Clarendon edition's gloss for "Forres" are respectively pronounced "Murray" and "Elgin" with a hard *g?* Would *Macbeth* be less intelligible if the characters had different names? Would it in fact matter very much if they all had Irish names? Latvian? Czech?[24] Would *Macbeth* be less "intelligible" if the characters were each identified by a different single letter (like the memorable French captains "E." and "G." of *All's Well*) or two or three letters or a single numeral, as speakers often are in the Folio and in other early modern printed scripts?[25]

So, too, one's attitude toward the "interest of modernity" seems a puzzling reason to change or preserve the Folio's proper names. G. K. Hunter continues,

> Names like *Seyton* and *Seyward* have been preserved in this form, as indicating their Shakespearian pronunciation. The fact that modern historians call the historical characters on whom these are based *Seaton* and *Siward* seems beside the point.[26]

Certainly, early orthography may preserve the hypothetical early pronunciation of proper names, and, certainly, an argument for a pun on *Seyton/*Satan has been made,[27] but if we regard indicating early modern pronunciation as a desirable feature of a modernized edition there are many words, not just proper names, that should retain the original quarto- or Folio-orthography.[28] Again, proper names, specifically personal names, have been given special treatment, as the editorial tradition did with "Soris" and *Sinells*. (Calling the historical Seaton and Siward "historical characters" seems to be a minor slip: they are not characters, they are dead people.)[29] There is, perhaps, a certain essentialism in the way editors accord personal names special treatment. If editors reproduce the early spelling or pronunciation, they grant those figures historical subjectivity, individuality, and thus retain their own (modern) subjectivity and individuality. Editorially, personal names and, much less frequently, place-names become transcendental signifiers.

Shakespeare's errors are Hunter's next subject, and here he sensibly violates Greg's "Rule 1":

> We should not correct Shakespeare's historical knowledge for him, change *Berowne* . . . into "Biron", or correct the spelling *Banquo* (= Banquho) into "Banwho"—no doubt the accurate modern notation; for Shakespeare's world is not that of the modern historian, but one created to stand by itself. . . . his *Birnan* is not the geographically precise modern Birnam, his [Thanes, later Earls, of] *Cathness* [actually, *Cathnes* and *Cath.*] and *Menteth* [or *Ment.*] are not the modern Caithness and Menteith but names he found in Holinshed. (189)

These are powerful arguments, eloquent and concise. But wait. If *Birnan* (TLN 2212), for example, "is not the geographically precise modern Birnam," what is it? Part of a world "created to stand by itself" comes the answer. Is *Birnan* not also a word for an imaginary place in that imaginary world? Could it not be called "Arden" or "Elgin" or "Tongue" or even the Folio's own Birnane (TLN 2283, 2295), *Byrnam* (TLN 1636), Byrnan (TLN 1642, 2181), or Byrnane (TLN 2216, 2356, 2368, 2471)[30] without defeating the play's power over its auditory?

Of course it could. Why not call it Birnam, then? Presumably because a few readers or spectators will possess "geographically precise" knowledge of "modern Birnam" and may be swayed toward thinking *Macbeth* concerns places in modern Scotland.[31] So, too, retaining *Cathnes[s]* and *Menteth* protects those readers and spectators who could locate Caithness or Menteith on an outline map of Scotland from thinking that *Macbeth* is not a "world created to stand by itself," or at least warns them they will have trouble finding *Cathnes* and *Menteth* in a modern atlas or in Debrett's. Since F1 prints *Cath.* and *Cathnes*, does not the editor have to know that F1's *Cathnes* means "Caithness" in order to print "Cathness"? (If the editor did not know *Cathnes* "meant" Caithness, the F1 spelling with one *s* would stand, but the edition reads "Cathness," which modernizes half of the word's orthography.) By now it must be clear who are the readers Hunter has in mind. They're geographically well-informed people, the majority Scots, just as George Hunter is.

Yet this project will fail even with so specifically limited a readership and audience when they open the New Penguin Shakespeare edition of *Macbeth* to Banquo/Banquho/Banwho's question and read, "How far is't called to Forres?" Forres, we recall from the Victorian Clarendon edition's gloss, "is near the Moray Frith, about halfway between Elgin and Nairn," or, as A. W. Verity, an early-twentieth-century (and, it would seem, mildly plagiarizing) editor more deliciously puts it, Forres is "about midway between Elgin and Nairn, near the Moray Firth; the railway runs through it."[32] When Verity adds the railway to the Clarendon gloss, he exemplifies my complaints about editorial behavior. Whether or not Shakespeare's first audiences could locate Forres on the map, whether or not they might have been puzzled by the Folio's "Soris," the railway ran through neither their map's Forres or their imagined world's Soris. Nor, I propose, has the railway ever run through any place in *Macbeth*. With or without its railway, "Forres" is not part of Shakespeare's "world created to stand by itself."[33] As part of such a world, "Soris" should presumably be allowed to remain, along with *Birnan*, *Cathnes[s]*, and *Menteth*. I suggest that readers of the New Penguin Shakespeare edition of *Macbeth* may be surprised to read "Forres"; they should be equally surprised to find that "Sinell's death," not Finel's, made Macbeth thane of Glamis in this edition of the play, as in so many others. *S* becomes *F* in one instance, but not the other.

According to Hunter's postulates, Holinshed's *Chronicles* is also a "world created to stand by itself," and, unlike most other modern editors of the play, Hunter rarely quotes Holinshed's version of events or even mentions Holinshed's text. His view of Holinshed's relevance coheres with his views on place-names and personal names:

> Shakespeare . . . treated his source with a degree of liberty that was not possible in the Histories. The "history" of *Macbeth* is, in fact, moral rather

factual history; just as the "Scotland" of *Macbeth* is a country of the mind rather than a real geographical location. Those who bring to the play experience of the country or the century [presumably the eleventh], beyond what the play provides, are in danger of distorting what is really there.[34]

Fair enough, consistent enough, and I agree.[35] But Hunter immediately turns to something more relevant to "what is really there": "More relevant is the image of Scottish history that appeared on Shakespeare's horizon via the mind of the new King of England—James I."[36]

How is King James I's mind revealed on Shakespeare's horizon? Through the new English king's writings, his texts (on kingship, witchcraft, etc.)—through his version of Holinshed, if you will. Or rather: we do not know how James's mind was revealed to Shakespeare. We know only texts by James VI and I that Shakespeare might also have known. If Holinshed's *Chronicles* has been denied relevance because the Scotland of *Macbeth* is "a country of the mind," I do not understand why James's texts should be any the less a world "created to stand by itself" than those *Chronicles* and any the less irrelevant. What makes one "world" transmitted through documents more relevant than another? There's a term missing from this admittedly compressed argument, some term distinguishing the Shakespeare-James relation from the Shakespeare-Holinshed relation. That distinction presumably places the Shakespeare-James relation in "the real world" or "history" or "wie es eigentlich gewesen ist," perhaps under the subheading "economic-political pragmatism," that is, the King's Men wanted to make money and avoid imprisonment for censurable acts. The distinction certainly cannot be the textual (Raphael Holinshed) or the nontextual (James VI and I) status of the information, because however Shakespeare's horizon may have been affected, our horizon—and our understanding of Shakespeare's horizon—can be influenced by, and our arguments supported by, texts and texts only. Moreover, to the degree that the "real world" or "economic-political pragmatism" is not hypothetical, the real world and the King's Men's economic-political pragmatism too are now textual.

I am not claiming that the historical William Shakespeare (not a "historical character" but a once-living person whose physical remains are now [probably] buried in Trinity Church, Stratford-upon-Avon, Warwickshire) could not or did not concern himself with the interests of the historical James VI and I, and I certainly would not contend that James VI and I did not live, did not rule, did not make mistakes. Our evidence for that concern, that existence, that rule, and those errors is, however, textual,[37] just as Shakespeare's evidence for Macbeth's existence, rule, and errors was also textual: the *Chronicles* of Raphael Holinshed. And yet Holinshed's text is rejected as irrelevant, James's accepted as relevant, to *Macbeth*.

꧁꧂

These examples need now to be considered in some larger contexts—
questions of reference, of representation, and the social construction of
texts.

Many deconstructionist arguments castigate opposing arguments for
holding a "reference" theory of language, a theory of homology, of "natural" (transparent, unproblematic) one-to-one correspondences between the
verbal (or signifier) and the nonverbal (or signified). In *Gulliver's Travels*,
Jonathan Swift caricatures a version of such a theory, as Plato had in the
Cratylus, and J. Hillis Miller has more recently described "the fiction of
the referential, the illusion that the terms of the poem refer literally to something that exists."[38] Behind Miller's modern assertion and others like it lies
(in more than one sense) this claim: "[T]he bases for historical knowledge
are not empirical facts but written texts, even if those texts masquerade in
the guise of wars or revolutions."[39] The proposed alternative is the Ferdinand
de Saussure-derived claim that signifiers function within a system of other
signifiers and achieve linguistic effect within that system and without necessary or specifiable reference to any nonverbal system, or "fact," or condition. This particular deconstructionist move can be and has been fairly
easily countered; much more sophisticated versions of reference theory
exist than have been answered by deconstructionist arguments.[40]

The examples from *Macbeth* enter this argument on both sides. G. K.
Hunter eschews the "geographically precise modern Birnam" and prints
one version of F1's place-name, *Birnan*, presumably to short-circuit crude
referentiality and to prevent audiences and readers from recalling/envi-
sioning/imagining a place in a Scotland where they live, or have visited, or
might live or visit, and to turn their imaginations to a *Birnan* "of the mind."
Here Hunter's view parallels the deconstructionist objection to the vulgar
theory of reference, and the position is similarly vulnerable. As F1's printing of *Birnan*, Birnane, Byrnan, Byrnane, and *Byrnam* shows, however,
the play of signifiers is everywhere apparent in Shakespearean place-names.
Early texts (quartos and the first four folios) offer, for example:[41] Marcellae,
Marsellis, Marcellus (i.e., the major Mediterranean seaport of France, the
contemporary city, Marseilles); Kymmalton and Kimbolten (for Holinshed's
Kimbalton, the place where Queen Katherine is held after her divorce in
the Fletcher-Shakespeare *Henry VIII*);[42] Elme, Elue, Elve (i.e., the Elbe,
the European river important in twentieth-century German-Polish-Soviet
relations). When F1's version of *All's Well* makes a French city (Marseilles)
resemble a character (Marcellus) in a Roman play, and quartos 1-3 and F1
of *Henry V* make a Central European river (the Elbe) resemble an English

tree (elm) or supernatural figure (elve), it is time to remember that "There is no fixed Elizabethan orthography, a condition also obtaining for foreign toponyms."[43] It is therefore equally difficult to assert that pronunciation of a specific spelling necessarily conveyed a "geographically precise" sense of place to the early audiences and that the spelling similarly conveys such a sense to a modern audience or that signifiers are not playing freely on the semantic field. For any member of the audience who knew Marseilles, for example, the early texts' spelling, and the actors' pronunciation, conveyed information (major Mediterranean seaport of France); for those who did not know Marseilles, no spelling, no pronunciation, could convey that information. And the same argument holds for modern readers and audiences: either the noise meaning "Marseilles-major-Mediterranean-seaport-of-France" evokes some mental response (experience or fantasy of the French city), or it does not. Tampering with the noise merely varies the ratio of listeners or readers who "know" Marseilles when they hear or see it to those who do not.

For some editors, this issue—how to treat foreign proper nouns in a modernized text of an imaginative work—can also end with what might be called the "first, do no harm" school of editorial choice. Stanley Wells, admitting that he might be "erring on the side of over-specificity," but preferring it "to the miasma of indeterminacy," argues at length for representing the forest of *As You Like It* as "Ardenne" rather than "Arden."[44] Wells reviews a number of details that suggest the Frenchness of certain characters and moments in the play and makes some related but possibly contradictory claims:

1. "we should deduce that if Shakespeare had any particular place in mind as he wrote 'Arden' (however he spelt it) it is likely to have been the French forest, not the English one"
2. "Shakespeare chose for his forest a name which must have suggested either England or Flanders or both"

and, finally,

3. "Shakespeare's geography is not predominantly realistic; but it is compounded of a mixture of realities, and those that can be identified may as well be."

With the first point, we are back in W. W. Greg's clairvoyant world, where the metaphysics of presence endorses editorial decisions, but the second claim detracts from or even undermines that certainty with what is self-evidently true: that "Arden" could suggest England, Flanders, or both. (That the word "Arden" "*must* [my emphasis] have" these suggestions is polemical exaggeration: there is and was plenty of geographical ignorance among modern, and early modern, audiences, and "Arden" could suggest or have suggested neither Flanders nor Warwickshire.) Finally, and here we arrive at the first-do-no-harm conclusion, the mixed realities (whatever they may be) of Shakespearean geography permit specificity some of the time, and "Ardenne" not "Arden" is one of those occasions. It may be. Wells's case is thought-provoking, but why does the Oxford *Complete Works* not pursue its logic and name the forest "Ardennes," the standard modern spelling, or why does that edition or its *Textual Companion* not offer late-sixteenth-century evidence for "Ardenne" as the then-preferred or more likely spelling?[45]

The question of representation also plays through these examples. Stephen Greenblatt's complicated argument for "the circulation of social energy" presumably applies to place-names and the names of historical individuals as much as it does to social practices, costume, objects, and coded phrases.[46] Again, the question returns to whether an early modern audience, or a modern one, would transfer some (or, for some audiences, all) of what the audience knows about an extant or once-extant place, or place-name, or historical individual, or personal name into its experience of a play citing those places or names.[47] As with the reference issues I have mentioned, the question of representation here turns on what stands for what, on which verbal stimulus invokes which response.

Finally, Shakespeare's texts, read or performed, do not and cannot "mean the same thing(s)" to a modern audience as they did to the original one, or to one in 1674, 1737, or 1899, because their meanings are socially constructed, created by the interaction of text, players, and audience here and now, not in some irrecoverable there and then.[48] This widely held view, usually treated as a (post)modern consequence of the poststructuralist demolition of immanentist criticism (e.g., the New Criticism),[49] in fact occurred, albeit untheorized, both to Shakespeare's contemporaries[50] and to modern editors.

In 1955, surely a year when New Criticism ruled the roost, an authoritative editorial voice admitted that Lewis Theobald's 1733 emendation, "scotched," of the first verb in F1's "We have scorch'd the Snake, not kill'd it" (*Macbeth*, TLN 1167) was "universally adopted," claimed it was invalid, lamented that Theobald's long-lasting change had made it "almost impossible to restore the Folio reading against proverbial use," and concluded, "On the whole, more would be lost than gained by preferring the less common spelling [i.e., the Folio's] to the more common [in editions after Theobald's] here."[51] "Proverbial use" and "the more common" reading testify to Theobald's success, whatever his lexical ignorance, but what "more would be lost" if an editor followed sense and lexicography and restored (or retained, rather) F1's "scorch'd"? The lost "more" is 250 years of speech from the stage and casual quotation (perhaps especially by people who do not know the phrase comes from "Shakespeare," much less *Macbeth*) of the emended text. In effect, users of the language, and not just people who know the line comes from *Macbeth*, have endorsed Theobald's emendation, not from conscious editorial conviction, but out of habit and ignorance. We, two and one-half centuries of us, have rewritten Shakespeare, and the proof is that "scotched," misunderstood as "frustrated" or "rendered inoperative" (*OED* Scotch v^2 b.—e.g. "She scotched my plan"; "He scotched the rumors"), is now common, and "scorch'd" refers to ironing or cooking only. We have endorsed and distorted one archaism, Theobald's, over another, Shakespeare's.[52]

By speaking of "users" of Shakespeare's text, I recall, for example, John Ellis's definitions of both literature and literary criticism.[53] C. J. Sisson's reluctant acceptance of Theobald's error and John Ellis's and many others' claim that what we, the audience/readers, make of a performance or text is what that performance or text *is*, have extensive consequences for the detailed editorial and textual choices we considered earlier. Think of those two thanes, *Cathnes* (or *Cath.*) and *Menteth* (or *Ment.*), or Caithness and Menteith. Most editors give the thanes their modern geographical titles and spellings. Acknowledging a plain illogic, one editor modernizes or retains F1's names and spellings because they are "intelligible" and are therefore not to be altered "in the interest of modernity, or historical accuracy." A further reason for reproducing the Folio's spellings, it seems, is that Scotland in *Macbeth* is "a country of the mind," peopled, it further seems, by persons "of the mind" rather than once-living individuals who left documentary traces. Could the first audiences of *Macbeth* have confused Shakespeare's characters with living beings? Were earls (not, of course, thanes) of Ca(i)thnes(s) and Mente(i)th known to London audiences in 1605-6 or so? Could the early Jacobean present infiltrate—or, to continue the chemical metaphor, contaminate—an audience's perception of a contemporary text about an ancient Scottish civilization? Could a dramatic text representing that ancient civilization generate associations with present Jacobean aristocratic, even political, realities? A glance at the *Complete Peerage* offers the Jacobean audience (and us) numerous possibilities. For example: George Sinclair, fifth earl of Caithness (1566–1643), who does not seem to have been prominent in English court or political life after James's accession and William Graham, seventh earl of Menteith (c. 1589–1661), who eventually was quite prominent although his father (c. 1569–98) had not been.[54] Presumably, both the Folio's spelling and the now standard ones are (or were) pronounced the same way, so any theatergoer or critic or editor, then or now, who happens to know that these early-seventeenth-century earls exist/existed might mingle fact with fiction.

⚜

To conclude, several points: the Folio's spellings of place-names and personal names will not stop the play of signifiers. However place-names and personal names are printed or represented or spoken, nothing will preclude an audience's thinking of the still-extant Scottish town, Forres, when they hear "How far is't called to Forres?" Nor will varied printings or speaking achieve more than a variable proportion of persons who do or do not understand "Marseilles" to be an extant place on France's Mediterranean coast. Similarly, no matter how we spell their names, certain characters in *Macbeth*, perhaps all or any of them, may invoke contemporary associations (be they eleventh-, or seventeenth-, or twentieth-century associations) with known persons, living or dead.[55]

NOTES

1. *Threnodia Augustalis*, lines 186–88, in *The Works of John Dryden*, ed. Earl Miner, and Vinton A. Dearing, The California Edition (Berkeley and Los Angeles: University of California Press, 1969), 3:97. Hereafter, all volumes in this edition are cited as *Works*; I take the publication data cited on pages 112–13 from the same volume, 536–37.

2. Ibid., 3:537; see note 6, below.

3. They are summarized in G. C. R. Morris, "Dryden, Hobbs, Tonson and the Death of Charles II," *N&Q* 220 (1975): 558–59.

4. See *Threnodia Augustalis*, line 160 and note in *Works*, vol. 3.

5. Morris, "Dryden, Hobbs, Tonson," 559.

6. The edition by Thomas Broughton (1743) and an anonymous London edition of 1767 accept the 1701 folio's reading. *The Miscellaneous Works*, 4 vols. (London: J. and R. Tonson, 1767), which reprints the 1701 version of *Threnodia Augustalis*, has a footnote to "Short and Hobbes [*sic*]": "Two Physicians who attended on the King" (1:274). Samuel Derrick's more meticulous edition, *The Miscellaneous Works of John Dryden*, 4 vols. (London: J. and R. Tonson, 1760), however, prints Q1685 without comment or note. Hugh Macdonald regards the 1767 edition as a "reprint" of Derrick's 1760 edition, but it is not. The 1767 edition (which seems unlikely to have been overseen by Derrick) plagiarizes (in *Threnodia Augustalis* and elsewhere) and prints on the page notes from Broughton and Derrick, but accepts the 1701 folio text. In these matters, Macdonald is wrong; see Hugh

Macdonald, *John Dryden: A Bibliography of Early Editions and Drydeniana* (Oxford: Clarendon Press, 1939), 85–87.

7. Alan Roper writes, "Editors [i.e., of the California edition], hitherto finding no reference to Hobbs's attendance on Charles, have rejected the variant as unauthorial. . . . But Tonson may have set 1701 from a copy marked by Dryden which reflected Dryden's later gratitude to Hobbs and his knowledge that Hobbs indeed attended Charles in February 1685. The change is certainly odd if it was not made by Dryden, especially as Hobbs was also dead by 1701" (*Works,* 6:1113). An unsystematic survey of editions suggests that most accept Q1's reading, although Robert Bell (1854) adopts the erratum reading ("They") and retains "Short himself." Collation of copies of the 1701 folio might reveal press variants to account for Bell's choice.

8. Alan Roper points out that I have omitted many steps from the argument for accepting 1701's reading as authorial, viz., when Dryden wrote *Threnodia Augustalis*, he may not have known that Hobbs attended Charles II; Hobbs attended Dryden as physician in 1697 and may have then or on another occasion told him of his royal duty twelve years before; the 1701 folio includes one text—the "Heads of an Answer to Rhymer"—never before published, apparently because Tonson held the manuscript; Dryden is known to have revised his published texts. I agree that the combination of fact and variant could be evidence for authorial revision, but further corroboration and a collation of substantive and semisubstantive variants in the early quartos and 1701 folio are needed.

9. T[hrough] L[ine] N[umbers] are cited from the facsimile of F1, ed. Charlton Hinman (New York: Norton, 1968). For the possibility that Macbeth and Banquo rode onto the Globe's stage, see Leah Scragg, "Macbeth on Horseback," *Shakespeare Survey* 26 (1973): 81–88.

10. William Shakespeare, *Select Plays: Macbeth*, ed. W. G. Clark and W. Aldis Wright, Clarendon Press Series (Oxford: Clarendon Press, 1869). Glossing Shakespeare's text, this edition often cites (untranslated) various Greek tragedies, hence my epithet "superior."

11. Kenneth Muir, in the revised Arden edition of *Macbeth* (London: Methuen, 1984), regards "Soris" as "probably" a compositor's error (xv).

12. Quoted from Geoffrey Bullough, comp., *Narrative and Dramatic Sources of Shakespeare*, vol. 7 (London: Routledge, 1973), 488.

13. Bullough, in ibid., 488 n. 3, opines that the copying error occurred in the thirteenth century, and it is uncertain whether Shakespeare could have known any texts with the now-accepted, historically accurate spelling. On the editorial problem of errors an author quotes from an erroneous source, see G. Thomas Tanselle, "External Fact as an Editorial Problem," *SB* 32 (1979): 12–13, 18–19; on the "historical" names in the *Macbeth* narrative and the Gaelic meanings of some (e.g., Macduff = "Mac Dubh—son of the black[-haired] man"), see the "Glossary of Personal Names" in Peter Berresford Ellis, *MacBeth, High King of Scotland, 1040–57* (London: Muller, 1980), 127–28.

14. The only modern edition of *Macbeth* I know to print "Soris" does not collate the change (but the commentary mentions "Forres" as a "Scottish castle") and prints "Sinel's" (F1: *Sinells*), also without collation. See John Andrews, ed., *Macbeth*, Everyman Shakespeare (London: Dent, 1993), esp. xxxviii (where "soris" erroneously appears) and 12; this edition is avowedly innovative, or imaginative, in retaining the Folio's spelling and indeed adding archaic orthographic conventions to that text (see xxvii–xxxvi).

15. One thing I should advise against is the annotation of "Sinell" as "Holinshed's name for Macbeth's father" (William Shakespeare, *Macbeth*, ed. Nicholas Brooke [Oxford: Oxford University Press, 1990], 1.3.71n). While indisputably true, this note conveys (a) the relationship between Macbeth and Sinell and (b) there's more here than meets the eye, but the reader isn't going to learn what, or as W. E. Gladstone wrote (31 March 1853) of Stonehenge, "It is a noble . . . relic, telling much, & telling too that it conceals more" (*The*

Gladstone Diaries, ed. M. R. D. Foot and H. C. G. Matthew, vol. 4 [Oxford: Clarendon Press, 1974], 510). Editors have been undecided about how to treat another proper name in Folio *Macbeth;* the speaker the Folio calls "Rosse" and *Rosse* (or *Ro.*, or *Ross.*) retains or loses, editorially, his final *e* with unexamined volatility (see, e.g., n. 26 below).

16. W. W. Greg, *The Editorial Problem in Shakespeare*, 3d ed. (Oxford: Clarendon Press, 1954), xi; see Stanley Wells, "The Oxford Shakespeare: Editorial Procedures" (typescript, 1978), 15. Greg's view persists outside Shakespearean studies; discussing Melville's *Moby-Dick*, Thomas Tanselle avers, "[S]ome of these erroneous readings [in quotations from other authors] may have been present in Melville's manuscript, but as long as they can be argued to be unintentional slips the case for emendation is not altered" ("External Fact," 7).

17. *Henslowe's Diary*, ed. W. W. Greg, vol. 1 (London: Bullen, 1904), xxiv.

18. Sunday performances were common at court during the reigns of Elizabeth and James VI and I, and for much of Charles I's. Church and civic authorities long objected to public performances of plays, bear-baitings, etc., on Sunday, and numerous decrees, orders, and proclamations forbade such events. Repetition probably marks failure: if something is not happening, it doesn't require continued iteration and suppression. Writing of a 25 July 1591 letter, E. K. Chambers says, "[T]he Privy Council had not merely to *insist once more* upon the due observance of Sunday . . ." (my italics; see *The Elizabethan Stage*, vol. 1 [Oxford: Clarendon Press, 1923], 255ff., quotation from 295). Authorities seem to have had more success at preventing performance "during the hours of divine service" (ibid., 313).

19. A few years after Greg wrote, Charles Johnson and Hilary Jenkinson's authoritative paleographic manual echoed his circular argument: "It will be found that the very possibility of seeing what is actually written often depends on the power of the reader to imagine for himself what ought to have been written, and to check his hypotheses by what he can see: indeed, it is not too much to say that you cannot read a word with certainty unless you know what it is" (*English Court Hand*, A.D. *1066 to 1500* [Oxford: Clarendon Press, 1915], xxxvii–xxxviii). Greg, Johnson, Jenkinson, and I all point to a fundamental paradox of reading; the reader must recognize the familiar before the unfamiliar may be known while at the same time accepting (and calculating) that the unfamiliar is precisely unknown, not familiar.

20. See Tanselle, "External Fact," 32ff. and Margreta de Grazia, "What is a Work? What is a Document?" and my comments in W. Speed Hill, ed., *New Ways of Looking at Old Texts* (Binghamton, N.Y.: MRTS, 1993), 199–207 and 223–24, respectively. Note that neither de Grazia nor I use "work" in the signification G. Thomas Tanselle wishes to give it in *A Rationale of Textual Criticism* (Philadelphia: University of Pennsylvania Press, 1989) and elsewhere.

21. See, for instance: Jürgen Schäfer, "The Orthography of Proper Names in Modern-spelling Editions of Shakespeare," *SB* 23 (1970): 1–19; Gary Taylor, "The Fortunes of Oldcastle," *Shakespeare Survey* 38 (1985): 85–100 and the numerous subsequent debates over Falstaff/Oldcastle examined in David Scott Kastan's contribution to the present volume.

22. William Shakespeare, *Macbeth*, ed. G. K. Hunter, The New Penguin Shakespeare (Harmondsworth, England: Penguin, 1967), 189. The next two block quotations are from the same page. Hunter's argument is necessarily apodictic, and on several occasions I have put words in his mouth as I try to fill out his views and extrapolate his reasons for holding them. Distortion is inevitable, and I apologize unreservedly.

23. A controversial feature of "the special semantic status of names" is their "capacity . . . to survive loss of lexical sense" (Cecily Clark, "Onomastics" in *Cambridge History of the English Language*, vol. 2, *1066–1476*, ed. N. F. Blake [Cambridge: Cambridge University Press, 1992], 593 and 600, respectively). Thus, for example, "Berger" and "Braunmüller" function efficiently as personal names though they are no longer "intelligible" as designations

of an individual's or a family's dwelling place or occupation: such names "have become so thoroughly onomasticized as to constitute only an otherwise 'meaningless' label" (ibid., 603). See also: Alan Gardiner, *The Theory of Proper Names: A Controversial Essay*, 2d ed. (Oxford: Oxford University Press, 1954), 38; the summary discussion in John M. Carroll, *What's in a Name: An Essay in the Psychology of Reference* (New York: Freeman, 1985), chap. 8; Michael Issacharoff, "How Playscripts refer," in *On Referring in Literature,* ed. Anna Whiteside and Michael Issacharoff (Bloomington: Indiana University Press, 1987), 84–94.

24. Of course, it is significant that Scotland is geographically contiguous with England, and of course, my suggestions are partly facetious. Still, it is remarkable how little now-recoverable "Scottishness" the F1 text conveys, though it is impossible to know how much was conveyed in performance (by accent, costume, imitated social practices regarded as distinctively Scottish, etc.). See my "*Macbeth* and Scottishness," seminar paper, Shakespeare Association of America meeting, Philadelphia, April 1989. I would have included Kurosawa's *Throne of Blood* and *Ran* here but for the fact that he so thoroughly transforms the play's cultural signs.

25. Numerals commonly differentiate among several type-named speakers (Gentlemen, Citizens, Fairies, Witches, etc.) in F. Speech prefixes of two or three letters are common in F, but single-letter prefixes occur in both F and the early Shakespearean quartos, and Edward Albee conducts *Three Tall Women* (1994) with characters named A, B, and C. Thus, in Shakespearean texts, *P.* is Pembroke in *John* TLN 2117 and *K.* the King of *1H6* and *2H6* (see TLN 1791 and 3053, 3078) and *M.* the "Mother" (i.e. Lady Capulet) of *Romeo* TLN 2602; the first quartos of *Love's Labour's Lost* and *Titus Andronicus* include such designations as *A.* (Armado), *B.* ("Braggart" for the same speaker), *M.* and *A.* and *N.* (for Marcus Andronicus and Aaron and the Nurse, respectively).

26. *Macbeth,* ed. Hunter, 189. Muir's Arden edition (see n. 11) does not discuss the issue of nomenclature and silently adopts a mixture of early modern and modern orthography: Rosse, Menteth, and Cathness, Siward and Seyton.

27. See, among many, J. M. Nosworthy, "*Macbeth, Doctor Faustus,* and the Juggling Fiends" in *Mirror up to Shakespeare: Essays in Honour of G. R. Hibbard,* ed. J. C. Gray (Toronto: University of Toronto Press, 1984), 216–17, and Alan Dessen, *Elizabethan Stage Conventions and Modern Interpreters* (Cambridge: Cambridge University Press, 1984), 6.

28. Such a principle operates in the Riverside Shakespeare, ed. G. Blakemore Evans (Boston: Houghton Mifflin, 1974). Compare: "[I]t is . . . questionable whether place-names in their Elizabethan form are compatible with a text that is in other respects fully modernized. The argument of preserving Elizabethan pronunciation does not seem really cogent since in all other cases the phonetic development of the English language is carefully reflected" (Schäfer, "Orthography," 5).

29. Hunter may use the word "characters" to indicate the "world created to stand by itself" (see below) of "modern historians" who use such spellings (*Macbeth,* ed. Hunter, 189; cf. Wells, "Editorial Procedures," 66, where he invokes a usage by "modern historians" to opposite effect), but the "world . . . of modern historians" is no less "created to stand by itself" than *Macbeth,* no less text-based and text-transmitted than Holinshed's *Chronicles* or F1.

30. As with the earlier details of *Cathnes* and *Menteth,* I owe specification of these variant place-names to T. H. Howard-Hill's indispensable "*Macbeth*": *A Concordance to the Text of the First Folio,* Oxford Shakespeare Concordances (Oxford: Clarendon Press, 1971).

31. For a more practical objection to Hunter's retaining *Birnan,* see: "The same [as Hunter says of Birnam/*Birnan*] might be said of London, or most other towns and countries" (Wells, "Editorial Procedures," 63).

32. William Shakespeare, *Macbeth*, ed. A. W. Verity, Students' Shakespeare (Cambridge: Cambridge University Press, 1902).

33. Different objections may be made to the superficially similar claim concerning personal names—*Cathnes, Menteth*—and they are discussed below.

34. *Macbeth*, ed. Hunter, 37–38.

35. Though I would not exempt the histories and their chronicle sources from liberal treatment, as Hunter does; see my "*King John* and Historiography," *ELH* 55 (1988): 309–32, esp. 311–21.

36. *Macbeth*, ed. Hunter, 38.

37. Coins, the Banqueting House, and Rubens's paintings survive as testimonies to James VI and I's existence, but it's an easy argument to make them "texts" too. I do not claim that texts fail to record a material reality nor deny the existence of that material reality, but I do claim that making *Macbeth* a different kind of text from Holinshed or the works of modern historians requires a rather complicated argument that few critics or editors provide. See next note.

38. *Gulliver's Travels*, ed. Louis A. Landa (London: Methuen, 1965), bk. 3, chap. 5: "An expedient was therefore offered, that since words are only names for *things*, it would be more convenient for all men to carry about them such *things* as were necessary to express the particular business they are to discourse on"; Edith Hamilton and Hamilton Cairns, eds., *Collected Dialogues of Plato*, Bollingen Series (Princeton: Princeton University Press, 1961), 389E, 440; J. Hillis Miller, "Stevens' Rock and Criticism as Cure" (1976), quoted in Jerome J. McGann, *Social Values and Poetic Acts: The Historical Judgment of Literary Work* (Cambridge: Harvard University Press, 1988), 119.

39. Paul de Man, *Blindness and Insight* (New York: Oxford University Press, 1971), 165; compare "The ambivalence of writing [including de Man's own oeuvre] is such that it can be considered both an act and an interpretative process that follows after an act with which it cannot coincide" (ibid., 152).

40. See, e.g., McGann, *Social Values,* 115–31 and more recently and effectively, Ora Avni, *The Resistance of Reference: Linguistics, Philosophy, and the Literary Text* (Baltimore: Johns Hopkins University Press, 1990), esp. chap. 6, and the helpful bibliography on reference in Whiteside and Issacharoff, *On Referring in Literature,* 205–8.

41. The following instances come from Jürgen Schäfer's appendix, "Survey of Readings" ("Orthography of Proper Names," 17–19).

42. R. A. Foakes's Arden edition (London: Methuen, 1957) adds "Kimoltoun" and "Guimolton" as sixteenth-century spellings (4.1.34n).

43. Schäfer, "Orthography of Proper Names," 5.

44. Stanley Wells, *Re-Editing Shakespeare for the Modern Reader* (Oxford: Oxford University Press, 1984), 28–30; subsequent quotations are taken from 29–30.

45. See, respectively, William Shakespeare, *The Complete Works*, ed. Stanley Wells and Gary Taylor (Oxford: Clarendon Press, 1986), and Stanley Wells and Gary Taylor with John Jowett and William Montgomery, *William Shakespeare: A Textual Companion* (Oxford: Clarendon Press, 1987). For a sensible discussion of both the spelling and the significance of the forest's geographical indeterminacy, see Alan Brissenden, ed., *As You Like It*, Oxford Shakespeare (Oxford: Clarendon Press, 1993), 39–42.

46. Stephen Greenblatt, *Shakespearean Negotiations* (Berkeley and Los Angeles: University of California Press, 1988), 1–20.

47. Compare the assertion that "Many of the original audience . . . would have known that the historical Oldcastle was eventually executed . . ." (Taylor, "Fortunes," 95).

48. The dates in this sentence are those of, respectively, the first printing of William Davenant's extensive adaptation of *Macbeth*, a significant Licensing Act, and the Boer War—each of which events had profound effects upon the social construction of Shakespeare's texts.

49. See, e.g., McGann, *Social Value.*

50. Shakespeare's contemporaries well knew an audience's constructive powers. Webster, for instance, angrily complained he lacked "a full and understanding auditory," "the only grace and setting out of a tragedy," when *The White Devil* first appeared at the Red Bull Theatre (John Webster, *The White Devil*, ed. J. R. Brown, 2d ed., The Revels Plays [London: Methuen, 1966], 2; cf. ibid., xxii–xxiii).

51. C. J. Sisson, *New Readings in Shakespeare*, vol. 2 (Cambridge: Cambridge University Press, 1955), 199. *OED* Scotch v^1 (= cut, score, gash) claims "identity with Scorch v^3 [where *Macbeth* is quoted] . . . is hardly possible." Sisson's claim is a small example of the editorial timidity Taylor, "Fortunes," 92–93, castigates.

52. The guild of scholars does not escape such transgressions against textual fact in favor of tradition. How many of us have said "to gild the lily," aware or unaware that we were misquoting Shakespeare? See *King John* 4.2.11: "To gild refined gold, to paint the lily."

53. John M. Ellis, *The Theory of Literary Criticism: A Logical Analysis* (Berkeley and Los Angeles: University of California Press, 1974).

54. The seventh earl of Menteith was indeed "prominent" in the crisis over James's succession; see Peter Ure, "A Pointer to the Date of Ford's *Perkin Warbeck*," *N&Q* 215 (1970): 215–17.

55. Earlier versions of this chapter survived scrutiny at a Shakespeare Association of America seminar chaired by F. J. Levy, where Phyllis Rackin offered valuable criticism, and at the H. E. Huntington Library, San Marino, California, through Roy Ritchie's generosity. Conversations with Alan Roper, Marion Trousdale, and Michael Warren have also improved this chapter, and I thank Vinton Dearing for returning to Drydenian labor he might justly have thought long finished. Laurie Maguire and Thomas Berger made bracing corrections, as did an anonymous reader. More than once, Billy Phelan checked, debated, and improved this argument.

6

The Problem of
Shakespeare's Text(s)

BARBARA A. MOWAT

It was in 1709 that Shakespeare's texts were first described as problematic. During the sixteenth and seventeenth centuries, many of the plays had been printed individually in quarto, and the plays had been collected in 1623 in folio; during the seventeenth century, new editions of the quartos continued to appear, and the folio collection was reissued in 1632, 1663–64, and 1685. In these early printed texts one finds attacks on the other versions— that is, some quartos claim on their title pages to be more complete than others, and the Folio letter to the readers accuses the quarto versions of being "maimed, and deformed"—but none talked about textual problems. Nicholas Rowe's edition of 1709, the first with a named editor, is the first to say that there is a problem with the texts and to define the problem: namely, that the manuscripts of the plays are lost. Rowe was certain that, had he only been able to locate the missing manuscripts, he could have given us Shakespeare's own words instead of having to reproduce the texts provided by the folios and quartos. As Rowe wrote in his dedicatory letter:

> I must not pretend to have restor'd this Work to the Exactness of the Author's Original Manuscripts. These are lost, or, at least, are gone beyond any Inquiry I could make; so that there was nothing left, but to compare the several Editions, and give the true Reading as well as I could from thence. This I have endeavour'd to do pretty carefully, and render'd very many places intelligible, that were not so before.[1]

Rowe found many differences between, for example, folio *Hamlet* (as he found it in F4) and quarto *Hamlet* (as he found it in Q1676),[2] and, in the absence of the *Hamlet* manuscript itself, saw as his editorial duty the comparing of the early editions, using material in one edition to supplement the other; in this way, he would, as he wrote, "restore" the "Work" as close "to the Exactness of the Author's Original Manuscripts" as he could.

Much has happened since Rowe published this statement in 1709. But as recently as 1964, Fredson Bowers continued to describe the central problem of Shakespeare's texts in terms of the recovery of the Shakespeare manuscripts—though, since the manuscripts themselves are still just as lost as they were in 1709, that recovery would have to be indirect. "One of the first tasks of any editor," wrote Bowers, "is to try to identify the kind of manuscript that served as printer's copy for a Shakespeare first edition and for any later authoritative form of the text." An authentic version of the Shakespeare text, according to Bowers, could only be created by the editor who would

> [b]y stripping the veil of print from the texts, . . . recover a number of the characteristics of the manuscript that was given to the printer. From such evidence one may eventually determine, not impressionistically as at present but scientifically, which were Shakespeare's own papers and which copies by . . . scribes.[3]

Bowers's belief that the day was coming when bibliographers would scientifically determine the nature of the manuscript lying behind any given early printed text of Shakespeare reflects the self-confidence that had been growing among bibliographers since the late-nineteenth century—the belief that an application of scientific method to the study of Shakespeare's early printed texts would eventually in effect give us back the lost manuscripts and give us, finally, the authentic Shakespeare.[4]

The belief of Bowers and other New Bibliographers remains current orthodoxy among Shakespeare editors, as one can see from the textual introductions to standard Shakespeare editions, where the editorial rationale is inextricably linked to the editor's view of "the manuscript" seen as lying behind the chosen early printed text. With *Hamlet*, for example, most editors base their edition on the *Hamlet* second quarto because (as the Riverside editor puts it) it was shown in 1934 "with near certainty that Q2 was printed from some form of Shakespeare's autograph."[5] In seeming contrast, the recent Oxford *Complete Works* bases its *Hamlet* on the Folio, but again the choice is made in terms of the putative underlying manuscript: according to the Oxford editors, Folio *Hamlet* prints Shakespeare's revised manuscript, the manuscript used in the theater as, in today's parlance, the "prompt-book."[6] Thus for G. B. Evans and for the Oxford editors—as for almost every editor of *Hamlet*—the decision about the text to be edited is made in terms of what is assumed about the manuscript underlying a given early printed text.

In recent years, scholars examining the extant manuscripts of Renaissance plays have shown that there are fallacies at the core of the New Bibliography—have shown, for example, that the very stigmata used by bibliographers to demonstrate that a play was printed from Shakespeare's autograph can be found in scribal and theatrical manuscripts as well.[7] As these scholars are demonstrating, scientific discovery of the kind of manuscript that was transformed in the printing house into a given (printed) playtext seems not to be possible (unless the manuscript, too, is extant), and our hopes of "stripping the veil of print from the texts" to reveal the manuscripts beneath are founded on sand rather than rock. It may take years for this heresy to become orthodoxy and for Shakespeare editors to acknowledge that the supposedly scientific links between early printed texts and their manuscript copy are based on questionable hypotheses. But in the meantime I would argue that there is another, equally large fallacy at work in our thinking about Shakespeare's text, a fallacy operative since at least 1709—the belief that obtaining manuscripts of the plays would unproblematize the text. I would argue, in other words, that there has been from the beginning an editorial sacralizing of lost authorial manuscripts that has made us frame the problem of Shakespeare's texts incorrectly.

Rowe's lament—"I must not pretend to have restor'd this Work to the Exactness of the Author's Original Manuscripts. These are lost . . ."—implies that, could Rowe have found the dramatic scripts in manuscript, he could have reproduced Shakespeare's exact words. An analogous assumption seems to lie behind Bowers's belief that we would have "the authentic text" once the authorial manuscript was scientifically unveiled. Yet there is clear evidence that having access to the manuscripts—having access even to Shakespeare and his fellow actors—did not guarantee publication of an unproblematic authorial work. To take a single example: if we assume that Shakespeare wrote out a manuscript of *Hamlet*, we must also assume that he had written it by 1603, since Q1 *Hamlet* was printed in that year. Q1 *Hamlet* claims on its title page to be the play as performed in London and elsewhere as written by William Shakespeare. Critics disagree about the provenance of the manuscript from which Q1 was printed—only a few link it directly to an authorial manuscript, since it seems a very garbled version of what one finds in the other two printings[8]—but whatever its provenance, Q1 is a printed witness to a manuscript of a play that is recognizably linked to the other two *Hamlets*. The 1604/5 Q2 *Hamlet* is much longer than Q1 ("enlarged to almost as much againe as it was," according to its title page); it makes a lot more sense than Q1; and it claims to be printed from "the true and perfect Coppie"—i.e., from Shakespeare's own manuscript (a claim, as I noted earlier, accepted by most editors today). Yet when Shakespeare's fellow actors collected his manuscripts for publication, they gave the printer a manuscript of *Hamlet* that differed in major ways from the manuscript behind Q2. As Rowe noted, the Folio version of *Hamlet* lacks many passages found in Q2; as Rowe did *not* note, it also contains passages missing from Q2 and it differs from Q2 in many hundreds of words. However, just as Q2 claims to be printed from "the true and perfect Coppie," the Folio advertises itself as publishing Shakespeare's manuscripts "perfect of their limbes" and "as [the author] conceived them." By 1623, then, the *Hamlet* text was as problematic as it is today. It existed, as it does today, in three printed forms that relate to each other in strange and interesting ways. Each claims to be the authentic text, but none carries any guarantee of authenticity, even though manuscripts of the play were obviously available at the time. Indeed, until 1616, the author himself was also available, as were, through the printing of the Folio, two persons who had performed in the play and who claimed to have "received from him" the very (unblotted) "papers" they had now "collected & publish'd."[9]

Further, there is abundant evidence that, should manuscripts of Shakespeare's plays come to light today, we would not thereby be guaranteed an unproblematic text. We see this in the experience of current editors of, for example, Renaissance women writers or coterie poets (writers and poets, that is, whose writings were largely published through manuscript circulation).[10] Publishing an "authentic" text of, say, the writings of Katherine Philips brings the editor up against problems that are amazingly like those facing those who edit Shakespeare from early printed texts. With manuscripts in hand, the editor must still make hard choices. Philips herself made more than one copy of individual poems and of collections of her poems; the poems are rarely exactly the same from manuscript to manuscript. The editor sometimes knows that one manuscript collection postdates another, but is even then left with the problem of whether a word or punctuation change represents revision or careless copying.[11] Philips's poems survive in many manuscript collections, copied there by scribes and friends who introduced the kinds of changes that routinely occur in manuscript transmission.[12] Here the editor must attempt to separate the changes that are, in fact, errors of transmission—omissions, word changes, additions—from those that might have come into the manuscript because the scribe had access to a different holograph. The facts of publication in manuscript form—i.e., that manuscripts themselves were copied and recopied, that copying inevitably introduces change—mean that editors with access to manuscripts are as hard pressed to publish "authentic" editions of their authors as is any Shakespeare editor.[13]

And the problem is only exacerbated when manuscripts exist alongside early printed editions. To cite once again the works of Katherine Philips: Elizabeth Hageman and Andrea Sununu, currently editing Philips's works,

have before them five versions of Philips's play *Pompey* that date from
Philips's lifetime or just after her death. Three printed versions (two quartos and the folio version) and one manuscript version (part of a larger transcription made for Philips's friend "Rosania") do not substantially differ
(the manuscript version being, in fact, a transcription of one of the printed
versions); a second manuscript transcription differs significantly from the
other versions. This second manuscript "is authorized by Philips's own
manuscript corrections and additions";[14] it includes many lines that are quite
different from the other four versions; and it dates from just before the play
was performed in Dublin and only a year and a half before Philips's death.
Since it is filled with Philips's own corrections, it would seem certainly to
represent—against the printed texts and the "Rosania" manuscript—the
author's "true Coppie." Through careful study of Philips's letters, of the
performance history of the play, and of the publication history of Corneille's
Pompée (which *Pompey* translates), the editors have determined (as best
one can) that this "authorized" manuscript is, in fact, an earlier version that
Philips later revised, while the printed texts and the "Rosania" transcript
actually represent Philips's "final version." Clearly, having Philips's playtext
in (an authorized) manuscript has not unproblematized the editorial process.

Nor (as I have already suggested when mentioning Philips's poems)
does having the author's holograph necessarily simplify the editor's problem nor guarantee the "Exactness" or the "true Reading" that Rowe and his
descendants have sought. John Shawcross describes the difficult editorial
decisions facing editors of John Donne's poems and says boldly that holographs would not—indeed, do not—help. After pointing out the many problems that arise from an editor's having to decide between depending on a
manuscript, with the usual scribal errors and idiosyncrasies, and a printed
version, with the usual compositorial interventions, Shawcross asks: "But
what if we had a manuscript in Donne's holograph? Would our problems
be solved? Well, no, they would not be, though some Donne scholars express dismay at such a statement. Probably they have not edited anything
other than from direct printed texts, and maybe not even looked at or studied a seventeenth-century manuscript." Shawcross writes that "The problems
if we had holographs would probably include . . . questions of accuracy on
Donne's part . . . and of the validity of readings"—and he illustrates his
point by discussing the difficulties that face the editor of Donne's one extant holograph poem.[15]

The kind of authorial inaccuracy alluded to by Shawcross is well documented in surviving playtext manuscripts. William B. Long shows how an
author, no doubt "confused by anticipating his next scene," "erroneously
entered" stage directions in the manuscript of *Thomas of Woodstock*; evidently, writes Long, "the book went to the company with this gross play-

wright's error in it. The players . . . restored the proper [directions], avoiding the chaos on stage that would have resulted if they had played as the
playwright had indicated." Long concludes that "among the many cautions
in dealing with texts must be added that of playwrights being subject to
lapsus calami in fair-copying their own work."[16] Trevor Howard-Hill describes the behavior of Thomas Middleton vis-à-vis the transcriptions of *A
Game at Chess,* where Middleton's cavalier treatment of his own play—
producing one error-filled authorial holograph that lacks a scene crucial to
the plot, and producing another authorially "completed" and "corrected"
manuscript in which Middleton (out of what appears to be sheer laziness)
patched together two parts of the manuscript in such a way that more than
230 lines of the text were simply left out, thus "mutilating the text" (to use
Howard-Hill's language) and creating a manuscript that "is error-ridden
and deliberately defective at just that point where the author was most closely
involved."[17]

  We know, then, that where several manuscript copies of a Renaissance
play have survived—as, for example, with *A Game at Chess*—one finds
countless differences from script to script. We know that actors made transcripts of plays to give as presentation copies to friends; we know that
playscripts were copied by professional scribes—and not just to provide a
"book" for the theatrical production.[18] Yet this knowledge does not carry
over into our thinking when faced with multiple-text Shakespeare plays—
with, for example, *Hamlet,* or *King Lear,* or *Richard III,* where (as we can
see in textual introductions to current editions) editors continue to debate
which version prints *the* authorial manuscript and which *the* theatrical
"prompt-book," or which prints the early holograph and which the holograph revision, and where a garbled early printed version can be accounted
for only as the result of an actor's memorial reconstruction or of a spectator's
shorthand thievery. *Othello* is unusual among Shakespeare plays in that
some editors allow for scribal transcripts as the basis for the two early
printed editions. But even here, editors who see both Q1 and F as printing
scribal versions of the play trace the transcriptions back to specific authorial manuscripts. Instead of considering the possibility that each version
may represent a printing of one of many manuscript copies of the play
circulating in the early 1620s, editors continue to try to link each version to
a particular holograph.[19] I would argue that it is this clinging to illusions
about "prompt-books" and "authorial manuscripts" that blinds us to the
possibility that there may have been a large flow of manuscript copies of
Shakespeare's plays, copies marked by the idiosyncrasies of manuscript
transmission, idiosyncrasies that would inevitably have made their way
into the printed copies.

  Where does that leave us? It leaves us where we've been for some centuries: that is, faced with different early printings of Shakespeare's plays—but also faced with the likelihood that certainty and authenticity will not be guaranteed at the end of a search for the manuscripts that lie behind those plays. This is an unacceptable thought to many Shakespeare editors, and, until a couple of decades ago, would probably have been a frightening thought to most Shakespeareans. Now, though, many Shakespeareans may be undisturbed by the suggestion that finding "the Author's Original Manuscripts" would give us only another possible text, another set of variants to consider, rather than "the exact Reading."

Such equanimity can be expected because so much of what was until recently believed about Shakespeare is now in question—and the result is a climate in which the pleasure taken in Shakespeare's plays need not depend on any link between the early printed texts and notions of the Bard and his manuscripts. Until the 1980s, I think it is fair to say, most Shakespeareans read and taught Shakespeare's plays and poems as Works—to use Roland Barthes's terminology. As Works they were tied to the author as father; as Works they were received as "defined objects" and offered themselves as closing in on the signified and thus open to study through philology (for those who thought the signified obvious) and to interpretation (for those who thought the signified hidden). As Works they were studied in terms of sources and influences, image patterns and themes, and, centrally, as Works they were seen as organic—whole, integral, fixed.[20] In that climate, questions about the authenticity of the text, certainty about the provenance of the manuscript lying behind the text, had a certain urgency.

Today, many Shakespeareans have moved away from the concept of the plays as Works. They see the plays as free of the process of filiation and (again to cite Barthes) read them "without the father's signature." They see them as subject not to interpretation but to explosion, dissemination; as woven from a "stereographic plurality of signifiers," of cultural languages. And they see them as the object not of philological or hermeneutic analysis, but as the object, instead, of *play*. "The Text itself *plays* (like a door on its hinges . . .); and the reader . . . plays twice over: playing the Text as one plays a game . . . he also *plays* the text in the musical sense of the term." The reader "opens it out, makes it go." When it is thus seen as plural, unfathered, a network rather than an organism, a Shakespeare play is linked inextricably to a pleasure (Barthes's term is *jouissance*) in which there is no separation between it and its reader or spectator.[21]

This shift in the perception of Shakespeare's plays has meant that the desacralizing of the lost manuscripts could well be seen as simply one more breaking of restrictive bonds, one more freeing up of the text. Each bond that has thus far been broken, with however much pain, has led to an unexpectedly fruitful opening out of the text. The setting aside of Shakespeare-as-Author, for example, has, in freeing the plays from the process of filiation, freed them as well from at least two centuries of moral encrustation. Whereas positing Shakespeare as author function[22] gave us a larger-than-life creator of a canon of texts that found coherence and organic integrity in his authorial persona—a bardic author around whom readings of "the canon" and of individual plays collected—scholars responding to the plays "without the father's signature" have challenged these earlier readings, finding in the plays significant ambiguities and intriguing moral complexities.[23] A similar shift in perception, a similar freeing of the text, occurs when critics place Shakespeare's plays among other documents of the period—literary, historical, cultural—viewing them, in Barthes's language, as networks rather than organisms. Immediately, the play is heard as separate, distinct voices, each voice making its claim, each fighting for its cultural and gendered place, instead of all being absorbed into the larger single voice that was for so long heard as Shakespeare's own.[24]

Editors themselves are responsible for a third breaking of restrictive bonds, though ironically they themselves have in general not followed the postmodern implications of the revolution they set in motion. I refer, of course, to the recent radical destabilizing of the received Shakespeare text. Until about 1980 most editors believed, with Nicholas Rowe, that behind a multiple-text play like *Hamlet* there once existed a single, larger text that had unfortunately and accidentally been fragmented, and that it was the duty of the editor to splice the pieces together into the original complete form. It has now been accepted by most Shakespeare editors that, instead, those plays that were printed in different versions—for example, the two texts of *Lear* and the three texts of *Hamlet*—must be considered in their individual printed versions. However, in attacking the traditional belief in the single Shakespeare play fragmented into multiple early printed versions, editors did not abandon their belief in the play as a Work—that is, as read "with the father's signature," as a "defined object," as organic—coherent, integral, fixed. They simply transferred that belief away from the ideal, lost, composite text to the separate, individual printing, and began to valorize one text of *Lear*, for instance, as a printing of Shakespeare's original manuscript, or to support the other as being a printing of his revised version, or to urge the superiority of one text of *Hamlet* as being printed from the author's original manuscript or to urge the authenticity of another because it was printed from the theater-manuscript promptbook.

In today's critical climate, where Shakespeare's plays are being accepted as simply playtexts, unfathered, sometimes multiple, many Shakespeareans will be untroubled by the idea that we cannot know whether the manuscript behind an early printed text is authorial, scribal, or theater-based; nor will they be disturbed at the suggestion that manuscript evidence—should any be found—would still have to be weighed with considerable care. For editors, however, such radical skepticism is much more troubling—and not only because the idea of an "ideal Work" lying behind given manuscripts and texts is deeply ingrained in the editorial mind, nor simply because the idea of "authorial intention" is, for many editors, at the heart of the editorial project. Even more to the point is that, as editors surely intuit, to abandon the figurative search for Shakespeare's manuscripts and to accept the fact that we have nothing but the printed texts themselves (texts into which have doubtless intruded the great variety of changes that occur in manuscript transmission as well as printing-house impositions and errors) will mean rethinking the foundations of Shakespeare editing—as my coeditor Paul Werstine and I have been learning as we edit Shakespeare's plays for the Folger Shakespeare Library.

As we think through each of the plays on the assumption that nothing is available to us except the early printed texts and the accumulated editorial and cultural traditions, we are discovering that the problems in the text are sorting themselves out in a different way than they have done for editors whose search has been for Shakespeare's veiled manuscripts. As a single example, take a moment in the text of *The Merchant of Venice*: in the play's final scene, Lorenzo and Jessica are alone onstage, waiting for the return of Portia and Bassanio. The Clown, Lancelet Gobbo, enters, speaks briefly, and exits. The textual moment in question is comprised by the Clown's exit line and Lorenzo's line that follows. Those two lines appear below as they are found in the Cambridge text of 1926 and substantially in almost all texts of the play today:

> *Lancelot.* . . . My master will be here ere morning. [*he runs off*
> *Lorenzo.* Sweet soul, let's in, and there expect their coming.
> (5.1.49–50)

Dover Wilson described the textual problem these lines present (as he and later editors have seen that problem) by noting that, in the quartos and the First Folio, the lines appear as:

> *Clown.* . . . my Maister will be heere ere morning sweete soule.
> *Lorenzo.* Let's in, and there expect their comming.

Wilson writes that here we have an unmistakable "textual irregularity" that "demands explanation: the words 'sweet soul', which should of course stand in line 50 at the beginning of Lorenzo's speech, have [in the early printed texts] been misplaced, and are printed by Q in line 49 at the end of Lancelot's speech." He saw this "irregularity" as "a clue of importance" about the nature of the manuscript underlying the quarto; Wilson's "own bias" was "in favour of an assembled text"—that is, a theatrical manuscript put together from players' acting parts. Since he did not want simply to follow his bias, he consulted Sir Walter Greg, asking Greg how he would "explain the misplacement of 'sweet soul' at 5.1.49 [of the quarto]." Greg responded with what he himself later called an "elaborate conjecture" about lines inserted into the manuscript on a slip of paper, and suggested there might have been some kind of "intermediate transcript." Wilson was delighted, since, as he wrote, "it will be noticed . . . how aptly Dr Greg's explanation of the puzzle falls in with our general theory" about the manuscript.[25]

Greg did not agree with Wilson that *The Merchant of Venice* was printed from a theatrical manuscript, but was sure that, instead, it was printed from the author's "foul papers." So he argued, in 1942, that the slip of paper might have been added to the manuscript "in foul papers as easily as in the prompt-book," and then in 1955 argued that "the facts" about the misplaced words "can be more simply explained by supposing" that Shakespeare wrote Lorenzo's name "too low, so that Lorenzo's 'sweete soule' got tacked on to the Clown's speech."[26]

Later editors have generally agreed with Dover Wilson that these lines in the text represent a significant textual problem, but have followed Greg in assuming that the text was printed from Shakespeare's manuscript; they have also agreed that one of Greg's explanations accounts for what Greg called "the facts" about this editorial problem—i.e., either that an addition to the manuscript on a separate slip of paper led to a miscopying or misprinting; or that Shakespeare wrote Lorenzo's name in the wrong place on the manuscript.

If one approaches the two problematic lines not as clues about the underlying manuscript but in terms of extant printed texts, one discovers that "the facts" may well be quite different from those implied in Wilson's question to Greg. Rather than asking how one would "explain the [quarto's] misplacement of 'sweet soul,'" as Wilson asked, one asks instead, "Why do editors move 'sweet soul' from where it appears in the quarto, giving it to a different speaker?" The answer, one discovers, traces back to the Second Folio, where a major printer's error changed the last word of the Clown's speech from "soul" to "Love." This error was reprinted in the Third and the Fourth Folios, and a comma was added before the word "sweet." Thus, when Rowe edited *The Merchant of Venice* from the Fourth Folio, he found the Clown either calling Lorenzo "sweet Love" or else referring to his master Bassanio by this unlikely epithet. Rowe obviously assumed the mistake was in the placing of the words "sweet love," so he moved them, assigning them to Lorenzo, who, in Rowe's edition, says to Jessica, "Sweet love, let's in and there expect their coming." Beginning with the 1785 Steevens-

Reed edition, editors restore the text's "sweet soul," but almost all editors continue to follow Rowe in assigning the words to Lorenzo. One or two editors recognize in their collations that Rowe followed a later Folio in printing "sweet Love";[27] the 1987 Oxford *Textual Companion* claims, erroneously, that Rowe "emended" "sweet soul" to "sweet love."[28] But editors in general continue to frame the problem in terms of a manuscript error and continue to solve this supposed problem by assigning the words to Lorenzo.[29]

This is one small example of what I see as the incorrect framing of the problem of Shakespeare's texts: when an editor's primary interest is in identifying and reproducing the manuscript he or she sees as underlying the early printed text, such obvious matters as contamination of texts through printers' errors are ignored while editors chase will-o'-the-wisp imaginary slips of paper or fantasize about authors' handwriting errors on imaginary manuscripts. Once one attends with full awareness to the early printed texts, textual problems begin to frame themselves differently, and new problems emerge. These problems fall into three related groups. Some—like Lorenzo's "sweet soul"—have to do with relationships among the early printed texts and with how those texts have entered the editorial tradition; a second group has to do with such surrounding matter as dramatis personae lists and editorially constructed character names and titles. To take a single example: in every edition of *Merchant* between 1709 and 1992, the Clown speaks under the name of "Lancelot"—this despite the fact that all the quartos and folios give the character's name as "Lancelet"—not in speech headings, where he is called "Clown," but in the dialogue of the text, where the name "Lancelet" is repeated some twenty-five times.[30] The word "lancelet" meant a "lancet" or "a small lance." If Shakespeare was playing with that word in Lancelet's name, no one between 1709 and 1992 heard the wordplay. Instead, with Rowe's change of the name to "Launcelot," we have heard instead other resonances, other allusions. (Some editors defend their following of Rowe in renaming the character on the grounds that the 1637 quarto prints "Lancelot" throughout the play, but that is simply not true. The name does appear as "Lancelot" in the dramatis personae list that was first added to *Merchant* in that quarto, but the text retains "Lancelet" throughout, as does the Fourth Quarto of 1652.[31])

The problem of Lancelet's name leads to the third group of problems that surface once one abandons the search for manuscripts and focuses on how one is to edit the extant texts. This third group grows out of the conflict between Shakespeare as presented in the early printed texts and the Shakespeare that has been editorially and culturally constructed, and, over the centuries, disseminated, acted, recited, quoted, loved. Each of Shakespeare's plays is, by now, a cultural as well as an editorial construct. Once

one abandons the notion of the authorial manuscript behind the early printing, one is again and again left with the choice of reproducing, on the one
hand, an early printing, with all its faults, and, on the other hand, the editorially, culturally constructed play. The problem of Shakespeare's texts becomes, then, how does an editor make choices? What does one choose?

What does one do, for example, about the name of Hamlet's mother?
As I mentioned earlier, Q2 *Hamlet* is now accepted by almost every editor
as the best text of *Hamlet*, since it seems to them to reproduce Shakespeare's
own manuscript. Most editors therefore use Q2 as the text on which to base
their editions. Yet each edition names Hamlet's mother not as she was named
in Q2, but as she was named in the Folio. That this character is known to us
as "Gertrude" is, again, the work of Nicholas Rowe, who thought of the
Folio as the superior text and therefore followed the Folio in naming her
"Gertrude." Had he followed the quarto instead of the Folio, we would
now know Hamlet's mother as Gertrard. She is "Gertrard" throughout the
stage directions and dialogue of Q2 *Hamlet*, and she was acted under that
name through 1703, where she appears as "Gertrard" in the text and the
dramatis personae list of the acting quarto printed in that year. The difference between the two names, of course, is in the sound—and since her
name is used in dialogue thirteen times, often at key emotional moments,
the use of the Folio's "Gertrude" creates quite different sound patterns in
thirteen lines of the play. Yet editors deeply committed to following Q2
Hamlet as copytext have continued to use F's "Gertrude."[32] They do so, I
suspect, for the same reason that Paul Werstine and I do in the New Folger
Hamlet: namely, because it is as Gertrude that she exists and has existed
for nearly three hundred years. That's who she *is* in the appreciations, criticisms, productions, and interpretations that comprise her social/cultural
life. In other words, we allow the "Shakespeare" that is culturally constructed to outweigh the Shakespeare that may be reflected in Q2 *Hamlet*,
and name her "Gertrude."

More editorial choices, of course, have to do with individual words
and phrases than with characters' names, and here one finds comparable
conflicts between the early printed texts and the inherited versions. To take
an example from *Othello*. More than one of this play's famous lines is, in
fact, an editorial construct, made, for example, from a Folio line with an
addition or substitution from Q. One that Werstine and I grappled with
reads, in the traditional text, "If she be false, O then heaven mocks itself!"
In the Folio (which we, along with most editors, chose as our copytext) the
line reads instead "If she be false, heaven mocks itself." The "O then" is
taken from the parallel line in the quarto and inserted, presumably to fill
out a short line. We decided that the "O then" is strictly padding and that it
weakens a line that is metrically short but rhetorically very strong indeed.

In fact, with the "O then" missing, an actor might so stress the last three words that the line would have the desired five beats: If **she** be **false, heaven mocks itself.** We therefore chose not to add the traditional padding. At another point, we decided instead to accept the familiar traditional reading as against the Folio. The line, which Desdemona gives in act 1, scene 3, reads in the Folio "That I love the Moor to live with him"; the traditional reading of the line includes an additional quarto word and reads "That I did love the Moor to live with him." This placing of the love in the past tense seemed to us problematic. But here it was harder to argue the rhetorical strength of the line as it appears in the Folio, and, finally, the weight of the familiarity of the line as we have inherited it from the editorial tradition became the deciding factor.

There is little that one can theorize about the editing of Shakespeare's texts once one abandons belief that one can determine the precise nature of the manuscript lying behind a given early printed text. Instead, one chooses which early printed text to edit, sticks to that text as closely as is feasible, and adds or substitutes variants or emendations only in specific circumstances, which one then spells out in one's textual introduction. The "problem" with Shakespeare's texts, in other words, is, for the editor today, no longer so much theoretical as practical, turning on questions of how one chooses. An important part of the process is paying attention to traditional emendations, checking each such emendation to see if the original word can, in fact, stand. A famous line at the end of *Romeo and Juliet*, for instance, is almost always emended to read, "I will raise her statue in pure gold." The word "raise" is found in the Fourth Quarto and the Folio, and is routinely substituted by editors for the word "raie"—i.e., "ray"—which appears in Q2, the text accepted by these editors as the basis for their editions. After checking early uses of *ray*, finding that it could be the short form of "array" or "decorate," checking the dialogue in which the line appears, which contains the declaration that Juliet's statue will *lie* by that of Romeo, and meditating on Shakespeare's other references to sarcophagi and their gilding (for example, Sonnet 55, with its reference to "the gilded monuments of princes"), we decided to break with tradition and retain Q2's *ray*. In the absence of a putative controlling manuscript, in other words, our problems are problems of research and careful thought. Our goal is to construct, with integrity, the best edition we can of a given early printed text.[33] The most difficult problem, it turns out, is how to shake off the eighteenth-century hand of Nicholas Rowe and those who have followed him, while still giving late-twentieth-century readers and audiences a text that is clear and that does not do violence to their "Shakespeare" merely in the interests of blindly following the errors of early modern scribes and typesetters.

I focus on the editorial work on the New Folger Library Shakespeare primarily because I believe that the problems we are facing are those that future editors will face. Like Rowe, editors working in a post–New Bibliography world will find that "there [is] nothing left, but to compare the several Editions," and then make the hard choices. Some of the mystique will have departed along with the lost manuscripts and the search for the "true Reading," but the editing will be even more challenging and the texts, we hope, will continue to give the pleasure they have always given—perhaps despite the work of the editor.[34]

NOTES

1. Nicholas Rowe, ed., *The Works of Mr. William Shakespear,* vol 1. (London: J. Tonson, 1709), A2–A2v.

2. See my "The Form of *Hamlet*'s Fortunes," *RD* 19 (1989): 97–126.

3. Fredson Bowers, "Today's Shakespeare Texts, and Tomorrow's," *SB* 19 (1966): 39–65, esp. 59–60. The paper was delivered as an address at Wayne State University, 10 March 1964.

George Walton Williams, the textual scholar to whom this volume is dedicated, presented a paper in 1969 that shares Bowers's positive view of the future of Shakespeare editing in the age of scientific advancement: "By knowing thoroughly the spelling patterns and variable practices of the compositors of a particular play, editors should be able with a reasonable degree of probability to reconstruct the original spellings used by Shakespeare and so to reconstitute, as it were, the lost manuscript of Shakespeare himself. For those plays in which a scribal transcript intervenes between the holograph and the print the task will be more difficult, but something may be said even of them. This hypothetical, recovered or reconstituted manuscript will be the finally definitive text of Shakespeare, in Shakespeare's own spelling" ("On Editing Shakespeare: *Annus Mirabilis*," *Medieval and Renaissance Studies* 5 [1971]: 61–79, esp. 73).

4. For a fascinating account of the rise of the "scientific bibliography" of Greg, McKerrow, and Pollard from Victorian "scientific" disintegrationism, see Hugh Grady, "Disintegration and its Reverberations," in *The Appropriation of Shakespeare*, ed. Jean I. Marsden (Hemel Hempstead, U.K.: Harvester Wheatsheaf, 1991), 111–27, esp. 119–20. Grady writes that, with the New Bibliography, "Science was now the guarantor of the integrity of the national culture. . . . [T]he unanimity with which the salvation of the received texts was hailed and implemented in subsequent editions of the works is remarkable and bespeaks powerful cultural forces at work, beyond whatever force of reason we care to assign to the new bibliographers" (120).

5. G. Blakemore Evans, ed., *The Riverside Shakespeare* (Boston: Houghton Mifflin, 1974), 1186.

6. See Stanley Wells and Gary Taylor, *William Shakespeare: A Textual Companion* (Oxford: Clarendon Press, 1987), 396–402, esp. 401.

7. See, e.g., William B. Long, "Stage Directions: A Misinterpreted Factor in Determining Textual Provenance," *TEXT* 2 (1985):121–38; and "'A bed/for woodstock': A Warning for the Unwary," *MaRDiE* 2 (1985): 91–118. See also Paul Werstine, "'Foul Papers' and 'Prompt-books': Printer's Copy of Shakespeare's *Comedy of Errors*," *SB* 41 (1988): 232–46; idem, "McKerrow's 'Suggestion' and Twentieth-Century Shakespeare Textual

Criticism," *RD* 19 (1989): 149–73; idem, "Narratives about Printed Shakespeare Texts: 'Foul Papers' and 'Bad' Quartos," *SQ* 41 (1990): 65–86, esp. 71. See also Anthony Hammond, ed., *Richard III* (London: Methuen, 1981), 11–12.

8. For an argument that Q1 is, in fact, an authorial version of *Hamlet*, see Steven Urkowitz, "'Well-sayd olde Mole': Burying Three *Hamlets* in Modern Editions," in *Shakespeare Study Today: The Horace Howard Furness Memorial Lectures* (1982), ed. Georgianna Ziegler (New York: AMS Press, 1986): 37–70.

9. John Heminge and Henrie Condell, "To the great Variety of Readers," *Mr William Shakespeares Comedies, Histories, & Tragedies, published according to the True Originall Copies* (London: Isaac Jaggard and Edward Blount, 1623), sig. A3.

10. For an interesting overview of manuscript publication of lyric poetry in Renaissance England, see Arthur F. Marotti, "The Transmission of Lyric Poetry and the Institutionalizing of Literature in the English Renaissance," in *Contending Kingdoms: Historical, Psychological, and Feminist Approaches to the Literature of Sixteenth-Century England and France*, ed. Marie-Rose Logan and Peter L. Rudnytsky (Detroit: Wayne State University Press, 1992), 21–41.

11. Elizabeth H. Hageman described these editorial problems in a paper, "Editing Katherine Philips," read at the Folger Shakespeare Library on 13 March 1992. See also Elizabeth H. Hageman and Andrea Sununu, "New Manuscript Texts of Katherine Philips, the 'Matchless Orinda,'" *English Manuscript Studies, 1100–1700* 4 (1993): 174–219.

12. For an extensive study of the kinds of errors typically made in the transcription of manuscripts, see James Willis, *Latin Textual Criticism* (Urbana: University of Illinois Press, 1972). "The principal kinds of corruptions in manuscripts" are summarized on pages 47–50. I am grateful to Paul Saengar of the Newberry Library for directing me to this book.

13. Arthur Marotti (cited in note 10, above) notes an interesting and important difference between publication in manuscript and in print. Pointing out the malleability of a text in manuscript transmission, he notes that "In the processes of manuscript transmission, texts are, of course, subject to errors of repeated copying; but they are also, by convention, open to reader emendation, supplementation, and answer-poem responses or parodies. . . . The conditions of manuscript transmission made it possible for a collector or reader to appropriate a text in ways that would be unthinkable in a highly developed print culture. . . . Individuals other than the author felt free not only to arrange and excerpt texts that came into their hands but also to rewrite and augment them as well" ("Transmission," 32).

The well-known "Dering manuscript" of Shakespeare's Henry IV plays (transcribed ca. 1623) shows that Marotti's "malleability" was not confined to manuscript transmission of lyric poetry. Sir Edward Dering's alterations, as he combined the two parts of the play into a single play, included not only the cuts necessary to bring the two plays into a single performable drama but also changes that seem to echo performances that Dering had seen, as well as changes of words that seem to have offended his particular religious sensibility. See the introduction to the Folger Facsimile Edition of *The History of King Henry the Fourth as revised by Sir Edward Dering,* prepared by George Walton Williams and Gwynne Blakemore Evans (Charlottesville: University Press of Virginia, 1974), vii–xi.

14. Hageman and Sununu, "New Manuscript Texts," 188.

15. John Shawcross, "A Text of John Donne's Poems; Unsatisfactory Compromise," *John Donne Journal* 2 (1983): 1–19, esp. 15. I am grateful to Steven May for calling this essay to my attention. See also Shawcross's edition of *The Complete Poetry of John Donne* (New York: New York University Press, 1968), xxi–xxii.

16. "'A bed / for woodstock.'" For a different ascription of the marginal notes that Long sees as authorial, see A. P. Rossiter, ed., *Woodstock: A Moral History* (London: Chatto and Windus, 1946), 170–74.

17. Trevor Howard-Hill, "The Author as Scribe or Reviser?" *TEXT* 3 (1987): 305–18.

For another reading of the evidence in the *Game at Chess* manuscripts, see Grace Ioppolo, *Revising Shakespeare* (Cambridge: Harvard University Press, 1991), 70–77.

18. See Werstine, "Narratives," 65–86, esp. 85–86. Werstine quotes the preface to the Beaumont and Fletcher First Folio, where Humphrey Moseley notes the actors' practice of making transcripts of plays for "private friends" (85). Werstine also cites Edward Knight's transcribing of *Bonduca* for a patron (72 and n. 23). Knight, who was bookkeeper of the King's company at the time, writes to his patron that certain scenes are missing from his transcription because "the booke where by it was first Acted from is lost: and this hath beene transcrib'd from the fowle papers of the Authors which were found." (See *Bonduca by John Fletcher*, ed. W. W. Greg, Malone Society Reprints [London: Malone Society, 1951], v, 90.) Knight's copying of the play for a patron and his note about what the patron would expect to find in the transcript make it fairly clear that plays were copied, just as poems were copied, for private readers. For further discussion on this topic, see Harold Love, *Scribal Publication in Seventeenth-Century England* (Oxford: Clarendon Press, 1993), 65–70.

19. Stanley Wells and Gary Taylor, for example, see Q1 as printing "a scribal copy of foul papers" and F as printing "a scribal copy of Shakespeare's own revised manuscript" (*Textual Companion,* 477). David Bevington takes the same position, writing that the quarto is "based probably on a scribal transcript of Shakespeare's working manuscript" while the Folio text "may have been derived (via an intermediate transcript) from a revision of the original authorial manuscript, in which Shakespeare himself copied over his work and made a large number of synonymous or nearly synonymous changes as he did so" (*The Complete Works of Shakespeare*, ed. David Bevington, 4th ed. [New York: Harper Collins, 1992], A-16). Norman Sanders, in his edition of the New Cambridge *Othello* (1984) sees Q1 as printing Shakespeare's own "hastily prepared and badly written manuscript" and F as printing a different manuscript that is probably also Shakespeare's holograph.

20. See Roland Barthes, "From Work to Text," trans. Josue V. Harari, in *Textual Strategies: Perspectives in Post-Structuralist Criticism*, ed. Josue V. Harari (Ithaca: Cornell University Press, 1979), 73–81; orig. pub. "De l'oeuvre au texte," *Revue d'Esthetique* 3 (1971).

21. Barthes, "From Work to Text," 79–80.

22. The term "author function" comes, of course, from Foucault, who distinguishes between the writer and "the author" and who argues that the concept of the author "serves to neutralize the contradictions that are found in . . . texts," because that which governs the author function "is the belief that there must be—at a particular level of an author's thought, of his conscious or unconscious desire—a point where contradictions are resolved, where the incompatible elements can be shown to relate to one another or to cohere around a fundamental and originating contradiction" (Michel Foucault, "What is an Author?" trans. Josue V. Harari, in Harari, ed., *Textual Strategies*, 141–60).

23. *Macbeth* provides a good example of the shift in critical perception of a play's moral climate. For the traditional view of the good-vs.-evil binary in the play, see, e.g., Kenneth Muir, who, in his introduction to the Arden edition of *Macbeth*, reprinted many times in the 1950s, '60s, and '70s, begins his own reading of the play by quoting approvingly these judgments of other noted critics: "*Macbeth* is Shakespeare's 'most profound and mature vision of evil'; it is 'a statement of evil'; it is 'a picture of a special battle in a universal war . . . ; and it 'contains the decisive orientation of Shakespearean good and evil.'" Recent critics who challenge this good-vs.-evil binary include Alan Sinfield ("*Macbeth*: history, ideology, and intellectuals," *Critical Quarterly* 28 [1986]: 63–77), Harry Berger Jr. ("Text against Performance in Shakespeare: The Example of *Macbeth*," in *The Power of Forms in the English Renaissance*, ed. Stephen Greenblatt [Norman, Okla.: Pilgrim, 1982], 49–79), David Norbrook ("*Macbeth* and the Politics of Historiography," in

Politics of Discourse, ed. Kevin Sharpe and Steven Zwicker [Berkeley: University of California Press, 1987], 78–116), and Susan Snyder ("*Macbeth:* A Modern Perspective," in *Macbeth,* ed. Barbara A. Mowat and Paul Werstine, The New Folger Shakespeare Library [New York: Washington Square Press, 1992], 197–207).

24. *Othello,* for example, seems a very different play when it is placed within—and in the process becomes—a polyphony of cultural languages. Critics begin to hear even Bianca, a character who is routinely listed in dramatis personae lists as "a courtesan," the designation given her in 1623 in the Folio, probably by someone in the printing house. When she is on occasion mentioned in earlier *Othello* criticism, her sexual availability is both assumed and judged. Richard Marienstras, for example, writes that "there are three women in *Othello* and . . . they are set at different levels on a moral scale. One of them, Bianca, is easy enough with everyone: 'A housewife that / by selling her desires / Buys herself bread and clothes' (IV, i, 94)"; at the opposite end of the moral spectrum, writes Marienstras, is the chaste Desdemona (*New Perspectives on the Shakespearean World* [Cambridge: Cambridge University Press, 1981], 132). This judgment of Bianca is challenged by Susan Snyder in her "*Othello*: A Modern Perspective," in *Othello,* ed. Barbara A. Mowat and Paul Werstine, New Folger Shakespeare Library (New York: Washington Square Press, 1993), 287–98. See also Lisa Jardine, "'Why should he call her whore?': Defamation and Desdemona's Case" in *Addressing Frank Kermode: Essays in Criticism and Interpretation,* ed. Margaret Tudeau-Clayton and Martin Warner (Urbana and Chicago: University of Illinois Press, 1991), 124–53. For a related discussion of Jane in Middleton's *A Trick to Catch the Old One,* see Valerie Wayne's essay in the present volume.

25. Dover Wilson, ed., *Merchant of Venice* (Cambridge: Cambridge University Press, 1926), 106–7. Greg's comment withdrawing his earlier "elaborate conjecture respecting an inserted slip" appears in his *The Shakespeare First Folio* (Oxford: Clarendon Press, 1955), 258, n.4.

26. See W. W. Greg, *The Editorial Problem in Shakespeare* (Oxford: Clarendon Press, 1942), 123, and Greg, *Shakespeare First Folio,* 258 n.4.

27. G. B. Evans's textual note to the Riverside edition of *Merchant* reads: "V.i.49 **Sweet soul**] arranged as in Rowe, who, however, reads *Sweet Love,* following F2; last words of Launcelot's speech, Q1–2, F1." Other modern editors read, for example: "48. **morning.**] Rowe; ~ sweete soule. Q, F. 49. **Sweet soul, let's**] VAR. 1785; Let's Q, F" (New Oxford, ed. Jay Halio); "48. **morning.**] Rowe; **morning sweete soule.** Q, F. 49. **Sweet soul let's**] Let's Q, F; **Sweet soul, let's** Var. '85" (New Arden).

28. The textual note on the lines reads: "48–49 morning. / LORENZO Sweete soule, let's] Steevens-Reed; morning sweete soule. / Loren<zo>. Let's Q, F. Rowe is the first to assign the epithet to Lorenzo, but he emends 'soule' to 'Love'."

29. M. M. Mahood, in her New Cambridge Edition of *Merchant* (Cambridge: Cambridge University Press, 1987), is almost alone in printing Lancelet's line as ". . . here ere morning, sweet soul." Her collation notes show that F2 reads "morning, sweet love," and that Rowe prints "Sweet love, let's." Her discussion of the placement of the words "sweet soul" quotes Greg's arguments, and quotes as well some suggestions from the Cambridge Associate General Editor Robin Hood defending the quarto placement of the two words at the end of Lancelet's line: "Robin Hood suggests that an interpolation had to be made when Shakespeare realised that Bassanio's homecoming needed to be announced, and that the passage was inserted between 38 and 49, with 'sweete soule' as the conclusion to Lancelot's speech, and 49 made a slightly short line to convey a sense of urgency."

30. The actual spelling of the name varies, sometimes being *Launcelet* and sometimes *Lancelet.*

31. M. M. Mahood writes (82 n. O SD): "**Lancelot** This name is always 'Launcelet' in Q1 (*au* being a typical Shakespearean spelling for nasalised *a*), and usually 'Lancelet' in

Q2 and F. 'Lancelot' occurs only once in Q2 (2.2.70), but it is the form throughout Q3." As noted, this statement about Q3 is in error. Mahood goes on to write, puzzlingly, "[Lancelot] is adopted here as more conformable to the editorial tradition than 'Lancelet' and as possibly meant by Shakespeare to be the name of the medieval romance hero."

32. See my "Nicholas Rowe and the Twentieth-Century Shakespeare Text," in *Shakespeare and Cultural Traditions: The Selected Proceedings of the International Shakespeare Association World Congress, Tokyo, 1991,* ed. Tetsuo Kishi, Roger Pringle, and Stanley Wells (Newark: University of Delaware Press, 1994): 314–22.

33. The operative word here is *edition.* One can, of course, choose to present an early printed version in facsimile or in a diplomatic reprint. An *edition* of a text involves more complicated decisions and takes into account intelligibility and audience.

34. A different version of this paper was presented at the 1995 Deutsche Shakespeare-Gesellschaft in Weimar, Germany, and published in *Shakespeare Jahrbuch* 132 (1996): 26–43 (printed here by permission of *Shakespeare Jahrbuch*).

7

Shakespeare's Most Neglected Play

RICHARD PROUDFOOT

Seldom can perception (or creation) of the cultural value of a secular author's works have so much depended on the establishment and defense of an authorized canon as in the case of William Shakespeare. Among the most widely noted results of this canonic endeavor, variously motivated by the various interests of those who have engaged in it, have been a dehistoricization of "Shakespeare's Works" (including a lack of curiosity about the theatrical repertoire of which they formed a part); a general neglect of the circumstances in which Shakespeare, in common with other playwrights of his time, must be supposed to have written his plays (notably the prevalence of collaborative authorship); and an undue tendency to regard the author's name on a title page as a principal criterion for valuing the play that follows (editions of *The Two Noble Kinsmen* published in "Complete Shakespeares" as "by William Shakespeare and John Fletcher" enjoy a commercial advantage over those which adopt the 1634 quarto's attribution to John Fletcher and William Shakespeare and are published independently of such series).

Is there a Shakespeare canon? Yes: the one established in 1623. Does it adequately define what it is generally accepted that Shakespeare wrote? No. To begin with, it omits his non-dramatic writings, quite apart from persistent questions about the authorship of some of the plays that the First Folio included and others that it left out. What then does the 1623 collection define? What Shakespeare's surviving colleagues regarded, or wished to have regarded, as his "comedies, histories and tragedies."

I

Of the various plays actually or ostensibly attributed to Shakespeare in the sixteenth and seventeenth centuries there is one whose position in scholarly debate has become somewhat anomalous. It was printed in 1605 with this information on its title page:

> THE L O N D O N Prodigall. As it was plaide by the Kings Maiesties seruants. By *VVilliam Shakespeare,* [device no. 299] LONDON. Printed by T.C. for *Nathaniel Butter,* and are to be sold neere *S. Austins* gate, at the signe of the pyde Bull. 1 6 0 5.

The anomaly, of course, is that it is the one remaining play for which attribution to Shakespeare is fully explicit and about which nothing approaching an orthodox hypothesis yet exists. In this it differs from its three comparable companions in the seven-play supplement to the Third Folio (1664). *Pericles* (1609) has been onboard the good ship Swan of Avon—even if regarded by a minority as a stowaway—since the late eighteenth century. *The First Part of Sir John Oldcastle* is satisfactorily—if not illuminatingly—attributed in Henslowe's *Diary* to Munday, Drayton, Wilson, and Hathaway (and in any case the "1600"=1619 attribution to Shakespeare is transparently a product of Thomas Pavier's attempt to publish a collected "Shakespeare" in that year). The third play, *A Yorkshire Tragedy* (1608), may belong in some way to a short period about 1605–6 during which Thomas Middleton worked for the King's Men and would appear to have collaborated with William Shakespeare.[1] Linguistic tests that point to Middleton's authorship can now be in some way reconciled with the attribution of this powerful one-acter to "VV. Shakspeare," despite the fact that the source of that attribution, both on the title page of the first edition and in the Stationers' Register entry, may once again be Thomas Pavier.

When Tucker Brooke wrote the one page of matter introductory to *The London Prodigal* (p. xxx) for his edition of *The Shakespeare Apocrypha* in 1908, he dutifully recorded the readiness of eighteenth-century reprints of the Folio supplement to ascribe the play to Shakespeare.[2] This readiness need surprise us the less when it is remembered that the vast majority of seventeenth-century attributions of plays to Shakespeare are of comedies, tragicomedies, and English histories. The nineteenth century yielded fewer champions: Brooke cites only Tieck, Schlegel, and A. F. Hopkinson. More to the point, he urges "the facts that *The London Prodigal* was performed by Shakespeare's company, and that the quarto was printed during the poet's lifetime for Butter, the publisher of *King Lear,*" though the conclusion that follows is as decisive as it may seem unexpected, namely, that "any theory which supports the play's authenticity may safely be branded as utterly untenable." The tone, of course, reflects assumptions that Brooke's next paragraph spells out: "Shakespeare's catholicity and psychological insight are conspicuously absent, and every principle of his dramatic morality is outraged in the treatment of the prodigal's career." More to the point is his cooler observation that this is a play that "deals entirely with humors and manners" and that is admirable for its "delineation of the externalities of contemporary life." The names that came to Brooke's mind as possible authors were John Marston and Thomas Dekker, "if he could be shown to have written for the King's Players just before 1605." Of the attribution to Shakespeare, the only explanation on offer is "that put forward by Mr Fleay; namely that Shakespeare 'plotted' the comedy roughly and then left his vague design to be very imperfectly executed by another."

What is perhaps most surprising about this brief discussion is the total failure of Tucker Brooke to acknowledge those aspects of *The London Prodigal* which might make one think of Shakespeare even if no question of alleged authorship existed. The plays that spring most immediately to mind are *Measure for Measure* and *All's Well that Ends Well*. Matthew Flowerdale, the prodigal of the title, follows a course of action which leads him in the end to a position strongly reminiscent of the equally rebarbative Bertram: like Bertram, he comes under strong suspicion of having murdered his wife—a wife for whom the prodigal has no use once he has appropriated her dowry to sustain his gaming and drinking. The plot depends on the machinations of his father, Old Flowerdale, who adopts in the opening scene a disguise that he sheds only in the play's closing moments. His sole confidant is his brother and Matthew's uncle—likewise a merchant—whose aim is to persuade the fond father of his son's dissolute and worthless character. Like Angelo, Young Flowerdale is safeguarded from the worst effects of his debauchery and meanness by an invisible safety net, once he employs his unknown father (supposedly dead on a trading voyage) as his servant.

The play has been discussed in the context of enforced marriage.[3] Where it differs from its Shakespearean analogues is that the reluctant spouse is not Flowerdale himself but his principal victim, Luce Spurcock, daughter of Sir Lancelot Spurcock. Luce's subsequently implausible loyalty to the unwanted husband whose only aim is to rob and reject her may well account for Tucker Brooke's claim that the play lacks psychological conviction— unless that conviction is to be sought rather in her virtuous and God-fearing opposition to an intolerant, inconsistent, and overbearing father, for whom she is quite as simply a possession as she can possibly seem to be for her rapacious husband.

The characters of this play bear a selection of significant names; Spurcock and his friend Weathercock embody belligerence and indecisiveness, while the servants Artichoke and Daffodil particularize on the herbal suggestion of Flowerdale. Multiplication of plot interest is achieved in a

somewhat desultory manner by giving Luce three further suitors: Sir Arthur
Greenshield, an impoverished but romantic soldier; Master Oliver, "the Devonshire man," a rich farmer; and the insubordinate servant, Daffodil. Two
younger sisters extend the plot laterally; one, the foolish Frances, or Frank,
accepts the advances of Master Civet; the other, Delia, renounces marriage.

Even this thumbnail sketch will justify a sense that this isn't what we
think of as Shakespeare's kind of play, despite the broad analogies noted
and despite the presence within the canon of those inconvenient and untidy
plays, *The Taming of the Shrew* and *The Merry Wives of Windsor*. Of course
Shakespeare is not the only dramatist of the period whose authorship of
The London Prodigal has been confidently proposed and as confidently
rejected. There can be few other plays of which it has been seriously proposed that they were written by Ben Jonson (mainly on the strength of its
affinities with *The Staple of News)*, John Marston, Thomas Dekker, Michael
Drayton, Thomas Middleton, George Wilkins, and John Fletcher. Either
the evidence is more than usually slippery, the attempts at attribution are
more than usually lacking in rigor, or the question of authorship is the
wrong question to address to this play.

II

The writing of *The London Prodigal* is variable. Its prose, especially in the
speeches of the prodigal himself, Matthew Flowerdale, has verve and energy; its verse ranges from the vestigial to the serviceable and even, lo-
cally, the fluent. Much of the energy of the writer(s) goes into creating the
comic idioms of the eight male humors of the play. But if the stylistic tex-
ture generally suggests little more than acceptable professional competence,
more credit is perhaps due to the plotting and scenic structure. The dy-
namic of the action stems from two false wills; its resolution depends on
the dropping of two disguises. Characters are for the most part grouped in
pairs, contrasting or complementary: Flowerdale's father and uncle; Sir
Lancelot Spurcock and his stooge Master Weathercock; Sir Lancelot's two
servants, Artichoke and Daffodil; Luce's two unsuccessful suitors, Sir Arthur
Greenshield and Master Oliver; Luce's (younger?) sisters, foolish Frances
and wise Delia; Frances and her uxorious bridegroom, Master Tom Civet;
the two bridegrooms, Civet and Flowerdale. This patterning extends even
to less important characters: the Lieutenant who attempts to press Oliver is
counterpoised by the Undersheriff who attempts to arrest Flowerdale; servants are twice dismissed, twice removing their masters' livery. In his final
husk-eating phase, the prodigal is twice cast off by ungrateful acquaintan-
ces and twice begs of passersby.

This tidiness of disposition is equally apparent in the three clearly marked phases of the plot (the classical protasis, epitasis, and catastrophe). Each culminates in a climactic scene involving more of the cast than the scenes that lead up to it. The protasis comprises scenes 1–3 (act 1.1–2; act 2.1) that introduce all the play's major characters but Delia, who will later emerge as spokeswoman for conservative standards of household economy and for a religious ideal of marriage unrealized in the action. The epitasis develops the theme of marriage through scenes 4–9 (act 2.2–4; act 3.1–3). Luce's preference for Sir Arthur and her father's for Oliver are superseded by Flowerdale's trick (suggested by his disguised father) of winning Sir Lancelot's support and Luce's hand with a false will. The climactic scene, scene 9, shows Flowerdale's arrest on emerging from the church where he has married Luce and proceeds to display the dilemma of his unhappy and enforced bride on learning of the trick. Choosing to stick by her unenthusiastic husband, Luce is first disowned by her father and then repudiated by Flowerdale himself, once her intercession with his uncle has led to the replenishment of his purse. The final phase of action (scenes 10–13 [act 4.1–3; act 5.1]) shows Flowerdale's descent into beggary and crime and Luce's simultaneous withdrawal into Dutch disguise and service in the house of the newlywed Civets. The last and longest scene brings Flowerdale from beggary to plotting the burglary of Civet's house with the inside help of the "Dutch" maid (doubtless assumed by Flowerdale to be "easy" enough to influence—as Marston had made clear, courtesans in London were frequently Dutch), and then to suspicion of murder of his vanished wife. The predicted removal of Luce's disguise triggers his penitence, though full reconciliation of the young couple with Sir Lancelot follows only after Old Flowerdale, the father, finally also removes the token disguise—a scar, presumably on his face—in which we have seen him from the start of the play.

If this high degree of patterning suggests a schematic play, then it must at least be conceded that the scheme is less clearly and simply didactic than is implied by critics who lay heavy stress on the play's old-fashioned moralizing. The ending in particular calls in question any easy satisfaction in resolving the themes of prodigality and of marriage. Flowerdale, the titular prodigal, professes reformation, thereby winning the support of a courageous wife and ample renewal of his squandered fortunes—and he does so with the muted backing even of his defeated rivals, Sir Arthur and Oliver. But the other newlywed couple, Civet and Frances, are just as surely set on a course of waste and prodigality as ever was Flowerdale, while the third daughter of Sir Lancelot, Delia, politely declines to tidy the ending by marrying Oliver, professing instead (like Diana in *All's Well*, though for different reasons) a commitment to single life and a rejection of "the care

and crosses of a wife, / The trouble in this world that children bring"
(5.1.465–66). Her conclusion is: "Husbands, howsoeuer good, I will haue
none" (468). She validates her decision by reference to "a vow . . . in heauen"
and concedes that marriage is "a sanctimonious thing" (467, 464). Not so
Oliver, who responds by heartily joining her in a commitment to celibate
life: "Che zet not a vig by a wife, if a wife zet not a vig by me. Come, shalls
go to dinner?" (470–71).

Like some of Shakespeare's comedies, then, *The London Prodigal* closes
on a hollow and uneasy cadence—though, to be fair, it more readily evokes
the perfunctoriness of *The Two Gentlemen of Verona* than the deeper unease of *Measure for Measure* or *All's Well*—and besides, Shakespeare holds
no monopoly on hollow comic endings.

III

I take it that *The London Prodigal* represents the workmanlike norm of
playwriting for the King's Men in the early years of the reign of James I.
Two further considerations may reinforce this impression. The first is certain, the second has still to be confirmed and refined on. *The London Prodigal* requires a minimum cast of only ten men (plus two or three walk-ons)
and three boys. Single-scene small parts can either be doubled by the ten
leading players or distributed among the walk-ons. Unlike the Shakespearean pattern (which is strongly hierarchical in the varying length of roles),
the leading parts, though indeed varying somewhat in length and in their
demands on performers, are closely comparable in terms of their shares of
the action. If the small parts are doubled, one adult actor (Sir Lancelot)
appears in eight of the thirteen scenes, five in seven scenes, two in six
scenes, and one in a mere four scenes. The three boys each appear in seven
scenes. Did not the paucity of female roles indicate otherwise, such a pattern and distribution of roles might suggest a play for a boys' company. If
this is indeed a play for the King's Men, then the inference that may perhaps be drawn is that it is very much of a company play, in which only two
roles (Young Flowerdale and Sir Lancelot) exceed a fairly modest length
and only three scenes involve enough actors at once to demand much en-
semble rehearsal.

The casting pattern and the sizes of the roles are facts; that the play was
written collaboratively by two writers who took almost equal shares is a
hypothesis—and a very recent one. It is proposed by Jonathan Hope[4] on
the sociolinguistic evidence of sharply divergent usage of relative forms
and constructions that separates scenes 8, 9, and 13 from the rest of the
play. As I have noted, these are the climactic scenes of the second and third

phases of the plot. If the play may be seen as having been written for rapid learning, rehearsal, and production, it may likewise have been written at some speed, one author composing the 895 lines of scenes 8, 9, and 13, while the other wrote the 1,062 lines of the remaining ten scenes. One or other would then have done some tidying (with less than 100 percent success)—and there was a play fitted.

We know nothing of the reception of *The London Prodigal,* and Thomas Creede would seem to have printed it from authorial papers—or a transcript thereof—acquired by Butter, rather than from copy in any way reflecting preparation of a prompt-book. Attribution to the King's Men and to William Shakespeare (in that order) may have been the selling point. If so, it wasn't a hugely successful tactic (whether or not either claim was made in good faith) as the play had to wait till 1664 for its first reprint. The extraordinary critical and scholarly neglect of the play has usually been seen, despite fluctuating assumptions about matters Shakespearean, as virtually inevitable. Whether or not the play demanded attention was dictated by your attitude to the attribution. The readiness of the late seventeenth and early eighteenth centuries to accept that attribution led easily to its inclusion in most major editions from the second issue of the Third Folio in 1664 until the 1730s. Thereafter it shifted into the Shakespeare apocrypha, its place assured as one of F3's supplement of seven plays. Uninquiring acceptance was presumably facilitated by acknowledged ignorance and by Shakespeare's early reputation as a writer of comedies and histories. An answering rejection, as universal—and nearly as mindless and uninquiring as the earlier acceptance—followed romantic revaluation of Shakespeare and the pronouncement of Malone in his *Supplement to the Edition of Shakespeare's Plays Published in 1778:*

> Concerning the origin of this play having been ever ascribed to Shakspeare, I have not been able to form any probable hypothesis. . . . One knows not which most to admire, the impudence of the printer in affixing our great poet's name to a comedy publickly acted at his own theatre, of which it is very improbable that he should have written a single line, or Shakspeare's negligence of fame in suffering such a piece to be imputed to him without taking the least notice of it.[5]

Of the little that has been written on the play since, much consists of hypothetical conjecture about its authorship. Otherwise, its thematic and structural affinities with a group of other plays, most of them also relatively obscure, have been pointed to and briefly commented on. The main points of contact proposed have been the "prodigal son" plot and the motif of enforced marriage, though other particulars have also been noted, among them the form of Oliver's Devonshire dialect (which resembles Edgar's brief burst of mummerset in *King Lear* 4.6). Malone's dating of it to 1603 or 1604 (2.449) has been generally accepted as having adequate internal support.

IV

Would we do best to try to forget the attribution of *The London Prodigal* to Shakespeare, or has the play some legitimate claim on the attention of Shakespeareans? That Shakespeare didn't write it, in any normal understanding of the word, has by now been amply argued and even demonstrated (though why the mere suggestion that he might have still provokes scholars to hot-collared indignation is hard to account for—Gary Taylor's "No serious scholar has taken the attribution seriously,"[6] for instance, seems gratuitous in making disbelief in the attribution a litmus test of scholarly seriousness). Such objective testing of linguistic features as has been undertaken points consistently to notable divergence from Shakespeare's observed norms.

But if a play, as we are increasingly urged to believe, is indeed the product of wide-ranging corporate activity on the part of writers, performers, theater managers, and audiences, then I would suppose that, like any other play associated with the early years of the King's Men, *The London Prodigal* might legitimately engage the interest of students of Shakespeare (as indeed it did that of Bernard Beckerman, who wrote one of the very few brief appraisals of it thirty-two years ago).[7] We are unlikely ever to know the nature and extent of Shakespeare's participation in the communal act of producing this play, whether as dramatist, dramaturge, plotter, actor, or sponsor of the play with his colleagues, but we are inescapably faced with a claim that he did in some way contribute to that production and that it took place early in the reign of James I. Indeed a useful, if preliminary, attempt to locate it in the early repertory of the King's Men has recently been made by Roslyn L. Knutson.[8]

Its place in the repertoire of the King's Men may be reflected in a minor feature of the extant text. The play is fairly well supplied with moments of Shakespearean reminiscence or premonition. Among the plays of which I have been fleetingly reminded while working on it are *Love's Labour's Lost*, *Henry V*, *Hamlet*, *Troilus and Cressida*, *All's Well that Ends Well*, *Othello*, *Measure for Measure*, and *Timon of Athens*. Affinities of plot or situation relate principally to *All's Well*, *Othello*, and *Measure* (recent plays in 1603–4) and all of these moments occur in the final scene, scene 13. Verbal similarities, some no doubt commonplace, range more widely, but of forty I have noted, only fifteen occur in the ten scenes assigned by Hope to author A while twenty-five are in author B's three scenes.

The question of who wrote *The London Prodigal* will doubtless continue to prompt some curiosity. One unexpected suggestion that has recently been propounded is that certain linguistic habits in the play fit better with the known norms of John Fletcher than with any other of the main candidates on offer as putative author. This finding came as very much of a surprise to its originator, Thomas Merriam.[9] He offers it by no means as an answer to the question of attribution, but as a hypothesis inviting validation or refutation. At first blush, it may seem easier to accept Dr. Merriam's negative findings—his data would rule out Shakespeare, Dekker, Middleton, and Wilkins—and he takes pains to point out some un-Fletcherian characteristics, including lack of the expected preferences for "ye" over "you," "does" and "has" over "doth," and "hath" and "'em" over "them." These lacks, except for "ye," are, however, shared by Fletcher's better-known "first play," *The Faithful Shepherdess*.

The simple and familiar point I have been trying to make is that—for all the contrary professions of critical theorists—a tendency to let questions of canon and authorship dictate what we read, what we print, and what we value still prevails. I make a small claim for *The London Prodigal* as a play of real interest and modest achievement that has been devalued as a result of its unhappy association with "our greatest poet's name" and of the critical unease that has resulted from the assumption that we need to be confident where we stand on the issue of authorship before we can engage with the play.

NOTES

1. Stanley Wells and Gary Taylor, with John Jowett and William Montgomery, *William Shakespeare: A Textual Companion* (Oxford: Clarendon Press, 1987), 140–41.

2. *The Shakespeare Apocrypha,* ed. C. F. Tucker Brooke (Oxford: Clarendon Press, 1908), xxix–xxx.

3. The most useful list of publications relating to the play is Anne Lancashire and Jill Levenson's "Anonymous Plays," in *The Popular School: A Survey and Bibliography of Recent Studies in Renaissance Drama,* ed. T. P. Logan and D. S. Smith (Lincoln: University of Nebraska Press, 1976), 220–24.

4. Jonathan Hope, *The Authorship of Shakespeare's Plays* (Cambridge: Cambridge University Press, 1994).

5. London, 1780, 2.449.

6. Wells et al., eds. *Textual Companion,* 138.

7. Bernard Beckermann, *Shakespeare at the Globe, 1599–1613* (New York: Macmillan, 1962), references listed in index, 246.

8. See Roslyn L. Knutson, *The Repertory of Shakespeare's Company, 1594–1613* (Fayetteville: University of Arkansas Press, 1991), chap. 4.

9. Thomas Merriam, "Modelling a Canon: A Stylometric Examination of Shakespeare's First Folio" (Ph.D. diss., University of London, 1992), chaps. 10 and 11.

Part III:
Contexts

8

Marriage and Divorce in 1613: Elizabeth Cary, Frances Howard, and Others

JEANNE ADDISON ROBERTS

Admirers of Elizabeth Cary, author of the only known original play by a woman published in Jacobean England, and students of the play, *The Tragedie of Mariam, Faire Queene of Jewry*, continue to be intrigued by two possibly unanswerable questions: When was the play written, and why was it published in 1613, probably years after its composition?

The likely limits for dating the composition are set by the publication in 1602 of Thomas Lodge's translation of Josephus's *Antiquities of the Jews*, Cary's chief source, and the entry of the play in the Stationers' Register in 1612. Cary's arranged marriage took place in 1602, and soon after she went to live with her unsympathetic mother-in-law while her husband was abroad. Meredith Skura has pointed out that all of Cary's datable writing dates either before her children were born or after they were taken from her; she guesses therefore that *Mariam* was written before 1609, when Cary's first child was born.[1] The period between 1602 and 1609 must, in any case, have been a time when marriage was much on Cary's mind while she tried to conform to her Protestant husband's expectations while pursuing her own literary concerns and her growing interest in Catholicism.

Marital tensions are abundantly evident in the play. The virtuous heroine, struggling to be a good wife without abdicating her identity, is killed by her husband, while the wicked Salome, already twice married, and now involved in a new liaison, argues for women's right to divorce:

> Why should such privilege to man be given?
> Or given to them, why barr'd from women then?
> Are men than we in greater grace with Heaven?
> Or cannot women hate as well as men?
> I'll be the custom-breaker: and begin

161

> To show my sex the way to freedom's door,
> And with an off'ring will I purge my sin;
> The law was made for none but who are poor.

$$(1.4.305-12)^2$$

And at play's end Salome (having arranged her husband's execution rather than a divorce) is prepared to live happily with husband number three.

Barry Weller and Margaret Ferguson have argued that Herod, the central male character of Cary's play, was associated widely with Henry VIII because Herod had divorced his wife to marry Herodias, his brother's wife. Weller and Ferguson further compare Salome, rather unconvincingly, to Anne Boleyn. Herod may have been a historical prototype of the divorcer, but it seems to me doubtful that Henry's 1533 divorce was still a live issue to most Englishmen when Cary probably wrote her play. It is Salome rather than Herod who becomes in the play the advocate of divorce. Of much greater contemporary interest than Henry would have been Penelope Rich, who, unhappy with her husband, left him to live with her lover, Charles Blount, in 1601, and then, by mutual consent, was divorced by her husband and married to Blount in 1605. Divorce and remarriage were current topics in 1605 because of Rich. Cary's play would have had contemporary resonance in that year, which I believe is a likely one for its composition.

Marriage and divorce were again urgent issues in 1613. The performance of Shakespeare's *Henry VIII* in that year signaled renewed interest in the king's memory; and Frances Howard's suit for the annulment of her marriage to the earl of Essex (nephew of Penelope Rich) and her rapid remarriage to Robert Carr fueled controversies about the legitimacy of divorce and remarriage. I will argue that these events created a climate which made the publication of Elizabeth Cary's play, focused on marriage and divorce, a likely venture for an enterprising publisher. Admittedly, I make use of gossip and speculation, but the hypothesis is worth considering as a plausible explanation of the 1613 publication.

⚜

The London of 1613 was the scene of an important marriage and an important divorce. On Valentine's Day the Princess Elizabeth married the elector palatine, Frederick of Bohemia, with great pomp and circumstance.[3] At precisely the same season Frances Howard and her family were planning proceedings to annul the marriage of Frances, countess of Essex, and Robert Devereux, third earl of Essex, on the grounds that he was impotent with her. They were also making plans for Frances's marriage to Robert

Carr as soon as the annulment was completed. Important as it was politically, Elizabeth's marriage followed conventional patterns, and, though celebrated with widespread rejoicing, receded into the background with the departure of the royal couple. The annulment and remarriage, on the other hand, were radical and controversial, provoking prolonged and strongly contradictory London responses that reverberated for years to come.[4] The legal process of annulment, officially initiated in May 1613, was concluded only at the end of September, and the extraordinary remarriage of the divorced Frances to Robert Carr, earl of Somerset, was solemnized on 26 December. The convergence of these events—the royal wedding and the divorce and remarriage involving three noble families—focused special attention on the pleasures and problems of marriage. A number of the dramatic works and other publications of 1612–13 seem to have relevance to the extended scandal of Frances Howard's divorce and precipitate remarriage.

Rightly or wrongly Frances Howard has suffered a very bad press. Almost without exception historians have repeated as either fact or strong conjecture the stories that after her allegedly unconsummated marriage to Essex in 1606 she "prostituted" herself to Prince Henry, that she was notoriously promiscuous, and that she had an affair with Robert Carr before she married him in 1613. Better substantiated events include her successful suit in 1613 to have her marriage to Essex annulled on the grounds that he was impotent with her and that she was still *virgo intacta*, her trial in 1616 for the murder of Sir Thomas Overbury, and her confession of complicity in that murder.[5] Although she has had her defenders, she certainly might have been thought of by some as an insatiate countess or a white devil. Whatever the truth—and, as usual, it is elusive—there can be no doubt of the scandalous contemporary reputation of Frances Howard. Married by her parents to Robert Devereux when she was thirteen and he fourteen, she lived with her family while he traveled abroad, returning to England in 1609. Almost immediately the marriage was clearly in trouble. By the beginning of 1610 Frances was thought to have become involved with both Prince Henry and Robert Carr, a favorite of King James, who had been granted the estate of Sir Walter Raleigh and was soon to become viscount Rochester and eventually earl of Somerset. Pressed by her husband to retire to Chartley Hall, his family estate, she declined, continuing active in court life and appearing in at least two court masques. In one of them, Samuel Daniel's *Tethys Festival*, a celebration in 1610 of the installation of Henry as Prince of Wales, she is identified with Essex; she portrays the Nymph of the River Lee, a river that bounded the county of Essex. But there is evidence that she and Carr met secretly and repeatedly in Essex's absence in a house in Hammersmith.[6]

After the investiture of Prince Henry in June 1610, Howard fled from Essex to her own family estate, Audley, while her husband retired to Chartley, where he contracted some disease, possibly smallpox. It is difficult in retrospect to separate Howard's predivorce reputation from the widespread condemnation that followed her admission of guilt in the murder of Overbury, an admission that had the effect of confirming earlier rumors of her supposed wantonness; but as early as 25 July 1610, one Samuel Calvert wrote a letter to an acquaintance warning that Essex's lady had laid plots to poison her husband.[7] Later, at the murder trial, copies of two letters written by Howard before September 1611 show requests to Anne Turner and Simon Forman for potions to win one Lord (Carr?) and inhibit the amorous desires of another (Essex?).[8]

The prospect of annulment of the Essex-Howard marriage must have been entertained before 1613. Bishop Goodman claimed that he had heard rumors "a year or two before the marriage was questioned";[9] and a detailed log of the efforts at consummation between husband and wife was compiled in 1612, presumably to demonstrate long-term mutual willingness, lack of success, and Essex's impotence with his wife.[10] All of these developments must have provided rich material for gossip. Lindley records descriptions of Frances as an adulteress, a Circe, a disobedient wife, a malicious woman, a mannish woman, and a witch. One popular poem identified Howard with the Roman sorceress Canidia to provide an explanation for her passing the virginity test performed at the time of the divorce. Like Canidia, she is:

> She that could reek within the sheets of lust,
> And there be searched, yet pass without mistrust;
> She that could surfle up the ways of sin
> And make strait posterns where wide gates had been.[11]

Robert Carr's name lent itself to obscene puns on the same subject:

> There was a court lady of late
> That none could enter she was so strait
> But now with use she is grown so wide
> There is a passage for a Carr to ride.[12]

Frances's notorious reputation endured. *The Changeling*, published in 1622, contains a farcical virginity test (4.1.40–127) involving a virgin substituted for a new wife, and this scene may be a satiric representation of what was believed to have happened at the trial.[13] Margot Heinemann suggests that Middleton's *The Witch* was "designed to appeal" to memories of the divorce proceedings.[14] Francis Osborne's play *The True Tragicomedy*, preserved in a manuscript and described as written for a court performance not earlier than 1654 (although almost certainly not actually performed at court), recapitulates the divorce case with its virginity test (the "wife's" face was covered) and has Frances openly declaring to a confidante that she was no virgin even before her marriage to Essex.[15] *The Five Years of James*, published in 1643 and dubiously attributed to Fulke Greville, describes Frances Howard as "unconstant, of a loose life" with a wish "to satisfie her insatiate appetite." The author elaborates that she was of "a lustful appetite, prodigal of expence, covetous of applause, ambitious of honour, and light of behaviour" (sigs. B2, B1v). Howard herself is said to have thought that Overbury's *The Wife* was written to contrast the ideal woman's behavior with hers and to warn off Carr from marrying her.[16] In view of the sensational and long-standing notoriety of Frances Howard, it seems worthwhile to look more closely at surviving publications of 1612–13 for insight into their attitudes toward marriage and divorce and their possible relation to the scandal.

It is true that George Chapman, Ben Jonson, John Donne, and Thomas Campion wrote poems celebrating the marriage of Howard and Carr, but all of them contain curious ambiguities.[17] Heather Dubrow dubs Jonson's twenty-six-line poem an aesthetic failure (with a wish that the bride be like the one in Overbury's *Wife*—a wish that can't have endeared him to the bride).[18] Dubrow judges that Donne vacillates between "blatant sycophancy" and trenchant criticism.[19] With the help of Virtue, Grace, and Eternity, Campion's *The Description of a Maske* (1614) banishes four enchanters: "Deformed *Error*," "wing-tongu'd *Rumor*," "*Curiositie* and *Credulitie*" (sigs. A3, B1, B2v). Banishing them, however, constitutes a recognition of their existence. Campion's masque includes a song in praise of fertility:

> Set is that Tree in ill houre
> That yields neither fruite not floure.
> How can man Perpetual be,
> but in his owne Posteritie?
>
> (sig. B3v)

Clearly a reference to her childless first marriage, the poem also echoes Howard's contention at the trial that she wanted to be made a mother.[20] Chapman's poem, *Andromeda Liberata or the Nuptials of Perseus and Andromeda* (1614), compares Howard to Andromeda chained to a "barren rock" and paints Carr as Perseus, her liberator. Chapman insists that Howard is a virgin (sig. A2) but admits the influence of the vulgar "whispering their scandals." He praises Howard's attributes:

> Her necke a chaine of orient pearles did decke,
> The pearles were faire, but fairer was her necke:

> Her breasts (laid out) show'd all enflamed sights
> Love, lie a sunning twixt two Crysolites. . . .
>
> (sig. B4v)[21]

But in praising her he also acknowledges gossip, urging her to

> . . . make our factions brood
> Whose forked tongs, would fain your honor sting
> Convert their venomd points into their spring;
> . . . arme your powers
> With such a seige of vertues, that no vice
> Of all your Foes, *Advantage* may entice. . . .
>
> (sig. ¶¶3)

and to combat "Bane-splitting Murmures and detracting Spels" (sig. B1v). Something about this poem offended readers (probably the seeming identification of Essex with a "barren rock") and Chapman was constrained to publish *A Free and Offenceless Justification of a Lately Publisht and Most Maliciously Misinterpreted Poem* (1614).

These rather muted celebrations of the Howard/Carr marriage were no doubt supported by the approval of King James and by Carr's favored position at his court. But other publications suggest much more negative views, especially of the lady.

The year 1613 saw the publication of two dramatic works that dealt with varieties of "divorces" and remarriages and that shared intriguing characteristics.[22] Both had almost certainly been written considerably earlier, and there is no evidence that either was performed as written. Both identified the author, an identification that was deleted in the course of printing. One play was Elizabeth Tanfield Cary's *The Tragedie of Mariam, The Faire Queen of Jewry*, written presumably between 1602 and 1612,[23] and containing in two surviving copies a poem dedicated to "Dianaes Earthlie Deputesse, my worthy sister, Mistress Elizabeth Carye." It is signed merely E. C. The leaf on which the poem appears was subsequently canceled and is lacking from all others of the twenty-two known extant copies. The other play was Q1 of *The Insatiate Countess*, identified in four of the eight extant copies as by John Marston. In the other four copies a cancel leaf with no mention of Marston has been substituted for the original title page. If the play is by Marston (the editor of the Revels edition, Giorgio Melchiori, posits a first draft by Marston, later revised for performance and publication by William Barksted, Lewis Machin, and perhaps others),[24] the first draft must be no later than 1608, when Marston retired from the stage.

These two plays are also linked by the fact that both deal with the dissatisfactions of marriage and desperate means of resolving them. A central character in each is a lascivious and unscrupulous woman. Cary's Salome has been responsible for the death of her first husband, contrived so that she could marry her second; and in the course of the play she resolves to rid herself of her second husband to make way for a third. She first contemplates divorce, arguing (in the lines quoted above) for women's right to this privilege.

Later Salome takes the simpler course of arranging the execution of her husband. At play's end she seems set to live happily with husband number three in spite of the violent vituperation against her and all women spewed out by her condemned husband (4.6.310–56). The play offers other variations on the divorce theme. Doris, Herod's embittered ex-wife, has been divorced by the king to make way for Mariam. She takes on particular importance because, as Meredith Skura points out, she does not appear in other Herod plays.[25] Cary has also added the virtuous lower-class virgin Graphina, who provides contrast to the more active principals, but whose dutiful passivity does not bring her happiness. In response to Doris's accusation that Mariam's marriage is adulterous, Mariam protests that this is not true because Moses's law permitted a man to divorce a hated wife (4.8.587–88). However, Mariam herself initiates a different kind of divorce, one not countenanced by Moses. She forswears her husband's bed in "revenge" for his murder of members of her family. When faced with death at Herod's order, she rather illogically blames Doris's curse for her fate; but she also repents her pride and her overconfidence in Herod's love, even while affirming her innocence and her chastity (4.8.556–63). The chorus, on the other hand, seems to blame both Doris and Mariam for being swayed by thirst for revenge. Mariam in particular is rebuked for "sullen passion" and for failing to perform her marital duty (4.8.648, 680). The cases of all four women raise problems; but, though the author flirts with the idea of rejecting patriarchal principles, such revolt finally seems to be condemned. From one perspective, Cary's play seems a meditation on the duties and hazards of matrimony.

Marston's countess, described by an early editor as "a truly disgusting wretch,"[26] begins as a widow, secretly marries a new husband, abandons him immediately, and enjoys the attentions of three paramours, setting one against another until a murder is committed. She is tried and condemned to death, repenting in the last minutes. The plot derives from an actual occurrence in Milan in 1526. The countess's story was told by Bandello and retold by Belleforest in a version translated by Painter in *The Palace of Pleasure*.[27] The play survives in only one version, probably bearing evidence of the hands of Marston, Machin, and Barksted. Although the original version must be 1608 or earlier, the play as revised was performed at White-Fryars some time between 1608 and its publication in 1613. The

authors make two notable departures from the sources, changes that make
the plot conform to Howard's cause more closely. In the sources the central
character, Isabella, is lowborn and only becomes a countess by marriage;
in the dramatic version she is a countess from the start, in spite of the fact
that her first husband was not a count. And the husband from whom she
flees on the morning after her marriage does not completely vanish from
the story, as he does in the sources. Both main plot and subplot deal with
unfaithful women, actual or imagined. Claridiana, one of the duped husbands, whose wife was in fact a model of fidelity, concludes with a typically misogynist peroration:

> Now I see great reason why
> Love should marry Jealousy
> Since man's best of life is fame,
> He had need preserve the same.
> When 'tis in a woman's keeping,
> Let not Argos' eyes be sleeping.
> The box unto Pandora given
> By the better powers of heaven,
> That contains pure chastity,
> And each virgin sovereignity,
> Wantonly she ope't and lost:
> Gift whereof a god might boast.
> Therefore shouldst thou Diana wed,
> Yet be jealous of her bed.

(5.2.223–36)

The central character, the countess, perhaps because she is manifestly guilty,
is clearly of great interest. Melchiori figures that she has one of the longest
female speaking parts in Jacobean drama—550 lines. He adds that none of
the male roles in the play reaches 250 lines.[28] It is especially striking that,
although there is no record of performance after 1613, the play was reprinted in 1616, the year Frances Howard confessed guilt for her part in the
murder of Sir Thomas Overbury.[29]

Both *Mariam* and *The Insatiate Countess* seem to condemn rebellion
against the patriarchy, but both depict such rebellion at considerable length.
It seems credible that both appeal at least in part because of perceived
contemporary relevance. It may also be worthy of note that John Webster's
The White Devil, performed unsuccessfully probably in 1612, was published by its author in 1612 and sold by Thomas Archer, who also sold *The
Insatiate Countess*. It is a compelling conjecture that the one inspired the
other. Although the direction of influence is not certain, *The Insatiate Countess* probably predates *The White Devil*. The latter also deals with a beautiful central character, Vittoria Corombona, who is a "devil in crystal," like

Cary's Salome and Marston's countess, "a painted sepulchre" (*Mariam* 2.4.325), adulterous and guilty of plotting the murder of her first husband in order to marry a second. Again the perils of marriage and of attempts to dissolve it are foregrounded. Bracchiano arranges the murder of his first wife, and Vittoria connives in the murder of her husband in order to be free to marry the duke. A trial, at which she defends herself eloquently, nonetheless condemns her (interestingly, not him), and she is consigned to a house of repentant whores. Although the title page describes *The White Devil* as the "Tragedy of Paolo Giordano Ursini, Duke of Bracchiano, with the Life and Death of Vittoria Corombona, the famous Venetian Courtesan," the running titles throughout mention only Vittoria Corombona. She has fewer lines than Marston's Isabella but, like Isabella, evokes an interest that seems to transcend her rather limited actions. (A sermon entitled *The White Devil, or the Hypocrite Uncased* was preached by Thomas Adams at Paul's Cross on 7 March 1613, entered in the Stationers' Register on 28 April, and published in the same year.)

A much earlier work by Marston, *The Metamorphosis of Pigmalion's Image,* was republished in 1613 after a long hiatus. Originally published in 1598 by Edmond Matts, copies were burned, according to the *DNB,* by the order of the archbishop of Canterbury, presumably because of their prurient interest. Richard Hawkins, a former apprentice to Matts, took over his business in 1613 and published both Cary's *Mariam* and a collection of erotic poems called *Alcilia: Philoparthens loving Folly.* The latter volume included Marston's *Metamorphosis* as well as another love poem entitled *The Love of Amos and Laura.* (The title page of this poem contains the same woodcut as that of *Mariam.*)[30] Like *The White Devil,* this volume, with its erotic appeal and its portrayal of a lover of virginity infatuated with Folly must have had a timely resonance.

Other possibly related publications of the period include George Wither's 1613 *Abuses Stript and Whipt* with chapters on fond love, lust, and hate. A poem on love describes a new husband who

> having got a dainty peece,
> Prouder then *Jason* with his golden fleece:
> Commends her *Vertues,* that has just as many,
> As a she-Baud that never yet had any.
> Yea sweares shes chast and takes her for no more,
> When all her neighbors know she is just a ———
>
> (sig. C2v)

Wither's work was phenomenally popular, going through five editions in 1613. The second edition reports that its author was imprisoned for serious offense to authorities. Thomas Overbury's *The Wife,* extolling wifely virtues, was entered in the Stationers' Register in December 1613 after Overbury's death and published in 1614 as *The Wife, Now The Widow*. Webster must have been sympathetic to the views of this work since he is thought to have contributed thirty-two character sketches to later editions. Ben Jonson also cites it as a model in his poem on the marriage of Howard and Somerset.[31] Samuel Hieron argued in his sermon *The Bridegroom*, printed in 1613, that marriage should last in perpetuity and could be severed only by adultery or death.[32] Henry Parrot in *Laquei ridiculosi; or, Springes for Woodcocks* (1613) claims he had "long left this work" and says it is printed without his "privitie," but his collection of 215 epigrams in the style of Ovid's *Amores* contains many female targets, and number 3 seems to have particular contemporary resonance:

> Two wooers for a wench were each at strife
> Which would enjoy her to his wedded wife:
> Quoth th'one, shee's mine, because I first her saw,
> Shee's mine, quoth th'other, by *Pye-corner* law;
> Where, sticking once a *Prick* on what you buy
> It's then your owne, which no man must deny.

William Est's *The Triall of True Tears* (1613), written he says "at the urgent importunitie of some of my best friends" (sig. A3), laments the sins of the age and particularly the consequences of adultery, citing the case of King David (sigs. E4–4v). Similarly Thomas Nashe's *Christ's Tears Over Jerusalem*, another diatribe against the sins of the age, last published in 1594, was reissued in 1613. Finally, Shakespeare's *Henry VIII*, performed in 1613, with its sympathetic portrait of the forcibly divorced Queen Katherine, resurrects the questions of the legitimacy of that divorce, or indeed of any divorce.

Although none of these works alone is proof of a contemporary climate, the convergence does suggest a strong interest in lustful women, the problems of marriage, and the acceptability of divorce. The annulment of the marriage of Howard and Essex and, especially, Howard's rapid remarriage to Carr must have been major determinants of this climate.

So far I have tried to establish that Howard was notorious considerably before the time of her actual divorce and that it was clear at least by 1610 and probably by 1609 when Essex returned to England that she had no intention of maintaining a traditional marriage with Essex. I think it is just possible that Marston, fond as he was of court satire, could have, as early as 1608, composed *The Insatiate Countess* with Howard in mind. In any case it seems very likely that the play performed sometime between 1608 and 1613 was revised by Machin and Barksted and published by Thomas Archer to take advantage of contemporary interest. By that time Marston, now in clerical orders, probably did not want to be further associated with the work and had his name removed from the title page. It seems even more likely that Webster, who was at least acquainted with Marston and his work, should have written and published *The White Devil* with the same popular relevance in mind and that Archer was interested in publishing it for the same reason. Similarly, I think Cary's *Mariam* was published to capitalize on the scandal and that, like Marston, the author wanted to avoid positive identification. The other works discussed above also seem to have strong contemporary relevance.

Whether Frances was in love with Robert Carr or was pressured by her family to form an alliance with James's powerful favorite, she was determined on divorce and remarriage rather than the more usual separation and/or illicit liaison. Her unwifely rejection of her husband on the tenuous ground that he was impotent but only with her (grounds that Essex accepted because they paved the way for his remarriage) seems to have precipitated not only gossip but also genuine concern about the legality of divorce. Her rapid remarriage was even more revolutionary. Donna Hamilton argues that the case brought back to the popular mind the controversy over Henry VIII's divorce from Katherine of Aragon and that this helps to account for Shakespeare's return to the long-abandoned genre of history plays.[33] If, as she suggests, Essex was identified with Katherine, unwillingly compelled into divorce, then Frances takes on something of the murky aura of Henry in Shakespeare's play. Her gender and lack of royal status, of course, make her action exponentially more shocking than his.

With the increasing interest in Elizabeth Cary's *Mariam*, critics have speculated as to why a play probably written considerably earlier and never performed should have been published in 1613. One theory is that the publication was prompted by John Davies's dedicatory letter to his *The Muses Sacrifice* (1612), where he refers to Cary as a pupil, now a threat to Minerva, and regrets the unpublished status of the works of Cary, Lucy, countess of Bedford, and Mary, Countess of Pembroke, remarking that

> Such nervy Limbes of Art, and Strains of Wit
> Times past neier knew the weaker Sexe to have;
> And Times to come, will hardly credit it,
> If thus thou give thy Works both Birth and Grave.

(sig. *3v)

Admittedly, however, the same poem speaks of the vulgarity of publication. Another theory is that the play was stolen for publication and may have been the work referred to in Cary's daughter's biography of her mother as stolen out of her sister-in-law's chamber and called in after publication by Cary herself.[34] The dedicatory poem appended to two extant copies of the play and addressed to "Dianaes Earthlie Deputesse, and my worthy Sister, Mistris Elizabeth Carye" probably refers to Cary's sister-in-law, so that this theory, because of the daughter's reference, has a certain appeal. If Cary wanted to call in the play, it seems unlikely that it would have survived in two different versions. The fact that twenty known copies of *Mariam* survive without the dedication casts doubt on the idea that the author intended to suppress the play. More plausible is the theory proposed by Elaine Beilin that the dedicatory poem may have been stolen and the dedication subsequently suppressed by the author to avoid overt indication of her identity.[35] This theory gains credibility from the survival of only two copies of the play with the poem and suggests that Cary may have been willing to have the play published but not to be positively identified as the author.

Cary's daughter reports that her mother was severely depressed, at one point neither eating nor drinking for fourteen days, while she was pregnant with her second and fourth children.[36] *Mariam* was entered in the Stationers' Register in December 1612. Whether or not Cary gave permission for its publication (and the number of surviving copies suggest that she at least acquiesced) she may well, like Virginia Woolf, have fallen into depression as her work actually became public. Publishing a play was a radical act for a woman, especially one of Cary's internal contradictions.[37]

It is clear that by 1613 Cary had acquired considerable visibility as a scholar, literary patron, and writer. As early as 1597 Michael Drayton had dedicated two of his poems in *England's Heroicall Epistles* to her. (She would have been approximately twelve.) He addressed her unmistakably as "my honoured Mistres, *Elizabeth Tanfelde*, the sole daughter and heyre of that famous and learned Lawyer, *Lawrence Tanfelde*, Esquire." And, although he refers to her "tender years," he praises her French and Italian, and nominates her as a new sister for the Graces and another Muse (I2v). In 1614 the publisher Richard More apparently enlists her patronage for the second edition of John Badenham's *England's Helicon*, addressing "the Truly Vertuous and Honourable Lady, the Lady Elizabeth Carie" as "England's *happy* Muse, / Learnings delight, that all things else exceeds" (sig. A2).

Her reputation as a patron apparently endured. In 1624 Richard Beling dedicated to "The truely vertuous and learned La: the Viscountess of Falkland" his addition of a sixth book to Sidney's *Arcadia*, claiming that "at the first birth" it was intended for her because "goodness can no where finde a more worthy patronesse." He acknowledges "many favours" and trusts that nowhere could his work have found a "more privileged Sanctuarie" than in her "favourable censure" (sigs. A2–2v). And as late as 1633 William Sheares dedicated to her his unauthorized collection of the plays of John Marston. (This does not necessarily indicate sympathy between Cary and Marston—the collection does not include either *The Insatiate*

Countess or *The Malcontent*, perhaps because both were thought to have multiple authors.) Sheares also addresses the "Viscountess Fawkland." He declares that she is "well acquainted with the Muses" and concludes that:

> Fame hath given out, that your Honour is the
> Mirrour of your sex, the admiration, not only
> of this Iland, but of all adjacent Countries and
> Dominions, which are acquainted with your rare
> Vertues, and Endowments. . . .
>
> (sigs. A4–4v)

As a patron Cary seems to have paid off, and as an author she must have seemed worth the risk of publication.

Mariam was the first book published by Richard Hawkins, a new London publisher who had taken over the shop of Edmond Matts, a London bookseller from 1597–1613 to whom Hawkins had been apprenticed since 1607. Matts was from Oxfordshire, as were Davies and Elizabeth Tanfield Cary's parents.[38] Matts had some literary concerns. In 1601 he had published, and in 1606 reprinted, *Discourses on Seneca* by Sir William Cornwallis, a fact that is of some interest, since Cary's daughter credits her mother with translating Seneca at an early age. In Matts's shop Cary may have found Lodge's 1602 translation of Josephus's *Antiquities of the Jews*, which was the chief source of her play. Matts had also published *Pigmalion's Image* in 1598, a work reprinted by Hawkins in 1613. Cary's daughter records her mother's reading as voluminous.[39] She must have known a bookseller or have had a very scholarly father, or both.

Matts himself may have had Catholic leanings. He published in 1606 a sermon preached by the then Anglican Benjamin Carier for Prince Henry. However, at some subsequent point Carier became a Catholic and left the country. His later works, supposedly published abroad, describe the miserable ends of those who have impugned the Catholic Church and explain why he abandoned Protestantism. An intriguing document by Carier with the imprint of Leidge 1614 includes "A Copy of a Letter written . . . beyond the Seas to some particular friends in England. Whereunto are added certaine collections found in his Closet, made by him (as is thought) of the miserable ends of such as have impugned the Catholic Church." In this work he says that he has left "lands and livings" for the honor of Christ and not in opposition to King James.

Matts continued as a bookseller from 1606 until 1613, but there is no record of books published by him in that period. One wonders whether he may not have been involved in secretly publishing recusant works during that period, although obviously this is sheer speculation.

About the publication of *Mariam*, my hypothesis is that Cary knew Matts and his apprentice Richard Hawkins, that they knew or knew of her play. When Hawkins took over the shop in 1613 he saw the opportunity for a publication with timely popular appeal, and persuaded Cary to agree to his publishing her play. Alternatively, if she knew Hawkins and had been persuaded by others to publish, she would naturally have turned to him as a publisher.

Certainly by 1613 and probably much earlier Cary had strong connections at court. In 1608 her husband was appointed gentleman of the king's bedchamber, master of the jewel house, and knight of Bath;[40] and Cary's daughter reports that her mother came frequently to live at his lodgings at court.[41] Her literary and religious interests, however, would have allied her more closely with the court of the queen than that of the king. Leeds Barroll has established that Anne's court was an important center of patronage and art. Her circle was dominated by what Barroll calls the "Essex group."[42] Among those included were the now-forgiven Penelope Rich, sister of the second earl of Essex, the countess of Bedford, the Sidneys, the dowager countess of Pembroke, and her son, the earl of Pembroke, leader of the queen's faction.[43] Davies had linked Cary with the countesses of Bedford and Pembroke, and Weller and Ferguson speculate credibly that Cary was associated with the literary salon of the Countess of Pembroke.[44] Lewalski reports[45] that Cary was also associated with a coterie of "Romanizing ladies" including Katherine Manners, who was later to become wife of the duke of Buckingham, patron of Henry Cary and enemy of Robert Carr.[46] Elizabeth's increasing interest in Catholicism may also have endeared her to Queen Anne, who was widely believed to be a closet Catholic.[47]

Cary's Catholic leanings and her association with the Essex group around the queen may have inclined her to oppose the Essex divorce and to side, as did the queen, with Essex in the divorce scandal. But religion was probably not the primary issue. Essex himself seems to have agreed to the divorce; and Henry Howard, earl of Northampton, archenemy of the queen's faction and uncle of Frances Howard, was both himself a crypto-Catholic and a prime mover in the divorce proceedings.[48] The king sided with Carr and the Howards for personal as well as political reasons. The motives of the two parties, though mixed, seem to have been shaped primarily by a struggle for power, but Cary herself may have had stronger religious feelings.

Even more controversial than the divorce was the question of the remarriage which was seen to be a way of cementing ties between the king, the Howards, and Robert Carr, already the royal favorite. The queen hated Carr, and at the very moment of the divorce was involved in a losing battle with him over control of some royal land.[49] Anne had opposed Carr's appointment as lord chamberlain, favoring the earl of Pembroke instead. The queen and Pembroke were also allied with Archbishop Abbott, described by one contemporary as a Romish metropolitan,[50] who was not only opposed to divorce but also a dissenting member of the commission that tried the case.

It seems not too fanciful to imagine that the queen and her court encouraged the publication of *Mariam* with its vivid portrait of the lustful Salome, vocal in her advocacy of divorce for women. Inevitably the play's character would have evoked the image of Frances Howard, even as it explored both the tensions of marriage and the evils of divorce.

In 1613 divorce and marriage were primary concerns of both court and country. As the foreign fortunes of Princess Elizabeth temporarily prospered, and Frances Howard approached the brief apogee of her career with her successful divorce and resplendent new marriage, Elizabeth Cary, pregnant with the fourth of her eleven children, perhaps in acute depression, added her own remarkable contribution to the public discussion of the liabilities of holy matrimony and the legitimacy of divorce and remarriage.[51]

Notes

1. Meredith Skura, "'Thy curse is cause that guiltless Mariam dies': What is Doris's Curse Doing in Elizabeth Cary's *Mariam*?" Unpublished manuscript.

2. All quotations from *Mariam* refer to *The Tragedy of Mariam, The Fair Queen of Jewry, with The Lady Falkland: Her Life by One of her Daughters*, ed. Barry Weller and Margaret W. Ferguson (Berkeley: University of California Press, 1994).

3. Many works of 1613 celebrate the marriage of Princess Elizabeth, and a number continue to mourn the death of Prince Henry in 1612.

4. The scope of interest in the annulment proceedings is suggested by the range of members of the commission that made the final judgment: the bishops of Winchester, Ely, Coventry, Lichfield, and Rochester (for), and the bishop of London and the archbishop of Canterbury (against), as well as six doctors, three on each side (*A True and Historical Relation of the Poysoning of Sir Thomas Overbury* [1651], 13–14). King James packed the court with two additional bishops after it became clear that the original commission was not likely to grant the divorce.

5. For negative views, see especially Edward LeComte, *The Notorious Lady Essex* (New York: Dial, 1969); Beatrice White, *Cast of Ravens: The Strange Case of Sir Thomas Overbury* (London: Murray, 1965); William McElwee, *The Murder of Sir Thomas Overbury* (London: Faber & Faber, 1952); and Philip Gibbs, *The King's Favourite: The Love Story of Robert Carr and Lady Essex* (London: Hutchinson, 1909). On the other hand, David Lindley (*The Trials of Frances Howard* [London: Routledge, 1993]) has argued persuasively, if not conclusively, that this account of Howard's career is largely unproven and conforms suspiciously to patterns of misogynist male stereotypes of women. He concludes that there is no proof of an affair with Prince Henry or of Frances's promiscuity. He suggests that she may in fact have been a virgin before her second marriage and may even have been innocent of involvement in the death of Overbury.

6. Lindley, *Trials*, 67–68.

7. Ibid., 43.
8. Ibid., 72.
9. Ibid., 43–44.
10. LeComte, *Notorious Lady Essex*, 55–57.
11. Ibid., 211.
12. Ibid., 133.
13. See James O. Halliwell, ed., *The Autobiography of Simonds D'Ewes during the Reign of James I and Charles I*, vol. 1 (London: Bentley, 1845), 90. References to *The Changeling* by Thomas Middleton and William Rowley are taken from the edition of George Walton Williams (Lincoln: University of Nebraska Press, 1966).
14. Margot Heinemann, *Puritanism and Theatre: Thomas Middleton and Opposition Drama under the Early Stuarts* (Cambridge: Cambridge University Press, 1980), 108–10. She points out that the most interesting character in the play is a sixteen-year-old girl named Francisca. Since she dates the play in 1616, she connects it with both the divorce and the Overbury trial. Elizabeth Schafer in the New Mermaid edition of *The Witch* (London: W. W. Norton, 1994) details six points of the play's relevance to Frances Howard. She favors a 1615–16 date and posits a connection to the scandal of the trial. Anne Lancashire, who has also argued for the relevance of the play to Howard, prefers a 1611 date for *The Witch* and therefore connects it specifically to the divorce; see *"The Witch*: Stage Flop or Political Mistake?" in *"Accompaninge the players": Essays Celebrating Thomas Middleton, 1580–1980,* ed. Kenneth Friedenreich (New York: AMS Press, 1983), 161–81 (164). Among other contemporary plays Lois Potter reports that she finds a possible echo of the scandal in *Two Noble Kinsmen*, probably written in 1613.
15. Francis Osborne, *The True Tragicomedy Formerly Acted at Court*, transcribed from the manuscript in the British Library by John Pitcher and Lois Potter, ed. Lois Potter (New York: Garland, 1983), 123, 54.
16. LeComte, *Notorious Lady Essex*, 65.
17. Lindley, *Trials*, chap. 4.
18. Jonson, *Hymenaei; or, The Solemnities of Masque and Barrier* (London: Thomas Thorp, 1606); Dubrow, *A Happier Eden: The Politics of Marriage in the Stuart Epithalamion* (Ithaca: Cornell University Press, 1990), 225–26.
19. Donne, "Eclogue" and "Epithalamion" (1613), in *The Complete Poetry and Selected Prose of John Donne and The Complete Poetry of William Blake,* ed. Robert S. Hillyer (New York: Random House, 1941), 92, 95; Dubrow, *A Happier Eden*, 133.
20. *A True and Historical relation of the Poysoning of Sir Thomas Overbury* (1651), sig. B2v. Campion's emphasis on sterility contrasts ironically with Jonson's epithalamion in his *Hymenaei*, a masque written to celebrate the Howard-Essex wedding in 1605. Jonson invokes the aid of Venus to assure the couple's fertility:

> . . . *Thou, with timely seede*
> (which may their after-Comforts breede)
> Informe the gentle Wombe;
> Nor, let it prove a Tombe:
> But, e'er ten Moones be wasted,
> *The* Birth, *by* Cynthia *hasted.*

(sig. D3)

21. Howard was famous for her décolletage; but, like the flowing hair she affected for her wedding, exposed breasts were a sign of virginity.
22. A third play, *Cynthia's Revenge* (1613), might fit this category. First published without an author's name on the title page, it was revised with the name of John Stephens as

author. It is a closet drama that reads like a political satire; but specific references are, if they exist, obscure.

23. For discussion of the dedication to Elizabeth Cary, see A. C. Dunstan and W. W. Greg, eds., *The Tragedy of Mariam* (London: Malone Society, 1914), viii–ix, and Weller and Ferguson, eds., *Mariam,* 54 n. 13. Identifying the different Elizabeth Carys is not simple. Seven so-named dedicatees are listed in the *Index of Dedications.* Obviously marriage often determined and/or altered the names of the possible candidates. In his Malone Society reprint Greg identified the dedication leaf as an addition but later recognized that it had in fact been canceled in most copies.

24. John Marston, *The Insatiate Countess*, ed. Giorgio Melchiori (Manchester: Manchester University Press, 1984), 1–16.

25. Skura, "'Thy curse is cause.'"

26. *The Insatiate Countess: A Tragicomedy* (London, 1820), xii.

27. *The Insatiate Countess*, ed. Melchiori, 17–30.

28. Ibid., 39.

29. As a proof of the eagerness of readers to perceive contemporary relevance, Tricomi points out that two seventeenth-century readers appended the names of eight English countesses to the 1631 quarto of *The Insatiate Countess* preserved in the National Library of Scotland. See Albert H. Tricomi, *Anticourt Drama in England, 1603–42* (Charlottesville: University Press of Virginia, 1989).

30. See Weller and Ferguson, eds., *Mariam,* 45 for a discussion of this emblem.

31. *Ben Jonson*, ed. C. H. Herford, Percy Simpson, and Evelyn Simpson, 11 vols. (Oxford: Clarendon Press, 1947–52). "To the most noble, and above his Titles, Robert, Earle of Somerset" (8:384).

32. Pp. 20–21.

33. Donna Hamilton, *Shakespeare and the Politics of Protestant England* (Lexington: University Press of Kentucky, 1992), 168, 178.

34. Weller and Ferguson, eds. *Mariam,* 190.

35. Ibid., 6; Elaine Beilin, "Elizabeth Cary and *The Tragedie of Mariam*," *Papers on Language and Literature* 16 (1980): 45–64.

36. Weller and Ferguson, eds. *Mariam,* 195. According to the Weller-Ferguson chronology (179–81), Cary gave birth in 1609, 1610, 1613, 1614, 1615, 1616, 1617, and frequently thereafter. She would probably have been pregnant with child number four in 1613.

37. See Barbara Kiefer Lewalski, *Writing Women in Jacobean England* (Cambridge: Harvard University Press, 1993), 180. Skura, "'Thy curse is cause,'" has a much more detailed analysis of Cary's conflicts.

38. Alexander Grosart reports in his introduction to Davies's works that Davies was a teacher of penmanship who probably resided for months at the homes of his patrons, tutoring his pupils. Grosart gives an interesting sidelight on Davies's acquaintance with the Tanfield family. He quotes a document of 1608 that tells how Judge Lawrence Tanfield, Cary's father, settled a complaint by Davies that he had been taxed on land that he did not own. Grosart also quotes Arthur Wilson's statement that Davies was a Catholic. See *John Davies of Hereford: The Complete Works,* ed. Alexander B. Grosart (1878; reprint, Hildesheim: Olms, 1968), x–xix.

39. Weller and Ferguson, eds., *Mariam,* 186.

40. Lewalski, *Writing Women,* 188.

41. Weller and Ferguson, eds., *Mariam,* 196.

42. J. Leeds Barroll, "The Court of the First Stuart Queen," in *The Mental World of the Jacobean Court,* ed. Linda Levy Peck (Cambridge: Cambridge University Press, 1991), 191–208 (see esp. 192). The reference to the "Essex group" is at p. 200.

43. There was at least one other Elizabeth Cary at court: the wife of Sir Robert and the

caretaker of Prince Charles; see Linda Levy Peck, *Northampton, Patronage and Policy at the Court of James I* (London: Allen & Unwin, 1982), 69.

44. Weller and Ferguson, eds., *Mariam,* 5.

45. Lewalski, *Writing Women,* 183.

46. Buckingham was introduced to King James in 1614 and soon began to replace Carr as the royal favorite.

47. For a discussion of Anne's religion see David M. Bergeron, *Royal Family, Royal Lovers: King James of England and Scotland* (Columbia: University of Missouri Press, 1991), 72–73.

48. For a discussion of Northampton's religion see Peck, *Northampton.*

49. Ibid., 74.

50. Lindley, *Trials,* 83.

51. I am indebted to Professor Lois Potter and her seminar at the Folger Shakespeare Library (1990) on the year 1613. The seminar was enormously helpful, and Professor Potter has since generously shared her knowledge and advice.

9

The Sexual Politics
of Textual Transmission

VALERIE WAYNE

Textual scholarship often still proceeds on the assumption that editorial decisions are objective, empirically based, and arrived at judiciously by experts who have devoted years of study to solving the mysteries of early English bibliography. The foundations of the objective status of editorial inquiry began to sink some time ago with the advent of sliding signifiers, and the edifice cracked in two, at least, when we learned that there could be more than one originary text of a Renaissance play. If there are still vestiges of belief in the impartial nature of the work, I want to question them here by calling attention to the gendered process of textual transmission, that is, the ways in which male compositors and editors have created texts that debase and efface women and members of other marginalized groups. One defense for an activity that has been called "feminist editing"[1] comes from the observation that editing has always been gendered, and that a feminist approach to texts offers an alternative to a tradition that has already exhibited its political investments. While a feminist text cannot, strictly speaking, "correct" previous editions, because it too operates from its own ideological commitments, it can problematize a history of received readings and interrupt previous forms of transmission by rendering a text in an alternative form. What I propose to offer here is an account of why such work is needed and what contributions it might make to our textual and cultural present.

Within the last decade I have edited Renaissance texts of two very different sorts: a dialogue on marriage of 1568—Edmund Tilney's *The Flower of Friendship*—that was published in a modern edition for the first time in 1992, and Thomas Middleton's city comedy first printed in 1608, *A Trick to Catch the Old One*, which has been edited sixteen times since

1815. As a feminist I recognized before I began this work that issues concerning women were likely to have been marginalized in the reproduction of these texts. But in neither instance did I anticipate the character of the bias that I found. Building on the Wife of Bath's question, "Who peyntede the leon, tel me who?"[2] I want to take a long look at who reproduced the lion for later generations and who touched it up under the guise of improving it. I will first discuss certain errors introduced by compositors in the seven editions of *The Flower*, then examine textual cruces and editorial decisions in *The Tempest* and *Othello*, and finally take up problems of speech tags, commentary, and stage directions as they relate to prostitution, slander, rape, and the law in *A Trick to Catch the Old One*. My plan is to seduce you, gentle reader, with the salacious appeal of these topics and then chasten you with the accompanying rhetoric, which will achieve such an ecstasy of zealous conviction that I end by invoking early modern laws on rape against current editorial practices.

⚜

Edmund Tilney's *The Flower of Friendship* sets forth the dominant—primarily humanist—ideology of marriage in 1568 within a dialogue that also articulates residual and emergent positions. My edition includes an introduction on the historical and theoretical implications of these ideologies and makes no pretense to objectivity. It offers instead a blatantly materialist feminist interpretation of the text's past and present. Yet if I was bold in my introduction and commentary, I was not bold editorially. The text is in old spelling and includes very few emendations, a decision that I still support given the plain style of the prose, the good condition of the text, and the likelihood that this will be the only edition available for some time. The "Note on the Text" is intentionally written in the voice of ungendered authority—distanced, supposedly universal, and therefore male. I drafted another note that more directly recounted my findings, but I abandoned that draft as too radical for the conservative community of Renaissance editors that I wanted to include as readers. Times change, though, and editors change with them. A politic silence on textual matters now seems to me far too easily read as supporting claims of a supposed neutrality.

The Flower was published in seven separate editions between 1568 and 1587. Three of these appeared within the first year of issue. My collation of the twelve consistent copies of the work that are extant (which does not address a thirteenth "made-up" copy) indicated that each edition was a paginary reprint of the immediately preceding edition, and I found deterioration among them more frequently than correction. The text was analyzed bibliographically by J. G. Tilney-Bassett in an article published in *The Library* in 1946 and edited as a dissertation for the University of Pittsburgh by Ralph Glassgow Johnson in 1960.[3] Neither of these editors had the advantage of the *Revised STC's* entry on all of the editions.[4] Nonetheless, both saw increasing correction rather than deterioration among those they analyzed. Most of the reasons for this discrepancy hinge on the word "flagrant," which they take to be a compositor's error for "fragrant," while I trace it from the Latin *flagrare*, "to burn," and interpret to mean "ardent, burning, eager; resplendent, glorious," as it is defined in *Cotgrave's Dictionary* of 1611.[5] More to the point, my research on that word was prompted by a difference of gender, for the first edition of this text is the only one that refers to Flora, the Roman goddess of flowers, with the pronoun "hir." All other texts print "hys" or "his."[6] Since Flora in this passage is cooperating with Phoebus in the conventional May morning project of clothing the world in the accoutrements of spring, and Phoebus contributes his "blissful rayes and comfortable beames," the gender of Flora is not blurred or unimportant, nor is the author likely to have mistaken "hir" for "hys/his."

Compositors, however, might easily have done so. The compositors who worked on *The Flower* were all men: Alice Clark found "no indication" in reviewing records of the Stationers' Company "that [women] were ever engaged in the manual processes of printing," and D. F. McKenzie lists no female apprentices to printers during the earliest period of his study, 1605–40.[7] According to Cyprian Blagden, the first woman to be formally apprenticed in the Stationers' Company was Joanna Nye, who was bound on 7 August 1666. Two years later Elizabeth Latham was admitted by patrimony, thereby becoming the first woman made free of the Stationers in her own right since 1541.[8] Only one compositor appears to have worked on each edition of this octavo text in five signatures. Those who set type had a clear indication of Flora's gender from her proper name; nonetheless, the compositor of the second edition substituted "hys" for "hir" and thereby decomposed Flora as woman: he erased the mark of her gender. He did so again in the dedication to Queen Elizabeth, where she is compared to "that Noble Alexander of Macedon" and then addressed as "redoubted Sovereigne ô noble Alexandra." In the second edition this gendered alteration of Alexander's name is returned to its male original.[9] Throughout the seven texts there were no comparable shifts from the masculine to the feminine form, an absence that indicates how fully the feminine is the marked and vulnerable term in each instance.

The compositor of the third edition made a different kind of change: he turned an equitable statement of marital obligations into support for the double standard in Elizabethan culture. The first two editions of *The Flower* say quite simply: "[T]he fayth that the woman oweth to hir husbande, the lyke fidelitie ought the man to repaye unto hys wyfe." The third edition reads: "[T]he fayth that the woman oweth to hir husbande, the lyke infidelitie ought the man to repaye unto hys wyfe."[10] O ye faithless compositor, who invoketh unjust social custom as moral law! Where was thy head when thou settedst type? Nay, where was thy member when thou settedst elsewhere?

The compositor of the fourth edition of 1571 prefers to debase the very bond of marriage itself. While all other texts say that "perfite love knitteth loving heartes, in an insoluble knot of amitie," this compositor loosens the bind when those loving hearts are knitted "in an in insoluble knot of amitie."[11] This same compositor also erases a difference in matters of age. Throughout Tilney's text marriage is constructed from an inequality of women's sexual control and men's wealth, with these criteria functioning as the gendered determinants of class. The speaker for the dominant ideology even proclaims that "the equalitie of age, I say, consisteth likewise in the inequalitie of yeares," because hierarchy is preserved if the wife is younger than the husband. But this compositor changed the statement to read that the equality of age consisted in the equality of years.[12] The three subsequent editions retained this reading, which elides a difference less of gender than of number, the latter being a consistent concern of compositors. The elision in this instance produces a more equitable statement, although one inappropriate to its larger context.

My favorite compositor is the one who set type for the sixth edition in 1577, for he validates women's righteous indignation. While the dominant spokeswoman in the dialogue manages to impose upon wives the persistent obligation of patience and even "dissembling" with what she calls an "importunate husband," adding that "hir honestie, hir good nature, and hir prayse is shewed in nothing more, than in tolerating of an undiscrete man," the sixth edition reads, "hir prayse is shewed in nothing more, than in intolerating of an undiscrete man."[13] I will follow this compositor in arguing that women should cultivate some intolerance of indiscreet men, including faithless compositors, by recognizing that the texts that have come down to us may perpetuate our erasure or other forms of our oppression in ways that are not even visible to those unfamiliar with their transmission—which means most feminists as well as other students of literature. I am not, of course, asserting that the changes made by these compositors were conscious, much less that they were malicious attempts to undermine authorial meaning and assert male dominance. The term "Freudian slip" is also inadequate to cover all of these instances, however appropriate it seems for the wayward compositor of the third edition. But I hope these examples do illustrate that a gender gap exists among those who set type as well as among those who write, and that editorial decisions as crucial as the choice of a copy-text may be influenced by recognizing how that difference is played out in the material reproduction of the text.

❧

The scope of the problem is larger than this account of nameless and long dead compositors might suggest. Editors, too, are guilty. Gary Taylor has observed that "women may read Shakespeare, but men edit him. . . . The works were written by Shakespeare and various male collaborators; copied by male scribes; annotated in the theater by male prompters, regulating the performances of male actors; edited in the printing shop by male publishers; set into type by male compositors; corrected by male proofreaders; supplied with prefatory matter by male literati."[14] Men's control over all of early modern printing was not quite so monolithic, since widows sometimes inherited printing shops from their husbands and ran them themselves or passed them on to later husbands or sons. Alice Clark finds three women among the twenty-two master printers of London named in 1630 and five of twenty-two in 1634, and there is evidence that this inheritance took place as early as 1540.[15] But no women were involved in the printing of Shakespeare's texts until the later seventeenth century,[16] and no edition of Shakespeare's *Complete Works* has ever been edited entirely by a woman. The first women who did edit Shakespeare were Elizabeth Inchbald in the *British Drama* collection of 1806–9, and Henrietta Maria Bowdler, who gave us *The Family Shakespeare* of 1807. Bowdler's text, which claims to have eliminated "everything that could give just offence to the religious and virtuous mind," is not one which would gladden a feminist's heart, except insofar as it shows how thoroughly women can become the receptacles and defenders of family values. She also published *Sermons on the Doctrines and Duties of Christianity,* which went through at least fifty editions by 1853![17] Yet whatever credit was due to Henrietta Maria was obscured when her edition of Shakespeare was published under the name of her brother Thomas, although he only made changes in the second edition of 1818.[18] The British Library's printed catalog of 1964 still credits him as the expurgator, which may explain why the *OED* traces the term "bowdlerize" from Thomas rather than Henrietta Maria.[19] In our own time women have become more fully involved in editing, sometimes with an explicitly feminist approach, and both men and women have begun to see the political implications of the work. But a history of editorial exclusion and gender bias has made its mark on our texts of the Renaissance, and the earlier partition between editing and theory did not help the project of revising the past.

Two examples from Shakespeare will serve to explore some of the problems of determining a text. The first concerns a crux in *The Tempest* that occurs after Prospero has presented Ferdinand and Miranda with the elaborate masque of Juno, Ceres, and Iris in honor of their impending marriage. Reacting with awe to the beauty of the performance, the future bridegroom, Ferdinand, says:

> Let me live here ever!
> So rare a wondered father and a wise
> Makes this place paradise.[20]

At least that is what he says in almost all twentieth-century editions of the play except David Bevington's *Complete Works* of 1980 and Stephen Orgel's 1987 edition of the play.[21] But it was not always so. Orgel observes that "critics since the eighteenth century have expressed a nagging worry about Ferdinand's celebrating his betrothal by including Prospero but not Miranda in his paradise."[22] Jeanne Addison Roberts reports that Nicholas Rowe emended "wise" to "wife" in 1709 and his reading was preferred throughout the century; Edmond Malone even altered "Makes" to "Make" in 1790 to bring about agreement between subject and verb. The return of "wise" was not consistent: John Payne Collier first printed "wise" in 1842 and then "wife" in 1853; Charles Knight opted for "wife" in 1838–43 and "wise" in 1842–44; Alexander Dyce preferred "wise" in 1858 but "wife" in 1864–67. Other nineteenth-century editors were more sure of "wise": that variant appeared in three editions by Hudson, Halliwell, and White published from 1851 through 1866. On 30 May 1865 the Philadelphia Shakespeare Society debated the issue and concluded that "either reading may stand . . . but the weight of the authority is in favour of 'wise.'"[23]

The editors of the Cambridge *Works* published from 1863 to 1895 and of the Globe edition of 1864 still preferred "wife"; yet William Aldis Wright, editing alone in 1874, chose "wise," observing that "*wife* seems to bring Ferdinand from his rapture back to earth again" and "the use of the word 'father' shows that Ferdinand regarded her as one with himself." But whose mundane associations with "wife" are being evoked here? And whose concept of paradise is alluded to through the marital incorporation of Miranda into Ferdinand? By the middle of the twentieth century, "wise" had become the reading of choice. Roberts finds it in editions by George Lyman Kittredge (1936), Peter Alexander (1951), Anne Righter (Barton) (1968), Irving Ribner (1966), Northrop Frye (1970), and G. B. Evans (1974).[24] It also appears in G. E. Bentley's edition of the play in the *Pelican Shakespeare* (1958, 1969) and in the Oxford *Complete Works* (1986).[25] Although none of these editorial decisions was made on bibliographical grounds, there was relevant evidence available, and Jeanne Addison Roberts claimed to recover it in 1978.

Roberts saw that the first Cambridge edition of 1863 recorded "wife" as a variant in the First Folio. In 1895 Furnivall printed a facsimile of the Folio that had a "damaged but recognizable 'f'" and his parallel text read "wife." However, Roberts adds, "no one seems to have pursued the implications." So she examined the Folger Folios and found two copies where "wife" is clearly visible and two more where the crossbar of the *f* was in the process of breaking. Charlton Hinman had recorded no press variant at this point in the text or in the forme; one of the Folio copies with "wife" had been collated by Hinman, the other had not. Both copies are plainly reproduced in facsimile in Roberts's article. Rejecting the possibility that a stop-press correction would account for these variants, Roberts concludes that "the letter began as an 'f' and broke in the process of printing." She adds that "bibliographical 'progress', in so far as it was based on partial knowledge, was [in this case] actually regress."[26] Stephen Orgel comments on her discovery that "we find only what we are looking for or are willing to see. Obviously wife is a reading whose time has come."[27]

But time marches on. John Jowett's note in the *Oxford Shakespeare*, published in the same year as Orgel's essay, considers Roberts's discovery and adds:

> Error is none the less so easy that the matter does not end there. Whereas previous critics were divided as to what F actually read, almost all preferred "wise" as the more convincing reading. F's pararhyme is suspicious; *wise/ paradise* is a Shakespearian rhyme. "Wife" gives trite sense and demands two grammatical licences: that "So rare a wondred" is extended to qualify "a wife," and that "Makes" has a plural subject.[28]

There are four objections to "wife" here: two on the grounds of grammar, one on rhyme, and one on "trite sense." I would argue that it is not difficult to accept the passage because of its error in subject-verb agreement. Singular verbs for compound subjects occur often in the texts of Shakespeare and his contemporaries without signaling textual problems. The minutes of the Philadelphia Shakespeare Society's debate show Asa I. Fish's contention that "the singular verb does not reliably support 'wise'" because "singular verbs and plural nominatives are too frequent in the F1 to found and determine a reading."[29] That position still holds. The extension of "so rare a wondred" to qualify "wife" as well as "father" is also not a serious impediment: Howard Staunton first observed that "wondred" might be related to Miranda's name, and the connection was supported by Dover Wilson, Kittredge, and Kermode in their editions of 1921, 1936, and 1954, respectively.[30] It is at least as easy to apply "wondred" to the admired Miranda[31] as it is to her more complicated father.

With the claim that *"wise/paradise* is a Shakespearian rhyme" we move into different territory, because the defense of the status quo depends on an interpretive account of what is or is not Shakespearean, a construct built up over the years by layers of male compositors and editors. Not all editors would agree with the judgment in any case. Morton Luce, writing in the Arden edition of 1901, remarks that "the rhyme of Paradise with wise is a blemish, and it could hardly have been intentional." Frank Kermode printed "wise" in his New Arden of 1954 but added that "Ferdinand must have said *wife*; and the rhyme is unexpected. . . . the true reading may be *wife* after all."[32] Authorities differ on what is Shakespearean, and the construct is a variable that can be evoked in support of anyone's preferences. Nor am I sure that the use of "wife" creates a "trite sense" if Ferdinand is speaking generally about the joy of having a wife at all. Nor is Ferdinand known for his depth of observation.

The kinds of arguments being adduced here can just as easily be gathered for the opposition, because they are interpretive and partial: there is no objective "Shakespearean" confirmation available to support them. My greatest concern about the Oxford note is the weight that it grants to tradition or what the Philadelphia Society referred to as "the weight of the authority,"[33] for it is all too predictable that those previous critics found "wise" the more convincing reading. For many of them, behind the burden of editorial evidence they bring to bear on their arguments lies a notion of paradise as more felicitously equipped with a wise father, alone, than one accompanied by the diviner's wife. Many utopias in our culture are created specifically without women, and most of our master narratives grant women at best a very tenuous status. Jowett's note in the *Oxford Shakespeare* shows that the greatest challenge for a female or a feminist editor of a canonical author may be in controverting the weight of tradition, which, for all of its expertise and refinement, is still largely unaware of its own gender bias. Perhaps the time has not yet arrived for this reading of "wife" in some quarters. But I would agree with Orgel that editors and bibliographers often "find only what [they] are looking for or are willing to see."

Jeanne Roberts's discovery was questioned again by Peter Blayney in his 1996 introduction to the second edition of *The Norton Facsimile*. After presenting Roberts's findings, Blayney comments, "As a typographer I cannot agree that what resembles a crossbar in Folger copies 6 and 73 is in fact part of the type at all, or that the marks in the supposedly intermediate copies were impressed by the remnants of a crossbar. But the way in which ink is deposited by metal type on damp paper is too specialized a subject to examine in detail here, and proper resolution of the matter must await a much more thorough discussion."[34] Blayney employed an electron microscope to view the Folger copies, so what Roberts saw with the naked human eye is called into question through the use of advanced scientific equipment and the specialized knowledge of typography. It is difficult to refute such cautious claims, especially in a culture so dependent upon the scientific discourse of technology, but that discourse is usually gendered as male, and deferring to it is no more mandatory than deferring to the weight of a masculinist editorial tradition. What counts as evidence in that discourse and how evidence is interpreted are still matters of individual judgment on which experts might disagree, especially if there are experts available to reflect diversity on this issue. Moreover, technology in this instance can only offer information about what was printed in the First Folio; it cannot achieve certainty about which word was used in the earliest performances or manuscript versions of the play. Since the manuscript for the Folio printing was a transcript, the possibilities for error in copying or typesetting this word remain extraordinarily high: long *s* and *f* could be confused in handwriting, and those letters lay side by side in the typecase. So the larger issue about whether "wise" or "wife" was used in the first productions or in playscripts or should appear in our own texts remains open to question and is not a material "fact" fully available to the assessments of science. The resistance to Roberts's sighting of this "wife" is instructive in its own right. Such a response is not disinterested, any more than her discovery was, and the editing of early modern texts would benefit greatly from more diversity of opinion and open debate about sexual/textual matters such as this one. What else will female and feminist editors, gay and lesbian editors, editors of different races and cultures, and other scholars willing to resist tradition see in the texts of Shakespeare that has been occluded by the labors of privilege? We won't know until we have the pleasures of their texts.

Another issue of editorial judgment occurs in that well-known crux in *Othello* about whose face is as fresh as Diane's visage. The First Folio of 1623 offers this version of what Othello says to Iago when he is beginning to question his wife's fidelity:

> I think my wife be honest, and think she is not.
> I think that thou art just, and think thou art not.
> I'll have some proof. My name, that was as fresh
> As Dian's visage, is now begrimed and black
> As mine own face.[35]

The passage does not appear in the First Quarto of 1622, so the Folio is the only text of these lines that can be traced to the earliest performances.[36] Thomas L. Berger has located the Folio's reading in only three modern texts of *Othello*—those by M. R. Ridley (1958), Lawrence J. Ross (1974), and Stanley Wells and Gary Taylor (1986).[37] Most other editions of the play, including the major *Works* most often used for teaching texts in the twentieth century, do not print this version. In editions by George Lyman Kittredge (1936), Peter Alexander (1952), G. E. Bentley (1958), Alice Walker and John Dover Wilson (1958), Kenneth Muir (1968), G. B. Evans (1974), David Bevington (1980), and Norman Sanders (1984),[38] Othello says to Iago:

> I think my wife be honest, and think she is not;
> I think that thou art just, and think thou art not.
> I'll have some proof. Her name, that was as fresh
> As Dian's visage, is now begrimed and black
> As mine own face.[39]

This second reading "blackens" Desdemona's name: it compounds Othello's later slander of his wife with an instance of textual defamation. It first appears in the Second Quarto of 1630, a text that combined portions of Q1 and F1 and was described by Charlton Hinman as having "no textual authority."[40] Berger has argued that editors should consult it nonetheless, for it is closer to Shakespeare's language and to theatrical conventions of the time.[41] But with regard to this passage, I would agree with Stanley Wells that the substitution of "Her" for "My" is "purely interpretative,"[42] whether it occurs in Q2 or in a modern edition. The change was probably introduced by whoever prepared the copy for Q2, or by a compositor, and either may have been trying to make the passage more accessible. But its accessibility is a function of the prevalence of the slander of women and racial Others in Western culture. When offered the choice of suspending a racialized reading of Othello or of projecting that reading onto Desdemona, most editors have chosen the second alternative. "Race" and gender become mutually implicating in that reading, and this option has been preferred over the separation of Othello's name from his "blackness" that is posited by the first passage.

The two passages pose the question of whose name is as "black" as Othello's face—Othello's or Desdemona's. Given Renaissance depictions of Diana, the goddess of chastity, as fair-skinned, and the generally negative and specifically racial codings of the word "black," the first passage says that Othello's reputation was, and no longer is, like a white woman's virtue in contrast to his own "blackness." The threat of Desdemona's infidelity has therefore changed his reputation to accord with the assumed color of his skin. Having been accepted and celebrated in a Venetian society that valued his work as a general, his racial identity has now been recognized and read back onto his reputation. In the second passage, Desdemona's name had been as pure as the face of the virgin goddess, but it became contaminated by the "blackness" of Othello, as if losing her virginity to him through marriage made her like him as a racial Other. Peter Stallybrass remarks that "through marriage, the woman's honor, like her property, is incorporated into her husband's," so these disputed readings "make equal sense" because "Desdemona's 'name,' like her handkerchief, is Othello's."[43] While that incorporative process can help one make sense of the endurance of these two readings, the My/Her crux begins by referring to a moment antecedent to their union, and the effects of the union were different for husbands than for wives: the husband's honor was only affected by his wife's when her sexual fidelity was at issue. The person whose reputation has been defamed remains different in each passage. In one, Othello has come to be *perceived* as "black" by white Venetians through the possibility of his being cuckolded; in the other, more common version, the estimation of Desdemona's worth has been changed to accord with the estimation of Othello's race.

The Folio's reading depends on acknowledging the possibility that Othello's name was at one time not perceived as "black" by the Venetians, which asks one to separate the negative from the explicitly racial codings of "black" in order to grant a difference between Othello's race and his earlier reputation. Some discussions of the play offer origins for this possibility in describing accounts of traditions that displace Othello's racial identity. Arthur L. Little Jr. observes an "unending exchange" in the play "between Othello's literal black presence and his metaphorical black absence," occasioned in part by "pre-textual histories of blackness as an essential absence,[44] and Karen Newman's account of the historical tradition of "washing the Ethiop white" is well known.[45] The Duke in the play confirms Othello's former reputation when he observes that he "is far more fair than black," but only "if virtue no delighted beauty lack";[46] that is, the Duke grants Othello's "fairness," his positive worth, only on the assumption that virtue is beautiful and beauty is never "black." His judgment uses what Kim Hall has called "the language of fairness and darkness," which she says "is always *potentially* racialized,"[47] as a means to displace Othello's racial identity by asserting his worth and beauty. The texts of Little, Newman, and Shakespeare's Duke all present maneuvers to disassociate Othello from "race" without avoiding racism, so one does not have to assume that the Venetians were impartial in assessing him (or that Shakespeare was impartial in representing the Venetians' assessment) in order to grant the Folio's reading. Michael Neill has even suggested that racial Otherness may have been in some senses "unutterable" to the early moderns in contemplating the events of this play.[48] But the eventual utterances of virulent racism have preceded modern editors, and Othello's racial identity has become harder for them to displace, making it difficult to conceive of a moment when he was not assessed on those terms. The increased visibility of racial Others in modern cultures, the tradition of associating Othello with them, and the explicit articulations of racial prejudice have all become obstacles to the acceptance of the Folio version.

A second obstacle is Othello's characterization of his earlier reputation as being "fresh as Dian's visage." Perhaps there are few contemporary, straight Caucasian men who would be pleased with such a comparison. But the word "fresh" could mean vigorous and eager or ready at this time;[49] and it did not yet have its associations of forward or impertinent behavior. Olivia describes Orsino as a "fresh and stainless youth" in *Twelfth Night*.[50] In this phrase, Othello associates himself with a figure of exemplary virtue, claiming that his name was once untarnished in the wars of reputation. There is a sexual innocence or inexperience evoked by the comparison that has feminine connotations, at least in our time, and may well be appropriate to Othello's sexual naïveté, but it does not sit well with racist stereotypes of "black" male libidos, whether early modern (like Iago's) or postmodern. Dian's face is juxtaposed in the passage with the later image of Othello's face, and a woman's presumed sexual guilt provides the transition between the two images: Desdemona's is the invisible visage that permits the movement from fresh Diana to "black" Othello, so the passage does evoke "her"—Desdemona—as an agent in the transformation. What it does not evoke is her "name."

Previous editors have argued for the Folio's reading for related reasons. Ridley observes, "Othello is maddened by the befoulment of his own honour; it is that which he will not endure, and which only revenge will clear." Yet he concedes that Q2's reading is "tolerable" because "later Othello does show himself moved by the stain on Desdemona's name as well as on his own."[51] Charles Knight, writing in his edition of 1841, is less conciliatory:

> In all the modern editions, except Rowe's, this has been changed into *her* name. There is probably not a more fatal corruption of the meaning of the poet amongst the thousand corruptions for which his editors are answerable. It destroys the master-key to Othello's character. It is his intense feeling of *honour* that makes his wife's supposed fault so terrific to him. It is not that *Desdemona's* name is begrimed and black, but that *his own name* is degraded.[52]

In addition to the focus on whose name is at issue in the passage, I find these remarks helpful in their assertion that the defense of Desdemona's honor cannot account for the intensity of Othello's response: he is haunted by that early modern male anxiety of being a cuckold. The main reason I would suppose that most male editors did not sympathize with that anxiety is that they perceived Othello as different from themselves.

Desdemona's name was the casualty of this difference. When presented with the choice of acknowledging a prior moment of Othello's unsullied reputation or of sullying Desdemona's, editors have usually impugned hers—by using a word with racial codings. She too becomes "black" and therefore doubly Other. This option has been preferred over granting that the racialized Other was once well-regarded. There are, on the other hand, many good reasons for retaining the Folio's reading, but they require that editors resist the reinscription of their own forms of racial and sexual prejudice onto the text. Such resistance is only possible when editors become aware of the political implications of the readings they select rather than proceeding on the assumption that the choice for either alternative is a "purely" literary or bibliographical matter.

As the first woman editor of Thomas Middleton's *A Trick to Catch the Old One*, I encountered a tradition of sixteen editions by fifteen editors who were convinced that this play is far more about men and money than women and marriage.[53] While, like most editors, I feel a strong gratitude to those who have preceded me for the painstaking work they have done and the meanings they have made evident, I am also surprised by a collective silence on what I perceive as some of the play's crucial issues. Even summarizing the plot of this play raises the question of what is important within it, and I will try to provide what I consider an inclusive account. The trick to catch the old one of the title is a plan begotten by Theodorus Witgood and bred by his former mistress[54] to pass the latter off as a rich widow interested in marrying him. The purpose of the trick is to entrap Witgood's uncle, Pecunius Lucre, into returning Witgood's mortgage to his property, which Lucre had assumed after paying innumerable debts for Witgood's profligate life. The ruse ends up entrapping not only Lucre, who returns the mortgage, but also Lucre's archrival, Walkadine Hoard, who discovers at the end of the play that the woman he has pursued and won in marriage is not a rich widow but Witgood's "whore." Witgood is thereby entirely free to marry the impalpable Joyce, a virginal niece of Hoard's. In the final scene, Hoard's coercion of a woman into marriage for money is exposed, while his new wife promises to shun any of the sexual wiles of married women and Witgood confesses the follies of his former, riotous life. This play has been successful on stage for many years: it offers the pleasure of watching two youthful, sexy characters outwit some avaricious old goats and dupe them into acts of uncharacteristic generosity.

In this summary the main female character of the play remains unnamed. I refer to her as Witgood's former mistress, later as his "whore," and finally as Hoard's wife. Those who are familiar with the play know her by the label of "Courtesan," which appears only in the speech headings and dialogue of the play, because there are no dramatis personae in the early quartos of 1608 and 1616. Yet identifying her in this way is not entirely satisfactory, for "courtesan" is a term that meant different things to an early modern audience than it means to us. To begin with, this character is not a professional prostitute but Witgood's mistress.[55] In the very first scene she makes it clear that she lost her virginity to Witgood, and in the very last scene Witgood says she has slept only with him.[56] She is a "loose" woman only in the sense that she is unmarried and is not a virgin, and there was no way of describing such a person in early modern England that is still relevant to our present categories. If she was neither maid (read "virgin"), wife, nor widow back then, she was considered a "whore," for a woman whose sexuality was not contained through a legal relation with a man was categorized as sexually available. A relentless binary opposition is at work in this way of thinking that is especially unfair in her case, because her sexuality has in effect been contained through her relation with Witgood. But because they are not married, she is a "whore." Unfaithful wives were also called "whores" without being professional prostitutes. Since the category was so often constructed through accusation and reputation rather than occupation, it is as unstable as her identity within this play.

When Walkadine Hoard discovers through his friends that he has married not a widow with lands and living but a "whore"—and here the rhyme between "whore" and Hoard becomes almost prophetic—his reaction results in a kind of defamation. He complains that he has been "daintily abused" and has married a "common strumpet."[57] Then Witgood objects. Having called her a "whore" himself just fifteen lines earlier, Witgood replies to Hoard:

> Nay, now
> You wrong her, sir. If I were she, I'd have
> The law on you for that. I durst depose for her
> She ne'er had common use, nor common thought.[58]

The sole gloss on this passage provided by all sixteen editions is Bryan Loughrey and Neil Taylor's note that "depose" means to "give evidence upon oath."[59] Neither the commentaries nor the critical interpretations point out that Hoard has committed an actionable offense: he has defamed Jane's reputation to a degree that would justify her seeking legal redress. Most cases for sexual slander were heard not in civil but in ecclesiastical courts, and Martin Ingram observes that they "formed one of the most prominent classes of litigation handled by the church courts in this period."[60] It was required that cases concern spiritual matters, such as sexual offenses; that they were not mixed with crimes over which the temporal courts had jurisdiction; and that no monetary damages were awarded, for the suit was "for the soul's health," in this case for clearing one's name. Public penance was often used as a remedy, although in extreme cases the defendant could be excommunicated.[61]

But how, you may ask, could a courtesan bring a case in a church court? The point is that the character is not a courtesan at this moment in the play despite the speech heading that fixes her as such in our minds, and Witgood recognizes the change in her status once she is married even if her editors do not. As a married woman, she had every right to bring an action against Hoard for his charge against her, which was different from calling her a "whore." "The Costomary of Tettenhall Regis" is an account of "the bye-laws made by the tenants of the manor at their Leet or Law-day" that is much older than the earliest extant copy of 1604.[62] As a civil rather than an ecclesiastical procedure, the document provides two separate penalties concerning sexual slander, one for calling "any man or woman whore," and another "if any man or woman call a wedded woman common strumpitt."[63] While the latter is a lesser offense, requiring a fine of twelve pence rather than two shillings, it is especially appropriate to a wife, and that is what she is at this moment in the play.

The difference between a whore and a common strumpet is related to the distinction between a courtesan and a common prostitute. This character "ne'er had common use, nor common thought": she was neither promiscuous nor had a reputation for being so, which is different from having had only one sexual partner. A common strumpet or prostitute was usually poorly compensated for her sexual services and worked with little protection or maintenance; as an insult the term "strumpet" implied, as Partridge puts it, "a (very) wanton woman."[64] The word "courtesan," on the other hand, is the feminine form of Italian *cortigiano*, and such a woman was originally attached to the court.[65] In Edward Sharpham's satire, *The Fleer*, of 1606, Fleer remarks, "Your whore is for euery rascall but your Curtizan is for your Courtier."[66] The term did not retain its exclusively upper-class associations: like the prostitutes who were so described, it was continually being reduced to its lowest common denominator. But it was more often used to name one who functioned as a mistress or had relatively few or sequential sexual partners; within G. R. Quaife's classification of English prostitutes, the courtesan was closest to a "private whore," others being vagrant, public, and village whores.[67] In the early part of the seventeenth century, those like Thomas Coryate who published accounts of their experiences with the famous courtesans of Venice—learned, beautiful, wealthy women who were compensated sometimes just for their verbal conversation—created exotic associations with the word.[68] But whether Italian or English, professional or private, courtesans were not usually seen as "common" and were very different from strumpets. Hoard's slander in the presence of witnesses is an actionable offense in early modern England.

The character he marries assumes three different subject positions in the play: she is Witgood's mistress, a feigned rich widow named Jane Meddler, and a wife named Jane Hoard. We never learn her "real" name. But the speech heading "courtesan" fixes her identity in a way that makes it difficult for readers to observe these shifts, especially modern readers who are accustomed to applying to an earlier period "essentialist conceptions of the self which only take effective hold in the Enlightenment," as Jonathan Dollimore puts it.[69] There is ample evidence that characters' positionalities in Renaissance texts were not nearly so fixed: the printing of plays without dramatis personae implied that characters did not exist before or apart from their speeches, and speech prefixes could also change within a play to mark different identities for the same figure.[70] Female characters were often presented as particularly unstable and spoke from conflicting subject positions, so they appeared as textually inconstant.[71]

In this play the original speech tags are consistent except for one stage direction where the character is referred to as "the Widow" and one speech assigned to "Lu." (for Lucre) clearly meant for her.[72] Yet the term "courtesan" stabilizes this character's sexual inconstancy, constructing for us a woman who makes her living by sexual commerce and is generally available to men. This situation has led most readers to think like Hoard about the character, which makes the correction and exposure of Hoard largely incomprehensible. An editorial fidelity to the original text thereby produces, for a modern audience, a de facto collusion with Hoard's view of Jane. Moreover, in the theater this character would have been constructed not by an abstract social label, but by the recurrence of a physical body. Members of a theatrical audience could alter their perceptions of the character as her situation changed more readily than a silent reader can, since the textual label is a constant reminder of her first identity. A familiar proper name, on the other hand, is about as individualized as a physical body without specifying a social role. For all of these reasons, I have altered the speech headings in my edition to "Jane" so that the subject positions of the character are associated with a name rather than a misleading occupational or sexual category.

An alternative to this procedure would have been to use variable speech headings to mark the different subject positions—courtesan, widow, and wife—that Jane assumes at various points in the play. This practice would have the advantage of creating the kind of "Dividual" character that Randall McLeod finds in Shakespeare's plays.[73] But a modern audience's associations with the word "courtesan" are still inappropriate for her, and if "Jane" is a fictional identity, so too are the fifty-four references to "the Widow" in the early quarto. The third possible speech heading of "Wife" is already used in the play for the wife of Lucre, so all three alternatives are objectionable in some respects. The history of commentary on the play reveals that so few people have been able to read the character *against* her speech heading that fidelity to the copy-text instead results in a lower assessment of the character and of the play. So my decision to call her "Jane" is a compromise within a range of unsatisfactory alternatives.

The decision prompts questions about the treatment of proper names in Renaissance drama. I agree with A. R. Braunmuller that "there is, perhaps, a certain essentialism in the way editors accord personal names special treatment,"[74] and in this instance my substitution of a name for a generic identity may have the effect of imposing a more inflexible approach onto a malleable text. Yet if the name "Jane" functions in this way, how much more does the label "Courtesan," with its misleading but unmistakable associations of sexual promiscuity? This seems to me a choice between inadequate essentialist forms, and I prefer the one that does not so categorically defame the character. Middleton also used "Jane" in *No Wit No Help Like a Woman's* and in *Fair Quarrel*, which he coauthored with William Rowley. *No Wit's* Jane "Sunset" is an undistinguished heroine whose primary function is to be interchangeable with Grace "Twilight" in the eyes of everyone except the two young heroes in love with one or the other. Jane Russell's role in *Fair Quarrel* is more ambiguous, for she, too, is charged with being a "whore" when she becomes pregnant by a man who turns out to have been her husband by a spousal that took place before the play began. Given the name's historical precursors—from Jane Shore, mistress of Edward IV, to Lady Jane Grey and Jane Seymour—its associations are at least appropriate in their range and complexity, although it is also possible that the name recommended itself because it was not weighed down with one, highly memorable antecedent.

Charles B. Lower also makes a persuasive case for the importance of generic terms over proper names in his essay "Character Identifications in Two Folio Plays" in this volume. Reading *Trick* according to what the theater audience would hear rather than what a reader would see, I find eighty references in the dialogue to the character's generic role and only eight mentions of her proper names. Within the three subject positions that she assumes, either generic or nominative references to her as a "courtesan," "whore," "quean," "strumpet," or "Dutch widow" appear thirteen times; mentions of her as a "widow" appear fifty-four times; and she is called a "wife" twenty-one times. So the heaviest weight is given to her fictional identity: forty of the references to "widow" occur in only two scenes, 2.1 and 3.1, where Lucre and Hoard are each vying for her wealth; and twenty-five mentions occur after she has already become a wife. The emphasis throughout is on what the male characters in the play take Jane to be, that is, on her identity as a wealthy widow.[75] Both the term "courtesan" and the name "Jane" each appear in the dialogue three times. However, "courtesan" has a kind of priority, because Middleton uses it twice in the first scene to establish her illicit relation with Witgood; only then does he occasion a lot of play with her signifiers in the remainder of the text, so that by the end we are still asking who, or what, she is. Since a speech heading serves as a kind of anchor for the free play of those signifiers, I would argue that in this case the emendation to a proper name allows that play to occur more fully than "courtesan" would, especially for a modern audience.

In the best of all possible textual worlds and in the interest of greater fidelity to the earliest texts, I would be willing to retain "courtesan" and use it to direct readers to a revised understanding of its meanings by disrupting its associations with professional prostitution. There is ample evidence of a need for this disruption in Jacobean drama. Middleton's own use of "courtesan" suggests a woman involved in an extramarital relationship between persons of some class standing, but it does not usually denote outright prostitution. The Jeweller's Wife in *The Phoenix* refers to herself as a "courtesan" even though she buys the sexual services of her "knight" rather than selling her own; Frank Gullmann, the courtesan in *A Mad World, My Masters*, is able to sell her maidenhead fifteen times only because she is not known as a prostitute but has been "kept" by various men; and the cost of keeping Florida, Antonio's courtesan in *The Witch*, is specified as four nobles (or £1.32) a week, a considerable sum in 1616, which he is said to have paid for at least five years.[76] A revision of our understanding of this word and early modern assumptions behind calling women "whores," "queans," and "strumpets" is badly needed, but I do not think a single edition of one play can bear the burden of that revision. In short, this is not the best of all possible textual worlds: it is still mad, for example, on the subject of women. Readers not only skip over introductions and commentary; they remain inclined to think the worst of a woman's sexual behavior unless they are persuaded otherwise.

It is, then, also for this reason that I interpellate the play's heroine as "Jane." The act does not clear her name but it does problematize it, and it also calls attention to the word "courtesan" in a way that no submission to the copy-text would have accomplished. Editing carries with it, here and elsewhere, a politics. When critics and editors challenge existing hierarchies, our politics become more visible and hence more open to objection; but using earlier terms not only evokes the ideological and historical structures that enabled former oppressions but may reinscribe those oppressions with a greater force now than then. Editing is in this sense a judgment call between the past and the present, and those who choose to conserve make political judgments alongside those who decide to emend.

Hopefully this change in the speech heading will make it clearer to contemporary readers that Jane could have brought a legal action against Hoard for his defamation. Although Witgood's defense of her extends only as far as that issue, Jane's defense of herself suggests that Hoard could also have been charged with a civil offense. She says to her husband:

> Despise me, publish me: I am your wife.
> What shame can I have now but you'll have part?
> If in disgrace you share, I sought not you.
> You pursued me, nay, forced me.
> Had I friends would follow it,
> Less than your action has been proved a rape.[77]

Rape is a short word with a large charge, and Jane makes it plainly here, with the beat falling on that last word. Why has nobody heard her, in all this time? The word and her accusation have never been glossed by any of the fifteen editors of this play. Two editions note that "publish" in the first line means to publicly denounce,[78] and one—Loughrey and Taylor again—glosses "follow" in the penultimate line as "prosecute the case," so there is some glimmer of legal proceeding that comes through in the spare commentary.[79] But does her charge seem so without foundation that no one has even bothered to assess its validity? Perhaps this editorial silence can be accounted for by a lack of knowledge about the law to which she refers. But is British law against rape so arcane and inaccessible that no one has even bothered to check, or to query the issue, as others are queried, in the notes?

I have to say, nay, "I will speak as liberal as the north,"[80] that the inattention granted to this concern in the play is far too like the centuries of silence that have greeted women's charges of sexual assault in nonfictional homes and streets and public arenas. There is a relation between this editorial silence and the lack of response in those other places. Texts are not produced and reproduced in isolation from other cultural events. Jane is careful to say that a case could only be proved on her behalf if she had "friends would follow it." The word "friends" here means kinsmen, near relations, or advisors,[81] those who would bring a suit on her behalf, since as a married woman she could not bring one herself in a civil court. In a modern sense, however, I am willing to act as such a friend, as most feminist editors would be. So I've spent some time in the law books on this issue.

> If in disgrace you share, I sought not you.
> You pursued me, nay, forced me.

In order to relate Jane's assertion to Sir Edward Coke's account of the legal history of forced marriages, or "carrying away a woman against her will,"[82] we must return to the pivotal scene where Jane is advised by Hoard and two gentlemen, named Lamprey and Spitchcock,[83] that Witgood has neither lands nor living and so is not worthy as a marital partner, which allows Hoard to step into his place. What occurs in this scene is a *spousal per verba de futuro*, a marital contract between Hoard and Jane that is later confirmed by a marriage and consummation. The only editor who has marked it as such is William Roy Dawson, whose 1969 edition of *Trick* as a dissertation for the University of Tennessee was never published.[84] Once Jane has agreed not to marry Witgood, both gentlemen, at Hoard's urging, move her, even push her, towards Hoard, and then Lamprey says, joining their hands in a traditional handclasp, "Come, clap hands, a match." This act is followed by Hoard's words,

> With all my heart, widow! Thanks, gentlemen.
> I will deserve your labour, and thy love.[85]

The "love" of the "widow" has been secured here through the labor of the gentlemen, and the future tense with which Hoard receives that "love" makes this a spousal *de futuro*. Jane is at first silent except for an important disclaimer:

> Alas, you love not widows but for wealth.
> I promise you, I ha' nothing, sir.[86]

She does not misrepresent her fortune to Hoard, which would have been subsequent grounds for him to challenge the validity of the marriage. Later she adds, "Now I must hope the best," and after Hoard has suggested how he will whisk her off to Cole Harbour for marriage by a priest, she replies, "In that it pleaseth you, it likes me well," to which Hoard responds with a kiss.[87] All the elements are here for a binding marital contract—verbal agreements before witnesses, a handclasp, and a kiss, after which Hoard calls

Jane "wife."[88] Those are also the elements necessary for an enforced marriage if the woman acted under duress.[89]

The degree of coercion that effects this action only becomes apparent afterwards, when Lamprey and Spitchcock are recollecting their success with Hoard. They discuss the spousal as if it were a sports event, with self-congratulation and some competition. Middleton devotes fourteen lines to this conversation:

Lamprey
Did not I use most art to win the widow?
Spitchcock
You shall pardon me for that, sir. Master Hoard knows I took her at best vantage.
Hoard
What's that, sweet gentlemen; what's that?
Spitchcock
He will needs bear me down that his art only wrought with the widow most.
Hoard
O, you did both well, gentlemen; you did both well. I thank you.
Lamprey
I was the first that moved her.
Hoard
You were, i'faith.
Spitchcock
But it was I that took her at the bound.
Hoard
Ay, that was you. Faith, gentlemen, 'tis right.
Lamprey
I boasted least, but 'twas I joined their hands.
Hoard
By'th mass, I think he did. You did all well,
Gentlemen, you did all well; contend no more.[90]

This boastful exchange of one-upmanship between Lamprey and Spitchcock makes it plain that Lamprey actually took the hands of Hoard and Jane and joined them himself in the earlier scene: it was not an act without his assistance or one in which Jane was the active agent, as the stage directions by Havelock Ellis and George R. Price, respectively, indicate. Loughrey and Taylor's text is again the only one to credit his counterpart with this action through a stage direction.[91] The conversation between Hoard and the gentlemen also justifies another stage direction that shows how they moved Jane toward Hoard. We need enough sense of their physical coercion to support Jane's later claim, "You pursued me, nay, forced me." Otherwise she appears to be making a charge without any foundation, a confusion that

Middleton specifically tried to avoid by including the men's exultant recollection of the spousal. To put it another way, the absence of such directions and commentary in previous editions can account for some of the inadequate response to Jane's speech in the last act, for without that support, especially for a modern audience accustomed to it, what she says appears incomprehensible or unsound.

On the other hand, I think this scene would have been more accessible to Renaissance audiences, because for them, the incidence of forced marriage and rape of women of substance was apparently not an anomaly. A statute of 31 Henry VI, passed in 1452–53, on "Abuses in compelling Women, to be bound by Obligations or to marry against their liking," makes this plain in a sequence of events quite like that in the play:

> Whereas in all Parts of this Realm divers People of great Power, moved with unsatiable Covetousness, against all Right, [Humanity, Integrity,] and good Conscience, have [sought] and found new Inventions, and them [continually] do execute, to the Danger, Trouble, and [great abusing] of all Ladies, Gentlewomen, and other Women sole, having any Substance of Lands, Tenements, or other moveable Goods within this Realm, perceiving their great [Weakness] and Simplicity, will take them by Force, or otherwise come to them, [seeming] to be their [great] Friends, promising them their faithful Friendship, and so by great Dissimulation, or otherwise, get them into their Possession, conveying them into such Places where the said Offenders be of most Power . . . until they will bind themselves to the said Offenders, or other Person or Persons to [their own] Use, in great Sums, by Obligation or Obligations, as well [simple] as conditional . . . ; also they will many Times compel them to be married by them, contrary to their own Likings, or otherwise they will levy the said Sum or Sums on their Lands and Goods, and put their Person or Persons in Danger, to their great Damage. . . .[92]

The party so compelled was permitted to sue a writ out of Chancery to make a complaint against the offender, and if the offenses were substantiated upon examination, the obligations entered into by the woman were found to be null and void. A statute of 3 Henry VII in 1486–87 made the offense "against takers for lucre, of maids, widows, or wives having substance of lands or goods, or being heirs apparent" a felony for "not only the takers, but the procurers, abetters of the felony, and receivers of the said woman";[93] another of 18 Elizabeth in 1575–76 withdrew benefit of clergy from those who raped by force; and one of 39 Elizabeth in 1596–97 withdrew it from those who raped by abduction.[94] Given the ease and speed with which spousals in England could be contracted before solemnization in church became the accepted practice, women of substance who were unmarried or *femes soles*[95] were at particular risk of being forced into marriage by men who wanted to gain control of their wealth. The function of act 3, scene 3, in the plot is to lend support to Jane's charge that she was so compelled. Although we know that she actually prefers to be married to Hoard (because that is her best option now that she has lost her virginity to Witgood and he refuses to marry her), Hoard does not know as much, so her legally valid charge represents a serious threat.

But her charge is not only of forced marriage:

> Had I friends would follow it,
> Less than your action has been proved a rape.

The relation between forced marriage and rape was especially strong because a woman who had been raped was permitted to demand the rapist for her husband, and sometimes she felt fortunate to be able to do so.[96] This resolution was sufficiently frequent that laws were passed under Richard II preventing the woman who so consented from claiming her inheritance, dowry, or joint feoffment.[97] The author of *The Lawes Resolutions of Womens Rights* of 1632 remarks of this law concerning the wife's consent: "This was a shrewd Statute. Till this time he that had rauished a woman might hope for a clemencie, at the least at her hands, because he had ventured his life for her sake, but what shall lusty leachers now doe? the more a woman is worthy to bee won, because shee hath or shall haue wherewith to keepe a man, the more danger it is to medle with her."[98]

Jane's charge of rape has also been dismissed because she was thought to have made her living by sexual commerce, and a "loose" woman in contemporary society is rarely believed when she makes such an accusation. The sexual history of the woman who brought a charge of rape against William Kennedy Smith was successfully used against her, both in court and by the media. But the early modern period appears not to have addressed the issue in such inflexible terms. The discussion of rape in Michael Dalton's *The Countrey Justice,* a compendium of law for justices of the peace published from 1618 to 1635, explains that "to rauish an harlot against her will, is felony."[99] Dalton cites a much-quoted passage from the thirteenth-century legal historian, Henry of Bracton:[100] "And if she was a whore before, she was not a whore then, since by crying out against his wicked deed she refused her consent."[101] The passage shows that the legal definition of a "whore" was also malleable: it depended upon the disposition of a woman's sexuality rather than her occupation. A woman who said "no" to a man was not sexually available and so was not, at that time, a "whore." This approach helps explain why the judges in the trial of the earl of Castlehaven in 1631 could reaffirm the same principle regardless of a woman's reputation and "resolve it to be a Rape, though committed on the body of a common strumpet; for it is the enforcing against the will which makes the Rape; and the common whore may be ravished against her will."[102]

Essentialist constructions of the self have occasioned a legal regress on
this issue in our own time. To allow modern readers to sustain their preconceptions about a woman like Jane being able to bring a charge of rape
against her molester if she had the support of "friends" is to ignore even
conventionally recognized obligations of an editor. Commentary on this
issue is as called for as glosses of the meanings of obsolete words, for the
same reasons.

The word "rape" during the early modern period also described two
different activities: what we would now call rape—forced sexual relations—
and the act of abduction.[103] The play provides little information relevant to
the former meaning except that Hoard claims to have "wedded her and /
Bedded her."[104] But her accusation more directly concerns Hoard's plan to
spirit her away from Witgood, "when, by some sleight removing him from
thee, we'll suddenly enter and surprise thee, carry thee away by boat to
Cole Harbour, have a priest ready, and there clap it up instantly."[105] Hoard
even plans to make this action *look* like an abduction. As far as I know, the
only person in all of the commentary on the play—critical and editorial—
who has seen any meaning in Jane's charge is Michael Shapiro, who remarks that Hoard's "abduction of her is tantamount to statutory rape."[106]
Hoard's feigned attempt at abduction is therefore at risk of being transformed into a legal reality by a very clever woman whose knowledge of
the law is so precise that she can use every opportunity that comes to hand
against him. And his total disregard for her wishes all along means he is
probably in doubt as to whether she did desire the spousal or participated
willingly in the abduction and its aftermath, the sexual consummation.

Hoard never denies Jane's accusation, and the only other person to
react to it is Onesiphorus Hoard, who says only, "Brother?" or "Brother!"
or however that word might be inflected by a modern editor.[107] Then Jane
weighs her own misdeeds against his and finds the loss of her virginity no
more reprehensible than his coercion. In response, he concedes that he was
driven by "spite" and "must embrace shame, to be rid of shame,"[108] an
admission that Jane's public dishonor and his own are now so inextricably
linked that their names can only be cleared by his treating her as a respectable wife. The "whoring" of Hoard therefore calls into question the opposition between good women and whores, as Anthony Dawson has observed,
because if a "whore" can play the role of rich widow so well that she actually becomes a wife, then the difference between the two collapses and the
very men who insisted on it, having taken the one for the other, become the
means by which the difference is undone.[109] Here the play offers an instance of what Dollimore has called "transgressive mimesis,"[110] where the
imitation of a legitimate woman in the marriage market by a marginal figure
like a "whore" highlights the way in which marriageable women are treated

as whores, because they also are bought and sold like property and for property. The malleability of women's identities in this play therefore begins to undermine the stability of some important social institutions—marriage, property, and inheritance. So it is not only usury that is exposed in *Trick;* it is the commodities market in women, with Hoard as its chief consumer. Jane and Witgood promise reform in the jingling, playful rhymes of the play's last lines, but it is Hoard whose "craft" has exposed him as the play's biggest "fool."[111]

Jane is no such fool. The text presents her as fully capable of defending herself in a battle of wills and bodies, if not in court, with this rich old man. And although she lacks "friends" to bring her suit, she does not need to seek legal redress, because she has what she wants: her marriage to Hoard is "sure," as she puts it,[112] and he has little choice but to remain her husband. Although this marriage is not an entirely happy union for either party, Jane has actively chosen it, perhaps because it is her best alternative in a world where she is characterized accurately, according to early modern usage, as a "whore" and must defend herself against the greater indignity of being called a "common strumpet." My impression of Jane by the end of this play is that she does not need a lot of help from anyone, except perhaps an editor. She is not without guilt or guile—indeed, she has displayed a wit as good or better than Witgood's in pulling off their ruse—but the weight of relative guilt between Jane and Hoard has been shifted by years of editorial treatment. In a sense Hoard's coercion and rape were permitted to decompose by centuries of silent inattention. As a feminist editor I have done what I can in my introduction, commentary, and text to ensure that the next time Jane makes a charge of rape, whether to a crowded theater or a private reader, somebody, somewhere, will sit up and listen. And I would remind those editors whose texts address issues like this one of the statute of 3 Henry VII about carrying away a wife against her will: that "not only the takers, but the procurers, abetters of the felony, and receivers of the said woman wittingly, knowing the same, be all adjudged as principall felons."[113]

NOTES

1. At the conference "Literary Theory and the Practice of Editing" held at the University of Liverpool on 10–12 July 1993, papers by Ann Thompson, Julia Briggs, Marion Wynne-Davies, and myself were given in a cluster called "Feminism and Editing." The term "feminist editing" came up frequently in this context. Ann Thompson talked on the topic at the meeting of the Shakespeare Association of America in 1988, and her New Cambridge edition of Shakespeare's *Taming of the Shrew* is one of the earliest examples of feminist editorial practice on an early modern text (Cambridge: Cambridge University Press, 1984). For more discussion of how editorial decisions have affected issues of gender and

performance in the past, see essays in the section, "Codifying Gender: the Disturbing Presence of Women," in *Reading Readings: Essays on Shakespeare Editing in the Eighteenth Century*, ed. Joanna Gondris (Rutherford, N.J.: Fairleigh Dickinson University Press, forthcoming), especially Laurie E. Osborne's "Editing Frailty in *Twelfth Night*: 'Where lies your Text?'" Many editions in the forthcoming *Collected Works of Thomas Middleton* and the ongoing Arden Shakespeare (third series) are being prepared by scholars who have committed themselves to various forms of political criticism, including feminism, so the production of alternative texts that I call for in this essay is already well underway.

Various projects devoted to editing the texts of early modern women have also posed questions about editorial procedures that have implications for feminist editing. See, for example, Sara Jayne Steen, "Behind the Arras: Editing Renaissance Women's Letters," in *New Ways of Looking at Old Texts*, ed. W. Speed Hill (Binghamton, N.Y.: MRTS, 1993), 229–38. These editing projects include two French Canadian on-line series directed by Diane Desrosiers-Bonin and Hannah Fournier; a series of translations edited by Albert Rabil Jr. and Margaret King for University of Chicago Press; the "Women Writers in English, 1350–1850" series edited by Susanne Woods and Elizabeth H. Hageman and published by Oxford University Press, which is an outgrowth of the Women Writers Project at Brown; and a series of facsimiles being edited for Scolar Press by Betty Travitsky and Patrick Cullen.

2. *The Wife of Bath's Prologue* in *The Riverside Chaucer*, ed. Larry D. Benson, 3d ed. (Boston: Houghton Mifflin, 1987), line 692.

3. J. G. Tilney-Bassett, "Edmund Tilney's *The Flower of Friendshippe*," *The Library*, 4th ser., 26 (1946): 175–81, and Ralph Glassgow Johnson, ed., "A Critical Third Edition of Edmund Tilney's *The Flower of Friendshippe*, published in 1577" (Ph.D. diss., University of Pittsburgh, 1960).

4. *A Short-Title Catalogue of Books Printed in England, Scotland, and Ireland and of English Books Printed Abroad, 1475–1640*, ed. Katharine F. Pantzer et al., 2d ed., rev. and enl., vol. 2 (London: Bibliographical Society, 1976), nos. 24076–77a.5.

5. "Note on the Text," in Edmund Tilney, *The Flower of Friendship: A Renaissance Dialogue Contesting Marriage*, ed. Valerie Wayne (Ithaca: Cornell University Press, 1992), 96.

6. Tilney, *Flower of Friendship*, n. to line 50 (p. 143).

7. Alice Clark, *Working Life of Women in the Seventeenth Century*, 3d ed. (London: Routledge, 1992), 165. D. F. McKenzie, *Stationers' Company Apprentices, 1605–40* (Charlottesville: Bibliographical Society of the University of Virginia, 1961).

8. Cyprian Blagden, *The Stationers' Company: A History, 1403–1959* (Cambridge: Harvard University Press, 1960), 162. I am grateful to Peter Blayney for this reference; he is also the source of the qualification regarding 1541.

9. Tilney, *Flower of Friendship*, 1.35 (p. 100) and n. to line 35 (p. 143).

10. Ibid., n. to line 524 (p. 144).

11. Ibid., lines 365–66 (p.110) and n. to line 366 (p. 144).

12. Ibid., lines 341–42 (p.109) and n. to line 342 (p. 144).

13. Ibid., lines 1207–10 (p. 135) and n. to lines 1209–10 (p. 145).

14. Gary Taylor, "Textual and Sexual Criticism: A Crux in *The Comedy of Errors*," *RD* 19 (1988):195–96.

15. Clark, *Working Life*, 162. See also Blagden, *Stationers' Company*, 162. Women appear as printers as early as 1540 in E. Gordon Duff's *A Century of the English Book Trade* (London: Bibliographical Society, 1948). There are also numerous women printers listed in R. B. McKerrow, ed., *A Dictionary of Printers and Booksellers in England, Scotland, and Ireland, and of Foreign Printers of English Books, 1557–1640* (London: Bibliographical Society, 1968). See also the list of "Women Printers, Publishers and Booksellers," in Hilda L.

Smith and Susan Cardinale, *Women and the Literature of the Seventeenth Century* (Westport, Conn.: Greenwood Press, 1990). For an account of women's more contemporary exclusion from the printing business, see Cynthia Cockburn, *Brothers: Male Dominance and Technological Exchange* (London: Pluto Press, 1983).

16. Stanley Wells and Gary Taylor, with John Jowett and William Montgomery, *William Shakespeare: A Textual Companion* (Oxford: Clarendon Press, 1987), 158–59 and textual introductions and notes to individual plays.

17. Ann Thompson and Sasha Roberts, eds., *Women Reading Shakespeare, 1660–1900* (Manchester: Manchester University Press, 1997), 3, 47, 46. See also British Museum, *General Catalogue of Printed Books, Photolithographic Edition to 1955,* vol. 24 (London: Trustees of the British Museum, 1964), col. 1190.

18. Thompson and Roberts, *Women Reading Shakespeare,* 46.

19. British Museum, *General Catalogue,* vol. 220, cols. 15–16. *Oxford English Dictionary,* 2d ed., s.v. "bowdlerize."

20. *The Tempest* 4.1.122–24 in William Shakespeare, *The Complete Works,* ed. Stanley Wells and Gary Taylor (Oxford: Clarendon Press, 1986).

21. *The Complete Works of Shakespeare,* ed. David Bevington, 3d. ed. (Glenview, Ill.: Scott, Foresman, 1980), 4.1.122–24 and *The Tempest,* ed. Stephen Orgel (Oxford: Oxford University Press, 1987), 4.1.122–24.

22. "Prospero's Wife," in *Rewriting the Renaissance: The Discourses of Sexual Difference in Early Modern Europe,* ed. Margaret W. Ferguson, Maureen Quilligan, and Nancy J. Vickers (Chicago: University of Chicago Press, 1986), 50–64 (63).

23. Jeanne A. Roberts, "'Wife' or 'Wise'—*The Tempest* 1. 1786," *SB* 31 (1978): 203–5.

24. Ibid., 205.

25. *William Shakespeare: The Complete Works,* ed. Alfred Harbage (London: Penguin, 1969) and *Complete Works,* ed. Wells and Taylor.

26. Roberts, "'Wife,'" 206–8.

27. Orgel, "Prospero's Wife," 64.

28. Wells et al., *Textual Companion,* note to *The Tempest,* 4.1.123/1579 (p. 616).

29. Roberts, "'Wife,'" 205.

30. Ibid., 204–5.

31. Orgel glosses Miranda's name as "literally 'wonderful,' 'to be wondered at'" in his *Tempest* at 1.2.0.1.

32. Roberts, "'Wife,'" 205.

33. Ibid. In "The Rhetoric of Textual Criticism," *TEXT* 4 (1988): 39–57, Gary Taylor remarks that "we often appeal to the authority of the editorial tradition. All such appeals employ a very simple strategy: 'You should be convinced by this argument, because other people have been convinced by this argument'" (46).

34. Peter W. M. Blayney, introduction to the second edition of *The Norton Facsimile: The First Folio of Shakespeare,* prepared by Charlton Hinman, 2d ed. (New York: W. W. Norton, 1996), xxxi. I am very grateful to Barbara Mowat and Stephen Orgel for providing me with information about Blayney's findings.

35. *Othello* 3.3.389–93, in *Complete Works,* ed. Wells and Taylor.

36. Stephen Orgel emphasizes that "we are *not* 'getting back to the author's original text'" when we use modern bibliographical methods, for the printed text is a collaborative and theatrical product owned less by the author than the company and publisher. See "What is a Text?" in *Staging the Renaissance: Reinterpretations of Elizabethan and Jacobean Drama,* ed. David Scott Kastan and Peter Stallybrass (New York: Routledge, 1991), 83–87, quote at 87.

37. Thomas L. Berger, "The Second Quarto of *Othello* and the Question of Textual

'Authority,'" in *Othello: New Perspectives*, ed. Virginia Mason Vaughan and Kent Cartwright (Rutherford, N.J.: Fairleigh Dickinson University Press, 1991), 32.

38. At ibid., Berger cites the editions by Alice Walker and J. D. Wilson (Cambridge), Kenneth Muir (New Penguin), G. B. Evans (Riverside), and Norman Sanders (New Cambridge). The others include *Complete Works*, ed. G. K. Kittredge (Boston: Ginn and Co., 1936); *The Complete Works*, ed. Peter Alexander (New York: Random House, 1952); *The Tragedy of Othello, the Moor of Venice*, ed. G. E. Bentley (Baltimore: Penguin, 1958), reprinted in *The Complete Pelican Shakespeare*, ed. Alfred Harbage (London: Penguin, 1969); and *The Complete Works*, ed. Bevington (1980).

39. Norman Sanders, ed., *Othello* (Cambridge: Cambridge University Press, 1984), 3.3.385–89.

40. Berger ("Second Quarto," 31) citing Charlton Hinman, "The 'Copy' for the Second Quarto of *Othello*," in *Joseph Quincy Adams Memorial Studies*, ed. James G. McManaway, Giles E. Dawson, and Edwin E. Willoughby (Washington, D.C.: The Folger Shakespeare Library, 1948), 388.

41. Berger, "Second Quarto," 26–47.

42. Wells et al., *Textual Companion*, n. to *Othello* 3.3.391/1838 (p. 480).

43. Peter Stallybrass, "Patriarchal Territories: The Body Enclosed," in *Rewriting the Renaissance*, ed. Ferguson, Quilligan, and Vickers, 123–42 (137).

44. Arthur L. Little Jr. "'An essence that's not seen': The Primal Scene of Racism in *Othello*," *SQ* 44 (1993): 304–24 (311, 309).

45. Karen Newman, "'And wash the Ethiop white': Femininity and the Monstrous in *Othello*," in *Shakespeare Reproduced: The Text in History and Ideology*, ed. Jean E. Howard and Marion F. O'Connor (New York: Methuen, 1987), 143–62.

46. *Othello* 1.3.289–90, in *Complete Works*, ed. Wells and Taylor.

47. Kim F. Hall, *Things of Darkness: Economies of Race and Gender in Early Modern England* (Ithaca: Cornell University Press, 1995), 261.

48. Michael Neill, "Unproper Beds: Race, Adultery, and the Hideous in *Othello*," *SQ* 40 (1989): 383–412.

49. *OED*, 2d ed., s.v. "fresh," 10a and 11a.

50. *Twelfth Night* 1.5.248, in *Complete Works*, ed. Wells and Taylor.

51. M. R. Ridley, ed., *Othello* (London: Methuen, 1958), n. to 3.3.392 (p. 117).

52. Charles Knight, ed., *The Pictorial Edition of the Works of Shakspere*, vol. 1 (1841; reprint, London: George Routledge and Sons, 1867), 296. Most of this passage is quoted in *Othello*, ed. Horace Howard Furness, The New Variorum Edition of Shakespeare (New York: Dover Publications, 1963), note to 3.3.445.

53. All of the editions of *Trick* are listed after the textual note to my edition in *Thomas Middleton and Early Modern Textual Culture*, the textual companion to Thomas Middleton, *Collected Works*, gen. ed. Gary Taylor (Oxford: Clarendon Press, forthcoming), where the text of my edition will appear. Citations from *Trick* below that do not identify an editor will be to my text. Since this edition is still in progress, there may be slight variations between the line numbers recorded here and those that appear when it is published.

54. After Witgood refers to the trick he has proposed as an "embryo" at 1.1.57, Jane replies, "Though you beget, 'tis I must help to breed," 1.1.61, so my language reflects the procreative terminology of the play.

55. Michael Shapiro makes a related observation when he says, "She is not a common harlot, but Witgood's mistress," in *Children of the Revels: The Boy Companies of Shakespeare's Time and Their Plays* (New York: Columbia University Press, 1977), 60. In "Middleton's Experiments with Comedy and Judgement," *Jacobean Theatre*, Stratford-upon-Avon Studies I (London: Edward Arnold, 1960), R. B. Parker refers to Witgood's courtesan, "who had been his mistress" (186).

56. *Trick* 1.1.36–38 and 5.2.159–60.

57. *Trick* 5.2.124–25.

58. *Trick* 5.2.125–28.

59. *A Trick to Catch the Old One*, in Thomas Middleton, *Five Plays* (Harmondsworth: Penguin Books, 1988), note to 5.2.110 (p. 67).

60. Martin Ingram, *Church Courts, Sex, and Marriage in England, 1570–1640* (Cambridge: Cambridge University Press, 1987), 292.

61. Ibid., 292–96 (quote at 296).

62. "General Note" on "The Costomary" in *English Gilds*, ed. Joshua Toulmin Smith and Lucy Toulmin Smith, Early English Text Society, no. 40 (London: Oxford University Press, 1870), 438.

63. Ibid., 434.

64. Eric Partridge, *Shakespeare's Bawdy*, 3d ed. (London: Routledge, 1968), 193.

65. *OED,* 2d ed., s.v. "courtesan," sb. 1 and a. and sb. 2.

66. Edward Sharpham, *A Critical Old Spelling Edition of the Works of Edward Sharpham*, ed. Christopher Gordon Petter, The Renaissance Imagination vol. 18 (New York: Garland, 1986), 2.1.184–85.

67. G. R. Quaife, *Wanton Wenches and Wayward Wives: Peasants and Illicit Sex in Early Seventeenth Century England* (New Brunswick, N.J.: Rutgers University Press, 1979), 146. In her dissertation in progress for the University of Alabama, Karen Pirnie relates the legal categories used to describe women imprisoned at Bridewell to the representations of whores and prostitutes in early modern drama. Her working title is "As she saith: Tracing Whoredom in Seventeenth-Century London from Bridewell to Southwark."

68. Thomas Coryate, *Coryat's Crudities*, vol. 1 (1611; reprint, Glasgow: James MacLehose and Sons, 1905), 402–9. See also Ann Rosalind Jones, "Italians and Others," in *Staging the Renaissance,* ed. Kastan and Stallybrass, 251–62.

69. Jonathan Dollimore, "Subjectivity, Sexuality and Transgression: The Jacobean Connection," *RD,* n.s., 17 (1986): 53.

70. Random Cloud [Randall McLeod], "'The very names of the Persons': Editing and the Invention of Dramatick Character," in Kastan and Stallybrass, eds., *Staging the Renaissance*, 88–96. See also Margreta de Grazia and Peter Stallybrass, "The Materiality of the Shakespearean Text," *SQ* 44 (1993): 255–83 (271–72), and Gary Taylor's "Proximities," the introductory essay to *Thomas Middleton and Early Modern Textual Culture*, forthcoming, which includes an extensive and revisionary account of dramatis personae lists in early English drama.

71. Catherine Belsey explores this issue in *The Subject of Tragedy: Identity and Difference in Renaissance Drama* (London: Methuen, 1985), 149.

72. See textual notes to 4.1.0.2. and 4.1.20 in *Trick,* ed. Wayne.

73. Cloud, "'The very names,'" 88.

74. See A. R. Braunmuller, "How farre is't call'd to Sorris?," p. **118** in this volume.

75. In "The Widow as Paradox and Paradigm in Middleton's Plays," *Journal of General Education* 34 (1982): 3–19, Renu Juneja recounts the coercive maneuvers used in the two remarriages of Margaret Dakin, where the countess of Huntington and Elizabeth Lady Russell played major parts. Juneja finds that Lady Russell "generally refers to Margaret simply as *the widow,*" which she sees as one sign that she is "treated like a commodity" (7, 5). Lady Russell's remarks are cited from *Fortesque Papers,* ed. S. R. Gardiner (London: Camden Society, 1871), x–xi, xviii–xix. I am grateful to Koreen Nakahodo-Tsuchida for this reference.

76. *The Phoenix*, ed. Lawrence Danson and Ivo Kamps, in *Collected Middleton,* ed. Taylor, 1.3.31; *The Witch,* ed. Marion F. O'Connor, also in *Collected Middleton,* 2.1.21 and n.

77. *Trick* 5.2.129–34.

78. Loughrey and Taylor, eds., *Trick*, note to 5.2.112 (p. 67), and William Roy Dawson Jr., "A Critical Edition of Thomas Middleton's *A Trick to Catch the Old One*" (Ph.D. diss., University of Tennessee, 1969), note to 5.2.141 (p. 314).

79. *Trick*, ed. Loughrey and Taylor, note to 5.2.110 (p.67).

80. Emilia in *Othello*, ed. Wells and Taylor, 5.2.226.

81. "Used in the plural, as 'my friends,' the word before the eighteenth century always meant no more than 'my advisors, associates and backers.' This category often indicated a relative, particularly a parent or an uncle by blood or marriage. But it could also include a member of the household, such as a steward, chaplain or tutor; or a neighbour; or a political associate sharing a common party affiliation; or a person of high status and influence with whom there was acquaintance and from whom there was hope of patronage" (Lawrence Stone, *The Family, Sex and Marriage in England, 1500–1800* [New York: Harper and Row, 1977], 97. I am grateful to Bob McHenry for this reference.

82. The phrase appears in the title of chapter 12 in Coke, *The Third Part of the Institutes of the Laws of England* (1644; reprint, New York: Garland, 1979), 61.

83. This scene is 3.1. Lamprey and Spitchcock remain unnamed in all other editions, producing a confusion between references to Lucre's friends, on the one hand, who appear in the quarto stage directions as "gentlemen" or "first and second gentlemen," and in speech tags as "1" and "2"; and Hoard's friends, on the other hand, who are referred to in the same way. A genuine conflict occurs in 4.1, when the character designated as "1" of that scene opens it by celebrating the marriage of Hoard and Jane and then vouches for Lucre's willingness to sign over the mortgage to Witgood at 4.1.72–74. I have removed this conflation of the friends of Lucre and Hoard by assigning speeches from Hoard's first and second gentlemen to Lamprey and Spitchcock, a change that is indicated by their support of Hoard's marriage when they appear in other scenes as named characters. Several previous editors proposed that the duplication should be emended in this way. See the textual note to 3.1.111.2 in *Trick*, ed. Wayne.

84. *Trick*, ed. Dawson, n. to 3.1.243–44 (p. 277).

85. *Trick* 3.1.203–4.

86. *Trick* 3.1.205–6.

87. *Trick* 3.1.208 and 227.

88. *Trick* 3.1.203–6 and 227; 202.1; 228; 234.

89. Ingram, *Church Courts*, 189–98.

90. *Trick* 3.3.22–35.

91. [Hoard *and* Courtesan *shake hands.*] in *A Trick to Catch the Old One* in *Thomas Middleton*, ed. Havelock Ellis (1887; reprint, St. Clair Shores, Mich.: Scholarly Press, [1969]), 3.1., p. 39; [*She takes* Hoord's *hand.*] in *Thomas Middleton: Michaelmas Term and A Trick to Catch the Old One*, ed. George R. Price (The Hague: Mouton, 1976), 3.1.196, p. 171. [Joins their hands.] in speech of Gentleman 1, in *Trick*, ed. Loughrey and Taylor, 3.1.199, p.31.

92. *The Statutes of the Realm*, vol. 2 (1816; reprint, London: Dawsons, 1963), 367–68, microfilm.

93. The first quoted phrase is from a description of the statute in T.E., *Lawes Resolutions of Womens Rights* (London: J. Grove, 1632), 384. It is a brief but accurate account of the statute as it appears in Coke, *Institutes*, 3:61, which is the source of the second quotation.

94. Coke, *Institutes*, 3:60–62; T.E., *Lawes*, 400–402.

95. "Feme-sole" is an Anglo-French term used in law for "a woman who has not the protection of a husband; an unmarried woman, a spinster; a widow," or "a married woman who with respect to property is as independent of her husband as if she were unmarried." The "feme sole" was contrasted to the "feme covert," "a woman under cover or protection

of her husband; a married woman." "Feme" in these uses comes from Old French. *OED*, s.v. "feme-sole," "feme covert," and "feme."

96. Coke attributes this practice to the Common Law and explores physical punishments (loss of eyes, castration, and death) meted out to the rapist "unlesse she that was ravished before judgement demaunded him for her husband; for that was onely in the will of the woman and not of the man" (*The Second Part of the Institutes of the Lawes of England* [1642; reprint, New York: Garland, 1979], 180–81). He specifically mentions the instance of the ravisher being a "nobleman" and the woman "base and ignoble." Suzanne Gossett examines this law and its dramatic applications in "'Best Men are Molded out of Faults': Marrying the Rapist in Jacobean Drama," *ELR* 14 (1984): 305–27.

97. Coke, *Institutes*, 2:434 and T.E., *Lawes*, 382–83.

98. T.E., *Lawes*, 382–83.

99. Dalton's book was published in 1619 and is reprinted in facsimile as *Countrey Justice, 1619*, Classical English Law Texts (London: Professional Books, 1973), 257.

100. In *Bracton: The Problem of His Text* (London: Bernard Quaritch, 1965), H. G. Richardson observes that "Bracton was not a real name at all" and that the author and judge was Henry of Bratton (1).

101. *Bracton on the Laws and Customs of England*, vol. 2, trans. Samuel E. Thorne (Cambridge: Belknap Press of Harvard University Press, 1968), 418. The Latin original is cited in Dalton, *Countrey Justice, 1619*, 257; in Sir Anthony Fitzherbert and Richard Crompton, *L'Office et Aucthoritie de Justices de Peace* (1584), Classical English Law Texts (London: Professional Books, 1972), 37; and in T.E., *Lawes*, 395, where it reads "Quia licit meretrix fuerit antea, certe tunc temporis non fuit, cum nequitiae eius reclamando consentire noluit."

102. *A Complete Collection of State Trials* [*Cobbetts State Trials*], vol. 3, ed. T. B. Howell (London: Longman, 1816), col. 414. For further discussion of this case and its implications, see Leah S. Marcus, "The Milieu of Milton's *Comus:* Judicial Reform at Ludlow and the Problem of Sexual Assault," *Criticism* 25 (1983): 293–327.

103. "Sect. xxi. Ravishment is in two sorts": this passage in T.E., *Lawes*, is most accessible in *Daughters, Wives, and Widows: Writings by Men about Women and Marriage in England, 1500–1640*, ed. Joan Larsen Klein (Urbana: University of Illinois Press, 1992), 55–56.

104. *Trick* 4.4.192–93.

105. *Trick* 3.1.224–28.

106. Shapiro, *Children of the Revels*, 63.

107. *Trick*, ed. Wayne, 5.2.135. The 1608 text follows the word with a question mark, but exclamations in that text are often signaled by question marks, and the punctuation there is not a reliable guide for an editor. My edition uses an exclamation mark, but it was a tough choice.

108. *Trick* 5.2.154–56.

109. Anthony B. Dawson, "Giving the Finger: Puns and Transgression in *The Changeling*," in *The Elizabethan Theatre 12*, ed. A. L. Magnusson and C. E. McGee (Toronto: P. D. Meany, 1993), 96.

110. Jonathan Dollimore, *Sexual Dissidence: Augustine to Wilde, Freud to Foucault* (Oxford: Clarendon Press, 1991), 284–93.

111. *Trick* 5.2.204.

112. *Trick* 4.1.18.

113. Coke, *Institutes*, 3:61.

Versions of this paper were presented at the Liverpool conference in 1993, the Women's Brown Bag Seminar Series and the Department of English at the University of Hawaii, and the meetings of the Rocky Mountain Medieval and Renaissance Association in 1994. I am grateful to many people in those groups for their responses and queries, including Roberta Krueger's question about whether women could be compositors. My work on *A Trick to Catch the Old One* was funded by an NEH Summer Stipend, the University of Hawaii Office of Research Relations, and the University of Hawaii Office of Women's Research. This last source supported the work of Paula Reeve, who collated four large notebooks of commentary on nine of the play's editions and helped with research on prostitution. Susan Amussen and Fran Dolan also offered crucial advice on rape and the law in early modern England in connection with this project. Tom Berger, Margo Hendricks, Jean Howard, Laurie Maguire, and Gary Taylor provided perceptive suggestions on the essay's revision. I am also thankful to Richard Tillotson and Sarah Anne Wayne Callies for their enthusiasm and engagement with these arguments as they took shape.

10

Killed with Hard Opinions: Oldcastle, Falstaff, and the Reformed Text of *1 Henry IV*

DAVID SCOTT KASTAN

> The struggle for the text is the text.
>
> —R. Cloud

No doubt, as has long been recognized, Shakespeare did not originally intend Hal's fat tavern companion to be named "Falstaff." As early as the 1630s, Richard James had noted that

> in Shakespeares first shewe of Harrie yᵉ fift, yᵉ person with which he vndertook to playe a buffone was not Falstaffe, but Sʳ Jhon Oldcastle, and that offence beinge worthily taken by personages descended from his title, as peradventure by manie others allso whoe ought to haue him in honourable memorie, the poet was putt to make an ignorant shifte of abusing Sʳ Jhon Fastolphe, a man not inferior of Vertue though not so famous in pietie as the other, whoe gaue witnesse vnto the truth of our reformation with a constant and resolute martyrdom, vnto which he was pursued by the Priests, Bishops, Moncks, and Friers of those dayes.[1]

Apparently objecting to the defamation of the well-known Lollard martyr, the fourth Lord Cobham (as Oldcastle became through his marriage to Joan Cobham in 1408), William Brooke, the tenth holder of the title,[2] seemingly compelled Shakespeare to alter the name of Sir John, acting either in his own right as lord chamberlain (as Brooke was from 8 August 1596 until his death on 5 March 1597) or through the intervention and agency of the queen (as Rowe claims: "[S]ome of the Family being then remaining, the Queen was pleas'd to command him [i.e. Shakespeare] to alter it").[3]

Pale traces of the original name, of course, seem to remain in the modified text. Hal refers to Falstaff as "my old lad of the castle" (1.2.40–41), the colloquial phrase for a roisterer seemingly taking its point from the name of its original referent; and a line in act 2—"Away, good Ned. Falstaff sweats to death" (2.2.102)—is metrically irregular with Falstaff's name but arguably not with the trisyllabic "Oldcastle"[4] (and the image itself is grotesquely appropriate for a man who notoriously did virtually sweat to death, being hanged in chains and burned at St. Giles Fields, the spectacular martyrdom grimly memorialized in one of the woodcuts in Foxe's *Acts and Monuments*). Also, in the quarto of *2 Henry IV*, a speech prefix at 1.2.114 has "Old." for "Falstaff," a residual mark somewhat like phantom pain in an amputated limb;[5] and, of course, the epilogue insists that "Oldcastle died a martyr, and this is not the man" (lines 29–30), a disclaimer that is meaningful only if it might reasonably have been assumed on the contrary that indeed "this" might well have been "the man."

I do not have any substantive quarrel with this familiar argument.[6] I have no new evidence that would confute it nor indeed any to confirm it. It seems certain that Shakespeare, in *1 Henry IV*, originally named his fat knight "Oldcastle" and under pressure changed it. The printing of the quarto in 1598 was perhaps demanded as proof of Shakespeare's willingness to respond to the concerns of the authorities.[7] Oldcastle thus disappeared from the printed texts of the play, though it is less certain that he disappeared in performance: Rowland White, for example, reports a production by the Lord Chamberlain's Men in March of 1600 for the Flemish ambassador, apparently at Lord Hunsdon's house, of a play referred to as *Sir John Old Castell*. Though some have thought this to be *The First Part of the True and Honorable History of the Life of Sir John Oldcastle* by Drayton, Hathaway, Munday, and Wilson, it is almost certainly Shakespeare's *1 Henry IV* rather than the play belonging to the Admiral's Men, which was unquestionably still in that company's possession (and so unavailable to the Lord Chamberlain's Men) at least as late as September 1602, when Henslowe paid Dekker ten shillings "for his adicions."[8]

Yet whatever play was performed for the ambassador, clearly the character we know as Falstaff was sometimes known as Oldcastle. In Nathan Field's *Amends for Ladies*, published in 1618, Seldon asks, obviously referring to Falstaff's catechizing of honor in act 5 of *1 Henry IV*: "Did you never see / The Play, where the fat knight hight *Old-Castlel*, / Did tell you truly what this honor was?" (sig. G1r). Presumably Field, for one, did see that play with "Falstaff's" catechism in Oldcastle's mouth, as seemingly did Jane Owen, who in 1634 similarly recalled "Syr Iohn Oldcastle, being exprobated of his Cowardlynes" and responding: "If through my persuyte of Honour, I shall fortune to loose an Arme, or a Leg in the wars, can Honour restore to me my lost Arme, or legge?"[9]

I am concerned here with what Oldcastle's elimination from and subsequent haunting of *1 Henry IV* means—both for a critic of the play interested in its religio-political valences in the late 1590s, and for an editor of the text, necessarily concerned with questions of composition and transmission. Gary Taylor, of course, has recently argued that at very least what this history means is that editions of *1 Henry IV* should return "Oldcastle" to the play, restoring "an important dimension of the character as first and freely conceived."[10] And notoriously the complete Oxford text does just that, although somewhat oddly the individual edition of *1 Henry IV* in The Oxford Shakespeare, edited by David Bevington, pointedly retains Falstaff's name, arguing sensibly that as Falstaff reappears in other plays, depending on familiarity with the name and character of the fat knight in *1 Henry IV*, he must be considered, as Bevington writes, "a fictional entity, requiring a single name. Since that name could no longer be 'Oldcastle', it had to be 'Falstaff', in *1 Henry IV* as in the later plays."[11]

I share Bevington's resistance to Taylor's provocative editorial decision (though for reasons somewhat different from Bevington's and on grounds that he might not accept), and hope that my argument here, which attempts to reconsider the historical circumstances, both ideological and textual, of the act of naming will lend it support. Nonetheless, Taylor's position has at least one solid stanchion. It cannot be denied that the name of Shakespeare's knight was initially "Oldcastle"; and therefore it may be helpful to consider that original act of naming. Critics who have commented on the "Oldcastle" name have usually focused on the perceived slight to the honor of the Cobham title and speculated either that Shakespeare intended an insult to William Brooke (usually, it is argued, because of Brooke's putative hostility to the theater);[12] or that Shakespeare intended no insult but unluckily chose his character's name, as Warburton argued in 1752: "I believe there was no malice in the matter. *Shakespear* wanted a droll name to his character, and never considered whom it belonged to."[13]

It seems to me unlikely that Shakespeare set out to mock or goad Lord Cobham, not least because, if the play was written, as most scholars assume, in late 1596 or early in 1597, Cobham, who became lord chamberlain in August 1596, was a dangerous man to offend; and no one has put forth any credible motive for the pragmatic Shakespeare to engage in such uncharacteristically imprudent behavior.[14] But Warburton's formulation can't be quite right either: that Shakespeare "*never* considered" to whom the name "Oldcastle" belonged. If the play does not use the fat knight to travesty the Elizabethan Lord Cobham, certainly it does use Sir John to travesty Cobham's medieval predecessor. Contemporaries seemed to have no doubt that Shakespeare's character referred to the Lollard knight. The authors of the 1599 *Sir John Oldcastle* consciously set out to correct the historical record Shakespeare had distorted: "It is no pampered glutton we present, / Nor aged Councellour to youthfull sinne, / But one whose vertue shone above the rest, / A Valiant Martyr, and a vertuous Peere" (prologue, 2.6–9). Thomas Fuller similarly lamented the travestying of the Lollard martyr by "Stage poets," and was pleased that "Sir John Falstaff hath relieved the memory of Sir John Oldcastle, and of late is substituted buffoon in his place."[15] George Daniel, in 1649, was another who saw through Shakespeare's fiction, like Fuller commending "The Worthy S^r whom Falstaffe's ill-us'd Name / Personates on the Stage, lest Scandall might / Creep backward & blott Martyr."[16]

If Shakespeare's fat knight, however named, is readily understood to "personate" the historical Oldcastle and "blott martyr," one might well ask what is at stake in his presentation as a "buffoon." Whatever Oldcastle was, he was hardly that.[17] Oldcastle had served the young Prince Henry in his Welsh command but had remained a relatively undistinguished Herefordshire knight until his marriage, his third, to Joan Cobham, the heiress of the estate of the third Baron Cobham. At last wiving wealthily, Oldcastle became an influential landowner with manors and considerable landholdings in five counties. He was assigned royal commissions and was called to sit in the House of Lords.

However, for all his newfound political respectability, Oldcastle remained theologically "unsound." Clearly he held heterodox views. He was widely understood to be a protector of heretical preachers, and was himself in communication with Bohemian Hussites and possibly sent Wycliffite literature to Prague. Perhaps inspired by the decision of the council at Rome early in 1413 to condemn Wycliffe's work as heretical and certainly encouraged by the newly crowned Henry V's need for ecclesiastical support, the English Church began vigorously to prosecute the Lollard heterodoxy, and Oldcastle himself was tried before Archbishop Arundel in September 1413 and declared a heretic. Oldcastle was, however, given forty days to recant his heresy, no doubt because of his long friendship with the king, and during this period of confinement he succeeded in escaping from the Tower. Following his escape, a rebellion was raised in his name and an attack on the king was planned for Twelfth Night. The king learned of the uprising and surprised and scattered the insurgent troops mustered at Ficket Field. Oldcastle fled and remained at large for three years, hiding in the Welsh marches. On 1 December 1417, news of his capture reached London. Oldcastle was carried to the capital, brought before parliament, indicted, and condemned. He was drawn through London to the newly erected gallows in St. Giles Field. Standing on the scaffold, Oldcastle, it was "popularly believed,"[18] promised that on the third day following his death he would rise again, whereupon he was hanged in chains and burned, as Francis

Thynne writes, "for the doctrine of wiclyffe and for treasone (as that age supposed)."[19]

Although it took considerably longer than three days, Oldcastle was finally resurrected. As the English Reformation sought a history, Oldcastle was rehabilitated and restored to prominence by a Protestant martyrology that found in his life and death the pattern of virtuous opposition to a corrupt clergy that underpinned the godly nation itself. Most powerfully in the five Elizabethan editions of Foxe's *Acts and Monuments* (1563–96), Oldcastle emerged, as Foxe writes, as one "so faithful and obedient to God, so submiss[ive] to his king, so sound in his doctrine, so constant in his cause, so afflicted for the truth, so ready and prepared for death" that he may "worthily be adorned with the title of martyr, which is in Greek as much as a witnessbearer."[20]

Foxe, however, must explain away the charge of treason if Oldcastle's life is to bear compelling witness to the truth of the emerging Protestant nation. For Oldcastle to serve not just as a martyr whose life testifies to the perpetual struggle of "the true doctrine of Christ's gospel" against the "proud proceedings of popish errors"[21] but also as the saving remnant on which the godly nation is built, his spiritual faith cannot be in conflict with his political loyalties. The heresy of his proto-Protestant Lollardy is easily dismissed by an emergent Protestant historiography but, since the Protestant cause in sixteenth-century England was inevitably tied to the monarchical claims of authority over the church, the charge of treason is less easily accommodated. Oldcastle's putative participation in a rebellion against the king puts at risk what Peter Lake has called "the Foxian synthesis" of "a view of the church centered on the Christian prince and one centered on the godly community."[22]

Foxe, of course, successfully locates Oldcastle within this synthesis. He erases the tension produced by the insurrection by erasing from the chronicle accounts Oldcastle's involvement in it.[23] Indeed the erasure is literal, though Edward Hall rather than Foxe is the agent. Foxe reports how Hall had echoed earlier chroniclers in writing of Oldcastle's conspiracy "against the king" and was preparing to publish his account, but, when a servant brought him "the book of John Bale, touching the story of the lord Cobham," which had "newly come over" from the continent, Hall, "within two nights after . . . rased and cancelled all that he had written before against sir John Oldcastle and his fellows."[24] For Foxe, the account of Hall's erasure of Oldcastle's treason is a conversion narrative that serves to guarantee Foxe's own debunking of the chronicle accounts of the Oldcastle rebellion.

Oldcastle's rebellion is finally for Foxe not an inconvenient fact but an outright invention of biased historians. He shows the inconsistencies and contradictions in the earlier accounts and concludes that it is merely "pretensed treason . . . falsely ascribed unto [Oldcastle] in his indictment, rising upon wrong suggestion and false surmise, and aggravated by rigour of words, rather than upon any ground of due probation." The invention, continues Foxe, is ideologically motivated, the charge rising "principally of his [i.e., Oldcastle's] religion, which first brought him in hatred of the bishops; the bishops brought him in hatred of the king; the hatred of the king brought him to his death and martyrdom."[25]

But even if Oldcastle is innocent of treason, Foxe still must inconveniently admit "the hatred of the king," thus exposing the fault line in a historiography that would appropriate Lollardy as the precursor of the national church. If Oldcastle is, as a Lollard, a martyr of the Protestant faith, he is, also, as one hated by the king, an uncomfortable hero of the Protestant nation. The unavoidable tension between Oldcastle's faith and royal authority makes impossible the identity of the True Church and the godly nation that Elizabethan England officially demanded.

Perhaps it is on this note that one can begin to assess the question of why it is that Shakespeare should ever have chosen to portray the historical Oldcastle as the irresponsible knight of his play. In 1752, an article in *Gentleman's Magazine*, signed only P. T., asked, "[C]ould *Shakespeare* make a pampered glutton, a debauched monster, of a noble personage, who stood foremost on the list of *English* reformers and Protestant martyrs, and that too at a time when reformation was the Queen's chief study? 'Tis absurd to suppose, 'tis impossible for any man to imagine."[26] P. T. undertakes to explain away the evidence that Falstaff ever was Oldcastle in Shakespeare's play, but since that evidence seems as incontrovertible as the evidence that Oldcastle, as P. T. says, "stood foremost on the list of *English* reformers and Protestant martyrs," one must assume that Shakespeare deliberately engaged in the very character assassination P. T. finds impossible to imagine.

Gary Taylor, committed to the original and the restored presence of Oldcastle in the play, has argued that Oldcastle's notoriety as a proto-Protestant hero is precisely that which demanded Shakespeare's travesty. John Speed, in *The Theatre of the Empire of Great Britaine* (1611), had objected to the presentation of Oldcastle as "a Ruffian, a Robber, and a Rebell" by the Jesuit Robert Parsons (writing as N. D.); he complained that Parson's evidence was "taken from the Stage-plaiers" and railed against "this Papist and his Poet, of like conscience for lies, the one euer faining, and the other euer falsifying the truth."[27] Marshaling evidence that purports to establish Shakespeare's sympathy to Catholic positions if not Shakespeare's commitment to the Catholic faith itself, Taylor, like Speed, takes the caricature of Oldcastle to suggest at very least Shakespeare's "willingness to exploit a point of view that many of his contemporaries would have regarded as 'papist.'" Noting other dramatic facts that admit of such an interpretation, Taylor concludes: "In such circumstances, the possibility that Shakespeare deliberately lampooned Oldcastle can hardly be denied."[28]

Certainly it can hardly be denied that Shakespeare has deliberately lampooned Oldcastle, but I think Taylor has somewhat misjudged the "circumstances" in which Shakespeare was writing and in which his play would be received. Whether or not Shakespeare was a Catholic or Catholic sympathizer,[29] Shakespeare's audience in 1596 or 1597 was far more likely to see the lampooning of Oldcastle as the mark of a Protestant bias rather than a papist one, providing evidence of the very fracture in the Protestant community that made the accommodation of the Lollard past so problematic. Lollardy increasingly had become identified not with the godly nation but with the more radical Puritans, the "godly brotherhood," as some termed themselves, that had tried and failed to achieve a "further reformation" of the Church of England. If in the first decades of Elizabeth's rule the Lollards were seen (with the encouragement of Foxe) as the precursors of the national church, in the last decades they were seen (with the encouragement of Bancroft and other voices of the Anglican polity) as the precursors of the nonconforming sectaries who threatened to undermine it.

No doubt recognizing that the radical Protestants were the inheritors of the doctrine and the discipline of the Lollards, as well as their reputation for sedition, John Hayward, in his *Life and Raigne of King Henrie IIII*, notes, as Daniel Woolf has observed, "with some regret the growth of Lollardy." The nonconformist community, the "favourers and followers of Wickliffes opinions," were consistently at odds with the crown, "which set the favour of the one and the faith of the other at great separation and distance." The political tensions existing at the end of Richard's reign and continuing through Henry's insure that Lollardy does not, in Hayward's history, comfortably anticipate the Protestant nation. "For Heyward," writes Woolf, "quite unlike John Foxe, Lollards were not early protestants but progenitors of Elizabethan Brownists, violators of the Reformation principle *cuius regio, eius religio*."[30]

But if Hayward recognized the nonconformist genealogy, he was not alone in doing so. In 1591, an almanac, written by a conforming astrologer identifying himself as "Adam Foulweather," predicted that "out of the old stock of heresies" would soon "bloom new schismatical opinions and strange sects, as Brownists, Barowists and such balductum devises, to the great hinderance to the unitie of the Church and confusion of the true faith."[31] And the separatist leader, Francis Johnson, writing defiantly from the Clink in 1593, himself confirmed his ties to "the old stock of heresies," proudly asserting that his opinions were identical to those that "were accounted

Lollardye and heresye in the holy servants and martirs of Christ in former ages," like "the Lord Cobham (who was hanged and burnte hanging)."[32]

Under the leadership of John Field (the father of Nathaniel Field, the author of *Amends for Ladies*), nonconforming Protestants had in the 1580s attempted the establishment of Presbyterianism by parliamentary authority, but by the mid-1590s, the government, led by Whitgift's rigorous promotion of uniformity and the queen's continuing insistence "upon the truth of the reformation which we have already,"[33] had succeeded in its campaign against the radicals. Christopher Hatton's appointment as lord chancellor, as Thomas Digges remembered, marked a change of policy whereby not merely papists but "puritans were trounced and traduced as troublers of the state,"[34] and by the early 1590s, radical Protestantism, conceived of by the government as a threat to the polity, was in retreat, at least as a political movement. The "seditious sectaries," as the 1593 "Act to retain the Queen's subjects in obedience"[35] termed the nonconformists, were driven underground or abroad; and advanced Protestantism, even as its evangelical impulse thrived, was, in its various sectarian forms, thoroughly "discredited," as Claire Cross has written, "as a viable alternative to the established Church in the eyes of most of the influential laity who still worked actively to advance a further reformation."[36] Whatever Shakespeare's own religious leanings, then, certainly most members of his audience in 1596 would most likely have viewed the travesty of a Lollard martyr not as a crypto-Catholic tactic but an entirely orthodox gesture, designed to reflect upon the nonconformity that the queen herself had termed "prejudicial to the religion established, to her crown, to her government, and to her subjects."[37]

Yet even if Taylor has mistaken the probable political implications of the lampooning of Oldcastle in 1596, what is for Taylor the more central bibliographical argument in favor of restoring the censored name "Oldcastle" to the text of *1 Henry IV* seemingly remains unaffected. Taylor argues that " the name 'Falstaff' fictionalizes, depoliticizes, secularizes, and in the process trivializes the play's most memorable character,"[38] and that argument would hold regardless of what the political valence of the suppressed "Oldcastle" actually is. Taylor's insistence that restoring "Oldcastle" effectively rehistoricizes the character of Sir John is compelling (even if I would rehistoricize it differently). What, however, is to me troubling about the editorial implications of this argument is that restoring "Oldcastle," if it rehistoricizes the character, effectively *de*-historicizes and in the process dematerializes the text in which he appears.[39]

Whether or not the travesty of Oldcastle would have shocked what Taylor calls "right-minded Protestants"[40]—and the answer clearly must depend upon what is understood to make a Protestant "right-minded"—whatever meanings attach to Shakespeare's fat knight, as Taylor's own argument shows, are not functions of an autonomous and self-contained text but are produced by the intersection of Shakespeare's text with something that lies outside it, a surrounding cultural text, what Roland Barthes calls "the volume of sociality,"[41] that the literary text both mediates and transforms. Yet if Taylor's critical response to the censored name "Oldcastle" ingeniously acknowledges the interdependency of the literary and social text, his reintroduction of "Oldcastle" to the printed text paradoxically works to deny it.

Taylor insists that we should restore the name "Oldcastle" to the play since the change "was forced upon Shakespeare" and the restoration allows us to return to "Shakespeare's original conception."[42] "Oldcastle" is what Shakespeare initially intended and, therefore, argues Taylor, what modern editions should print. "So far as I can see," Taylor writes, "the chief, indeed the *only* objection to restoring the original reading (Oldcastle) is that the substituted reading (Falstaff) has become famous."[43] But there is at least one other substantive objection to the restoration: that is, that all the authoritative texts print "Falstaff" and none prints "Oldcastle." "Oldcastle" may return us to "Shakespeare's original conception," but literally "Oldcastle" is not a "reading" at all.[44]

To disregard this fact is to idealize the activity of authorship, removing it from the social and material mediations that permit intentions to be realized in print and in performance. It is to remove the text from its own complicating historicity.[45] The restoration of "Oldcastle" enacts a fantasy of unmediated authorship paradoxically mediated by the Oxford edition itself. Taylor here privileges "what Shakespeare originally intended"[46] over the realized text that necessarily preserves multiple (and sometimes contradictory) intentions. While Taylor's commitment here to authorial intention is obviously not in itself an unknown or unproductive theoretical position,[47] what is undeniably odd about this particular exercise of it is that it seemingly rejects what is the central achievement of the Oxford Shakespeare, which differentiates itself from its predecessors by acknowledging the fact that dramatic production in Shakespeare's England was never an autonomous authorial achievement but a complex social and theatrical activity in which authorship was only one determinant. The Oxford Shakespeare is, in Taylor's words, "an edition conspicuously committed to the textual and critical implications of the recognition that Shakespeare was a theatre poet, whose work found its intended fruition only in the collaborative theatrical enterprise for which he wrote."[48]

Obviously Gary Taylor understands better than most editors that dramatic texts are produced by multiple collaborations, and the Oxford edition uniquely attempts to register these, presenting not "the literary, pretheatrical text" but a text as it appears "in the light of theatrical practice."[49] Yet what allows him in the case of the disputed name of Falstaff/Oldcastle to privilege Shakespeare's original intention over the operations of "the collaborative theatrical enterprise," the necessarily multiple and dispersed intentionalities of Renaissance playmaking, is Taylor's certainty that the change from "Oldcastle" in *1 Henry IV* was "forced upon" the playwright; that is, the replacement of "Oldcastle" is taken as evidence of an unsolicited and irresistible interference with the author's intentions rather than as a symptom of the inevitable compromise and accommodation that allow a play to reach the stage or the bookshop. For Taylor the issue is clear: "The change of name is not an instance of revision but of censorship."[50] And as an instance of censorship it is a "depredation" to be editorially undone.

Indeed, it does seem certain that Shakespeare originally intended to call his character "Oldcastle," and it seems equally obvious that Shakespeare was, in some fashion, compelled to change the name. But the necessary vagueness of that "in some fashion" suggests a problem with the appeal to intention. If Taylor is correct to say that we "know what Shakespeare originally intended," his secondary premise is more vulnerable: that we know "why that intention was abandoned."[51] In fact we do not. If it does seem clear that political pressure was applied, it is less so in what form it was exerted. Taylor speaks confidently of "the censor's intervention,"[52] but there is no record of any such action. It seems probable that Richard James's account is largely correct, that the Elizabethan Lord Cobham took "offence" at the travesty of a former holder of the title. But it is worth remembering that the scholarly James is writing well after the fact and with no obvious connection to any of the participants; and, although Nicholas Rowe's testimony is offered as "independent confirmation that the Cobhams were responsible" for the censorship,[53] Rowe is writing at even a further remove from the events, and Rowe, as we've seen, actually says not that the Cobhams but that "the Queen" commanded the alteration, suggesting another source of pressure and muddying our sense of the nature of the interference with Shakespeare's text.[54]

My point is not to deny that governmental authorities were unhappy with the parody of the Lollard martyr, Oldcastle, but only to indicate that the available evidence does not allow us to say precisely why "Oldcastle" disappeared from the text of *1 Henry IV*. An influential family seems unquestionably to have objected to the name "Oldcastle," but it is less certain that the elimination of that name was a result of the operations of a process we can confidently and precisely identify as censorship. This is not to split hairs but to move to the heart of the bibliographical argument. If we have an example of the external domination of authorship, any edition of *1 Henry IV* that was committed to the recovery of Shakespeare's artistic intentions might well introduce—though certainly not *re*introduce—"Oldcastle" into the printed text; although an edition, like Oxford's, that insists "that Shakespeare was a theatre poet" could plausibly, even in the case of such censorship, have found "Falstaff" to be the appropriate reading, since censorship was one of the inescapable conditions of a theater poet's professional existence.

But we do not in fact know that the replacement of "Oldcastle" with "Falstaff" was an effect of governmental imposition rather than an example of the inevitable, if arguably undesirable, compromises that authors make with and within the institutions of dramatic production. In the absence of documentation, we cannot tell whether we have a text marred by forces beyond the author's control or a text marked by the author's effort to function within the existing conditions in which plays were written and performed. It does seem certain that Lord Cobham objected to the scurrilous treatment of Oldcastle in the play, but we do not have the evidence that would tell us whether "Falstaff" is evidence of Shakespeare's subsequent loss of control over his text or of his effort to keep control of it; that is, we cannot be certain whether "Falstaff" resulted from the play's censorship or from its revision.

But the very uncertainty is as revealing as it is frustrating, suggesting that often no rigid distinction between the two can be maintained. Authority and authorship were usually not discrete and opposed sources of agency but instead were interdependent activities that helped constitute the drama in Elizabethan England.[55] No doubt some form of interference from above led Shakespeare to change Oldcastle's name to "Falstaff," but scrutiny and regulation were among the determining circumstances of playmaking no less than were boy actors in the theater or casting off copy in the printing house. Playwrights worked with and around censors to get their texts to the stage and into the shops. Finding what was acceptable to the censor was as necessary as finding out from the actors what played well. We cannot then say that "Falstaff" represents the "domination of the author's meaning."[56] "Falstaff" seems rather the evidence of the author's desire to have his meanings realized on stage and in print. Certainly the use of "Falstaff" in subsequent plays, suggests that Shakespeare, however happily, accepted the compromise of his artistic integrity, brilliantly incorporating it into his own intentionality.

Obviously we do not know what Shakespeare and his company thought about the change of name in *1 Henry IV*, but, claims Taylor, "the later intentions of Shakespeare and his company only matter in relation to a single question: would he (or they) have restored 'Oldcastle' to Part 1 if given the chance."[57] For Taylor the answer, of course, is "Yes," confirming his decision to print "Oldcastle" in the edited text of the play. The stage history that apparently shows *1 Henry IV* occasionally performed "with the original designation intact," even after *2 Henry IV, The Merry Wives of Windsor*, and *Henry V* were written with the character of Sir John named "Falstaff," serves for Taylor as evidence that Shakespeare or Shakespeare's company continued to imagine the fat knight of *1 Henry IV* as "Oldcastle."[58]

But the argument from the stage history is at best inconclusive. Even ignoring the fact that intentions other than those of Shakespeare or his company might determine the choice of name especially in a private performance, simply on the basis of the frequency of allusions to Falstaff in the seventeenth century (more than to any other Shakespearean character),[59] it seems clear that the play was far more frequently played with the new name in place than with the residual "Oldcastle." The popularity of the character known as Falstaff was virtually proverbial. Sir Thomas Palmer remarks Falstaff's ability to captivate an audience as one benchmark of theatrical renown: "*I could . . . tell how long* Falstaff *from cracking nuts hath kept the throng,*" he says in a prefatory poem to the 1647 Beaumont and Fletcher folio, to indicate a standard against which to measure the collaborators' putatively greater success.[60] And Leonard Digges writes: "When let but *Falstaffe* come / *Hall* [*sic*], *Poines*, the rest—you shall scarce have a roome / All is so pester'd."[61] Sir Henry Herbert's office-book registers Falstaff's impressive cultural currency, referring to the play itself, as performed by the King's men at Whitehall on "New-years night" of 1624–25, as *The First Part of Sir John Falstaff.*[62]

Nonetheless, a bibliographical argument against Taylor's claim that Shakespeare or at least his company continued to think of Sir John as "Oldcastle" seems finally more compelling even than the theatrical one: his friends and fellow sharers were in fact "given the chance" to restore the censored name and manifestly decided *not* to return Oldcastle to the play. With the decision to collect and publish Shakespeare's plays in a Folio edition, Heminges and Condell had the perfect opportunity to reinstate "Oldcastle." Indeed, they advertise the virtue of the 1623 Folio as repairing the defects of the earlier quartos, curing texts previously "maimed, and deformed" and printing them now "as he [i.e. Shakespeare] conceiued them."[63] At the time of the printing of the First Folio, no Cobham was around to enforce the change of name demanded by the tenth Lord Cobham's sensitivity in 1596: Henry Brooke, the eleventh Lord Cobham, had been found guilty of treason in 1603 for his activity in a plot to place Arabella Stuart on the throne, and he remained confined in the Tower until his death in 1619. The Cobham title then remained unfilled until 1645. Yet in 1623, with the Cobham title discredited and vacant, Heminges and Condell did not see the restoration of "Oldcastle" to the text of *1 Henry IV* as a necessary emendation to return the text to the uncontaminated form in which it was first "conceiued."

Taylor offers a conjectural argument that perhaps they "tried unsuccessfully" to reinstate the "Oldcastle" name: "The delay in printing Folio *Henry IV* could easily have risen because of an attempt to secure permission from the new Master of the Revels . . . to restore the original surname." Taylor, however, is forced to concede: "If Heminges and Condell did attempt to restore 'Oldcastle', they obviously failed. . . ." Yet in the absence of any evidence that they in fact did try to restore the name or any that they were likely to have failed had they so tried, it is hard to resist the all too obvious conclusion that Taylor strenuously works to avoid: "that Heminges and Condell, as Shakespeare's literary executors, were happy enough to perpetuate 'Falstaff' in *Part 1*."[64] But so it seems they were. With no obvious impediment to reinstating "Oldcastle," Heminges and Condell retained the name "Falstaff," providing evidence not of Shakespeare's original intention, no doubt, but of the complex interplay of authorial and nonauthorial intentions that allowed *1 Henry IV* to be produced (indeed that allows any text to be produced), providing evidence, that is, that the play is not autonomous and self-defined but maddeningly alive in and to the world. "Falstaff" is the mark of the play's existence in history, and, perhaps in their most telling bibliographical decision Heminges and Condell wisely left his "rejection" to Hal.[65]

NOTES

1. Samuel Schoenbaum, *William Shakespeare: A Documentary Life* (Oxford: Oxford University Press, 1975), 143. James's account appears in the dedicatory epistle to his manuscript edition of Thomas Hoccleve's "The legend and defence of ye Noble knight and Martyr Sir Jhon Oldcastel" (Bodleian Library, MS James 34). The epistle was first published in 1841 by James Orchard Halliwell [-Phillipps], and the entire manuscript was printed in *The Poems Etc., of Richard James, B.D.*, ed. Alexander B. Grosart (London: Chiswick Press, 1880). In his "William Shakespeare, Richard James and the House of Cobham," *RES*, n.s., 38 (1987): 334–54, Gary Taylor dates the manuscript in "late 1633 or early 1634" (341).

2. Following the *DNB*, most commentators identify William Brooke and his son Henry as the seventh and eighth Lords Cobham, but see *The Complete Peerage of England, Scotland, and Ireland*, by G .E. C[ockayne], rev. ed., ed. Vicary Gibbs, vol. 3 (London: St. Catherine Press, 1913), 341–51, where they are identified as the tenth and eleventh holders. See also the genealogical tables in David McKeen, *A Memory of Honour: The Life of William Brooke. Lord Cobham*, vol. 2 (Salzburg, Austria: Universität Salzburg, 1986), 700–702.

3. Nicholas Rowe, "Some Account of the Life, &c. of Mr. William Shakespear," in *The Works of Mr. William Shakespeare*, vol. 1 (London: Jacob Tonson, 1709), ix.

4. In his "Revision in Shakespeare's Plays," in *Editing and Editors: A Retrospect*, ed. Richard Landon (New York: AMS Press, 1988), 72, Stanley Wells says that this is "the only verse line in which [Falstaff's] name occurs" and notes that it "is restored to a decasyllable if 'Oldcastle' is substituted for 'Falstaff.'" But it is worth observing that at least in the early editions this is not "a verse line" at all. The line appears as verse only

following Pope. In all the early quartos, as well as in the Folio, the line appears in a prose passage. In "'This is not the man': On Calling Falstaff Falstaff," *Analytical and Enumerative Bibliography*, n.s., 4 (1990): 59–71, Thomas A. Pendleton contests the assertion that the missing syllable argues for a merely perfunctory revision, pointing out how metrically rough the entire section is (and recognizing that it is printed as prose in the earliest editions), and how many simple ways there are to regularize the line if one only sought to substitute "Falstaff" for "Oldcastle" (62–63).

5. The text's "Old." could, however, stand for "Old man" ("I know thee not, old man") rather than "Oldcastle."

6. There has, of course, been much discussion of the name change, most notably Gary Taylor's "The Fortunes of Oldcastle," *Shakespeare Survey* 38 (1985): 85–100; idem, "William Shakespeare, Richard James and the House of Cobham" *RES*, n.s., 38 (1987): 334–54; E. A. J. Honigmann, "Sir John Oldcastle: Shakespeare's Martyr," in "*Fanned and Winnowed Opinions*," ed. John W. Mahon and Thomas A. Pendleton (London: Methuen, 1987), 118–32; Pendleton, "'This is not the man'"; Jonathan Goldberg, "The Commodity of Names: 'Falstaff' and 'Oldcastle' in *1 Henry IV*," in *Reconfiguring the Renaissance: Essays in Critical Materialism*, ed. Jonathan Crewe (Lewisburg, Pa.: Bucknell University Press, 1992), 76–88; and Eric Sams, "Oldcastle and the Oxford Shakespeare," *N&Q*, n.s., 40 (1993): 180–85. See also Rudolph Fiehler, "How Oldcastle Became Falstaff," *MLQ* 16 (1955): 16–28; and Alice-Lyle Scoufus, *Shakespeare's Typological Satire: A Study of the Falstaff-Oldcastle Problem* (Athens: University of Ohio Press, 1978).

7. See E. K. Chambers, *William Shakespeare: A Study of Facts and Problems*, vol. 1 (Oxford: Oxford University Press, 1930), 382, though it is perhaps worth noting that *The Famous Victories of Henry the Fifth*, in which Oldcastle appears, was published by Thomas Creede also in 1598.

8. See *Henslowe's Diary*, ed. R. A. Foakes and R. T. Rickert (Cambridge: Cambridge University Press, 1961), 216. Gary Taylor (in "Fortunes," 90) has similarly suggested that the performance for the ambassador (reported in a letter of 8 March 1599/1600 to Robert Sydney, in *Letters and Memorials of State*, ed. Arthur Collins, vol. 2 [London, 1746], 175) must be Shakespeare's play, but Eric Sams ("Oldcastle and the Oxford Shakespeare") has, energetically, if not entirely convincingly, argued that "there is no objective reason to suppose that the text was not copied, or borrowed, or indeed commandeered, by the court company, the Lord Chamberlain's men" (182).

9. The reference from Jane Owen's *An Antidote Against Purgatory* (1634) is reported by R. W. F. Martin, "A Catholic Oldcastle," *N&Q*, n.s., 40 (1993): 185–86.

10. Stanley Wells et al., *William Shakespeare: A Textual Companion* (Oxford: Clarendon Press, 1987), 330. John Jowett has argued, on somewhat similar grounds, that Peto and Bardolph were names "introduced at the same time as Falstaff," and that their original names, Harvey and Russell (present in Q1 at 1.2.158), like Falstaff's, should be restored in modern editions. See his "The Thieves in *1 Henry IV*," *RES* 38 (1987): 325–33.

11. *1 Henry IV*, ed. David Bevington (Oxford: Oxford University Press, 1987), 108.

12. See, for example, J. Dover Wilson, "The Origin and Development of Shakespeare's *Henry IV*," *The Library*, 4th ser., 26 (1945–46): 1–16 (13), who argues that Cobham was "a man puritanically inclined and inimical to the theatre." See also E. K. Chambers, *The Elizabethan Stage* (Oxford: Clarendon Press, 1923), 1:297. William Green, however, in *Shakespeare's "Merry Wives of Windsor"* (Princeton: Princeton University Press, 1962), has demonstrated that during Cobham's term as lord chamberlain "not one piece of legislation hostile to the theater was enacted" and, in fact, between 1592 and his death in 1597, Lord Cobham "was absent from every meeting of the Council at which a restraining piece of theatrical legislation was passed" (113–14).

13. *The Works of Shakespear*, ed. William Warburton, vol. 4 (1747), 103.

14. See Robert J. Fehrenbach, "'When Lord Cobham and Edmund Tilney were att odds': Oldcastle, Falstaff, and the Date of *1 Henry IV*," *Shakespeare Studies* 18 (1986): 87–101. But see also Honigmann, "Sir John Oldcastle," who argues that the play was intended "to annoy the Cobhams" and "to amuse Essex" (127–28), and suggests that the play "was written—or at least begun" in the first half of 1596 "before Lord Cobham became Lord Chamberlain" (122).

15. Thomas Fuller, *The Church History of Britain* (London, 1655), bk. 4, 168.

16. George Daniel, *Trinarchodia*, in *The Poems of George Daniel, esq. of Beswick, Yorkshire*, ed. Alexander B. Grosart, vol. 4 (privately printed, 1878), 112.

17. The best account of the life of Oldcastle is still W. T. Waugh's "Sir John Oldcastle," *English Historical Review* 20 (1905): 434–56, 637–58. See also the entry on Oldcastle in the *DNB* written by James Tait. The following paragraphs are indebted to both.

18. See *DNB*, s.v. "Oldcastle, Sir John." Stow, in his *Annales of England* (1592), reports that "the last words that he spake, was to sir Thomas of Erpingham, adjuring him, that if he saw him rise from death to life again, the third day, he would procure that his sect might be in peace and quiet" (572).

19. Quoted in McKeen, *Memory of Honour*, 1:22. Thynne's "treatise of the lord Cobhams" was written to honor Lord Cobham's admission to the Privy Council on 2 February 1586 for inclusion in the 1586/7 edition of Holinshed's *Chronicles*, but was excised from the edition along with other parts that touched on contemporary political events. Thynne presented an elegant manuscript version (British Museum MS Add. 37666) to William's son, Henry, in December 1598. See David Carlson, "The Writings and Manuscript Collections of the Elizabethan Alchemist, Antiquary, and Herald Francis Thynne," *HLQ* 52 (1989): 203–72, esp. 210–11, 235–36.

20. John Foxe, *Acts and Monuments*, ed. Josiah Pratt, in *The Church Historians of England* (London: Seeleys, 1855), 3:350.

21. Ibid., 2:265.

22. Lake, "Presbyterianism, the Idea of a National Church and the Argument from Divine Right," in *Protestantism and the National Church in Sixteenth-Century England*, ed. Peter Lake and Maria Dowling (London: Croom Helm, 1987), 193–224 (195).

23. Annabel Patterson has kindly shared with me a draft of a forthcoming essay, "'All Affections Set Apart': Sir John Oldcastle as Symbol of Reformation Historiography," that more extensively treats much of this material. Patterson's interest in the story of Oldcastle, however, is less for its implications for understanding developments in English Protestantism than for understanding the development of Renaissance historiography.

24. Foxe, *Acts and Monuments,* 3:377–78.

25. Ibid., 3:543.

26. P. T., "Observations on Shakespeare's Falstaff," *Gentleman's Magazine* 22 (October 1752), 459–61. Rudolph Fiehler, in "How Oldcastle Became Falstaff," has suggested that it is "not inconceivable" that P. T. was actually William Warburton (19).

27. John Speed, *The Theatre of the Empire of Great Britaine* (1611), 637.

28. Taylor, "Fortunes," 99.

29. I remain unpersuaded that Shakespeare was a Catholic, though for a recent argument making a provocative case for a "Catholic Shakespeare" (126), see E. A. J. Honigmann, *Shakespeare: The "Lost Years"* (Manchester: Manchester University Press, 1985).

30. D. R. Woolf, *The Idea of History in Early Stuart England* (Toronto: University of Toronto Press, 1990), 109. The two parts of Hayward's *Life and Raigne of King Henrie IIII* have recently been published by the Camden Society, ed. John J. Manning (London: Royal Historical Society, 1991), and the quoted material is on 90–91. For an account of the association of Lollards with sedition, see Margaret Aston, "Lollardy and Sedition 1381–1431," *Past and Present* 17 (1960): 1–44.

31. Quoted in John Booty, "Tumult in Cheapside: The Hacket Conspiracy," *Historical Magazine of the Protestant Episcopal Church* 42 (1973): 293.

32. "That Fraunces Johnson For His Writing Is Not Under The Danger Of The Statute Of 35 Elizabeth, Chapter I . . . ," in *The Writings of John Greenwood and Henry Barrow*, ed. Leland H. Carlson (London: George Allen and Unwin, 1970), 463. An incomplete version of the document (Lansdowne MSS. 75, item 25, fols. 52–53) appears in John Strype, *Annals of the Reformation*, vol. 4 (Oxford: Clarendon Press, 1824), 192–94.

33. See J. E. Neale, *Elizabeth I and her Parliaments, 1584–1601* (New York: Norton, 1966), esp. 58–83; and Patrick Collinson, "John Field and Elizabethan Puritanism," in *Godly People: Essays on English Protestantism and Puritanism* (London: Hambledon Press, 1983), 335–70. The quotation from Elizabeth appears in Neale, *Elizabeth I and her Parliaments*, 163.

34. Quoted in Patrick Collinson, *The Elizabethan Puritan Movement* (1967; reprint, Oxford: Clarendon Press, 1990), 388.

35. 35 Eliz. c. 1; in J. R. Tanner, *Tudor Constitutional Documents* (1922; reprint, Cambridge: Cambridge University Press, 1951), 197–200. Neale sees the harsh turn against the Protestant sectaries, equating schism with sedition, "as a revolution in parliamentary policy" accomplished by Whitgift and his party. See *Elizabeth I and her Parliaments*, 280–97.

36. Claire, Cross, *Church and People, 1450–1660: The Triumph of the Laity in the English Church* (Glasgow: Fontana, 1976), 152. Nonetheless, if "further reformation of the Church of England was, for the moment, out of the question," we must recognize what Patrick Collinson has called "the paradox that the miscarriage of the further reformation coincided with the birth of the great age of puritan religious experience" (Collinson, *Elizabethan Puritan Movement*, 433).

37. Quoted in Neale, *Elizabeth I and her Parliaments*, 2:163.

38. Taylor, "Fortunes," 95.

39. Jonathan Goldberg, in his essay in *Reconfiguring the Renaissance* (see n. 6), similarly argues that the restoration of the name "Oldcastle" works to "remove the traces of the history that produced the earliest texts of *1 Henry IV*" (83).

40. Taylor, "Fortunes," 97.

41. Roland Barthes, "The Theory of the Text," in *Untying the Text: A Post-Structural Reader*, ed. Robert Young (Boston and London: Routledge, 1981): 31–47 (39).

42. Taylor, "Fortunes," 88.

43. Ibid., 89; my emphasis.

44. In this regard it is notably different from the expurgation of profanity in the Folio text. The uncensored forms exist in the 1598 quarto as readings that can be *restored*.

45. James Thorpe, in a seminal essay, "The Aesthetics of Textual Criticism," *PMLA* 80 (1965): 465–82, argued that in every work of art "the intentions of the person we call the author . . . become entangled with the intentions of all the others who have a stake in the outcome." Jerome J. McGann offers perhaps the most influential and sustained account of the literary text as a "social product," first in *A Critique of Modern Textual Criticism* (Chicago: University of Chicago Press, 1983) and most recently in his *The Textual Condition* (Princeton: Princeton University Press, 1991). See, however, the essay by G. Thomas Tanselle, "Historicism and Critical Editing," *SB* 39 (1986): 1–46, esp. 20–27.

46. Taylor, "Fortunes," 90.

47. See G. Thomas Tanselle, "The Editorial Problem of Final Authorial Intention," *SB* 32 (1979): 309–54.

48. Gary Taylor and John Jowett, *Shakespeare Reshaped: 1606–1623* (Oxford: Clarendon Press, 1993), 237.

49. Gary Taylor, *Reinventing Shakespeare: A Cultural History from the Restoration to the Present* (New York: Weidenfeld & Nicolson, 1989), 311.

50. Taylor, "Fortunes," 88.

51. Ibid., 90.

52. Ibid., 85.

53. Ibid., 87.

54. It is worth wondering about how much weight to attach to Rowe's "confirmation." Rowe follows Richard Davies in recording the apocryphal story about Shakespeare's "frequent practice of Deer-stealing" in "a Park that belong'd to Sir *Thomas Lucy* of *Cherlecot*"; and the very passage that comments on the alteration of the name of "Oldcastle" includes the probably fanciful account, derived from John Dennis, of Queen Elizabeth's delight with the "Character of Falstaff" and her order to Shakespeare to write "one Play more, and to shew him in Love" ("Some Account of the Life," v, viii–ix).

55. in "Buc and the Censorship of *Sir John van Olden Barnavelt* in 1619," *RES*, n.s., 39 (1988): 39–63 (43), T. H. Howard-Hill has claimed, for example, that Tilney's "relationship with the players although ultimately authoritarian was more collegial than adversarial." For a full account of the mechanisms of censorship, see Richard Dutton, *Mastering the Revels: The Regulation and Censorship of English Renaissance Drama* (Iowa City: University of Iowa Press, 1991). See also Annabel Patterson, *Censorship and Interpretation: The Conditions of Writing and Reading in Early Modern England* (Madison: University of Wisconsin Press, 1984), who, while less interested in the processes of control than in its effects, sees the necessity for "assuming some degree of cooperation and understanding on the part of the authorities themselves" (11); and Janet Clare, *"Art made tongue-tied by authority": Elizabethan and Jacobean Dramatic Censorship* (Manchester: Manchester University Press, 1990), who similarly understands that censorship "is perhaps the most potent external force which interacts with the creative consciousness" (215).

56. Taylor, "Fortunes," 92.

57. Ibid., 90.

58. Ibid., 91.

59. Gerald Bentley writes: "Falstaff was clearly most famous of all the characters of Shakespeare and Jonson in the seventeenth century. This fact ought to surprise no reader familiar with the literature of the time, but the overwhelming dominance of his position has perhaps not been so obvious" (*Shakespeare and Jonson: Their Reputations in the Seventeenth Century Compared*, vol. 1 [1945; reprint, Chicago and London: University of Chicago Press, 1969], 119; see also 120 and 126).

60. Thomas Palmer, "Master John Fletcher his dramaticall Workes now at last printed," in *Comedies and Tragedies, written by Francis Beaumont and John Fletcher, Gentlemen* (London, 1647), sig. f2V.

61. Digges, "Upon Master William Shakespeare, the Deceased Authour, and his Poems," in *Poems, written by Wil. Shake-speare, Gent.* (London, 1640), Sig.*4r.

62. Joseph Quincy Adams, ed., The *Dramatic Records of Sir Henry Herbert, 1623–1673* (New Haven: Yale University Press, 1917), 52. That this was not an entirely anomalous practice is revealed by a notation on a scrap of paper from the Revels Office that has been dated ca. 1619: "nd part of Falstaff. . ." See Bentley, *Shakespeare and Jonson*, 2:1.

63. "To the great Variety of Readers," in *The Norton Facsimile: The First Folio of Shakespeare*, ed. Charlton Hinman (New York: Norton, 1968), 7.

64. Taylor, "Fortunes," 92.

65. A version of this paper was delivered at the Shakespeare divisional meeting at the MLA in 1991. 1 would like to thank John Austin, David Bevington, Margaret Ferguson, Donna Hamilton, Peter Lake, Jesse Lander, Annabel Patterson, Steven Pincus, Phyllis Rackin, Jim Shapiro, Richard Strier, and, especially, G. Thomas Tanselle for comments, criticism, and encouragement on that occasion or subsequently that have helped me in the development of this essay.

Part IV:
Readings

11

Character Identifications in Two Folio Plays: *Coriolanus* and *All's Well*: A Theater Perspective

CHARLES B. LOWER

Shakespeare's naming of characters in *Coriolanus* and *All's Well that Ends Well* is only a little patch of ground in any comprehensive appreciation of either play, but I hope, with much preparation, to suggest ways in which that naming is worth more than an eggshell to critics and editors.

When I say "Shakespeare's naming," do not misunderstand: the "text" now is convincingly understood as "problematized,"[1] and no one today can—or should—have the naive faith that the authorial intent is an achievable goal of textual studies: neither is it achievable nor is it now really the goal. Yet one cannot employ this understanding in the everyday world, for it would effectively stop all editing of Shakespeare . . . and all reading of Shakespeare except of the original quartos and First Folio. However fraught with uncertainties, to read and to discuss critically "Shakespeare" necessitates some, hopefully not arbitrary, starting point, *a* text. The Folio texts of *Coriolanus* and *All's Well* reflect some one moment in the transitory, volatile (and largely unknowable) history of the collaborative effort from playwright to theater company and its ever-changing, never stable script from one performance to the next, from first performance to another year's revival, each likely slightly different both by design and by accident. The Folio text of these plays provides us with our only access to this ephemeral process. The pure principle of a "problematized" text would permit only its own perpetual reiteration; one must act—read, criticize, edit—using the Folio's unique preservation of a moment of these two playtexts.

My commitment is to *an* early-seventeenth-century public-theater performance of *Coriolanus* and of *All's Well*, to understanding features of what is so largely unreconstructible because, like all performance (before film documentation), it is ephemeral. But we must not throw out the baby with the bathwater: that the whole of an original performance is irrecoverable should not mean ignoring what residual evidence the printed Folio text offers of features of that performance. The one feature I propose considering can stand untainted by the vast vacuum of information about the totality of such a stage production. We can and do know the spoken English likely *heard* by some early-seventeenth-century audience, as represented in the 1623 Folio. I begin with this hard fact.[2] Any full-fledged commitment to Shakespeare's theatricality, to "What the text makes the actors make the audience do," should, I think, include investigation of Shakespeare's character identifications.[3]

The hard "facts" of the Folio naming in *Coriolanus* and *All's Well* are already familiar, yet I find justification for examining them in how often published criticism ignores them. My concern is simple and, I would add, obvious except that I have found only occasional awareness and use of it: *only what's in the dialogue matters*. The rubrics—the pre-performance instructions—of stage directions, speech prefixes, and dramatis personae lists are not part of the auditory experience of a theater audience.

So who—or what—are the characters in *Coriolanus* and *All's Well*? what are their "names"? what information does an audience have for identifying the stage characters? In the early-seventeenth-century public theater, the theater audience had, of course, no access to what is so familiar and inescapable to us as readers today—a list of characters, stage directions, and speech prefixes that, insofar as possible in editorial tradition and practice, use as specific and exact a name as possible for almost all characters.

These two Folio plays involve some problematic evidence, so I begin by revisiting a 1967 article of mine that concentrates on some of the clearest-cut instances of Shakespeare not providing a single dialogue use of a major character's name, so at odds with his usual practice that it points to intentionality, dramatic purpose.[4]

Fundamentally, my concerns are these: precisely how does a theater audience know, for example, that "he's Hamlet," "she's Countess of Rossillion," or "he's Malvolio"? And when do generic visual considerations of a characterization, briefly or infrequently alluded to in the dialogue, serve as part of the audience's *continual* visual impression of that character? That is, what generic visual considerations, such as the youthfulness of Arthur in *King John*, the deformity of Richard III, or the Moorness of Othello (rather than the unique features of a single production, such as brocade, blue, and actor's build)[5] supplement—or substitute for—an audience's appellative recognition of a character? Editors regularize character identification in the rubrics of a text (in the stage directions and speech prefixes); consequently, we as readers tend to identify characters by (merely) names. But my two questions suggest that no such uniformity exists in the experience of a theater audience. Note the credits at the end of almost any movie: minor roles are identified generically, the likes of "bartender," "clerk," "paperboy," "policeman at switchboard." Likewise in Shakespeare, sometimes the theatrical identification of a character is something more— and sometimes less—than "a name."

Costume, incidental dialogue references, and the dramatic situation sometimes provide indications of theatrical type, such as "clownish" or "malcontent," which would continually and forcefully be part of the audience's visual experience. But such considerations provide identification only in terms of social status, vocation, dramatic function, or theatrical type. Essentially three other means cooperate to provide the individualizing of *a name*, and the bulk of evidence from Shakespeare's plays points, I think, to his scrupulous care in naming much of the time.[6] First, a person's name can appear in the dialogue at or near his first entrance, either in announcement ("Here comes Signior Claudio") or direct address ("That thou, Iago . . ."). Secondly, dialogue references prior to a character's entrance can create anticipation, so that the audience immediately associates a character on entrance with the earlier use of his name: for example, Montague, Lady Montague, and Benvolio's discussion in the first scene centers on the yet unseen "Romeo." And thirdly, the title of a play, together with costuming (and repertory casting practices), may provide an audience with individualized identification (as with identifying "King Lear" in the play's opening scene).

Generally, Shakespeare presents prominently and frequently the name of a major character within the dialogue. The name "Romeo" is known first from the title; the discussion of his whereabouts and condition prior to his first entrance is introduced by "O, where is Romeo"; "See, where he comes" breaks up this discussion at his entrance. Romeo's name appears naturally and frequently, at least eighty times, in the conversation of the play. Macbeth's name is mentioned prior to his entrance—by the witches, the bleeding soldier, and King Duncan. Almost immediately upon his first entrance, Macbeth is identified by his name, which, by then, contains much anticipated interest.[7] In the dialogue of *Much Ado*, "Claudio" appears more than fifty times, and "Benedick," "Hero," and "Beatrice" appear about forty times each.

On the other hand, very minor and supernumerary roles are not usually individualized with names. The identity of such characters, coming through costuming, grouping in relationship to major characters, and manner of participation in the narrative action of major characters, is exclusively in terms of social status *(a lord),* vocation *(a soldier),* dramatic function *(a messenger)*, and relationship to a major character *(his servant)*. Usually in such instances a name does not appear in the dialogue; but, even when it does, its lack of prominence and frequency makes it an incidental feature of the conversation and situation of the stage personage rather than the means by which an audience identifies him or her. For example, the stage direction *Enter a Roman and a Volsce* in *Coriolanus* 4.3 accurately reflects the theatrical experience of a "mirror" or "choric" scene with two anonymous characters narratively unrelated to the events of the primary story— even though the names "Adrian" and "Nicanor" appear once each in the dialogue of the scene. Here a reader provided with the rubrics "A Roman" and "A Volsce" will likely find less trouble, more clarity dramatically.

Editions in their stage directions and speech prefixes have frequently been misleading because they have preserved or added names that are not theatrically memorable and significant for minor characters (as in the two choric figures in *Coriolanus*) and for the unusual major characters like the Prince in *Romeo,* where "Escalus" is never used in the dialogue and thus is never heard by an audience. In performance, he is this play's (nameless) "prince." Similarly, critics in their discussions have frequently misled because they have given prominence to a character name unknown to a theater audience. The opening scenes of *Measure for Measure* present fifteen or sixteen characters, almost invariably identified in modern editions as Vincentio the Duke, Angelo, Escalus, Lucio, Mistress Overdone, Pompey, Claudio, the Provost, Juliet, Isabella—all appearing frequently in the play— and two gentlemen, officers, Friar Thomas, and Francisca a nun. In modern editions we get all these names first in the dramatis personae list preceding 1.1.[8] But how would these various characters be identified by a theater audience? That is, what appellative identifications are contained within the dramatic dialogue of the first act? Unquestionably, "Angelo" and "Claudio" are memorable names in the theater: the dialogue contains sixty-one instances of "Angelo" and forty-three instances of "Claudio," including the prominent devices of anticipation, announcement, and direct address. But the dialogue in the first four scenes does not provide an instance of the names "Mistress Overdone," "Pompey," "Friar Thomas," or "Francisca." Thus, theatrically, these do not exist as *named characters*. Rather, we have—using the terminology of the Folio speech prefixes—a *Bawd*, a *Clown*, a *Friar*, and a *Nun;* probably immediately recognized by costuming, this foursome's dramatic significance resides in social status, vocation, and association with conventional theatrical types.

More surprisingly the name "Vincentio" never occurs in the dialogue; our only knowledge of this name comes in the Folio's list of "The names of all the Actors" at the end of the playtext; the Duke's significance resides in *what* rather than *who* he is. A theater audience doesn't—can't—know of a

"Vincentio." Do not critics using "Duke Vincentio" and "Vincentio," as they frequently do, distort by introducing a nuance of both familiarity and intimacy that in performance the nameless Duke doesn't have?

A detour into the *Hamlet* playtext may clarify what's at stake. *Hamlet* offers a struggle between "mighty opposites" in which "'Tis dangerous when the baser nature" of not only a Rosencrantz and a Guildenstern but also a Polonius "comes between." The titular Hamlet is one mighty opposite. From beginning to end a theater audience hears his name, at least seventy-five times, thirty-four as direct address, ten times as "Lord Hamlet." The other mighty opposite is Hamlet's uncle (and his new stepfather), the new husband of Hamlet's mother, the reigning king.

Period. The all too familiar "Cl——" word, a personal name used for Hamlet's "mighty opposite," does not appear even once in the dialogue of Q1, Q2, or F. However attentive to, or even desirous of, a personal name for Hamlet's adversary, no audience member would hear such a name.

Not surprisingly, Polonius, Rosencrantz, and Guildenstern never address the king with a (his) proper name. Their formality serves as a nuanced fillip in characterizing their unctuous sycophancy. Hamlet's antagonism exists from before his first appearance; he is a youth out of sorts with the man whom his mother marries, the man he does not wish to acknowledge as stepfather, so Hamlet's never addressing him with a proper name is consistent with larger matters within the dramatic world. But what of the husband-wife relationship within that world? The new husband addresses his new wife as "Gertrude" a dozen times. But she does not reciprocate. Given the abundance of other characters using names in direct address as a "realistic" feature of the play and given these uses of "Gertrude," isn't it for the audience a conspicuous silence from the Queen, this "Gertrude," that she never replies in direct address with a name for *him?*

Whatever it may suggest to us about their relationship, I suggest that her silence—added to the absence of any other dialogue use, even a nonce use, of a proper name—must suggest that Shakespeare deliberately didn't give the play's other "mighty opposite" a proper name. A number of critics have noted the absence of "Cl——" from the dialogue, but as if it were a mere curiosity—because each uses "Cl——" elsewhere in the very criticism that notes this absence.[9] But it needs to be more than a curiosity. If no one ever in the playworld speaks to the king by name and no one ever in the playworld outside of his (intimidating?) presence refers to him with a personal name, a theater audience can't give him a name.

Over the years, I've refused even once to use "Cl——" in my classroom teaching. Once I played the "game" silently, pointing to my practice only on an exam problem; most often I make some ado about it, attempting to sell a class on Shakespeare's withholding that information from his early-seventeenth-century audience as something we all should honor. I had students who listened to my distinction; it wasn't unusual to have a student interrupt himself or herself, "Cl——, no I mean the King." This past term, never. Why not? Surely, it was my choice of G. R. Hibbard's Oxford University Press edition, in which all the speech prefixes are "Cl——." I stood nakedly alone, at odds with my students' reading experience. The Oxford Shakespeare counsels its editors on speech prefixes: "In general, personal names are preferred to generic ones." That guideline, which Hibbard follows in introducing "Cl——" speech prefixes, creates "a significant divergence between the reader's apprehension of that character and the spectator's."[10]

Critics of *Hamlet* are too abundant in their use of "Cl——" to admonish or to seek to reform. But, by comparison, editors of *Hamlet* are few in number, so I'll preach to future editors: a Shakespeare edition, in the imperfect mode of only printed words, should seek accord with the aural and visual experience of a theater audience, and in *Hamlet* the speech prefix *King* fosters this accord.

Shakespeare's audience could gain familiarity with character names from dialogue alone—and Shakespeare was sufficiently the theater professional to know that. So, with likely purposefulness, an audience never learns the names of the Prince in *Romeo and Juliet*, of the two soldiers opening *Antony and Cleopatra*, nor of a number of Scottish lords in *Macbeth*. Shakespeare's dialogue contains not even a single use of "Escalus," "Demetrius," "Philo," "Angus," "Caithness," and "Lennox." *Our* familiarity with these names results exclusively from stage directions and speech prefixes. And an audience hears "Hamlet" repeatedly but never a name for his adversary: to a theater audience, he's Hamlet's uncle and, with the emphasis of costuming and stage grouping, *the King*.

With this preparation, we're ready to examine the complexity in naming found in *Coriolanus* and *All's Well*. Prior to entering, Caius Martius is named in *Coriolanus* 1.1 as the nub of the citizens' dispute; when first entering, he is identified by name. "Martius" occurs five times in the final eleven lines of 1.1. Shakespeare batters his audience with the protagonist's name, thirty instances prior to his gaining the approbation "Coriolanus." But four major characters in *Coriolanus*—Sicinius Velutus, Junius Brutus, Volumnia, and Virgilia—receive surprisingly untypical treatment.

Names for the tribunes appear in only two passages, and these in performance do not—cannot—associate characters with names, names with characters; they will not serve for an audience's recognition of a "Sicinius Velutus" and a "Junius Brutus." The reference in 1.1, Martius's

> Five tribunes to defend their vulgar wisdoms,
> Of their own choice. One's Junius Brutus,
> Sicinius Velutus, and I know not. 'Sdeath,

> The rabble should have first unroofed the City
> Ere so prevail'd with me!

is neither direct address nor an instance of "look-where-he-comes" identifying; the two names are passing specifics drowned by what's louder and clearer, Martius's personal and patrician invective, disgust.[11] No tribune has yet appeared, so this naming isn't sufficiently prominent to foreshadow; nor is it sufficiently prominent to use subsequently to yoke with entering characters, especially when no use of names accompanies the tribunes' first appearance, at 1.1.222. Even their end-of-scene duologue includes no "natural" direct address. This "name" silence surely points to a purposeful namelessness.

The only other dialogue use of the names, in 3.1, has a moment of direct address:

> *They all bustle about Coriolanus.*
>
> ALL
>   Tribunes!—Patricians!—Citizens!—What ho! Sicinius!—Brutus!—
>   Coriolanus!—Citizens! Peace!—Peace!—Peace!—Stay!—Hold!—
>   Peace!
> MENENIUS
>   What is about to be?—I am out of breath.—
>   Confusion's near.—I cannot speak.—You tribunes,
>   To th'people!—Coriolanus, patience!—
>   Speak, good Sicinius.
> SICINIUS
>   Hear me, people, peace!
>
> (3.1.186.1–193)

But association with specific characters isn't likely, for the "Sicinius!—Brutus!" occurs amidst multiple-voiced shouting—the stage situation less orderly than the sequential printed script.[12] Menenius's direct address gets a response, "Sicinius" speaking a line next. In that moment it offers character identification, but its singularity surely makes it seem merely local and transitory. Furthermore, 3.1 is too late: an audience has had (necessarily) to identify the tribunes as a pair in generic terms in 1.1, 2.1, and 2.2.

Dramatic situation after situation has invited a name, yet "Speak, good Sicinius" in 3.1 is the only clear instance. The recurring appellations are "tribunes of the people" and "Masters o' th' people." This aural identification accords with and reinforces our larger experience. In eight scenes the two enter and exit together. Names (and characterization) fail to distinguish between the two. They are a single political force, "the tribunes." Criticism giving prominence to "Brutus" and "Sicinius" deceives by failing to stress the generic. Shakespeare's unusual practice in avoiding memorable,

identifying naming of the two (together with a chariness in dialogue naming of the various Patricians) reinforces what criticism recognizes, that
Coriolanus exists within a political context—citizens an anonymous rabble,
Patricians (to a considerable degree) a corporate dramatic being, and two
Tribunes inseparable and indistinguishable one from the other. The editorial tradition of the speech prefixes *Sicinius* and *Brutus* throughout offers
yet again only "a significant divergence between the reader's apprehension
of [these two characters] and the spectator's." How much better would be
First Tribune and *Second Tribune* throughout (including even at the reply
to Menenius's "Speak, good Sicinius").

"Virgilia" and "Volumnia," prominent in stage directions and speech
prefixes of the Folio (and throughout *Coriolanus* criticism), are names found
in the play's dialogue only once each: "Prithee, Virgilia, turn thy solemness
out o' door, and go along with us" (1.3.110), and "This Volumnia / Is worth
of consuls, senators, patricians, / A city full" (5.4.52–54). Such isolated,
incidental references will not serve for memorable, certain audience char-
acter-identifying. Because the nonce use of "Virgilia" comes during her
first appearance, there's a good possibility of a name-seeking audience
member noting it, albeit after most of the scene has been experienced without
it, but there are no name references in her subsequent scenes to reinforce
this once. Contrasted against so many characters for whom Shakespeare
hammers home a name, this one use of "Virgilia" seems slim support for
believing a name her central identification. The singular use of "Volumnia"
in 5.4 may well have the local significance of the sort Anne Barton argues
for—an audience appreciating her now having earned a name from her
successful efforts in Rome's behalf in 5.3. But any such strikingness is a
local 5.4 effect, an effect depending on her generic/relational identity as
Coriolanus's mother theretofore. A reader today gains (or misses) such an
effect from the "This Volumnia . . ." encomium in 5.4 only after experiencing an editing that does not anticipate (and thereby destroy) that effect
through speech prefix and stage direction use of "Volumnia" consistently
from 1.3 onward.

Anne Barton is a rarity in recognizing this singular dialogue use and
then finding it critically significant. But she is, I believe, wrong in arguing
that this 5.4 moment argues against the use of *Coriolanus's Mother*, or
Mother in speech prefixes and stage directions. After only a single example
(that of Timon's steward, where she finds the Riverside speech prefix
"Flavius" based on a nonce dialogue-naming "novelistic" tampering),
Barton moves to the limits of what play readers "can be asked to tolerate—
or imagine," citing as good editing decisions the speech prefixes "VIOLA"
in *Twelfth Night* and "VOLUMNIA" in *Coriolanus,* even though "these
personal names are held back in the dialogue until late in Act V" and "In

neither case does the long delay in their release look accidental" (that is, Shakespeare deliberately withheld the names from his theater audience). But Barton offers only unexplained (and, I think, unconvincing) certitude when she claims that

> to have tried to duplicate on the printed page the theatrical effect of such belated revelations would have been to run the risk of misinterpretation: of imposing a false suggestion of type upon characters for whom, unlike those of *The Noble Gentlemen*, it would be inappropriate.[13]

Would the speech prefixes *Coriolanus's Mother* misrepresent the character, distort a reader's experience (then akin to a playgoer's)? Is there any suggestion of "type" here? (There would be in *Patrician Lady*, and there would be a reader's likely confusion about her relationship to Caius Martius, but the temptation Barton suggests an editor might have is "Mother"). Two pages earlier Barton notes that "Namelessness need not . . . emphasize the generic over the individual," and cites two *All's Well* characters who are never given proper names in the dialogue: "[B]oth the self-willed and stubborn King and the remarkably individual Countess . . . are nameless without being in the least 'types.'"[14] Barton does not object—cannot, of course— to an editor's generic speech prefixes with them. I can see no reason why *Coriolanus's Mother* would restrict a reader's individualizing "her" through the play any more than with *King (of France)* and *Countess (of Rossillion)*. And *Coriolanus's Mother* does not widen the distance between reader's and playgoer's experiences.[15] "Brutus," "Sicinius," "Volumnia," and "Virgilia" are meaningful specifics in historical narrative, in North's Plutarch. But criticism and editions that use these four names misrepresent Shakespeare's design for the theater experience.

Turning from *Coriolanus* to *All's Well* brings more complex, and more subtle, problems in evaluating the dialogue's use of character names—but it also brings an able predecessor who has done so much of the work beautifully, Susan Snyder, in "Naming Names in *All's Well that Ends Well*."[16] Her opening page is eloquent in setting out the issue as she chafes at the guidelines to Oxford Shakespeare editors to prefer "personal names . . . to generic ones" in speech prefixes. Her discussions of "Rinaldo" and "Lavatch" I can only wish to second. Her ultimate concern is a large interpretive matter, expressed in her final paragraph:

> The names of Helen and Diana, then, are suggestive about larger currents and issues of *All's Well*. Mythically resonant and variously underlined in dialogue, they will be highlighted all the more for the reader as well as the viewer if character names of minimum importance are not featured in the text.[17]

Because this interpretive concern so dominates, Snyder slights, with but selective attention, the dialogue use of names for Bertram, his mother the Countess, and even Helen: only with these three names is there room for anyone walking in Snyder's footsteps.

All's Well, conforming to a general Shakespearean pattern, names its major characters and identifies many minor characters only generically— *soldiers*, "divers young Lords," *attendants*—as background credibility for military and court moments.[18] Snyder rightly proposes adding to these generic characters a Clown and a Steward: the single dialogue instance of "Lavatch" (late, 5.2, after an audience has experienced him nameless in 1.3, 2.2, 2.4, 3.2, and 4.5) and two instances of "Rinaldo" in his second (and last) appearance, 3.4, do not justify the speech prefixes *Lavatch* and *Rinaldo*. The stage direction at the beginning of 3.5 identifies a "Violenta" and a "Mariana," but a theater audience hears neither name. *Who* these two are (only one with even a bit of dialogue in the scene) matters not; as many have noted, there's a gender bond, a strength in numbers, with the focus exclusively on "Diana."

If editing continues to add a dramatis personae before the playtext, that for *All's Well* should have fewer named characters:

> *A Steward and a Fool, servants to the Countess of Rossillion*

(rather than, as in the Riverside, "RINALDO, a steward" and "LAVATCH, a clown"; this change also avoids the servants' contrast with "PAGE" and "GENTLEMAN, an astringer," the pair immediately following in the Riverside).

> *Diana, of Florence*
> *Her widowed mother*
> *Two women neighbors and friends of Diana's mother*

(rather than, as in the Riverside, "An old WIDOW of Florence," "DIANA, daughter to the Widow," and "VIOLENTA and MARIANA, neighbors and friends to the Widow").[19]

No major character in *All's Well* comes to a theater audience in the way the tribunes, Coriolanus' wife, and his mother are experienced in a performance of *Coriolanus*. Shakespeare lets a theater audience hear the names "Bertram," "Helen," and "Parolles"—and memorably so. But—and the starting point for possibly fruitful exploration—these names are *not* heard frequently. There is a striking paucity of dialogue naming in *All's Well*— Parolles's name only thirteen times, "Helena" once, "Helen" sixteen times, and "Bertram" only eight times.

All's Well is, of course, centrally the "story" of Helen and Bertram, and the early uses of their names make those appellative identifications memorable play-long: they *are* "Helen" and "Bertram."[20] But the evidence of published criticism suggests that most of us read a playtext indiscriminately, drawing upon dialogue, speech prefixes and stage directions, and editorially supplied dramatis personae, so the infrequent dialogue presence of "Helen" and "Bertram" seems unnoticed and deserves some foregrounding.

Five of the eight uses of "Bertram" in the play's dialogue are in the opening two scenes:

> (1) *Countess.* Be thou blest, Bertram, and succeed thy father
> In manners, as in shape,
>
> (1.1.61–62)
>
> (2) *Countess.* Heaven bless him [the sick king]. Farewell, Bertram,
>
> (1.1.74)

as her last line before exiting; (3 and 4) in Helen's first soliloquy, 1.1.75ff.:

> I have forgot him [my father]. My imagination
> Carries no favour in't but Bertram's.
> I am undone; there is no living, none,
> If Bertram be away.

(5) in the formulaic "Look who's there" at his entrance to the King of France in 1.2.17–19):

> *King.*   What's he comes here?
>   *Enter Bertram, Lafew, and Parolles.*
> *1 Lord.*   It is the Count Rossillion, my good lord,
>   Young Bertram.

These five uses of "Bertram" are early, prominent, memorable—sufficient to identify this character by name (through the rest of a performance). This identifying is similar to that of many major characters in Shakespeare. What's unusual with "Bertram" is that the name occurs but three times in the rest of the play. It is heard twice at the plot-important moment of Helen's choice of husband:

> *Helen.*   . . . This is the man.
> *King.*   Why then, young Bertram, take her; she's thy wife.
> *Bertram.* My wife, my liege? I shall beseech your highness,
>   In such a business give me leave to use
>   The help of mine own eyes.

> *King.*   Know'st thou not, Bertram,
> What she has done for me?
>
> (2.3.105–110)

The king's conjoined "young"—the same association of name and attribute heard in the "look who's there" identifying formula in 1.2—is invitingly conspicuous. Snyder has already commented astutely on this association, adding those instances of mere youthfulness without the name:

> The achievement of independent manhood proves no easier at court [1.2, 2.1, and 2.3] with his substitute parent than at home with the real one [1.1]. The King first forbids Bertram to go to the Italian wars ("Too young . . ." and "'tis too early") [2.1.28] and then commands him to marry Helen, marking parental care and authority here with his repeated "Bertram" as the Countess did earlier. When Bertram rejects Helen, both King and Countess call him "boy"—"Proud, scornful boy" (2.3.152), "rash and unbridled boy" (3.2.28)— reinforcing the sense of wayward youth already generated by their early emphatic use of Bertram's Christian name.[21]

The only other use of "Bertram" in the entire play is his signature on the letter to his mother, read by her in 3.2.26 ("Your unfortunate son, Bertram").

Not unlike the "Bertram" usage, Helen's first two appearances in the play, in 1.1 and 1.3, provide over half—nine of the seventeen—dialogue instances of "Helen/Helena" in the play. Six times "Helen" occurs as direct address; the other three occurrences are in the context of her being sent for to speak with Bertram's mother (1.3), all prior to the Steward's "she love[s] your son." These nine are more than enough, in their strategic positioning, to make an audience's character identification play-long be appellative, as "Helen."

After 1.3 (after Helen has left Bertram's mother, has set out for Paris), there's a paucity of dialogue uses of "Helen." Five of the remaining eight instances of the name occur in the play's final scene (which is without a single use of Bertram's name)—once by Lafew, the other four by the King (all concerned with either Helen's presumed death or identifying the King's ring). Therefore, between 1.3 and 5.3 a theater audience experiencing the Folio playtext hears "Helen" but three times:

(1) In 2.2 the Fool ("Lavatch") and Countess engage in fifty-five lines of banter at the scene's beginning, then:

> *Countess.* An end, sir! To your business: give Helen this,
> And urge her to a present answer back.
>
> (2.2.59–60)

With the abrupt change of topic the pronoun "her" would have puzzled; certain identification was needed, and "Helen" is the most direct and natural.

(2) In 2.3.45 the entrance of the King, cured, able "to lead her a coranto," is met with—and verbally highlighted by—Parolles's "Mort du vinaigre! Is not this Helen?"

(3) Bertram uses her name in direct address in his leaving for the wars: "You must not marvel, Helen, at my course" (2.5.58).

An audience recognizes the play's mating pair as "Bertram" and "Helen" from the forceful dialogue use of the names in the opening scene, "Helen" amply reinforced in 1.3, "Bertram" in the "here comes" formula in 2.1. If Shakespeare's appellative usage were typical, the names would appear thirty times or more, scattered throughout the play. But both these names (except for "Helen" in the final scene) almost disappear after 2.1. Helen never speaks to Bertram as "Bertram" in direct address, and Bertram never uses "Helen" outside her presence and only once in direct address (perhaps a lapse, a careless anomaly?). Readers may not notice, since the eyes see both names frequently in stage directions and speech prefixes. But an early seventeenth-century theatergoer's ears would, and in consequence would sense the impersonality of many dramatic moments.

For example, in 2.1 Helen introduces herself to the King with "Gerard de Narbon was my father" (99). She does not volunteer her own name, nor does the King inquire what it is; his direct address to her is "maiden" and "kind maid." This scene has 210 lines; it contains only one appellative, "Parolles," a part of the Lords' leave-taking. In "Shakespeare," it is difficult to find any sequential two hundred lines devoid of appellatives. Here Helen's credentials (her father's identity) and not her unique personhood matter to the moment, to the King, to the risk of an attempt to cure; the impersonality lends a nuance to the heightened "ritual" dimension of the moment, adds a nuance of preparation for the mysteriousness, even miraculousness, often assigned critically to Helen's curing the King.

In 2.3 the cured king enters—in startling contrast to his earlier appearances; most modern productions and most critics see the visual of this entrance governed by Lafew's "Why, he's able to lead her a coranto." This spectacular moment is delayed and thus anticipated in the first thirty-five lines of talk of "miracles" and "great transcendence." That visual surprise is punctuated (two lines later) with Parolles's "Is not this Helen?" to Lafew and, more importantly, to an audience. Yet the King continues to use "Fair maid," not her name, in direct address to the character we know to be Helen, and she introduces herself to the various Lords she rejects as husband-choice with

I am a simple maid, and therein wealthiest
That I protest I simply am a maid,

(67–68)

without supplying to them her name. After she has selected Bertram, and after the King's "Why then, young Bertram, take her; she's thy wife" (106), Bertram never uses her name—not in his protests, not in his eventually forced taking of her hand. This appellative silence is a fact of the Folio text viewed as a theater event; it is available as a tidbit grist for mill for any critic, especially I would think one emphasizing Bertram as a callow youth or as a social snob.

Neither does the King use "Helen" anywhere in 2.3 (or elsewhere). His uninterrupted twenty-eight-line persuasion speech countering Bertram's "A poor physician's daughter my wife?" (116) begins "'Tis only title thou disdain'st in her" and contains only the pronouns *she* and *her*: for example, "She is young, wise, fair" and "Virtue and she / Is her own dower." Such is the fact of the Folio text experienced as audible theater event; it is a fact worth recognizing and dealing with critically. How does it augment or nudge ajar your own reading of this moment? It's often observed that *All's Well* inverts the comic formula of *senex* as "blocking" figure providing obstacles to young love; Bertram's mother, Lafew, and the King—all the "old folk" of the play—are advocates of Helen's married-love agenda, the "blocking" figure being instead Bertram himself. Whereas Bertram's mother offers female bonding supportiveness, treating Helen as a daughter and happily anticipated daughter-in-law, the King's advocacy is "beyond" the personal, the uniqueness signaled in a proper name: *what* Helen represents and embodies is his valuation of her.

My sense from much published *All's Well* criticism is that many readers have been inured by the omnipresence of names in stage directions, speech prefixes, and previous criticism to fail to find remarkable a moment such as this one between Bertram and Parolles in 2.5:

> *Bertram [to Parolles].* Is she gone to the king?
> *Parolles.* She is.
> *Bertram.* Will she away to-night?
> *Parolles.* As you'll have her.
> *Bertram.* I have writ my letters, casketed my treasure,
> Given order for our horses; and to-night,
> When I should take possession of the bride,
> End ere I do begin—
>
> (2.5.20–27)

She thrice, *her*, and the *bride*—the referent perfectly clear to us—yet to the ear experiencing only dialogue, there's conspicuousness in the absence of the antecedent noun—the name—for the pronouns. This dialogue prepares us well for the oft-appreciated "Here comes my clog" at Helen's entrance twenty-five lines later. Then comes the singular play-long use of Helen's name from Bertram's mouth ("You must not marvel, Helen, at my course"), but it is followed by a formal description of a husband's obligations presented by this Bertram as "a business" only. The significance of "Helen" here is not, of course, fact but a matter of interpretation. I would, however, be surprised if many readers found it personalizing or respectful of the personhood of Helen, particularly when heard in the context of Bertram's never having used her name before, either to or about her.

In 2.5 Helen is deferential toward Bertram: she three times uses "Sir" in direct address to Bertram, twice "my lord," and never his name. But this absence is not restricted to their leave-taking; in her important thirty-one-line soliloquy that ends 3.2, Helen refers to him as "Rossillion" (twice) and "my lord" but never as "Bertram." Should a critic embrace her man more familiarly than Helen herself does?

Everyone but his mother and the King (and the First Lord in reply to the King in 1.2) speaks of "Count Rossillion."[22] For example, in 3.5, the introduction of *old Widow of Florence, her Daughter, Violenta, and Mariana*, we find only titles—"the French count" and "this French earl"—and pronouns in the warnings to the daughter Diana. Helen enters as religious pilgrim, and in response to "Here you shall see a countryman of yours / That has done worthy service," she asks, "His name, I pray you?" Diana answers with the title, "The Count Rossillion." The anonymous Frenchmen in 3.6 speak to Bertram with "my lord" and "your lordship" repeatedly, a dozen times. In 4.2 Diana speaks to Bertram as "my lord." 4.3 begins with a Lord asking "You have not given him his mother's letter?" and continues with frequent pronoun references until, after the subject of the settlement of wars, there's "Count Rossillion" when a pronoun would be muddling for an audience. Bertram's entrance is accompanied by "Here's his lordship now" and direct address "my lord" and "your lordship."

I have been leading up to a question each interpreter of the play must weigh on sensitive scales, for there is no bold, obvious answer. The play is replete with "lord" and "lordship" addresses to Bertram, and in 1.2 when the King asks "What's he who comes here?" the answer is "It is the Count Rossillion, my good lord, Young Bertram." "Rossillion" is heard thirteen times in the play. In ten of those it is "(the) Count Rossillion," and twice in her 3.2 soliloquy Helen speaks of "Rossillion." Only once, from the Gentleman/Astringer in 5.1, answering Helen's question of the whereabouts of the King ("Rossillion"), is the word not Bertram's title. To respect the theater experience of *Measure for Measure*, a critic should speak of "The Duke" and not "Vincentio" or even "Duke Vincentio." In *All's Well* an audience experiences Bertram as "Bertram"—from his mother and the King. But more often—twelve times over against eight—and acutely so in the latter portions of the play, he is "Count Rossillion." Thus, criticism is empowered by the playtext to use both "Bertram" and "Count Rossillion." I've glanced back through a dozen articles and find that they consistently, invariably use "Bertram"—even when the critical emphasis falls on social-rank disparity between Helen and him, where the connotations of "Count Rossillion" would provide the appropriate flavoring. Criticism usually finds this male a rather cold fish, yet consistently criticism uses "Bertram," which implies intimacy, familiarity. I wonder if this usage isn't (largely) a regrettable instance of criticism's inertia. And is "Bertram" a tiny signal of a critic's desire to gain ascendance over the play, to control?

Let me briefly suggest a related revision in nomenclature. While stage directions and speech prefixes (including those of the Folio) refer to "Countess" and "Countess of Rossillion," her social ranking would come to a theater audience visually, with costuming, and not verbally: the title "Countess" is never heard in performance. Costuming is an ephemeral feature of an early-seventeenth-century public-theater play (beyond deductions and speculations from pictures, Henslowe, and occasional stage directions), but it is worth asking whether stage costuming would go beyond a generic "aristocrat" or "nobility" to the precision of *Countess*. The *words* of the play deal with her role—the mother-son relationship. Might criticism better reflect the play by speaking of her as *Bertram's mother* and/or *Count Rossillion's mother?*

Most editions offer their readers a number of generic functionaries at the end of the dramatis personae list. In the Riverside we find "LORDS, OFFICERS, SOLDIERS, *etc., French and Florentine*"; in Bevington's edition, *"Lords, Attendants, Soldiers, Citizens."* But a reader is offered a deceptively indiscriminate picture when earlier the listing has with equal "billing" noted King of France, Bertram, Parolles, Rinaldo, Lavatch, Page, Helena, Diana, Violenta, Mariana. An audience's auditory experience of the Folio text would include among the generic functionaries a Page, a Steward, a Clown or Fool, and women accompanying Diana and her mother. A dramatis personae for *All's Well*, of editorial origin, exists to assist a reader. If an edition today continues to use this convention, its list should provide a reader with an accurate reflection of the relative prominence of the play's various characters and of the play's variety in prominence in appellative identification. The use of "Rinaldo, Lavatch, Violenta, and Mariana" distorts.[23]

A reader's experience of the playscript is, consciously or unconsciously, partly fashioned from speech prefixes (and names in stage directions). But attention solely to dialogue—a theater perspective—will, I think, suggest a rather different hierarchy, different emphases, and raise questions about how we should think and talk about even the major characters. Shakespeare wrote plays, wrote for performance. Should not a popular edition reflect that fact as accurately as the printed word can and as fully as reasonable certainty about such performance permits in its apparatus (dramatis personae lists) and its rubrics (speech prefixes and stage directions)? Should not criticism, whatever its ilk, reflect the precritical basics of who's who, what names, in some approximation of what some early-seventeenth-century public-theater audience heard and saw? Examination of the Folio texts of *Coriolanus* and *All's Well* offers, I think, some salutory building blocks that suggest we have room to improve our appellative identifications in editing and in "doing" criticism about these two plays.

NOTES

1. This view is now rather commonplace; for a pure instance (that, significantly, does not seek to answer the practical problems of how one now edits), see Stephen Orgel, "What is a Text?" in *Staging the Renaissance: Reinterpretations of Elizabethan and Jacobean Drama*, ed. David Scott Kastan and Peter Stallybrass (London: Routledge, 1991), 83–87. In various ways, the familiar work of such scholars as Michael Warren and Randall McLeod represents those who seek the "unediting" of Shakespeare, "a radical stripping away of editorial encrustation, for a reliance instead upon photographic facsimiles of the earliest extant texts" (citation from Gary Taylor, "The Renaissance and the End of Editing," in *Palimpsest*, ed. George Bornstein and Ralph G. Williams [Ann Arbor: University of Michigan Press, 1993], 123). See, for example, McLeod, "UnEditing Shakspeare," *Sub-Stance* 33/4 (1982): 28–55. In this essay, I seek considerable editorial intervention—but intervention grounded in, more faithful to, the 1623 Folio.

2. This is, of course, problematized a bit by compositor studies, but such concerns do not impact on the dialogue presence or absence of particular names.

3. The quotation comes from J. L. Styan, *The Elements of Drama* (Cambridge: Cambridge University Press, 1960), 2.

4. "Character Identification in the Theatre: Some Principles and Some Examples," in *Renaissance Papers 1967* (Durham, N.C..: Southeastern Renaissance Conference, 1968), 57–68.

5. On costume see G. K. Hunter, "Flatcaps and Bluecoats," *Essays and Studies*, n.s., 33 (1980): 16–47. I am grateful to A. R. Braunmuller for calling my attention to this reference.

6. Harry Levin offers a delightful potpourri of Shakespeare's pleasures in naming ("Shakespeare's Nomenclature," in *Shakespeare and the Revolution of the Times* [1965; reprint, Oxford: Clarendon Press, 1976], 51–77). Anne Barton is among those who highlight the counterbalance of Shakespeare's occasional indifference to naming. For example, "Although his comedies are dotted with inspired coinages . . . , for the most part he seeks out neutral praenomens regularly employed by other dramatists of the time, and reuses

them across a range of plays. There are, for instance, four comic characters in Shakespeare named 'Sebastian,' four 'Balthazar,' two 'Ferdinand,' four 'Helen,' two 'Claudio,' two 'Angelo,' three 'Katherine' and no fewer than seven 'Antonio'" (*The Names of Comedy* [Toronto: University of Toronto Press, 1990], 96).

7. A. R. Braunmuller points out (personal communication) that Macbeth is not identified by name for ten lines after the actor's appearance on stage, possibly leading the audience to ponder "which actor is Macbeth, which Banquo?"

8. Since E. K. Chambers and W. W. Greg, little attention has been given to dramatis personae lists; exceptions are E. A. J. Honigmann and Randall McLeod. Honigmann examines the Folio "dramatis personae" lists in *The Stability of Shakespeare's Text* (Lincoln: University of Nebraska Press, 1965), 44–46. Writing as Random Cloud, McLeod criticizes the editorial tradition of "inflicting" such lists on plays: "These editorial lists have now become as sacrosanct as the very body of Shakespeare's playtext" ("'The very names of the Persons': Editing and the Invention of Dramatick Character," in Kastan and Stallybrass, eds., *Staging the Renaissance*, 95).

9. For example, early in his *To Be and Not to Be: Negation and Metadrama in "Hamlet"* (New York: University of Columbia Press, 1983), 8–9, James Calderwood notes that the king's single name "does not exist in any performance," is not spoken in the play's dialogue. Yet throughout subsequent chapters of this book about *Hamlet*, Calderwood uses "Cl——" frequently, uninfluenced by his own second chapter, "Names and Identities." The only *Hamlet* study I recall using "the king" exclusively is Martin Holmes, *The Guns of Elsinore* (London: Chatto and Windus, 1964).

10. Susan Snyder, "Naming Names in *All's Well that Ends Well,*" *SQ* 43 (1992): 265–79 (265). I quote the Oxford guideline from 265.

11. I cite *Coriolanus*, ed. R. B. Parker, The Oxford Shakespeare (Oxford: Clarendon Press, 1994), 1.1.212–16.

12. Editors in the twentieth century have generally assigned the two lines following the stage direction to ALL; in the Folio, they are without a speech prefix, implying a continuation of the line from the Second Senator preceding the stage direction. See E. A. J. Honigmann, "Re-enter the Stage Direction: Shakespeare and Some Contemporaries," *Shakespeare Survey* 29 (1976): 120–22, for a convincing discussion of the speech prefix *All* as multiple-voiced and contrapuntal rather than, as in the appearance of the printed text, sequential. R. B. Parker's note on this passage is "The following three lines must be divided amongst the various groups on stage, taking care not to separate them too clearly into two camps because, not only are the Senators divided into those calling for weapons and those trying to make peace, but Plutarch says some of the Citizens also favoured restraint. . . . The effect must be of confusion, not polarization," p. 256.

13. Barton, *Names of Comedy*, 95. Barton is commendable in resisting in general the editorial goal of proper names. She agrees with L. A. Beaurline's criticism of previous editors in the "gradual shift" from generic to proper names in *The Noble Gentleman*. In endorsing Beaurline, Barton sees the pre-Beaurline shift as "a reminder of how persistently readers . . . have wanted to resist an anonymity which, in the theatre, rarely seems troubling" (94), citing Beaurline's textual introduction to *The Noble Gentleman* in *The Dramatic Works in the Beaumont and Fletcher Canon*, ed. Fredson Bowers, vol. 3 (Cambridge: Cambridge University Press, 1976), 11–20. Here I think Barton's "readers" misleads, since most "readers" have the given of an edited text; it is *editors* who have resisted anonymity.

14. Barton, *Names of Comedy*, 93.

15. I have some discomfort in pursuing this issue further, since Barton's subject is, as expressed in her title, the names of comedy. *Coriolanus* is peripheral for her, yet I must suggest that evaluation of her dismissal of *Mother* needs consideration of "Virgilia," a naming she does not mention. Curiously, Barton's final discussion of the dialogue use of "Viola"

as being purposefully withheld until 5.1.241—where it then, for her, has the force of "restorative: returning the anonymous 'lady,' the pretended 'Cesario,' to her family, her social identity, and estate" (138)—has no mention of the dilemma for an editor in selecting speech prefixes for *Twelfth Night*.

16. See note 10. In effect, I have moved a step backward, concentrating on the preliminaries on which Snyder is building a particular critical discussion. I remain precriticism, essentially. I don't engage in possible critical avenues such as Snyder's "There is [at 2.3.276–80] a kind of pre-Freudian economy of libido operating here." Snyder rather too quickly concentrates on the complexity of the conflict of goddesses, the allusions to chastity and desire—a far piece from "naming."

On the other hand, precriticism Snyder puts forth some telling blows against "editorial inertia" in both suggesting that editors should reject "Lavatch" for Clown just as they have rejected "Angelica" in favor of Nurse in *Romeo and Juliet* and noting that even the Oxford editors don't add "Capilet" to "Widow" for Diana's mother, since its singular appearance— the last name signed on the petition presented to the king in the play's final scene—is a "purely local purpose."

17. Snyder, "Naming Names," 279.

18. There has been a robust number of attempts to solve the business of "the brothers Dumain" (and?) "The French Lords" in the Folio speech prefixes. None, I think, has been fully convincing. Whoever and however many these characters are, they are background and generic characters, and the dialogue use of "Dumain" is purely local.

19. I agree with the criticism of dramatis personae lists expressed by McLeod in "'The very names'": "Edition after edition suggests that editors do not read Shakespeare's text afresh to compile such lists. No, they read and crib them from other editors, in a tradition that stems from Pope's appropriation of Rowe" (96). Though this editorial convention has little historical justification, and none for its front-end location, McLeod's mocking is extreme: "Why editors should inflict dramatis-personae lists on plays, and not novellae-personae lists on novels or sonnetae-personae lists on sonnet sequences, is not clear to me." The model is, as it has been, subsequent theater history: readers of Shakespeare attending most theater events receive a programme with a cast list. The editorial dramatis personae list is not in itself a "novelistic intrusion." But contemporary programme lists might have a salutary influence on editors, since usually the programmes make restrictive use of names for dramatic characters—with extensive use of the generic, parallel to the closing credits in films. *If* useful in advance for a reader, such a list should reflect the play's restricted number of major parts. A "Rinaldo" or a "Mariana" misleads.

In an otherwise interesting and appreciative study called *Bit Parts in Shakespeare's Plays* (Cambridge: Cambridge University Press, 1992), M. M. Mahood pushes in the wrong direction about dramatis personae lists when she suggests that their concluding with "Lords, Gentlemen, Attendants, Citizens, Messengers, Soldiers . . . may indicate that the editor has been unable to decide how many of these generically named characters there are or to establish where one bit part ends and another begins" (8). A reader's or a playgoer's local appreciation of a bit part does not warrant its inclusion in a thorough dramatis personae list.

20. My choice of "Helen" is the clear choice of the dialogue. Yet criticism (and editing) is replete with "Helena." Snyder's Oxford edition (Oxford: Clarendon Press, 1993) deserves commendations for its use of "Helen."

21. Snyder, "Naming Names," 271.

22. Snyder notes that the dialogue use of "Bertram" belongs "mainly to his mother and to the King." But she suggests, I think misleadingly, that the play's decided preference is for name over against title: "With Bertram, whose name Shakespeare adapted from Boccaccio's Beltramo, the significance is not so much in the name as in the prominence of its use. He could have gone by his title, and indeed he is 'Count' or 'Rossillion' at times in

stage directions and speech prefixes and in dialogue. But at several points in the text and even more frequently in stage directions and speech prefixes, he is designated by his Christian name. It is understandable, of course, that Helen in her doting attachment should use his personal name, and that a play primarily about mating rather than war or politics should stress this individual aspect rather than the more public one implied by his title" (270–71). Snyder then pursues the emphasis on Bertram's youthfulness quoted (and endorsed) above. But Snyder seems to give dialogue and rubrics equal weight, exaggerates Helen's use of "Bertram," and ignores the frequency of dialogue references to "Lord" that reinforce the twelve dialogue references to the play's young protagonist as "Rossillion."

23. The dialogue use of the names Parolles and Lafew deserves brief mention. "Parolles" is heard thirteen times in the Folio dialogue, including direct address twice in 1.1, both as "Monsieur Parolles." It occurs three other times, and six times he is addressed as "Monsieur"—while the play uses "Monsieur" with no other character in the play except "Mr. Lavatch" at 5.2.1. Snyder is convincing in reading the Folio's "Mr." as "Monsieur" rather than as the usual "Master": "Formerly, as the companion of counts and lords, Parolles used 'thou' and 'knave' in talking with the Clown, aping his betters; now down and out, and indeed newly determined himself to live by fooling, he sees this same Clown as the back door into noble patronage. Parolles thus marks their new relationship by giving him not only the respectful 'you' but a title and a name, the first *we* have heard 'Lavatch'" ("Naming Names," 68). "Lafew" occurs only five times in the dialogue. A single direct-address instance in 2.1 occurs prior to his participation in 2.3 and 2.5. Shakespeare doesn't build a large edifice of name significance on so slight, so singular, a foundation; our concern should be to understand what Lafew as this (only incidentally named) "old Lord" (3.6.103) contributes.

12

The Taming of a Shrew and the Theories; or, "Though this be badness, yet there is method in't"

STEPHEN MILLER

Arguably the most persistent and difficult of the textual questions relating to Shakespeare's *The Taming of the Shrew*, first published in the Shakespeare folio of 1623, is the question of its relationship to *The Taming of a Shrew,* printed twenty-nine years earlier in 1594 by Peter Short. During the twentieth century critics have found it difficult to agree upon a theory to account for the variation between the two versions. The "bad quarto" theory, which at first seemed to offer an easy answer, in fact created a knotted debate. Perhaps rather surprisingly, given the seriousness with which critics developing the New Bibliography approached textual theory, they allowed the prejudicial overtones of their term "bad quarto" (surely influenced by the vivid adjectives of that famous sentence by Heminge and Condell: "stolne," "surreptitious," "maimed," "deformed," "injurious") to color their understanding of the textual position of plays so categorized. This appears to be the case regarding *The Taming of a Shrew*. If we examine the debate over *A Shrew* earlier in the twentieth century with the benefit of hindsight, we can locate some of the problems associated with the "bad quarto" theory, including the odd fact that labeling the variant material "bad" tended to direct attention *away* from any close examination of it. This essay will look at two issues associated with *A Shrew*. It will examine the difficulties critics have experienced with the ambiguity of the "bad quarto" theory, which in the case of plays associated with Shakespeare has acted in the past to turn interest away from the parts of the text not found in "good" versions; and it will examine the "bad" parts of *A Shrew*, suggesting that its compiler may have amended the plot of Shakespeare's *The Shrew* deliberately and have added new material in the "romantic" style to produce what could best be called an adaptation of Shakespeare's play. By closely examining these "bad" sections we can, in fact, discover important and surprising new details in *A Shrew*.

Structurally, *A Shrew* is quite similar to *The Shrew* in its three plot strands: the main plot of the taming of Kate the shrew, the subplot of the wooing of her sister(s), and the separate framing plot of a trick played by a lord on the drunkard, Sly, who is made to think he is a lord being shown the taming play. However, despite the similar titles and many similarities of plot and occasionally of language, *A Shrew* shows many striking differences from *The Shrew*. *A Shrew* is just over half the length, about 60 percent that of *The Shrew*, and, except for Kate and Sly, all the characters have different names. *A Shrew* is set in Greece, not Italy, it has a conclusion to the Sly frame tale not found in *The Shrew*, and its subplot differs in many particulars from *The Shrew*, most notably in giving Kate two sisters instead of one. *A Shrew*, then, offers textual critics a dilemma: Why, when *A Shrew* is so similar to *The Shrew*, does it have such a large amount of material that is different?

In the two centuries of criticism after Pope first took notice of *A Shrew*, a host of theories was enlisted to account for its differences from *The Shrew*, with changing critical fashions offering *A Shrew* a new niche from time to time. Pope apparently considered it an alternative version of *The Shrew* filled with actors' corruptions, but preserving some lines of Shakespeare missing from the Folio.[1] Though he degraded some of the Folio lines in *The Shrew*, he incorporated into it lines from *A Shrew*, especially the Sly frame material not found in *The Shrew*, and subsequent editors retained them for about half a century. Though many modern editors agree that the Sly scenes unique to *A Shrew* reflect something that Shakespeare probably wrote, they lack the textual confidence Pope displayed in incorporating them into *The Shrew*. When interest in source study blossomed in the eighteenth century, it is perhaps not surprising that *A Shrew* was declared a source play, and when scholars began to postulate lost source plays, apparently spurred by Malone's suggestion that Shakespeare began his career by revising the plays of others, Charles Knight suggested that both *A* and *The Shrew* must have derived from a lost source play.[2] Surveying the textual criticism of *A Shrew* we discover a changing response that tends to mirror the broader critical interests of each period—good evidence of the ambiguous nature of the relationship between the two plays. Given this critical background, it was surely inevitable that a piece such as *A Shrew*, clearly containing material from Marlowe, and probably Shakespeare, in a mix not found elsewhere, would be labeled a "bad quarto" after the theory of memorial reconstruction was advanced by the New Bibliographers early in the twentieth century. However, the label adhered poorly.

By the early 1900s, in addition to the theoretical discussion, critical examination of the internal evidence in the two plays had turned up a few important facts: (1) it had been discovered that several quotations and paraphrases of plays by Marlowe were incorporated into the text of *A Shrew* in addition to lines that seemed to be imitations of Marlowe or other contemporary playwrights;[3] (2) Alfred Tolman had pointed out that George Gascoigne's play, *Supposes*, of 1566 (and also, perhaps, Ariosto's *I Suppositi* from which Gascoigne translated his play) lay behind the subplot not only of *The Shrew*, but of *A Shrew* as well, although textually *Supposes* is closer to *The Shrew* than *A Shrew*.[4] These arguments led Wilhelm Creizenach to assert that *A Shrew* was the work of a "plagiarist" of Shakespeare. (The more neutral term "compiler" is adopted in this paper, since it indicates the use of borrowed material in *A Shrew* without pinning onto the sixteenth-century writer a label conveying our modern distaste for authorial borrowing.) Creizenach's work, along with the work of W. W. Greg and other New Bibliographers who proposed "memorial reconstruction" as an origin for a class of plays called "bad quartos," led to Peter Alexander's single-page article in the *TLS* in 1926 proposing that *A Shrew* was a "bad quarto" reliant solely upon Shakespeare's *The Shrew*. Alexander had previously argued that the texts of *The Contention* and *Richard, Duke of York* were "bad quartos" of 2 and 3 *Henry 6*; and although his opinions of the *Henry 6* plays were taken up with approval by many critics, the case of *A Shrew* proved a different matter.[5] In retrospect, it seems that Alexander's comments on *A Shrew* provoked a crisis for the textual criticism of *A Shrew* and *The Shrew,* a crisis possibly containing implications for the whole "bad quarto" theory.

At first Alexander's opinions seemed to find acceptance. Dover Wilson accepted them in his edition of *The Shrew* edited for Cambridge in 1928, and B. A. P van Dam welcomed them.[6] However, the 1930s saw a strong negative reaction. When E. K. Chambers, who had accepted Alexander's arguments for 2 and 3 *Henry 6,* came to consider whether *A Shrew* was a "bad quarto," he pronounced: "I am quite unable to believe that *A Shrew* had any such origin."[7] For him *A Shrew* remained a source play. T. W. Baldwin rejected the notion in a review of Dover Wilson's edition.[8] Leo Kirschbaum delivered a setback to Alexander's theory in his influential article, "A Census of Bad Quartos," by specifically refusing to include *A Shrew* in his list of more than twenty texts that he suspected of being "bad quartos."[9]

The 1940s saw the appearance of arguments that varied the "bad quarto" theory by arguing that *A Shrew* reported a different, lost version of *The Shrew*, probably by Shakespeare—a theory that Alexander had rejected in his *TLS* article without supplying any compelling reason. This variant "bad quarto" theory was argued by Raymond Houk and more memorably by G. I. Duthie, who is most closely associated with it in the minds of critics.[10] At its simplest, this theory seems to be a "revision" theory arguing that Shakespeare (or somebody) revised *The Shrew* and that the alternative version only survives as reported in *A Shrew*. Although Greg was attracted to this idea, no one after Duthie showed much interest in developing the theory or defending it from attack.[11] The notion that Shakespeare revised his own work found little favor among scholars pursuing the principles of the New Bibliography. At about this time the theoretical debate begun by Alexander's *TLS* article seems to have turned into a struggle among three entrenched positions. It became customary to refer to the textual problem of *A Shrew* as a debate among three theories—the source theory, the "bad quarto" theory, and the "ur-*Shrew*" theory (as the Duthie theory was dubbed). This tripartite model has not entirely passed from currency. The 1930s, '40s and '50s provided no major editions of *The Shrew* that might have produced a reassessment of the critical debate; nor did any edition of *A Shrew* appear.

A thaw came in the 1960s when the Pelican and Penguin editions of *The Shrew* appeared, edited, respectively, by Richard Hosley and G. R. Hibbard. Hosley supported Alexander's original "bad quarto" theory; Hibbard supported Duthie's alternative "bad quarto" theory. Thereafter, the three important new editions of *The Shrew* in the early 1980s—by Brian Morris for the New Arden, H. J. Oliver for the Oxford single-volume Shakespeare, and Ann Thompson for the New Cambridge Shakespeare—followed Alexander with the exception of Oliver, who nodded in the direction of Duthie's "revision" theory. These texts provide a more detailed summary of the history of the modern textual debate than is possible here.[12] But Morris, whose discussion is fullest, is not completely content with any theory, remarking:

> Unless new, external evidence comes to light, the relationship between *The Shrew* and *A Shrew* can never be decided beyond a peradventure. It will always be a balance of probabilities, shifting as new arguments and opinions are added to the scales. Nevertheless, in the present century the movement has unquestionably been towards acceptance of the Bad Quarto theory, and this can now be accepted as at least the current orthodoxy.[13]

The "current orthodoxy" is a description most critics would give to theories that they do not entirely trust to last. Morris is probably right in his pessimism, and nothing that I have to offer, either here or in my edition, much alters the truth of his argument that the relationship between the *Shrew* plays is extremely complex and cannot be resolved finally without the discovery of new external evidence. I do not feel, though, that the issue of the crisis precipitated by Alexander's first article has been thoroughly analyzed. What is needed is another hard look at the implications of Alexander's applying to *A Shrew* the "bad quarto" theory in his first *TLS* article, which still serves as the basis for the "current orthodoxy." I would argue that Alexander's treatment of the important differences between *The Shrew* and *A Shrew* is inadequate.

Many critics would now admit that "bad quarto" is an unfortunate label and it seems to me that the tale of twentieth-century criticism of *A Shrew* offers a prime example of why that label is unsatisfactory—particularly because labeling a text as "bad" seems to have a chilling effect upon readers of that text, including textual critics.

One problem is that the term "bad quarto" can be understood in at least two senses: one specifically Shakespearean, the other not. A. W. Pollard in 1909 had introduced the term "bad quarto" in a specifically Shakespearean context in *Shakespeare Folios and Quartos* to characterize the earliest quartos of *Romeo*, *Henry V*, *Hamlet,* and *Merry Wives,* which showed many verbal variants from later "good" texts by Shakespeare despite obvious similarities (he included *Pericles,* though no "good" version survives of the "bad" part). Pollard's aim was positive—to show that Heminge and Condell were not condemning all quartos as "stolne and surreptitious" in the Folio preface. Only a handful of the quartos were "bad." A keen interest in how these "bad" texts came into being led to the surmise that they were "stolne" from stage performances either by memory or stenography.[14] Memorial reconstruction came to be favored, and W. W. Greg's analysis of *The Battle of Alcazar* and *Orlando Furioso* in 1923 implied that memorially reconstructed plays were not confined to Shakespearean texts and could vary significantly from their originals. A non-Shakespearean "bad quarto" might reveal itself in a text found to exhibit characteristics of memorial reconstruction such as repetition and inclusion of parts of other plays. *A Shrew* could qualify as this sort of "bad quarto." Certainly the compiler of *A Shrew* could be seen to rely upon memory (and, possibly, notes), because he quotes *Dr Faustus,* a play not yet in print in 1594. If *The Shrew* had never appeared in the Folio, it is probable that the anonymous *A Shrew* would have fallen under strong suspicion anyway of being a "bad quarto" of Greg's type. But *The Shrew* was printed and when *A Shrew* was compared with it, although it appeared to have many features of a memorially derived text, it showed greater variation from its "good" version than other Shakespearean "bad quartos" did from theirs. Critics who took a narrow view of what constitutes a "Shakespearean bad quarto" would not admit it to the club. This, it seems to me, is what lies behind Kirschbaum's very terse comment upon *A Shrew*. He does not discuss whether *A Shrew* might be a memorially based text as he has with the "bad quartos" he allows into his list, but says: "Despite protestations to the contrary, *The Taming of a Shrew* does not stand in relation to *The Shrew* as *The True Tragedie*, for example, stands in relation to *3 Henry VI*."[15] A "*Shakespearean* bad quarto" must not show a great deal of variation, then.

Underpinning the notion of a "Shakespearean bad quarto" is the assumption that the motive of whoever compiled that text was to produce, deferentially, a verbal replica of what appeared onstage. If we find lines that differ from the "good" text, they fall under suspicion of being corrupt. Hence, Alexander seems to pay little attention to the variant matter in *A Shrew*. Ideally it should not be where it is. According to Alexander, the compiler relied only upon *The Shrew* but proved unable to re-create the complex intrigue of Shakespeare, so he simplified the story line and borrowed passages from other plays to give his renamed characters some dialogue. Here I believe Alexander falls under the negative influence of the term "bad quarto." Critics other than Alexander in the 1920s who were reading *The Shrew* and *A Shrew* and noticed the differences must have felt the need for a better explanation of variations than an incompetent compiler. This, I believe, is the prime reason for the persistence of doubt over *A Shrew* among twentieth-century critics. Some of the subplot variations have real substance. For instance, unlike Lucentio and Bianca in *The Shrew*, their parallels in *A Shrew*—Aurelius and Phylema—are from different social ranks, he being a prince of Sestos. What is more, when the prince's father, the duke of Sestos, appears, he explodes in haughty anger to find his noble son married to a girl of the merchant class. Vincentio, the duke's parallel in *The Shrew*, is of the merchant class himself and seems rather inclined to reassure Baptista of his son's worth than question Bianca's (5.1.124, New Arden). The issue of rank does not become a point of contention in *The Shrew*. Perhaps we can say of *A Shrew*, though this be badness, yet there is method in't. Such coordination in *A Shrew* between the later actions of a noble father and the earlier actions of his son suggests that the compiler might be following some intelligent plan, but Alexander does not investigate further than to satisfy himself of the compiler's incompetence. In his last article on *A Shrew*, printed in 1969, Alexander revealed that his position on the variant matter in *A Shrew* had altered little in over forty years:

> The compiler of *A Shrew* while trying to follow the sub-plot of *The Shrew* gave it up as too complicated to reproduce, and fell back on love scenes in which he substituted for the maneuvers of the disguised Lucentio and Hortensio extracts from *Tamburlaine* and *Faustus*, with which the lovers woo their ladies.[16]

Evidently the variant material is the "bad" part of "bad quarto," and as a consequence, not of much interest.

The troubled reception of Alexander's "bad quarto" theory for *A Shrew* in the decades since he first presented it might have caused critics over forty years later to ponder. There are two points that throw doubt upon Alexander's hypothesis that the compiler was a bungler and simplifier only:

1. If critics found that the subplot of *A Shrew* were only simpler than that of *The Shrew*, who would protest at labeling it a "bad quarto" report? The subplot contains elements and scenes not found in *The Shrew*. The difficulty with the subplot is not its simplicity but its complexity and differences.

2. The more incompetent the critic paints the compiler as being, the more he strengthens the argument that the compiler would have been incapable of inventing all of the differences found in the subplot of *A Shrew* and developing them consistently. To argue that he is incompetent, ironically, strengthens the hands of those who argue in support of the revision theory: that there must have been another version from which this weak compiler took his new plot details.

In fact, there is evidence of coherent variation in the subplot of *A Shrew* that seriously undermines Alexander's hypothesis of a weak compiler. In editing *A Shrew* I made a close inspection of the "corrupt" parts of the subplot, and I believe that although the love story of the shrew's two sisters is simpler than the Bianca plot of *The Shrew*, *A Shrew* does contain another coherent plot strand not found in *The Shrew*. As hinted above, it turns upon the consequences of distinguishing as noblemen two of the characters, father and son. Since Aurelius, the young nobleman, winds up wooing and marrying one of the "shrewish" sisters of the final wager scene, the theme appears to be that marriage outside one's rank is fraught with danger. Rather than trace out the lines of the alternative plot in argument, I offer the following parallel synopses of the variant subplots. In order to make clearer the comparison, generic labels have generally been substituted for character names.

In *The Shrew* the subplot tells a tale of a well-to-do merchant's son who, arriving from elsewhere to study, falls in love at first sight with the younger of two daughters of a rich gentleman (the older daughter being a shrew). The woman he admires is of roughly equivalent status to himself. Because she is already pressed by two wooers—one young, one old—he divides his resources by disguising himself as a tutor of lower rank and giving his servant his identity. In his disguise, the son competes with the younger of the woman's wooers and triumphs. His servant, taking the son's name, outbids and displaces the older wooer by promising the woman's father a superior marriage settlement. It remains only to find a False Father to verify the servant's promises. This done, the young man secretly marries the woman. However, as soon as they have married, the son's True Father arrives. Though surprised at the mixed identities, he is pleased to find his son and soon assures the woman's anxious father that his son is a worthy match.

The subplot in *A Shrew* tells a tale of a young nobleman, prince of Sestos, who arrives from elsewhere to study. He is greeted by a friend who has already fallen in love with the youngest of the three daughters of a rich merchant (the oldest being a shrew). Upon seeing the three daughters, the prince falls in love at first sight with the middle daughter, who apparently has no other suitors. This woman the prince admires is a woman of lower status than he himself—a merchant's daughter. The prince presents himself as a merchant, someone of equal rank. He disguises his servant as prince of Sestos—his own rank. The prince (as a merchant) woos and wins the woman in the same scenes in which his friend woos and wins the youngest daughter, making two parallel couples. The prince wins over the father by finding and presenting to him a False Father, a merchant (apparently also from Sestos) who offers assurances of great wealth to his son and bride. Before their wedding, when the two parallel couples are pledging their mutual loves, the prince tests the woman he loves by asking her whether she would not rather marry the rich prince of Sestos (his servant). She says she would not, and the couples wed as planned. As soon as they have married, the son's True Father, the duke, arrives. He explodes in fury to find his son marrying beneath himself and rounds on all, particularly the woman's father, who protests ignorance. All beg the duke's forgiveness, and he at last relents, accepting the marriage.

Plot summaries are rough tools but undeniably useful in the case of these plays. The first observation is that the two subplots contain many parallels. In both *A Shrew* and *The Shrew* most of the points of intersection between the main plot and the subplot are similar in both versions—examples are the shrew's wedding, which subplot characters attend in both versions, and the encounter of the tamer and shrew with the true father on the road to Padua/Athens. These parallel structural links suggest an intimate knowledge of the original text by whoever created the alternative version. In addition to the element of a nobleman wooing in disguise, the subplot of *A Shrew* shows him testing the faithfulness of his bride-to-be. Plots based upon the testing of women, such as the tale of Griselda, are of venerable date, and this aspect of the subplot of *A Shrew* is compatible with the end of the play when the subplot and taming plot of both plays combine in the testing of three women for obedience to their husbands.

Another important observation is that the alternative subplots are different in comic type. That of *The Shrew*, as is well known, follows the classical style of Latin comedy with an intricate plot involving deception, often kept in motion by a clever servant such as Tranio. (Shakespeare took the names Tranio and Grumio from the *Mostellaria* by Plautus—just such a Latin comedy.) *Supposes*, from which both subplots derive, is another such play, although it derives from a Renaissance Italian imitation of Latin comedies. On the other hand, the subplot of *A Shrew* has many elements more associated with the romantic style of comedy popular in London in the 1590s. The theme of a nobleman falling in love with a woman of lesser rank appears in romantic comedies such as Greene's *Friar Bacon and Friar Bungay*, *Fair Em*, and other plays. Scenes between wooing lovers are also found in romantic comedies. Lucentio and Bianca have scarcely six lines of lovemaking "alone" in *The Shrew* (4.2.6–10); in fact, Hortensio and Tranio are eavesdropping even then. By contrast, the audience of *A Shrew* at a similar juncture is treated to a full scene of the most elaborate promises of love between the shrew's two sisters and their lovers.[17] Although Shakespeare employs the conventions of romantic comedy by including in *The Shrew* occasional passages of elaborate description and classical allusion, such passages in *A Shrew* seem plentiful and extravagant almost to the point of parody, with offers of

> A thousand massie ingots of pure gold,
> And twise as many bares [bars] of siluer plate[18]

The importation into *A Shrew* of extravagant language from the popular plays of about 1590—especially Marlowe's—has long been known. I suggest that the subplot of *A Shrew* was also indebted to the structural principles of the popular romantic comedies for the character of some of its plotting where that differs from *The Shrew*. To me it seems that *A Shrew* is an adaptation of *The Shrew*. Alexander's incompetent compiler should be dismissed in favor of a compiler more willing to intervene in the structure of the play.

Probably the single instance offering the clearest evidence of a process of adaptation between *A Shrew* and *The Shrew* is provided by a parallel passage between the subplots, indicated in print as early as 1886 in the margin of the Praetorius facsimile of *A Shrew*.[19] It occurs after Kate's wedding in a scene found between her arrival at the tamer's house and the scene in which Kate is tempted with food by his servant: scene 10 in Bullough's edition of *A Shrew;* scene 7, lines 23–37 in my edition quoted below (parallels begin with the word "tame"):

> *[Valeria.]* But tell me my Lord, is *Ferando* married then?
> *Aurelius.* He is: and *Polidor* shortly shall be wed,

> And he meanes to tame his wife erelong.
> *Valeria.* He saies so.
> *Aurelius.* Faith he's gon vnto the taming schoole.
> *Valeria.* The taming schoole: why, is there such a place?
> *Aurelius.* I: and *Ferando* is the Maister of the schoole.
> *Valeria.* Thats rare: but what *decorum* dos he vse?
> *Aurelius.* Faith I know not: but by som odde deuise or other,

In *The Shrew* the equivalent passage is found at TLN 1900–1909 (4.2.50–58), the Folio scene in which Lucentio and Tranio inform Bianca that Hortensio has abandoned wooing her:

> *Tra.* I'faith hee'l haue a lustie Widdow now,
> That shalbe woo'd, and wedded in a day.
> *Bian.* God giue him ioy.
> *Tra.* I, and hee'l tame her.
> *Bianca.* He sayes so *Tranio*.
> *Tra.* Faith he is gone vnto the taming schoole.
> *Bian.* The taming schoole: what is there such a place?
> *Tra.* I mistris, and *Petruchio* is the master,
> That teacheth trickes eleuen and twentie long,
> To tame a shrew, and charme her chattering tongue.

The five lines, beginning with Tranio's "I, and hee'l tame her," constitute the closest verbal parallel between the two subplots. If the characters in *The Shrew* followed their equivalents in *A Shrew*, the conversation would be between Lucentio and Tranio, with Lucentio taking the lead and Tranio playing the uninformed party, instead of the version in the Folio in which Tranio takes the lead and Bianca plays the uninformed party or "straight man." Since the speakers in *A Shrew* are not their customary equivalents in *The Shrew*, these verbal parallels also provide strong evidence that one version is an adaptation of the other: the verbal correspondence is too close to have been arrived at independently. The writer of one version necessarily had direct knowledge of the other version, at least in this passage. The other borrowings in *A Shrew* suggest that the most economic explanation of indebtedness is to propose that whoever compiled *A Shrew* borrowed the lines from Shakespeare's *The Shrew*, or a version of it, and adapted them to a reorganized subplot.

It may seem heresy to suggest that a contemporary of Shakespeare's would create the sort of adaptation that we associate with the late seventeenth century. While it is difficult to know the motivation of the adapter, we can reckon that from his point of view an early staging of *The Shrew* might have revealed an overly wrought play with "possibilities" from a writer trying to establish himself with a play that, however, challenged too far the current ideas of popular comedy. *The Shrew* is long and complicated with three plots, the subplot being in the swift Latin or Italianate style with several disguises. Its language is at first stuffed with difficult Italian quotations, but its dialogue must often sound plain when compared to the mouth-filling lines and images that on other afternoons were drawing crowds to Marlowe's thunder or Greene's romance. An adapter might well have seen his role as that of a "play doctor," improving *The Shrew*—while cutting it—by stuffing it with the sort of material currently in demand in popular romantic comedies, including characters from the nobility: in other words, glamorizing it.

It is difficult to avoid the suspicion that the anomalous nature of *A Shrew* is related, somehow, to the date of its appearance. *A Shrew* was the first comedy associated with Shakespeare to be printed. It was entered on 2 May 1594, so that its printing must date from the first few months of the publication of Shakespeare's plays. The two other Shakespearean plays surviving in editions of 1594 are *Titus Andronicus* (entered 6 February) and *The Contention* (entered 12 March). This was a confused time for London acting companies suffering the long closure of the playhouses because of the plague. A large number of plays came to the presses in 1594, perhaps as many as half in texts that modern critics have singled out as possibly including material derived memorially from the stage. As far as we know, after *Titus* no "good" versions of a play by Shakespeare appeared until 1597. Ideally, investigating this difficult but crucial period for Shakespeare's development should be a priority for scholars. Certainly during the whole of the period the acting companies must have exerted whatever control they could over releasing plays to the press.

Shakespeare's comedies, particularly, seem to have escaped early printing. By 1600, besides *A Shrew*, only *Love's Labour's Lost* had been printed as far as we know (given our ignorance of the history of *Love's Labour's Won*). The three "good quarto" comedies of 1600, a notable exception, may have been released to help finance the construction of the Globe. Thereafter only the "bad" *Merry Wives* and *Pericles* (omitted by the Folio) were printed before the Folio. Of the four "good" Folio comedy texts that appeared in quarto, none was reprinted before 1623, except for the two included among the "Pavier quartos" of 1619, which were falsely dated with the years of their first editions to disguise the fact that they were reprints.

Although the argument presented here is that the variations discovered in *A Shrew* seem best explained as the work of an adapter of *The Shrew*, I do not believe that the revision theory—the notion that *A Shrew* is a "bad quarto" of an alternative version of *The Shrew*—can be dismissed out of hand, although it has long been largely ignored by critics. This was Duthie's version of events, but Duthie was a careful scholar and he seems not to have been entirely certain whether the alternative subplot was by Shakespeare or someone else. The difficult task is to find any lines in *A Shrew* not paralleled in *The Shrew* that could certainly be identified as Shakespeare's. Scholars would have to surmount this teasing difficulty in order to convince us that Shakespeare himself might have produced an alternative version of *The Shrew*. Certainly some of the romantic elements and themes of *A Shrew*, not found in *The Shrew*, appear in Shakespeare's other plays. However, while romantic comedy was a vein that Shakespeare exploited brilliantly in his subsequent plays, its themes were not exclusively his. Without certainty about his words, we can prove nothing.

To conclude, *The Taming of a Shrew* has always suffered low esteem in comparison to the more verbally brilliant text of *The Shrew*. Nevertheless, I believe that *A Shrew* contains more of interest than critics have so far discussed. We benefit greatly from accepting *A Shrew* as a viable comic text of its period even if it is, as it seems, memorially derived in large part from *The Shrew*. What the bibliography of the later twentieth century has to say to that of the early twentieth century is that the "bad quarto theory" has value, but has had the surprising and negative effect of diverting scholarly attention away from much of what is most interesting about *A Shrew* and ultimately from the play itself. Instead of an embarrassment, *A Shrew* provides fascinating testimony to the taste of its time and possibly a critical reaction to an early Shakespearean comedy by another writer expressed through adaptation. In examining the "corruption" of *A Shrew*, we find a mine of information about theatrical taste of 1594, a taste that Shakespeare was busily building upon and reacting against.

NOTES

1. Alexander Pope, ed., *The Taming of the Shrew,* in *The Works of Shakespear,* vol. 2 (London: Jacob Tonson, 1723–25), 351.

2. E. A. J. Honigmann, "Shakespeare's 'Lost Source-Plays,'" *MLR* 49 (1954): 293–307 (esp. 293); *The Taming of the Shrew* in *The Comedies, Histories, Tragedies, and Poems of William Shakspere,* ed. Charles Knight, 2d ed. ("Library" ed.), vol. 2 (London: Charles Knight and Co., 1842), 119–20.

3. *The Taming of the Shrew,* ed. Knight, 114–19.

4. Alfred Tolman, "Shakespeare's Part in *The Taming of the Shrew,*" *PMLA* 5 (1890): 201–78; an offprint of this was issued, repaginated, as a book.

5. Wilhelm Creizenach, *Das Englische Drama im Zeitalter Shakespeares,* in *Geschichte des Neuern Dramas,* vol. 4 (Halle: Max Niemeyer, 1909), 686–98; and Peter Alexander, *"The Taming of a Shrew,"* TLS, 16 September 1926, 614.

6. B. A. P. van Dam, *"The Taming of the Shrew,"* English Studies 10 (1928): 97–106.

7. *William Shakespeare: A Study of Facts and Problems,* vol. 1 (Oxford: Clarendon Press, 1930), 372.

8. T. W. Baldwin, review of *The Taming of the Shrew*, ed. Sir Arthur Quiller-Couch and J. D. Wilson, *JEGP* 31 (1932): 152–56.

9. Leo Kirschbaum, "A Census of Bad Quartos," *RES* 14 (1938): 20–43 (esp. 43).

10. Raymond A. Houk, "The Evolution of *The Taming of the Shrew*," *PMLA* 57 (1942): 1009–38, and G. I. Duthie, "*The Taming of a Shrew* and *The Taming of the Shrew*," *RES* 19 (1943): 337–56.

11. W. W. Greg, *The Shakespeare First Folio* (Oxford: Clarendon Press, 1955), 211–12.

12. Historical surveys are found in the editions of Brian Morris for the New Arden Shakespeare (London: Methuen, 1981), 12–50ff.; H. J. Oliver for the Oxford Shakespeare (Oxford: Clarendon Press, 1982), 13–57; and Ann Thompson for the New Cambridge Shakespeare (Cambridge: Cambridge University Press, 1984), 9–17, 160–85. My edition of *A Shrew* ("A Critical, Old-spelling Edition of *The Taming of a Shrew*, 1594" [Ph.D. diss., University of London, 1993]) includes a survey more focused upon that text .

13. *The Taming of the Shrew*, ed. Brian Morris, The New Arden Shakespeare (London: Methuen, 1981), 45.

14. For an analysis of the development of this theory see Paul Werstine's essay in this volume.

15. Kirschbaum, "A Census," 43.

16. Peter Alexander, "The Original Ending of *The Taming of the Shrew*," *SQ* 20 (1969): 111–16 (114).

17. See scene 14 in Geoffrey Bullough's reprint edition of *The Taming of a Shrew* in *Narrative and Dramatic Sources of Shakespeare*, vol. 1 (London: Routledge, 1957), 97–98; in my edition of *A Shrew* this is scene 11.

18. Bullough, *Narrative and Dramatic Sources*, 1:57; 9.30–31 in my edition.

19. Pp. 30–31.

13

Looking for Cousin Ferdinand:
The Value of F1 Stage Directions for a
Production of *The Taming of the Shrew*

RALPH ALAN COHEN

In 1983, after teaching Shakespeare for ten years, I had the chance to codirect a production of *The Taming of the Shrew*.[1] Much about my first experience as a director surprised me—the long hours, the organizational problems, the dedication of student actors who in my English classes seemed incapable of working at all—but nothing surprised me more than the helpfulness of the Folio text in staging our production. I began the process in the expectation that I could use the nearly three centuries of editorial work on the play as a crutch; I shortly found that much of what editors have done is an obstacle to staging the work, that editorial misconceptions about the stage played into editorial preconceptions about the play, and that the resulting editorial decisions have had the cumulative effect of changing the play. What follow are some insights about stage directions born of wrestling with a production of *The Shrew*.

To set the scene for my observations, let me contrast the opening of act 4 as it appears in the Folio with the same moment as it appears in the New Cambridge Shakespeare. The Folio reads: *"Enter Grumio."* The New Shakespeare reads:

> The hall of Petruchio's house in the country; stairs leading to a gallery; a large open hearth; a table, benches, and stools; three doors, one opening on to the porch without.
>   GRUMIO enters the house, his shoulders covered with snow, his legs with mud. Grumio [throws himself upon a bench].[2]

George Bernard Shaw would hardly have told us more than does John Dover Wilson. But such flagrant imposition of an editor's conception, so open and obtrusive, is not as subversive as the accretion of small stage directions legitimized over the years by much more conservative editors. Brian Morris's edition for New Arden provides an excellent perspective on the problem. Though offering fewer stage directions than most editions, the Arden *Shrew* provides one hundred fifty-nine stage directions, forty-eight more than in F1. Of those forty-eight, twenty-one can be traced to Rowe (1709), eight to Theobald (1733), one to Hanmer (1744), one to Johnson (1765), six to Capell (1767), one to Malone (1790), two to the Cambridge (1863), seven to Hibbard (1968), and one to Morris himself.[3] These editorial additions are carefully considered, and the great majority of them no doubt reflect accurately what happened on Shakespeare's stage; but anyone directing *Shrew* should be careful to view such stage directions in the light of the Folio. Doing so avoids staging problems created in the editor's study, provides simple answers to the question "what is going on?" and, in a few cases, helps us see the work free from centuries of theatrical assumptions.

Editors make six kinds of changes in the stage directions of *The Shrew*: (1) most rarely, they omit directions from F1; (2) they change punctuation and wording; (3) they add asides; (4) they add actions; (5) they assign locales; and (6) they add and reposition entrances and exits.[4] Together these changes have a powerful influence on the shape and feel of the play. This observation may sound obvious; it once did for me, but now—after my experience as a director—it is a proposition that for me has graduated from a platitude to an axiom.

OMISSIONS FROM F1

Two stage directions in *The Shrew*—both in 4.4—have had trouble surviving: 4.4. 18 (TLN 2200–2201), *"Pedant booted / and bare headed"* and 4.4 (TLN 2253), *"Enter Peter."* Morris preserves the latter but omits *"booted and bare headed,"* a change first made by Rowe. As Alan Dessen tells us, the Elizabethans used boots as stage shorthand either for hasty departures or for recent arrivals.[5] Morris explains that he omits the stage direction because "the Pedant has been on stage for 18 lines, and was carefully described at the start of the scene as *'dressed like Vincentio.'"* Morris conjectures that the scene "originally opened at this point" and was only "partially corrected."[6] Perhaps; but from the point of view of staging the scene, the Folio stage direction at that point in the text has a value of its own.

We found the plot complication of the Bianca-Lucentio story after act 4 a major weakness of the play. Partly because Kate and Petruchio have become overwhelmingly the center of interest and partly because so much of the plot explanation is compressed into the glib lines of Tranio, audiences lose interest in 4.4. They have not, after all, even met the real Vincentio, so all they *see* is yet another introduction of an out-of-towner to Baptista (who in the course of the play is introduced to six strangers). Morris assumes that "dressed like Vincentio" (4.4.s.d.) means "booted and bare headed" and that therefore the stage direction at line 18 is redundant. Not in stage value. Since we have not yet seen Vincentio, that opening stage direction will have meaning only after his entrance in the next scene. What the scene needs is a visual reminder of the plotting going on, and that is what the stage direction provides. When Tranio says to the Pedant, "Here comes Baptista. Set your countenance, sir," the Pedant (who has long been in town), by busying himself with a pair of boots (to look newly arrived) and by doffing his hat to begin his pitch to Baptista, reminds the audience that the plot calls for him to impersonate Vincentio.

Morris retains (but Hosley, Oliver, and Thompson, for example, do not) the stage direction at 4.4.68—"Enter Peter."[7] That entrance comes in the midst of stage business that has provided a knot of editorial problems. Baptista, pleased with the pseudo-Vincentio's "plainness and shortness," agrees to a betrothal but rather inexplicably refuses to have it take place at his home.[8] F1 prints the following:

> *Tra.* Then at my lodging, and it like you,
> There doth my father lie: and there this night
> Weele passe the businesse priuately and well:
> Send for your daughter by your seruant here,
> My Boy shall fetch the Scriuener presentlie,
> The worst is this that at so slender warning,
> You are like to haue a thin and slender pittance.
>   *Bap.* It likes me well:
> *Cambio* hie you home, and bid *Bianca* make her readie
>   straight:
> And if you will tell what hath hapned,
> *Lucentios* Father is arriued in *Padua*,
> And how she's like to be *Lucentios* wife.
>   *Biond.* I praie the gods she may withall my heart.
>   *Exit.*
>   *Tran.* Dallie not with the gods, but get thee gone.
>   *Enter Peter.*
> Signior *Baptista*, shall I leade the way,
> Welcome, one mess is like to be your cheere,

Come sir, we will better it in *Pisa.*
     Bap. I follow you.   *Exeunt.*
      Enter Lucentio and Biondello.
     Bion. Cambio.
     Luc. What saist thou *Biondello.*

                          (TLN 2237–60)

The passage contains an inordinate number of instructions and implicit stage directions: the entire party plans to go to Lucentio's lodgings, Baptista is to send a servant to Bianca, Tranio (pretending to be Lucentio) is to send his "boy" (presumably Biondello) to get a scrivener, Baptista chooses Cambio (the real Lucentio) to go to Bianca to tell her to "make readie straight." In 1709, Rowe gave the line "I praie the gods she may withall my heart" to Lucentio and then had Lucentio exit instead of Biondello. Theobald (1733) then established the tradition of omitting the stage direction, *"Enter Peter."* Who is Peter? What is happening on the stage?

The only Peter named previously in the play is a servant of Petruchio whose hat needed blacking. Quiller-Couch and Dover Wilson (in the New Shakespeare, p. 171) suggest that Peter was the name of an actor in the company. In staging *The Shrew*, our initial impulse was to simplify matters by assuming that there is no entrance and no Peter at that point in the play. Our problem then became what to do with Biondello's exit and his almost immediate reentry with Lucentio. They could not have gone far because Biondello explains that Tranio "has left mee here behinde" (TLN 2264), an indication that their exchange takes place where the whole group had just been. We found the only way to observe the geography implied in that line was to have Biondello make a false exit, reenter upstage, and motion to Lucentio (as Cambio) to remain behind as the others "exeunt."[9] What's more, our solution to the staging of this business was perfectly in keeping with F1 if the Peter that the New Shakespeare suggests is an actor who was playing Biondello. In that case, Biondello, the mischievous servant, after some relatively interesting mugging with Tranio, doubles back and waits for the group to leave. His appearance upstage would not, moreover, be a distraction from important matters, since there is no substance whatever in Tranio's lines after the stage direction, *"Enter Peter."* Indeed, like the Pedant's onstage preparation to meet Baptista, Biondello's false exit provides visual underscoring for the plot at a time when the show is going flat.[10] Thus the stage direction *"Enter Lucentio and Biondello"* is a direction for the two to come forward from the upstage or fringe position on the stage, and Biondello's words "here behinde" make perfect sense. Again, we find F1, however thorny as a readers' text, smoother going on the stage than those texts which would simply remove the problem by omitting the stage direction.

CHANGES IN WORDING

For the most part, editors have taken care to preserve the Folio's wording of stage directions, but the stage direction at the beginning of act 5 (TLN 2379–80), *"Gremio / is out before,"* was changed by Rowe to *"walking on one side,"* and that version more or less prevailed until this century. In our desire to keep the show moving as quickly as possible, we flirted with Rowe's variation, which saves time by having Gremio's entrance largely simultaneous with that of Biondello, Lucentio, and Bianca. But the Folio direction in its entirety—*"Enter Biondello, Lucentio, and Bianca, Gremio / is out before"*—suggests the afterthought of a good dramatist who, imagining his action as he wrote, discovered what it took us several attempts at staging to find out.[11] Gremio's earlier entrance solves two dramaturgical problems. First, it makes less severe the difficulties of having Gremio and the threesome miss seeing each other. When Gremio comes out first, he can move to an imagined nook in the stage, stand behind a pillar, or station himself virtually anywhere so that it does not strain credulity to think that Biondello, Lucentio, and Bianca would miss him. His own concentration or misplaced attention can be established so that he in turn would not see the people for whom he is in fact looking. The alternative of a simultaneous entrance is, by contrast, a choreographic nightmare in terms of keeping the two oblivious to one another. The second, more narrative, advantage of an early Gremio entrance is that it provides an opportunity for the audience to readjust its perspective and resume its involvement in the Bianca-Lucentio subplot. As I suggested above, Shakespeare made the mistake of complicating the subplot long after it is clearly of secondary interest. To have the old suitor of Bianca lurk suspiciously about the stage is to recall for the audience the original conflict. That one figure reminds the audience of the only obstacle left to Bianca and Lucentio's marriage— Gremio's hope that Lucentio's father will not give his financial support to the union.

Underlying the editorial change from "Gremio is out before" to "walking on one side" or "stands aside" or "discovered"[12] or even "Gremio seated under the trees, nodding"[13] are theatrical assumptions conditioned by the proscenium stage and the curtain it made possible. Without realizing it, these editors may simply have been imagining that a curtain hid Gremio until he was in place, an easy solution to all the blocking problems related to getting him and the three other characters onto the stage in ignorance of one another. But the uncurtained thrust stage the dramatist was imagining meant that an audience would have to see Gremio get into position and demands adherence to the Folio wording.

ADDITIONAL ASIDES

The most frequently added stage direction in *The Shrew* is the word "aside."
Editors rightly perceive that one reader-friendly intrusion can do wonders
to clarify the text. Take for example this passage from 4.3:

> *Petr.* Eate it vp all *Hortensio*, if thou louest mee:
> Much good do it vnto thy gentle heart:
> *Kate* eate apace. . . .
>
> (TLN 2032–34)

To a reader, those lines are confusing. Is Petruchio telling Hortensio to eat
all his portion? To whose "gentle heart" is he wishing "much good"? Do
the words "Kate eate apace" mean that Petruchio is having Kate compete
with Hortensio? In short, to whom is Petruchio speaking and to what purpose? When editors add "aside to Hortensio" before the first line and "to
Kate" before the second line,[14] they help the reader immeasurably in seeing the action. Without that tool, an editor would have a terrible time leading a reader through the narrative tangle of almost any Renaissance plot.
From the standpoint of the director, however, the "aside" stage direction
carries a great deal more than narrative weight.

In his article on stage directions, E. A. J. Honigmann lists asides as one
of the areas that editors need to reevaluate in their treatment of stage directions:

> When an editor adds "Aside" he often implies that the speaker would not
> have dared to utter the same words openly; in short, he passes judgment on
> the relationship of two or more dramatic characters.[15]

In *The Shrew*, a comedy so full of pranks and disguises, the weight of the
accumulated editorial asides is considerable enough to sink some of the
characters. For example, Rowe makes Biondello's comment on the resemblance of the Pedant to Vincentio—"as much as an Apple doth an oyster"[16]—an aside. All editors have followed Rowe in this addition, but the
main feature of Biondello's character is his impudence; repeatedly he teases
his masters in the play, most notably when he is describing Petruchio's
approach for the wedding. In our production, we tried Biondello's "as much
as an apple doth an oyster" as an aside to the audience, but it seemed uncharacteristically indirect for Biondello. Then we tried the line as an aside
to Tranio, an improvement, but less successful than our eventual decision
to make the line a typically impertinent comment to all on stage (though to

no one in particular). Not only did that choice preserve Biondello's character, but it also forced Tranio into a comically more awkward situation. In
theatrical terms removing the aside "raised the stakes" for all the actors
onstage: the actor playing Biondello had to find the right level of imperti-
nence, the actor playing Tranio had to deal with both his unruly servant and
the Pedant, while the actor playing the Pedant had to decide how much
Biondello's gibe would slow his surrender to Tranio's con. To achieve this
much richer theatrical moment all we had to do was ignore an editorial
sense of propriety.

ADDED ACTIONS

The Shrew, with its madcap hero, its roughhouse courtship, and its numerous descriptions of violent action—Hortensio's account of his music les-
son with Kate, Gremio's description of the wedding, Grumio's tale of the
journey back to Verona —suggests a world of extreme physicality and makes
a particularly inviting text for the addition of explicit stage directions for
actions that seem implied by the text. A director faced with the meeting of
Kate and Petruchio, for example, will find that a virtually blank canvas
awaits his blocking. In some cases, the implied action is so specific that
from Rowe on, editors have not hesitated to describe the action. For example, in 5.2.122, when Petruchio tells Kate,

> *Katerine*, that Cap of yours becomes you not,
> Off with that bable, throw it underfoote.

(TLN 2677–78)

editors have reasonably followed Rowe's stage direction, "She pulls off
her Cap and throws it down." [17]
    Less obvious but probably no less accurate is Rowe's direction that
Petruchio "throws the Meat, &c about the Stage"[18] in 4.1. F1 gives no direction following Petruchio's line, "There, take it to you, trenchers, cups,
and all," and the next line, "You heedlesse iolt-heads, and vnmanner'd
slaues" (TLN 1797–98), gives no real clue as to what Petruchio does other
than to reinforce his apparent anger. If the actor, for example, simply handed
back to a servant a tray holding "trenchers, cups, and all," he would satisfy
the literal requirements of the text. But the mood of the scene and the weight
of theatrical tradition make Rowe's addition a unanimous choice of succeeding editors, and a director who does less than Rowe's stage direction
dictates loses one of the play's most energetic moments.
    Nonetheless, remembering that F1 is not the source of that specific
action can help us look more critically at the accretion of other actions

attributed to Petruchio by editors following Rowe's assumption that Petruchio is the kind of character who "throws the Meat, &c. about the stage." For example, Hibbard renders 4.1 (TLN 1772–84) in this way:

> [Petruchio] Off with my boots, you rogues! You villains,when?
> *He sings*
> > It was the friar of orders grey,
> > As he forth walkèd on his way—
> Out you rogue! You pluck my foot awry.
> *He strikes the Servant*
> Take that, and mend the plucking of the other.
> Be merry, Kate. Some water here. What ho!
> *Enter one with water*
> Where's my spaniel Troilus? Sirrah, get you hence,
> And bid my cousin Ferdinand come hither.
> > *Exit another Servingman*
> One, Kate, that you must kiss and be acquainted with.
> Where are my slippers? Shall I have some water?
> Come, Kate, and wash, and welcome heartily.
> *He knocks the basin out of the Servant's hands*
> You whoreson villain, will you let it fall?
> *He strikes the Servant*

Of the six stage directions, only "Enter one with water" appears in F1. The F1 italics and the verse form of the rhyme about the Greyfriars certainly support the conjecture that Petruchio is singing.[19] Petruchio's "take that" may indicate, as Rowe first suggests, that "he strikes the servant," but he could just as well be giving him—or hurling at him—the boot the servant removed "awry." Hibbard's suggestion that Petruchio "knocks the basin out of the Servant's hands" could account for Petruchio's accusation that the servant "let it fall," but he might just as simply have bumped into the servant or tripped him (our solution). Finally, the text gives no support to Capell's idea that Petruchio strikes the servant who let the water fall. Kate's protest, "Patience I pray you, 'twas a fault unwilling" (TLN 1785), needs no more provocation than Petruchio's epithet, "You whoreson villain."

The accumulated weight of the three added stage directions describing Petruchio's contact with the servants loads the character in a single direction: he is a man who hits people. In fact, nowhere in the Folio text is there any evidence that Petruchio strikes anyone on stage. He does threaten to "knock" Grumio's pate, but instead "he rings him by the eares"—an altogether more proprietary and comic action. He warns Kate, "I sweare Ile cuffe you, if you strike againe" (TLN 1097), but, apparently deciding he means what he says, she gives him no opportunity to prove it. True, Grumio tells Curtis that Petruchio beat him on their way to Padua, but such a report

(1) from a character eager to "tell the tale," (2) in a story full of comic exaggeration, and (3) about an offstage action does not tell on the character of Petruchio like a single one of Hibbard's conjectural directions. Here the matter of degree is all important, because the audience that *sees* Petruchio hit people experiences quite another range of possibilities from the audience that hears him threaten to hit someone or hears his comic servant (or Gremio) report that he has done so.

Editors and directors have difficulty escaping from the mythic Petruchio produced by the layers of such reasonable but not inevitable stage directions. Louis B. Wright's old Folger paperback, for example, depicts Petruchio holding a whip in his hand,[20] though F1 makes no mention of such a prop. Pity the reader who would read that edition without preconceptions about the character and, by extension, of course, the meaning and the tone of the play. In short, F1 leaves room for another, more subtle, sort of Petruchio, one who poses as a madman and a bully, creating not only the sort of false havoc of 4.1 but a fictitious self as well.[21]

In that connection, Hibbard's direction, *"Exit another Servingman,"* after Petruchio says, "bid my cousin Ferdinand come hither," may alter a major aspect of the comedy of 4.1. As H. J. Oliver points out, "Conceivably the servants know that there is no such person [as Ferdinand], for F1 provides no exit here, and editors spoil the joke by inserting one."[22] Much in the scene suggests precisely this kind of absurd joke. From a production point of view, we found it impossible to take literally Petruchio's claims about his serving staff, or for that matter those of his surrogate, Grumio. For example, though five servants appear—Nathaniel, Philip, Joseph, Nicholas, and Peter have lines after F1's *"Enter foure or fiue seruingmen"* (TLN 1733)—Grumio names no less than six others—Walter, Sugarsop, Gabriel, Adam, Ralph, and Gregory. Were we really to take seriously the production problems—and cost—of eleven serving men, "their blue coats brushed"? And if "there were none fine but Adam, Ralph and Gregory," why is it that Nathaniel, Philip, Joseph, and Nicholas appear? And who answers "here" for Gregory? Is he the fifth serving man, and if so, is Peter, who has the line "I," the sixth serving man? Is there a spaniel in the play? Cousin Ferdinand?

Our solution was to make it clear by the servants' amusement and confusion that Petruchio is improvising as he goes along. Such an understanding of Petruchio is quite in accord with the man who claims that in their first meeting Kate "hung about my neck . . . and won me to her love," who stages a "rescue" of his bride from her own wedding, who contradicts the clock and the sun, and who greets an old, rich man with "good morrow, Gentle mistress." It sorts less well with a Petruchio who strikes his servants. As for the stage direction that a servant exits following Petruchio's request to see his cousin, we found that there, as well as with his spaniel and his slippers, the bewildered servant, scratching his head, looking desperately around, not knowing which way to go, and mugging for help to his fellows, made the scene funnier and reinforced Petruchio's game of make-believe. F1 allows that interpretation as well as the more traditional, while the accretion of stage directions over the centuries has slowly restricted the possibilities to a less imaginative, bully Petruchio ordering a small army of servants to perform real tasks.

ASSIGNING LOCALE

Decisions editors have made with regard to the imagined locale of a scene can also influence an audience's sense of character. Just as with asides, such editorial assistance, designed as a help to readers, quickly translates to the stage and by a forged process back into the myth of the play. Strictly speaking, of course, a locale, like a scene designation, is not a stage direction. F1, in fact, gives no locales at all but relies on lines of the characters to fix the identity of a scene's whereabouts. This is a hard fact for actors and directors of Shakespeare, since even productions on a bare stage must begin with a sense of place. Such basic distinctions as inside and outside dictate the way a character speaks and moves, what costumes he wears, how likely he is to be observed or to meet another character, how private or public his actions and words are—all of which have significant influence on the mood, the tone, and even the meaning of the scene. Directors, therefore, pounce on any information that can tell them where the action is happening.

The opening of the play proper provides a good illustration of the suggestive power of locale. Pope, who first named the "Induction," prefaces the entrance of Lucentio and Tranio with "The Taming of the Shrew / Act I. Scene I. Padua."[23] But where in Padua? Theobald provides "a street in Padua," and in so doing assures the public nature of the proceedings. But not so public as Quiller-Couch would have it: "Padua, the houses of Baptista, Hortensio and others opening upon a public square . . . 'Lucentio and his man Tranio' enter the square." Such a setting (essentially a Palladian *mise en scène*) heightens much in the scene: Lucentio's opening effusiveness is all the more gushing in so public a locale, his falling in love at first sight all the more ridiculous; Baptista's bias toward Bianca all the more blatant, his humiliation of Kate all the more painful; and the exchange of clothes between Lucentio and Tranio with Biondello's comment, "Where are you?" (TLN 529–30), all the more comic. In this case, then, editorial tradition appears to have served the dramatic requirements of the scene without imposing any particular reading on the characters.

Less innocent is another locale originally assigned by Rowe on the page with the dramatis personae and provided by Pope immediately before 4.1: "Petruchio's Country House." From the seemingly trivial word "country" has sprung the assumption of most modern productions that Petruchio is somewhere between an Elizabethan Marlboro Man and an Italian hillbilly. His house in scenes 1 and 3 of act 4 is usually depicted as the neglected cabin of a backwoods hermit or, at best, as a rustic, rambling villa à la Ponderosa. What is the source of this conception? Not, I think, a fair reading of F1.

Petruchio's first words—"*Verona,* for a while I take my leaue" (TLN 566)—tell us he is from a town, not from some rural place. Later he introduces himself to Baptista as a "gentleman of *Verona*" (TLN 908), and his often-repeated connection with his father and his father's property further suggests that his family is from Verona and "well knowne throughout all Italy" (TLN 930). The only suggestion the text gives that Petruchio's house is in any way associated with the country is his remark to Grumio (TLN 1757–58), "Did I not bid thee meete me in the Parke / And bring along these rascal knaues with thee?" (the correct answer to which is probably "No"). The use of the word "rascal" suggests that Petruchio is referring to a deer park, but such preserves adjacent to the homes of wealthy men did not exclude the possibility that the house was in some way a part of the town and by no means meant that it was isolated. At the end of 4.3 Petruchio orders Grumio to "bring our horses vnto Long-lane end, / There wil we mount, and thither walke on foote" (TLN 2168–69). These instructions imply an urban setting with enough congestion in the street to persuade Petruchio that he and his party had best walk to the end of the street before mounting their horses.

Without the authority of F1, the assumption that Petruchio is somehow from the country appears debatable, and the evidence of the text that Petruchio is a city man has a profound effect on the conception of his character. His behavior as a "madcap ruffian" (TLN 1168) and a "mad-braine rudesby" (TLN 1398) becomes, like his wedding costume in 3.2, deliberately chosen, not ingrained by a life away from civilization. After all, his message to Kate is that appearances do not matter—"is the Iay more precious then the Larke? / Because his feathers are more beautifull?" (TLN 2158–59). To ignore, therefore, the traditional editorial assumption about the location of Petruchio's house is to sharpen our sense of Petruchio as a game player and as a man with a healthy contempt for appearances. Followed to its logical conclusion, that approach to Petruchio's character has the effect of inverting our view of him. The man who seems maddest but is the wisest is certainly a corollary of the woman he chooses, who appears to be a shrew but makes the best wife. Further corollaries can shed even more interesting light on the play: the man who appears to be a brute can be the gentle husband; the wife who makes a public speech about subservience to a husband might privately be an equal partner.[24] The point is not that this view of the play, though I believe in it, is preferable to traditional interpretations, but that one effect of editorial decisions with respect to locale—and, as we have seen, to asides and to added actions—is that they have foreclosed other possibilities.

Added or Moved Exits and Entrances

In the case of the servant sent for Cousin Ferdinand we have already seen how an exit assumed by an editor can change the tone and meaning of a scene. Editors, however, cannot avoid contributions in this area because here, more clearly than with other sorts of stage directions, F1 simply makes mistakes. Of the fourteen exits added by Rowe and Theobald (ten and four, respectively), thirteen are undebatably necessary to the stage business. In almost all cases, the issue is not whether or not there is an exit, but when exactly it takes place. For example, just before the first encounter of Kate and Petruchio, F1 follows Baptista's question, "Signior *Petruchio*, will you go with vs, / Or shall I send my daughter *Kate* to you" (TLN 1034–35), with "*Exit. Manet Petruchio.*" The problem with that stage direction is that Hortensio at least is still with Baptista, so editors have changed the stage direction to the plural "exeunt." They assume as well that the others—Gremio, Tranio, and Biondello—also wait until then to exit. If so, none of them—all garrulous characters—has said a word during the sixty lines of dialogue. In our production we did not know what to do with these characters. It seemed unlikely that Gremio or Tranio, both chronic interrupters, would stand quietly by during Petruchio's negotiations with Baptista when both of them have so much at stake. We solved the problem by moving the exit of that threesome fifty-six lines earlier, following Baptista's invitation to "go walke a little in the Orchard" (TLN 976). He points the way, tells his guests "you are passing welcome," and begins to follow them offstage when Petruchio calls him back with "Signior *Baptista*, my businesse asketh haste" (TLN 979). Thus the stage direction, "Exeunt Gremio, Tranio, and Biondello," at 2.1.112, without contradicting F1, solves the unlikely silence of three noisy characters by removing them from the stage.

Although in this case an ingenious director might be able to make the more traditional exit work without damaging the characters of Gremio, Tranio, and Biondello, the placement of the exit or entrance can sometimes alter the meaning of the scene. The passage in *The Shrew* where editors have most confidently repositioned an F1 exit shows the impact that such decisions can have on character and theme. After the duel between Petruchio and Kate,

F1 provides the stage direction, *"Enter Baptista, Gremio, Trayno"* (TLN 1155), following Petruchio's line, "Thou must be married to no man but me." Beginning with Pope, editors moved the entrance first five lines later to follow the end of Petruchio's speech and then, following Capell, back one line to come after Petruchio says, "Heere comes your father." Though this placement still holds sway, some editors have returned to the F1 position.[25] Oliver explains:

> The placing of the direction in F1 indicates another entrance from the back of the deep Elizabethan stage. The audience sees the other characters approaching before Petruchio sees them.[26]

But on the stage we discovered another and more interesting reason for the F1 entrance.

From the moment of Kate's entrance Petruchio puts on a rhetorical show from the coarsest puns to the most overwrought compliments, all the while maintaining such complete fictions as that he has heard her "mildness praised in every town," that she is "slow in speech" and "soft and affable." But he begins his final lines alone to her as if to dismiss the game he has been playing: "and therefore setting all this chat aside, / Thus in plaine termes . . ." (TLN 1147–48). The form and content of what follows are in sharp contrast to all that has gone before:

> your father hath consented
> That you shall be my wife; your dowry greed on,
> And will you, nill you, I will marry you.
> Now *Kate*, I am a husband for your turne,
> For by this light, whereby I see thy beauty,
> Thy beauty that doth make me like thee well,
> Thou must be married to no man but me[.]
>
> (TLN 1148–54)

The language here is "plaine" and unadorned; the content is true. At this point in F1, Baptista, Gremio, and Tranio enter. What we noticed in staging the scene was that immediately following the F1 entrance, Petruchio returns to the rhetorical mode of his opening gambit, the rapid repetition of Kate's name, and the puns. It may be, as Oliver suggests, that Petruchio has not yet seen Baptista and company, but by having him see them we found an explanation for the change in his speech. The lines

> For I am he am borne to tame you *Kate*,
> And bring you from a wilde *Kate* to a *Kate*
> Comfortable as other household *Kates:*
>
> (TLN 1156–58)

are meant for Baptista and the suitors, and the line "Heere comes your father, neuer make deniall" is an aside to Katherine before he finishes with "I must and will haue *Katherine* to my wife" (TLN 1160).

Such a reading, based on the F1 placement of the stage direction, has profound implications for the play. First, it strongly suggests the gamester in Petruchio by showing him in and out of his verbal disguise. Second, it throws into sharp contrast the theme of his undisguised and private voice (the deal is made, I will marry you, we are a good match, you are beautiful, I like you) with the theme of his disguised and public voice (I am your tamer, I want you to be like other wives). Third, it makes clear Petruchio's willingness to be undisguised with Kate while he maintains his mask with her society and thus establishes his distance from them and their view of the "taming"—an attitude he will later make clear: "If she and I be pleas'd, what's that to you?," "Be madde and merry, or goe hang yourselues" (TLN 1183, 1612)

This understanding of the issues in the play, of Petruchio's game and his contempt for the people in Kate's background, is connected as well to the final stage direction in the play—or, more precisely, to its absence. In F1 the final lines look like this:

> *Pet.* Come *Kate*, weee'le to bed,
> We three are married, but you two are sped.
> 'Twas I wonne the wager, though you hit the white,
> and being a winner, God giue you good night.
> *Exit Petruchio*
> *Horten.* Now goe thy wayes, thou hast tam'd a curst Shrow.
> *Luc.* Tis a wonder, by your leaue, she wil be tam'd so.
> (TLN 2743–50)

Rowe first allows the bride to leave with her groom when he emends the stage direction at 2747 to "Exeunt Petruchio and Katherine," an addition with which it is hard to quarrel. Pope added the Sly material from *A Shrew* in place of the last sixteen lines. Theobald then removed the interpolated material, restored the last lines, and finished the play with *"Exeunt Omnes."* That "exeunt," which survives in all successive editions, does not appear in F1. It clearly reflects the assumption of a proscenium stage, where the arch and the flats made the exit of a minimum of nine remaining characters, all of whom are at a wedding feast, at least a possibility. But such a mass exit makes no sense on an Elizabethan stage.

Since Shakespeare frequently left characters on the stage, such an ending changes the nature of the play without sufficient justification. Although F1 empties the stage at the end of seven of the twelve comedies, Puck remains on the stage to ask for applause in *A Midsummer Night's Dream*, a dance ends *Much Ado About Nothing*, Feste sings his song at the end of *Twelfth Night*, and *Measure for Measure* ends with everyone on stage. The text makes clear that Petruchio and Katherine leave the wedding gathering, but nothing in the two last lines suggests that anyone follows. Indeed, Hortensio's "goe thy wayes" are the words of a man who is staying put. More important, the point of the scene is, at least in part, the dismissal of the others by a triumphant Petruchio. The departure of the rest of the party, in whatever direction, undercuts that point. Lucentio, moreover, follows Hortensio's attempted summation—"thou hast tam'd a curst Shrow" (TLN 2748–49)—with a line that leaves that interpretation open to question: "Tis a wonder, by your leaue, she wil be tam'd so." These words, by raising the possibility that Kate is a partner to her reformation, contradict the viewpoint of Petruchio's admirers, who sit or stand abandoned by the couple who has "a world elsewhere." More intriguingly, Lucentio's line, the final words in the play, also contradicts the play's title and might have discomforted the larger audience outside of the play.

In our production we had originally ended the play with Petruchio's last line and the couple's exit. We guessed correctly that the exchange between Hortensio and Lucentio prevented a "big finish" by returning the focus to the losers at the feast. Gradually, though, we became aware of the degree to which Petruchio's battle is not with Kate but with Kate's world, and we decided that the uncomfortable and deflated party left behind was as integral to Shakespeare's purpose as Feste's melancholy song in *Twelfth Night*. In restoring the last two lines and in omitting, as does F1, the "exeunt," we not only found the staging simpler and more logical, we also discovered a play that seems to challenge the assumptions of its audience, and we preserved a complexity lost to the editorial stage direction. In other of his plays, with perhaps less popular traditions, such complexity is called Shakespearean.

NOTES

1. My codirector was Professor Roger Allan Hall, of James Madison University's Department of Theatre and Dance. Whenever I say "we" in this essay, I'm referring to our joint decisions. Subsequently, I have served as a consultant for Jim Warren's 1989 Shenandoah Shakespeare Express production of the play and for Mary Hartman's 1994 SSE production.

2. Charlton Hinman, *The Norton Facsimile of the First Folio of Shakespeare* (New York: W. W. Norton, 1968), p. 238; *The Taming of the Shrew*, ed. Sir Arthur Quiller-Couch and John Dover Wilson, The New Shakespeare (1928; reprint, Cambridge: Cambridge University Press, 1953), p. 57.

3. *The Taming of the Shrew*, ed. Brian Morris (London: Methuen, 1981). Other editions of the play cited: *The Works of Mr. William Shakespeare*, ed. Nicholas Rowe (1709); *The Works of Shakespeare*, ed. Lewis Theobald (1733); *The Works of Shakespear*, ed. Thomas

Hanmer (1744); *The Plays of William Shakespeare*, ed. Samuel Johnson (1765); *Mr William Shakespeare, his Comedies, Histories, and Tragedies*, ed. Edward Capell (1767); *The Plays and Poems of William Shakespeare*, ed. Edmond Malone (1790); *The Works of William Shakespeare*, ed. William George Clark and William Aldis Wright (Cambridge and London, 1863); *The Taming of the Shrew*, ed. G. R. Hibbard, (Harmondsworth: Penguin, 1968); *The Taming of the Shrew*, ed. H. J. Oliver (Oxford: Clarendon Press, 1982); *The Taming of the Shrew*, ed. Barbara A. Mowat and Paul Werstine (New York: Washington Square Press, 1992).

4. I have not included the imposition of act and scene divisions in my consideration of stage directions because—with the exception of Pope's interpolation from *A Shrew*—such editorial decisions do not show up in the stage action, per se. Obviously, editorial decisions about act and scene divisions *could* affect the staging of a play, but normally the only performance matter at issue is the location of the interval (or whether or not to have one).

5. Alan Dessen, *Elizabethan Stage Conventions and Modern Interpreters* (Cambridge: Cambridge University Press, 1984), 39.

6. *The Shrew*, ed. Morris, 270–71.

7. *The Taming of the Shrew*, ed. Richard Hosley, The Pelican Shakespeare (Baltimore: Pelican, 1964); *The Taming of the Shrew*, ed. Ann Thompson, The New Cambridge Shakespeare (Cambridge: Cambridge University Press, 1984).

8. His excuse that "*Gremio* is harkning still, / And happilie we might be interrupted" (TLN 2235–36) seems unnecessarily to avoid a suitor who has already been dispatched in the dowry competition for Bianca.

9. We felt confident ascribing the "I praie the gods" line (TLN 2250) to Biondello, who is impudent throughout the play, but I agree with Stanley Wells that this "exit-line comes even better from Lucentio," since he has the most direct interest in having Bianca wed. Our 1983 production also followed Wells's view that Tranio's "'Dallie not with the gods, but get thee gone' is obviously addressed to [Biondello]" (Wells et al., *William Shakespeare: A Textual Companion* [Oxford: Clarendon Press, 1987], 170), but in the 1994 SSE production of *The Shrew* Tranio (supposed Lucentio) took the line to Lucentio (trapped in his guise as Cambio) with wonderful comic effect. The servant was jumping at an opportunity to scold the master.

10. Morris cites R. Warwick Bond's suggestion that Peter has come to tell Tranio dinner is served seems most unlikely in terms of efficient use of personnel. Why would Shakespeare waste an actor on such a peripheral chore when Tranio's announcement serves equally well?

11. I agree with Oliver's view, based on such stage directions, "that *The Taming of the Shrew* was set up in print from Shakespeare's own manuscript" (*The Shrew*, ed. Oliver, 10).

12. William J. Rolfe, ed., *The Taming of the Shrew* (New York: Harper and Brothers, 1897).

13. *Taming of the Shrew*, ed. Quiller-Couch and Dover Wilson (1928).

14. Or to the third line, since Petruchio might also be wishing "much good" to Hortensio's heart.

15. E. A. J. Honigmann, "Re-enter the Stage Direction: Shakespeare and Some Contemporaries," *Shakespeare Survey*, 29 (1976): 117–25 (120). Thus the Hamlet who says "A little more than kin and less than kind" to Claudius's face is a different character from the Hamlet who says it so that no one else on stage can hear (and the latter is different from a Hamlet who says the line only for the benefit, say, of his mother; and so on).

16. *Works of Mr. William Shakespeare*, ed. Rowe, 2:343.

17. Ibid., 361. Hibbard's less specific "she obeys" (p. 154) seems to me an improvement that allows more to the imagination of the director or actor. Kate might, for example,

decide to drop, toss, flip, hurl, or pitch the cap instead of obeying the letter of Petruchio's law.

18. Ibid., 338.

19. Cf. P. J. Croft, "The 'Friar of Orders Gray' and the Nun," *RES* 32 (1981): 1–16.

20. As does the title page of the Kittredge Shakespeare. Even the cover of Ann Thompson's New Cambridge edition of the play has C. Walter Hodges's drawing of 4.1 as it might have appeared on the theater stage. Petruchio is just about to throw the meat and beneath his legs is a fallen whip.

21. For a good discussion of this aspect of the play, see C. C. Seronsy, " 'Supposes' as the Unifying Theme in *The Shrew*," *SQ* 14 (1963): 15–30.

22. *The Shrew*, ed. Oliver, 184n.

23. *The Works of Mr. William Shakespear*, ed. Alexander Pope (1723).

24. Coppélia Kahn asks, "Would [Petruchio] enjoy being married to a woman as dull and proper as the Kate who delivers that marriage sermon? From all indications, no. Then can we conclude that Petruchio no less than Kate knowingly plays a false role in this marriage, the role of victorious tamer and complacent master? I think we can . . ." (*Man's Estate: Masculine Identity in Shakespeare* [Berkeley, Los Angeles, and London: University of California Press, 1981], 117).

25. The New Shakespeare (Quiller-Couch and Wilson, eds.) follows Capell; the Oxford Shakespeare (Oliver, ed.) follows F1.

26. *The Shrew*, ed. Oliver, 184n.

Bibliography

Adams, Joseph Quincy, ed. *The Dramatic Records of Sir Henry Herbert, 1623–1673*. New Haven: Yale University Press, 1917.

Adams, Thomas. *The White Devil, or the Hypocrite Uncased*. London, 1613.

Alcilia: Philoparthens Loving Folly. London, 1613.

Alexander, Peter. "The Original Ending of *The Taming of a Shrew*." *SQ* 20 (1969): 111–16.

———. *Shakespeare's Henry VI and Richard III*. Cambridge: Cambridge University Press, 1929.

———. "*The Taming of the Shrew*." *TLS*, 16 September 1926, 614.

Allen, Michael J. B., and Kenneth Muir, eds. *Shakespeare's Plays in Quarto*. Berkeley: University of California Press, 1981.

Andrews, John, ed. *Macbeth*. London: Dent, 1993.

Arber, Edward. *A Transcript of the Registers of the Company of the Stationers of London, 1554–1640*. 5 vols. London and Birmingham, 1875–94.

Aston, Margaret. "Lollardy and Sedition, 1381–1431." *Past and Present* 17 (1960): 1–44.

Avni, Ora. *The Resistance of Reference: Linguistics, Philosophy, and the Literary Text*. Baltimore: Johns Hopkins University Press, 1990.

Babula, William. "Fortune or Fate: Ambiguity in Robert Greene's 'Orlando Furioso.'" *MLR* 67 (1972): 482–85.

Bagrow, Leo. *History of Cartography: Revised and Enlarged by R. A. Skelton*. London: Watts and Co., 1964.

Baldwin, T. W. Review of *The Taming of the Shrew*, edited by Arthur Quiller-Couch and J. Dover Wilson. *JEGP* 31 (1932): 152–56.

Barker, Nicholas, and John Collins. *A Sequel to An Enquiry Concerning Certain Nineteenth-Century Pamphlets by John Carter and Graham Pollard*. London: Scolar Press, 1983.

Barroll, J. Leeds. "The Court of the First Stuart Queen." In *The Mental World of the Jacobean Court*, edited by Linda Levy Peck, 191–208. Cambridge: Cambridge University Press, 1991.

Barthes, Roland. "From Work to Text," translated by Josue V. Harari. In *Textual Strategies: Perspectives in Post-Structuralist Criticism*, edited by Josue V. Harari, 73–81. Ithaca: Cornell University Press, 1979.

———. "Theory of the Text." In *Untying the Text*, edited by Robert Young, 31–47. Boston and London: Routledge, 1981.

Barton, Anne. *The Names of Comedy.* Toronto: University of Toronto Press, 1990.

Beaurline, L. A. Textual introduction to *The Noble Gentleman.* In *The Dramatic Works in the Beaumont and Fletcher Canon,* edited by Fredson Bowers, 3:11–20. Cambridge: Cambridge University Press, 1976.

Beckerman, Bernard. *Shakespeare at the Globe, 1599–1613.* New York: Macmillan, 1962.

Beilin, Elaine. "Elizabeth Cary and *The Tragedie of Mariam.*" *Papers on Language and Literature* 16 (1980): 45–64.

Beling, Richard. *A Sixth Booke to the Countess of Pembrokes Arcadia.* Dublin, 1624.

Belsey, Catherine. *The Subject of Tragedy: Identity and Difference in Renaissance Drama.* London: Methuen, 1985.

Benson, Larry D., ed. *The Riverside Chaucer.* 3d ed. Boston: Houghton Mifflin, 1987.

Bentley, G. E. *The Profession of Player in Shakespeare's Time, 1590–1642.* Princeton: Princeton University Press, 1984.

———. *Shakespeare: A Biographical Handbook.* New Haven: Yale University Press, 1961.

———. *Shakespeare and Jonson: Their Reputations in the Seventeenth Century Compared.* 2 vols. 1945. Reprint, Chicago and London: University of Chicago Press, 1969.

Berger, Harry, Jr. "Text against Performance in Shakespeare: The Example of *Macbeth.*" In *The Power of Forms in the English Renaissance,* edited by Stephen Greenblatt, 49–79. Norman, Okla.: Pilgrim, 1982.

Berger, Thomas L. "The Second Quarto of *Othello* and the Question of Textual 'Authority.'" In *Othello: New Perspectives,* edited by Virginia Mason Vaughan and Kent Cartwright, 26–47. Rutherford, N.J.: Fairleigh Dickinson University Press, 1991.

Bergeron, David M. *Royal Family, Royal Lovers: King James of England and Scotland.* Columbia: University of Missouri Press, 1991.

Bevington, David M. *From "Mankind" to Marlowe.* Cambridge: Harvard University Press, 1962.

———, ed. *The Complete Works of Shakespeare.* 3d ed. Glenview, Ill.: Scott Foresman, 1980.

———. *1 Henry IV.* Oxford: Oxford University Press, 1987.

Blagden, Cyprian. *The Stationers' Company: A History, 1403–1959.* Cambridge: Harvard University Press, 1960.

Bodenham, John. *England's Helicon.* London, 1614.

Bonham–Carter, Victor. *Authors by Profession.* Vol. 1. Los Altos, Calif.: William Kaufman, 1978.

Booty, John. "Tumult in Cheapside: The Hacket Conspiracy." *Historical Magazine of the Protestant Episcopal Church* 42 (1973): 293–317.

Bowers, Fredson. "Today's Shakespeare Texts, and Tomorrow's." *SB* 19 (1966): 39–65.

Bracton, Henryde. *Bracton on the Laws and Customs of England.* Translated by Samuel E. Thorne. Vol. 2. Cambridge: Belknap Press of Harvard University Press, 1968.

Bracy, William. *The Merry Wives of Windsor: The History and Transmission of Shakespeare's Text.* University of Missouri Studies 25, no. 1. Columbia: Curators of the University of Missouri, 1952.

Bradley, David. *From Text to Performance in the Elizabethan Theatre.* Cambridge: Cambridge University Press, 1992.

Braunmuller, A. R. "*King John* and Historiography." *ELH* 55 (1988): 309–22.

———. "*Macbeth* and Scottishness." Paper, Shakespeare Association of America meeting, 1989.

Briggs, William. *The Law of International Copyright.* London: Stevens and Hayes, 1906.

Brissenden, Alan. "*Romeo and Juliet,* III.iii.108: The Nurse and the Dagger." *N&Q,* n.s., 28 (1981): 126–27.

British Museum. *General Catalogue of Printed Books, Photolithographic Edition to 1955.* London: Trustees of the British Museum, 1964.

Brooke, C. F. Tucker, ed. *The Shakespeare Apocrypha.* Oxford: Clarendon Press, 1908.

Brooke, Nicholas, ed. *Macbeth.* Oxford: Oxford University Press, 1990.

Brown, J. D. "Practical Bibliography." *The Library,* 2d ser., 4 (1903): 145–46.

Brown, Lloyd A. *The Story of Maps.* London: Cresset Press, 1951.

Bullough, Geoffrey. *Narrative and Dramatic Sources of Shakespeare.* 8 vols. London: Routledge, 1957–75.

Burkhart, Robert. *Shakespeare's Bad Quartos: Deliberate Abridgments Designed for Performance by a Reduced Cast.* The Hague: Mouton, 1975.

Calderwood, James. *To Be and Not to Be: Negation and Metadrama in "Hamlet."* New York: Columbia University Press, 1983.

Campion, Thomas. *The Description of a Maske.* 1614.

Capell, Edward, ed. *Mr William Shakespeare, his Comedies, Histories, and Tragedies.* 1767–68.

Carier, Benjamin. *A copy of a letter.* Liège, 1615.

Carlson, David. "The Writings and Manuscript Collections of the Elizabethan Alchemist, Antiquary, and Herald Francis Thynne." *HLQ* 52 (1989): 203–72.

Carlson, Leland H., ed. *The Writings of John Greenwood and Henry Barrow.* London: George Allen and Unwin, 1970.

Carnegie, David. "Actors' Parts and the 'Play of Poore.'" *Harvard Library Bulletin* 30 (1982): 5–24.

———, ed. "The Part of Poore." In *Collections XV.* London: Malone Society, 1993.

Carroll, John M. *What's in a Name: An Essay in the Psychology of Reference.* New York: Freeman, 1985.

Carter, John. *Taste and Technique in Book Collecting.* 4th ed. New York: Bowker, 1948. Reprint, London: Private Libraries Association, 1970.

Carter, John, and Graham Pollard. *An Enquiry Concerning Certain Nineteenth-Century Pamphlets.* 2d ed. London: Scolar Press, 1983.

Cary, Elizabeth. *The Tragedy of Mariam, The Fair Queen of Jewry.* London, 1613.

Chambers, E. K. "Abridged Play–texts." Review of *Two Elizabethan Stage Abridgements,* by W. W. Greg. *The Library,* 4th ser., 4 (1923–24): 242–48.

———. *The Elizabethan Stage.* 4 vols. Oxford: Clarendon Press, 1923.

———. *William Shakespeare: A Study of Facts and Problems.* 2 vols. Oxford: Clarendon Press, 1930.

Chapman, George. *Andromeda Liberata; or, The Nuptials of Perseus and Andromeda.* 1614.

Clare, Janet. *"Art made tongue–tied by authority": Elizabethan and Jacobean Dramatic Censorship.* Manchester: Manchester University Press, 1990.

Clark, Alice. *Working Life of Women in the Seventeenth Century.* 3d ed. London: Routledge, 1992.

Clark, Cecily. "Onomastics" In *Cambridge History of the English Language,* vol. 2, *1066–1476,* edited by N. F. Blake, 542–606. Cambridge: Cambridge University Press, 1992.

Clark, William George, and William Aldis Wright, eds. *The Works of William Shakespeare.* Cambridge and London: Cambridge University Press, 1863.

———. *Select Plays: Macbeth.* Oxford: Clarendon Press, 1869.

Clayton, Thomas, ed. *The "Hamlet" First Published (Q1 1603): Origins, Form, Intertextualities.* Newark: University of Delaware Press, 1992.

Cloud, Random. *See* McLeod, Randall.

C[ockayne], G. E. *The Complete Peerage of England, Scotland, and Ireland.* Revised by Vicary Gibbs. Vol. 3. London: St. Catherine Press, 1913.

Cockburn, Cynthia. *Brothers: Male Dominance and Technological Exchange.* London: Pluto Press, 1983.

Coke, Sir Edward. *The Second Part of the Institutes of the Lawes of England.* 1642. Reprint, New York: Garland, 1979.

———. *The Third Part of the Institutes of the Laws of England.* 1644. Reprint, New York: Garland, 1979.

Collins, J. Churton, ed. *The Plays and Poems of Robert Greene.* 2 vols. Oxford: Clarendon Press, 1905.

Collinson, Patrick. *The Elizabethan Puritan Movement.* 1967. Reprint, Oxford: Clarendon Press, 1990.

———. "John Field and Elizabethan Puritanism." In *Godly People: Essays on English Protestantism and Puritanism,* 335–70. London: Hambledon Press, 1983.

Cornish, W. R. *Intellectual Property: Patents, Copyright, Trade Marks, and Allied Rights.* London: Sweet and Maxwell, 1981.

Coryate, Thomas. *Coryat's Crudities.* Vol. 1. 1611. Reprint, vol. 1, Glasgow: James MacLehose and Sons, 1905.

Creizenach, Wilhelm. *Das Englische Drama im Zeitalter Shakespeares.* In *Geschichte des Neuern Dramas,* 4:686–98. Halle: Max Niemeyer, 1909.

Croft, P. J. "The 'Friar of Order Gray' and the Nun." *RES* 32 (1981): 1–16.

Crone, G. R. *Maps and their Makers: An Introduction to the History of Cartography.* London: Hutchinson's University Library, 1953.

Cross, Claire. *Church and People, 1450–1660: The Triumph of the Laity in the English Church.* Glasgow: Fontana, 1976.

Crupi, Charles W. *Robert Greene.* Boston: Twayne, 1986.

Dalton, Michael. *Countrey Justice, 1619.* Classical English Law Texts. London: Professional Books, 1973.

Daniel, Samuel. *A Free and Offenceless Justification.* London, 1614.

———. *Tethys Festival.* London, 1610.

Danson, Lawrence, and Ivo Kamps, eds. *The Phoenix.* In *Collected Middleton* (Oxford: Oxford University Press, forthcoming).

Davies, John. *The Muses Sacrifice.* 1612.

Dawson, Anthony B. "Giving the Finger: Puns and Transgression in *The Changeling.*" In *Elizabethan Theatre 12,* edited by A. L. Magnusson and C. E. McGee, 93–112. Toronto: P. D. Meany, 1993.

Dawson, William Roy, Jr. "A Critical Edition of Thomas Middleton's *A Trick to Catch the Old One.*" Ph.D. diss., University of Tennessee, 1969.

de Grazia, Margreta. "What is a Work? What is a Document?" In *New Ways of Looking at Old Texts,* edited by W. Speed Hill, 199–207. Binghamton, N.Y.: Medieval and Renaissance Texts and Studies, 1993.

de Grazia, Margreta, and Peter Stallybrass. "The Materiality of the Shakespearean Text." *SQ* 44 (1993): 255–83.

de Man, Paul. *Blindness and Insight.* New York: Oxford University Press, 1971.

Dessen, Alan. *Elizabethan Stage Conventions and Modern Interpreters.* Cambridge: Cambridge University Press, 1984.

Digges, Leonard. "Upon Master William Shakespeare, the Deceased Authour, and his Poems." In *Poems, written by Wil. Shake-speare, Gent.* London, 1640.

Dillon, Janette. "Is there a Performance in this Text?" *SQ* 45 (1994): 74–86.

Dollimore, Jonathan. *Sexual Dissidence: Augustine to Wilde, Freud to Foucault.* Oxford: Clarendon Press, 1991.

———. "Subjectivity, Sexuality and Transgression: The Jacobean Connection." *RD,* n.s., 17 (1986): 53–81.

Donovan, Kevin J. "Recent Studies in Robert Greene (1968–1988)." *ELR* 20 (1990): 163–75.

Doran, Madeleine. *Henry VI, Parts II and III: Their Relation to "The Contention" and the "True Tragedy."* University of Iowa Humanistic Studies 4, no. 4. Iowa City: University of Iowa Press, 1928.

Drayton, Michael. *England's Heroicall Epistles.* 1597.

Dryden. John. *The Miscellaneous Works.* 4 vols. London: J. and R. Tonson, 1767.

———. *The Miscellaneous Works of John Dryden.* Edited by Samuel Derrick. 4 vols. London: J. and R. Tonson, 1760.

———. *The Miscellaneous Works of John Dryden.* London, 1767.

———. *Works.* Edited by Thomas Broughton. London, 1743.

Dubrow, Heather. *A Happier Eden: The Politics of Marriage in the Stuart Epithalamion.* Ithaca: Cornell University Press, 1990.

Duff, E. Gordon. *A Century of the English Book Trade.* London: Bibliographical Society, 1948.

Dunstan, A. C., and W. W. Greg, eds. *The Tragedy of Mariam.* London: Malone Society, 1914.

Duthie, G. I. *The "Bad" Quarto of Hamlet: A Critical Study.* Cambridge: Cambridge University Press, 1941.

———. *"The Taming of a Shrew* and *The Taming of the Shrew."* *RES* 19 (1943): 337–56.

Dutton, Richard. *Mastering the Revels: The Regulation and Censorship of English Renaissance Drama.* Iowa City: University of Iowa Press, 1991.

E., T. *The Lawes Resolutions of Womens Rights.* London: assignes of J. More, 1632.

Ellis, Havelock, ed. *A Trick to Catch the Old One.* In *Thomas Middleton.* 1887. Reprint, St. Clair Shores, Mich.: Scholarly Press, 1968.

Ellis, John M. *The Theory of Literary Criticism: A Logical Analysis.* Berkeley and Los Angeles: University of California Press, 1974.

Ellis, Peter Berresford. *MacBeth, High King of Scotland, 1040–57.* London: Muller, 1980.

Evans, G. Blakemore, ed. *The Riverside Shakespeare.* Boston: Houghton Mifflin, 1974.

Fehrenbach, Robert J. "'When Lord Cobham and Edmund Tilney were att odds': Oldcastle, Falstaff, and the Date of *1 Henry IV."* *Shakespeare Studies* 18 (1986): 87–101.

Fiehler, Rudolph. "How Oldcastle Became Falstaff." *MLQ* 16 (1955): 16–28.

Fitzherbert, Sir Anthony, and Richard Crompton. *L'Office et Aucthoritie de Justices de Peace.* 1584. London: Professional Books, 1972.

Foakes, R. A., and R. T. Rickert, eds. *Henslowe's Diary.* Cambridge: Cambridge University Press, 1961.

Foot, M. R. D., and H. C. G. Matthew, eds. *The Gladstone Diaries.* Vol. 4. Oxford: Clarendon Press, 1974.

Foucault, Michel. "What is an Author?," translated by Josue V. Harari. In *Textual Strategies: Perspectives in Post-Structuralist Criticism,* edited by Josue V. Harari, 141–60. Ithaca: Cornell University Press, 1979.

Foxe, John. *Acts and Monuments,* edited by Josiah Pratt. In *The Church Historians of England,* vol. 3. London: Seeleys, 1855.

Francis, F. C. "The Bibliographical Society: A Sketch of the First Fifty Years." In *The Bibliographical Society, 1892–1942,* edited by F. C. Francis, 1–22. London: The Bibliographical Society, 1945.

Friedenreich, Kenneth, ed. *"Accompaninge the players": Essays Celebrating Thomas Middleton, 1580–1980.* New York: AMS Press, 1983.

Fuller, Thomas. *The Church History of Britain.* London, 1655.

Gardiner, Alan. *The Theory of Proper Names.* 2d ed. Oxford: Oxford University Press, 1954.

Gardiner, S. R., ed. *Fortesque Papers.* London: Camden Society, 1871.

Gelber, Norman. "Robert Greene's 'Orlando Furioso': A Study of Thematic Ambiguity." *MLR* 64 (1969): 264–66.

Gibbons, Brian, ed. *Romeo and Juliet.* London: Methuen, 1980.

Gibbs, Philip. *The King's Favourite: The Love Story of Robert Carr and Lady Essex.* London: Hutchinson, 1909.

Gillies, John. *Shakespeare and the Geography of Difference.* Cambridge: Cambridge University Press, 1994.

Goldberg, Jonathan. "The Commodity of Names: 'Falstaff' and 'Oldcastle' in *Henry IV.*" In *Reconfiguring the Renaissance: Essays in Critical Materialism,* edited by Jonathan Crewe, 76–88. Lewisburg, Pa.: Bucknell University Press, 1992.

Gondris, Joanna, ed. *Reading Readings: Essays on Shakespeare Editing in the Eighteenth Century.* Rutherford, N.J.: Fairleigh Dickinson University. Forthcoming.

Gossett, Suzanne. "'Best Men are Molded out of Faults': Marrying the Rapist in Jacobean Drama." *ELR* 14 (1984): 305–27.

Grady, Hugh. "Disintegration and its Reverberations." In *The Appropriation of Shakespeare,* edited by Jean I. Marsden, 111–27. Hemel Hempstead, U.K.: Harvester Wheatsheaf, 1991.

Green, William. *Shakespeare's "Merry Wives of Windsor."* Princeton: Princeton University Press, 1962.

Greenblatt, Stephen. *Shakespearean Negotiations.* Berkeley and Los Angeles: University of California Press, 1988.

Greg, W. W. "The Bibliographical History of the First Folio." *The Library,* 2d ser., 4 (1903): 258–85.

———. "Bibliography—An Apologia." *The Library,* 4th ser., 13 (1932–33): 113–43.

———. *The Editorial Problem in Shakespeare.* 1942. 3d ed. Oxford: Clarendon Press, 1954.

———. "On Certain False Dates in Shakespearian Quartos." *The Library,* 2d ser., 9 (1908): 396–97.

———. "Principles of Emendation in Shakespeare." *Proceedings of the British Academy* 14 (1928): 147–73.

———. Review of *The Bad Quarto of Romeo and Juliet,* by Harry Hoppe. *RES,* n.s., 1 (1950): 64–66.

———. Review of *The Plays and Poems of Robert Greene,* edited by J. Churton Collins. *MLR* 1 (1905–6): 238–51.

———. *The Shakespeare First Folio.* Oxford: Clarendon Press, 1955.

———. *Two Elizabethan Stage Abridgements: The Battle of Alcazar & Orlando Furioso.* London: Malone Society, 1922.

———, ed. *Bonduca,* by John Fletcher. London: Malone Society, 1951.

———. *Dramatic Documents from the Elizabethan Playhouse.* Oxford: Clarendon Press, 1931.

———. *Henslowe's Diary.* London: Bullen, 1904, 1908.

———. *The History of Orlando Furioso, 1594.* London: Malone Society, 1907.

———. *Shakespeare's Merry Wives of Windsor, 1602.* Oxford: Clarendon Press, 1910.

Greville, Fulke. *The Five Years of James.* 1643.

Grosart, Alexander B., ed. *John Davies of Hereford: The Complete Works.* 1878. Reprint, Hildesheim: Olms, 1968.

———. *The Poems of George Daniel, esq. of Beswick, Yorkshire.* Privately printed, 1878.

———. *The Poems Etc., of Richard James, B.D.* London: Chiswick Press, 1880.

Hageman, Elizabeth H. "Editing Katherine Philips." Paper read at the Folger Shakespeare Library on 13 March 1992.

Hageman, Elizabeth H., and Andrea Sununu. "New Manuscript Texts of Katherine Philips, the 'Matchless Orinda.'" *English Manuscript Studies, 1100–1700* 4 (1993): 174–219.

Halio, Jay, ed. *The Merchant of Venice.* Oxford: Oxford University Press, 1993.

Hall, Kim F. *Things of Darkness: Economies of Race and Gender in Early Modern England.* Ithaca: Cornell University Press, 1995.

Halliwell, James O., ed. *The Autobiography of Simonds D'Ewes during the Reigns of James I and Charles I.* Vol. 1. London: Bentley, 1845.

Hamilton, Donna. *Shakespeare and the Politics of Protestant England.* Lexington: University Press of Kentucky, 1992.

Hamilton, Edith, and Huntington Cairns, eds. *Collected Dialogues of Plato.* Princeton: Princeton University Press, 1961.

Hammond, Anthony, ed. *Richard III.* London: Methuen, 1981.

Hanmer, Thomas, ed. *The Works of Shakespear.* 1744.

Harari, Josue V., ed. *Textual Strategies: Perspectives in Post–Structuralist Criticism.* Ithaca: Cornell University Press, 1979.

Harbage, Alfred, ed. *William Shakespeare: The Complete Works.* London: Penguin, 1969.

Harley, J. B., and David Woodward. *The History of Cartography.* Vol. 1. Chicago and London: University of Chicago Press, 1987.

Hart, Alfred. *Stolne and Surreptitious Copies.* Melbourne: Melbourne University Press, 1942.

Harvey, Paul, comp. and ed. *Oxford Companion to English Literature.* 2d ed. Oxford: Oxford University Press, 1937.

Hayashi, Tatsumaro. *A Textual Study of Robert Greene's "Orlando Furioso" with an Elizabethan Text.* Ball State Monographs 21, Publications in English 15. Muncie, Ind.: Ball State University Press, 1973.

Hayward, John. *Life and Raigne of King Henrie IIII.* Edited by John J. Manning. London: Royal Historical Society, 1991.

Heinemann, Margot. *Puritanism and Theatre: Thomas Middleton and Opposition Drama under the Early Stuarts.* Cambridge: Cambridge University Press, 1980.

Heminge, John, and Henry Condell. *Mr William Shakespeares Comedies, Histories, & Tragedies.* London: Isaac Jaggard and Edward Blount, 1623.

Hendricks, Margo, and Patricia Parker, eds. *Women, "Race" and Writing in the Early Modern Period.* London and New York: Routledge, 1994.

Hereford, C. H., Percy Simpson, and Evelyn Simpson, eds. *Ben Jonson.* 11 vols. Oxford: Clarendon Press, 1947–52.

Hieron, Samuel. *The Bridegroom.* 1613.

Hill, W. Speed, ed.*New Ways of Looking at Old Texts.* Binghamton, N.Y.: MRTS, 1993.

Hillyer, Robert S., ed. *The Complete Poetry and Selected Prose of John Donne and The Complete Poetry of William Blake.* New York: Random House, 1941.

Hinman, Charlton. "The 'Copy' for the Second Quarto of *Othello.*" In *Joseph Quincy Adams Memorial Studies,* edited by James G. McManaway, Giles E. Dawson, and Edwin E. Willoughby, 373–89. Washington, D.C.: Folger Shakespeare Library, 1948.

———. *The Printing and Proofreading of the First Folio.* 2 vols. Oxford: Clarendon Press, 1963.

———, ed. *The Norton Facsimile: The First Folio of Shakespeare.* New York: W. W. Norton, 1968.

———. *The Norton Facsimile: The First Folio of Shakespeare.* With a new introduction by Peter Layney. New York: W. W. Norton, 1996.

———. *Richard II, 1597.* Shakespeare Quarto Facsimiles No. 13. Oxford: Clarendon Press, 1966.

Holderness, Graham, and Bryan Loughrey, eds. *The Tragicall Historie of Hamlet.* Lanham, Md.: Barnes and Noble, 1992.

Holmes, Martin. *The Guns of Elsinore.* London: Chatto and Windus, 1964.

Honigmann, E. A. J. "Re-enter the Stage Direction: Shakespeare and Some Contemporaries." *Shakespeare Survey* 29 (1976): 117–25.

———. *Shakespeare: The "Lost Years."* Manchester: Manchester University Press, 1985.

———. "Shakespeare's 'Lost Source-Plays'." *MLR* 49 (1954): 293–307.

———. "Sir John Oldcastle: Shakespeare's Martyr." In *"Fanned and Winnowed Opinions,"* edited by John W. Mahon and Thomas A. Pendleton, 118–32. London: Methuen, 1987.

———. *The Stability of Shakespeare's Text.* Lincoln: University of Nebraska Press, 1965.

Hope, Jonathan. *The Authorship of Shakespeare's Plays.* Cambridge: Cambridge University Press, 1994.

Hoppe, Harry R. *The Bad Quarto of Romeo and Juliet.* Ithaca: Cornell University Press, 1948.

Horwood E. C., and R. E. C. Houghton, eds. *Othello.* Oxford: Oxford University Press, 1968.

Hosley, Richard, ed. *The Taming of the Shrew.* Baltimore: Pelican, 1964.

Houk, Raymond A. "The Evolution of *The Taming of the Shrew.*" *PMLA* 57 (1942): 1009–38.

Housman, A. E. *Selected Prose.* Edited by John Carter. Cambridge: Cambridge University Press, 1961.

Howard–Hill, T. H. "The Author as Scribe or Reviser?" *TEXT* 3 (1987): 305–18.

———. "Buc and the Censorship of *Sir John van Olden Barnavelt* in 1619." *RES*, n.s., 39 (1988): 39–63.

———. *"Macbeth": A Concordance to the Text of the First Folio.* Oxford: Clarendon Press, 1971.

———, ed. *Shakespeare and "Sir Thomas More."* Cambridge: Cambridge University Press, 1989.

Howell, T. B., ed. *A Complete Collection of State Trials [Cobbetts State Trials].* Vol. 3. London: Longman, 1816.

Hunter, G. K. "Flatcaps and Bluecoats." *Essays and Studies,* n.s., 33 (1980): 16–47.

———, ed. *Macbeth.* Harmondsworth: Penguin, 1967.

Ingram, Martin. *Church Courts, Sex and Marriage in England, 1570–1640.* Cambridge: Cambridge University Press, 1987.

Ingram, William. "The Costs of Touring." *MaRDiE* 6 (1993): 57–62.

Ioppolo, Grace. *Revising Shakespeare.* Cambridge: Harvard University Press, 1991.

Irace, Kathleen O. *Reforming the "Bad" Quartos.* Newark: University of Delaware Press, 1994.

Isidore of Seville. *Etymologies.* Augsburg, 1472.

Issacharoff, Michael. "How Playscripts Refer." In *On Referring in Literature,* edited by Anna Whiteside and Michael Issacharoff, 84–94. Bloomington: Indiana University Press, 1987.

Jardine, Lisa. "'Why should he call her whore?': Defamation and Desdemona's Case." In *Addressing Frank Kermode: Essays in Criticism and Interpretation,* edited by Margaret Tudeau–Clayton and Martin Warner, 124–53. Urbana and Chicago: University of Illinois Press, 1991.

Johnson, Charles, and Hilary Jenkinson. *English Court Hand, A.D. 1066 to 1500.* Oxford: Clarendon Press, 1915.

Johnson, Gerald. *"The Merry Wives of Windsor* Q1: Provincial Touring and Adapted Texts." *SQ* 38 (1987): 154–65.

Johnson, Ralph Glassgow, ed. "A Critical Third Edition of Edmund Tilney's *The Flower of Friendshippe,* published in 1577." Ph.D. diss., University of Pittsburgh, 1960.

Johnson, Samuel, ed. *The Plays of William Shakespeare.* 1765.

Jones, Ann Rosalind. "Italians and Others." In *Staging the Renaissance,* edited by David Scott Kastan and Peter Stallybrass, 251–62. New York and London: Routledge, 1991.

Jonson, Ben. *Cynthia's Revels.* 1613.

———. *Hymenaei.* 1606.

Josephus. *The Most Famous and Memorable Works of Josephus.* Translated by Thomas Lodge. London, 1602.

Jowett, John. "The Thieves in *1 Henry IV.*" *RES* 38 (1987): 325–33.

Juneja, Renu. "The Widow as Paradox and Paradigm in Middleton's Plays." *Journal of General Education* 34 (1982): 3–19.

Kahn, Coppélia. *Man's Estate: Masculine Identity in Shakespeare.* Berkeley: University of California Press, 1981.

Kastan, David Scott, and Peter Stallybrass, eds. *Staging the Renaissance*. New York and London: Routledge, 1991.

King, T. J. *Casting Shakespeare's Plays: London Actors and their Roles, 1590–1642*. Cambridge: Cambridge University Press, 1992.

Kinney, Arthur, and Dan Collins, eds. *Renaissance Historicism (Essays from ELR)*. Amherst: University of Massachussets Press, 1987.

Kirschbaum, Leo. "A Census of Bad Quartos." *RES* 14 (1938): 20–43.

Klein, Joan Larsen, ed. *Daughters, Wives, and Widows: Writings by Men about Women and Marriage in England, 1500–1640*. Urbana: University of Illinois Press, 1992.

Knight, Charles, ed. *The Comedies, Histories, Tragedies, and Poems of William Shakspere*. 2d ed. London: Charles Knight and Co., 1842.

———. *The Pictorial Edition of the Works of Shakspere*. Vol. 1. 1841. Reprint, London: George Routledge and Sons, 1867.

Knutson, Roslyn. *The Repertory of Shakespeare's Company, 1594–1613*. Fayetteville: University of Arkansas Press, 1991.

Lakatos, Imre. *Proofs and Refutations, the Logic of Mathematical Discovery*. Edited by John Worrall and Elie Zahar. Cambridge: Cambridge University Press, 1976.

Lake, Peter. "Presbyterianism, the Idea of a National Church and the Argument from Divine Right." In *Protestantism and the National Church in Sixteenth-Century England*, edited by Peter Lake and Maria Dowling, 193–224. London: Croom Helm, 1987.

Lancashire, Anne. "*The Witch*: Stage Flop or Political Mistake?" In *"Accompaninge the players": Essays Celebrating Thomas Middleton, 1580–1980*, edited by Kenneth Friedenreich, 161–181. New York: AMS Press, 1983.

Landa, Louis A., ed. *Gulliver's Travels*. London: Methuen, 1965.

Lawrence, W. J. *Those Nut–Cracking Elizabethans*. London: Argonaut, 1935.

LeComte, Edward. *The Notorious Lady Essex*. New York: Dial, 1969.

Lee, Sidney, ed. *Shakespeare's Comedies Histories, & Tragedies, Being a Reproduction in Facsimile of the First Folio Edition, 1623*. Oxford: Clarendon Press, 1902.

Levin, Harry. *Shakespeare and the Revolution of the Times*. Oxford: Clarendon Press, 1976.

Lewalski, Barbara Kiefer. *Writing Women in Jacobean England*. Cambridge: Harvard University Press, 1993.

Lindley, David. *The Trials of Frances Howard*. London: Routledge, 1993.

Little, Arthur L., Jr. "'An essence that's not seen': The Primal Scene of Racism in *Othello*." *SQ* 44 (1993): 304–24.

Logan, T. P, and D. S. Smith, eds. *The Popular School: A Survey and Bibliography of Recent Studies in Renaissance Drama*. Lincoln: University of Nebraska Press, 1976.

Long, William B. "'A bed / for woodstock': A Warning for the Unwary." *MaRDiE* 2 (1985): 91–118.

———. *Co-operative Ventures: English Manuscript Playbooks, 1590–1635*. Forthcoming.

———. "Stage Directions: A Misinterpreted Factor in Determining Textual Provenance." *TEXT* 2 (1985): 121–38.

Loughrey, Bryan. "Q1 in Recent Performance: An Interview." In *The "Hamlet" First Published (Q1 1603)*, edited by Thomas Clayton, 123–136. Newark: University of Delaware Press, 1992.

Loughrey, Bryan, and Neil Taylor, eds. *A Trick to Catch the Old One*. In *Five Plays*, by Thomas Middleton. Harmondsworth: Penguin Books, 1988.

Love, Harold. *Scribal Publication in Seventeenth–Century England*. Oxford: Clarendon Press, 1993.

Lower, Charles B. "Character Identification in the Theatre: Some Principles and Some Examples." In *Renaissance Papers, 1967* (Durham, N.C.: Southeastern Renaissance Conference, 1968), 57–68.

Macdonald, Hugh. *John Dryden: A Bibliography of Early Editions and Drydeniana*. Oxford: Clarendon Press, 1939.

MacLean, Sally–Beth. "Tour Routes: 'Provincial Wanderings' or Traditional Circuits?" *MaRDiE* 6 (1993): 1–14.

Maguire, Laurie E. *Shakespearean Suspect Texts: The "Bad" Quartos and their Contexts*. Cambridge: Cambridge University Press, 1996.

Mahood, M. M. *Bit Parts in Shakespeare's Plays*. Cambridge: Cambridge University Press, 1992.

———, ed. *The Merchant of Venice*. Cambridge: Cambridge University Press, 1987.

Malone, Edmond. *Supplement to the Edition of Shakespeare's Plays Published in 1778*. 2 vols. London, 1780.

———, ed. *The Plays and Poems of William Shakespeare*. 1790.

Marcus, Leah S. "The Milieu of Milton's *Comus:* Judicial Reform at Ludlow and the Problem of Sexual Assault." *Criticism* 25 (1983): 293–327.

Marienstras, Richard. *New Perspectives on the Shakespearean World*. Cambridge: Cambridge University Press, 1981.

Marotti, Arthur F. "The Transmission of Lyric Poetry and the Institutionalizing of Literature in the English Renaissance." In *Contending Kingdoms: Historical, Psychological, and Feminist Approaches to the Literature of Sixteenth–Century England and France*, edited by Marie–Rose Logan and Peter L. Rudnytsky, 21–41. Detroit: Wayne State University Press, 1992.

Marston, John. *The Insatiate Countess*. 1613.

———. *The Insatiate Countess*. Edited by Giorgio Melchiori. Manchester: Manchester University Press, 1984.

———. *The Insatiate Countess: A Tragicomedy*. London, 1820.

———. *The Metamorphosis of Pigmalion's Image*. 1598. Reprinted in 1613 as *Alicia: Philoparthens loving Folly*.

———. *The Workes of Mr. J. Marston*. London, 1633.

Martin, R. W. F. "A Catholic Oldcastle." *N&Q*, n.s., 40 (1993): 185–86.

McElwee, William. *The Murder of Sir Thomas Overbury*. London: Faber & Faber, 1952.

McGann, Jerome J. *A Critique of Modern Textual Criticism*. Chicago: University of Chicago Press, 1983.

———. *Social Values and Poetic Acts: The Historical Judgment of Literary Work*. Cambridge: Harvard University Press, 1988.

———. *The Textual Condition*. Princeton: Princeton University Press, 1991.

McKeen, David. *A Memory of Honour: The Life of William Brooke, Lord Cobham*. 2 vols. Salzburg, Austria: Universität Salzburg, 1986.

McKenzie, D. F. *Stationers' Company Apprentices, 1605–40*. Charlottesville: Bibliographical Society of the University of Virginia, 1961.

McKerrow, R. B., ed. *A Dictionary of Printers and Booksellers in England, Scotland, and Ireland, and of Foreign Printers of English Books, 1557–1640*. London: Bibliographical Society, 1968.

McLeod, Randall [Random Cloud, pseud.]. "The Marriage of Good and Bad Quartos." *SQ* 33 (1982): 421–31.

———. "UnEditing Shakspeare." *Sub-Stance* 33/4 (1982): 28–55.

———. "'The very names of the Persons': Editing and the Invention of Dramatick Character." In *Staging the Renaissance,* edited by David Scott Kastan and Peter Stallybrass. New York and London: Routledge, 1991.

McMillin, Scott. "Casting the *Hamlet* Quartos: The Limit of Eleven." In *The "Hamlet" First Published (Q1 1603),* edited by Thomas Clayton, 179–94. Newark: University of Delaware Press, 1992.

Merriam, Thomas V. N. "Modelling a Canon: A Stylometric Examination of Shakespeare's First Folio." Ph.D. diss., University of London,1992.

Miller, Stephen R. "A Critical, Old–spelling Edition of *The Taming of a Shrew,* 1594." Ph.D. diss., University of London, 1993.

Miner, Earl, and Vinton A. Dearing, eds. *The Works of John Dryden.* Vol. 3. Berkeley and Los Angeles: University of California Press, 1969.

Moore, Miriam. "Circumscribing the East: Cartography and the Body in *Othello.*" Paper, Shakespeare Association of America meeting, 1994.

Morris, G. C. R. "Dryden, Hobbs, Tonson and the Death of Charles II." *N&Q* 220 (1975): 558–59.

Mowat, Barbara A. "The Form of *Hamlet*'s Fortunes." *RD,* n.s., 19 (1989): 97–126.

———. "Nicholas Rowe and the Twentieth–Century Shakespeare Text." In *Shakespeare and Cultural Traditions: The Selected Proceedings of the International Shakespeare Association World Congress, Tokyo, 1991,* edited by Tetsuo Kishi, Roger Pringle, and Stanley Wells, 314–22. Newark: University of Delaware Press, 1994.

Mowat, Barbara A., and Paul Werstine, eds. *The Taming of the Shrew.* New York: Simon and Schuster, 1992.

Mukherjee, Sujit Kumar. "The Text of Greene's *Orlando Furioso.*" *Indian Journal of English Studies* 6 (1965): 102–7.

Murray, J. T. *English Dramatic Companies, 1558–1642.* 2 vols. London: Constable, 1910.

Nashe, Thomas. *Christ's Tears Over Jerusalem.* 1594. Reprint, 1613.

Neale, J. E. *Elizabeth I and her Parliaments, 1584–1601.* New York: Norton, 1966.

Negt, Oskar, and Alexander Kluge. *Geschichte und Eigensinn.* Frankfurt: Zeitausendeins, 1981.

Neill, Michael. "Unproper Beds: Race, Adultery, and the Hideous in *Othello.*" *SQ* 40 (1989): 383–412.

Newman, Karen. "'And wash the Ethiop white': Femininity and the Monstrous in *Othello.*" In *Shakespeare Reproduced: The Text in History and Ideology,* edited by Jean E. Howard and Marion F. O'Connor, 143–62. New York: Methuen, 1987.

Nietzsche, F. *The Birth of Tragedy and The Genealogy of Morals.* Translated by Francis Goffing. Garden City, N.Y.: Anchor, 1956.

Norbrook, David. "*Macbeth* and the Politics of Historiography." In *Politics of Discourse,* edited by Kevin Sharpe and Steven Zwicker, 78–116. Berkeley: University of California Press, 1987.

Nosworthy, J. M. "*Macbeth, Doctor Faustus,* and the Juggling Fiends." In *Mirror up to Shakespeare: Essays in Honour of G. R. Hibbard,* edited by J. C. Gray, 208–22. Toronto: University of Toronto Press, 1984.

O'Connor, Marion. *William Poel and the Elizabethan Stage Society.* London: Chadwick–Healey and the Consortium for Drama and Media in Higher Education, 1987.

———, ed. *The Witch.* In *Collected Middleton.* Oxford: Oxford University Press, forthcoming.

Orgel, Stephen. "Prospero's Wife." In *Rewriting the Renaissance: The Discourses of Sexual Difference in Early Modern Europe,* edited by Margaret W. Ferguson, Maureen Quilligan, and Nancy J. Vickers, 50–64. Chicago: University of Chicago Press, 1986.

———. "What is a Text?" In *Staging the Renaissance,* edited by David Scott Kastan and Peter Stallybrass, 83–87. New York and London: Routledge, 1991.

———, ed. *The Tempest.* Oxford: Oxford University Press, 1987.

Osborne, Francis. *The True Tragicomedy Formerly Acted at Court.* Transcribed from the manuscript in the British Library by John Pitcher and Lois Potter and edited by Lois Potter. New York: Garland, 1983.

Osborne, Laurie E.. "Editing Frailty in *Twelfth Night:* 'Where lies your Text?'" In *Reading Readings: Essays on Shakespeare Editing in the Eighteenth Century,* edited by Joanna Gondris. Rutherford, N.J.: Fairleigh Dickinson University, forthcoming.

Overbury, Thomas. *The Wife, Now the Widow.* 1614.

Palmer, Thomas. "Master John Fletcher his dramaticall Workes now at last printed." In *Comedies and Tragedies, written by Francis Beaumont and John Fletcher, Gentlemen,* sig. f2v. London, 1647.

Parker, R. B. "Middleton's Experiments with Comedy and Judgement." In *Jacobean Theatre,* 179–99. Stratford-upon-Avon Studies 1. London: Edward Arnold, 1960.

Parrot, Henry. *Laquei Ridiculosi; or, Springes for Woodcocks.* 1613.

Patrick, D. L. *The Textual History of "Richard III."* Stanford University Publications, Language and Literature 6, no. 1. Stanford, Calif.: Stanford University Press, 1936.

Partridge, Eric. *Shakespeare's Bawdy.* 3d ed. London: Routledge, 1968.

Patterson, Annabel. "'All Affections Set Apart': Sir John Oldcastle as Symbol of Reformation Historiography." Forthcoming.

———. *Censorship and Interpretation: The Conditions of Writing and Reading in Early Modern England.* Madison: University of Wisconsin Press, 1984.

Patterson, Lyman Ray. *Copyright in Historical Perspective.* Nashville, Tenn.: Vanderbilt University Press, 1968.

Peck, Linda Levy. *Northampton, Patronage and Policy at the Court of James I.* London: Allen & Unwin, 1982.

Peckham, Morse. "Reflections on the Foundations of Modern Textual Editing." *Proof* 1 (1971): 122–55.

Pendleton, Thomas A. "'This is not the man': On Calling Falstaff Falstaff." *Analytical and Enumerative Bibliography,* n.s., 4 (1990): 59–71.

Poel, William. "The First Quarto 'Hamlet.'" *The Athenaeum* 3776 (10 March 1900): 316.

Pollard, A. W. "New Fields in Bibliography." Reprinted in John Dover Wilson, "Alfred William Pollard," *PBA* 31 (1945): 381–409.

———. "Our Twenty–First Birthday." *Transactions of the Bibliographical Society* 13 (1913): 9–27.

———. Review of *Book Prices Current. The Library,* 2d ser., 9 (1908): 215–16.

———. *Shakespeare Folios and Quartos.* London: Methuen, 1909.

———. *Shakespeare's Fight with the Pirates.* 2d ed. Cambridge: Cambridge University Press, 1920.

————, ed. *Shakespeare's Hand in the Play of Sir Thomas More*. Cambridge: Cambridge University Press, 1923.

Pollard, A. W., and G. R. Redgrave. *A Short-Title Catalogue of Books Printed in England, Scotland, and Ireland, 1475–1640*. Enlarged by W. A. Jackson and F. S. Ferguson. Completed by K. Pantzer. 3 vols. London: The Bibliographical Society, 1976–91.

Pollard, A. W., and J. Dover Wilson. "The 'Stolne and Surreptitious' Shakespearian Texts." *TLS,* 9 and 16 January 1919, 18, 30.

Pope, Alexander, ed. *The Works of Shakespear*. London: Jacob Tonson, 1723–25.

Price, George R., ed. *Thomas Middleton: Michaelmas Term and A Trick to Catch the Old One*. The Hague: Mouton, 1976.

Quaife, G. R. *Wanton Wenches and Wayward Wives: Peasants and Illicit Sex in Early-Seventeenth-Century England*. New Brunswick, N.J.: Rutgers University Press, 1979.

Rhodes, R. Crompton. *Shakespeare's First Folio*. Oxford: Blackwell, 1923.

Richardson, H. G. *Bracton: The Problem of His Text*. London: Bernard Quaritch, 1965.

Roberts, Jeanne A. "'Wife' or 'Wise'—*The Tempest* 1.1786." *SB* 31 (1978): 203–5.

Robinson, Arthur H., and Barbara Bartz Retchenik. *The Nature of Maps*. Chicago: University of Chicago Press, 1976.

Rose, Mark. *Authors and Owners: The Invention of Copyright*. Cambridge: Harvard University Press, 1993.

Rose, Mary Beth. *Women in the Middle Ages and the Renaissance*. Syracuse, N.Y.: Syracuse University Press, 1986.

Rosenberg, Marvin. "The First Modern English Staging of *Hamlet* Q1." In *The "Hamlet" First Published (Q1 1603)*, edited by Thomas Clayton, 241–48. Newark: University of Delaware Press, 1992.

Rossiter, A. P., ed. *Woodstock: A Moral History*. London: Chatto and Windus, 1946.

Rowe, Nicholas, ed. *The Works of Mr. William Shakespear*. London: J. Tonson, 1709.

Sams, Eric. "Oldcastle and the Oxford Shakespeare." *N&Q*, n.s., 40 (1993): 180–85.

Schäfer, Jürgen. "The Orthography of Proper Names in Modern–spelling Editions of Shakespeare." *SB* 23 (1970): 1–19.

Schafer, Elizabeth, ed. *The Witch*. London: W. W. Norton, 1994.

Schoenbaum, Samuel. *William Shakespeare: A Documentary Life*. Oxford: Oxford University Press, 1975.

Scoufus, Alice–Lyle. *Shakespeare's Typological Satire: A Study of the Falstaff–Oldcastle Problem*. Athens: University of Ohio Press, 1978.

Scragg, Leah. "Macbeth on Horseback." *Shakespeare Survey* 26 (1973): 81–88.

Seronsy, C. C. "'Supposes' as the Unifying Theme in *The Shrew*." *SQ* 14 (1963): 15–30.

Shakespeare, William. *As You Like It*. Edited by Alan Brissenden. Oxford: Clarendon Press, 1993.

————. *The Comedy of Errors*. Edited by R. A. Foakes. London: Methuen, 1962.

————. *Coriolanus*. Edited by R. B. Parker. Oxford: Clarendon Press, 1984.

————. *Henry VIII*. Edited by R. A. Foakes. London: Methuen, 1957.

————. *Macbeth*.Edited by A. W. Verity. Cambridge: Cambridge University Press, 1902.

————. *Macbeth*. Edited by Kenneth Muir. Rev. ed. London: Methuen, 1984.

————. *The Merchant of Venice*. Edited by John Russell Brown. 1955. Reprint, London: Methuen, 1961.

————. *The Merchant of Venice*. Edited by M. M. Mahood. Cambridge: Cambridge University Press, 1987.

————. *Othello*. Edited by Alice Walker and John Dover Wilson. Cambridge: Cambridge University Press, 1957.

————. *Othello*. Edited by Horace Howard Furness. Philadelphia: J. B. Lippincott, 1886.

————. *Othello*. Edited by M. R. Ridley. London: Methuen, 1958.

————. *Othello*. Edited by Norman Sanders. Cambridge: Cambridge University Press, 1984.

————. *Plays and Poems of William Shakespeare*. Edited by Edmond Malone. 1790.

————. *Romeo and Juliet*. Edited by Brian Gibbons. London: Methuen, 1980.

————. *The Taming of the Shrew*. Edited by Ann Thompson. Cambridge: Cambridge University Press, 1984.

————. *The Taming of the Shrew*. Edited by Arthur Quiller-Couch and John Dover Wilson. 1928. Reprint, Cambridge: Cambridge University Press, 1953.

————. *The Taming of the Shrew*. Edited by Brian Morris. London: Methuen, 1981.

————. *The Taming of the Shrew*. Edited by G. R. Hibbard. Harmondsworth: Penguin, 1968.

————. *The Taming of the Shrew*. Edited by H. J. Oliver. Oxford: Clarendon Press, 1982.

————. *The Taming of the Shrew*. Edited by Richard Hosley. Baltimore: Pelican, 1964.

————. *The Taming of the Shrew*. Edited by William J. Rolfe. New York: Harper and Brothers, 1897.

————. *The Tempest*. Edited by Stephen Orgel. Oxford: Oxford University Press, 1987.

Shapiro, Michael. *Children of the Revels: The Boy Companies of Shakespeare's Time and Their Plays*. New York: Columbia University Press, 1977.

Sharpham, Edward. *A Critical Old-Spelling Edition of the Works of Edward Sharpham*. Edited by Christopher Gordon Petter. The Renaissance Imagination, vol.18. New York: Garland, 1986.

Shawcross, John. "A Text of John Donne's Poems; Unsatisfactory Compromise." *John Donne Journal* 2 (1983): 1–19.

————, ed. *The Complete Poetry of John Donne*. New York and London: New York University Press, 1968.

Shirley, Rodney W. *The Mapping of the World: Early Printed World Maps, 1472–1700*. London: Holland Press, 1987.

Shrimpton, Nicholas. "Shakespeare Performances in London and Stratford–Upon–Avon, 1984–85." *Shakespeare Survey* 39 (1985): 191–98.

Sinfield, Alan. "*Macbeth:* History, Ideology, and Intellectuals." *Critical Quarterly* 28 (1986): 63–77.

Sisson, C. J. *New Readings in Shakespeare*. Vol. 2. Cambridge: Cambridge University Press, 1955.

Skura, Meredith. "'Thy curse is cause that guiltless Mariam dies': What is Doris's Curse Doing in Elizabeth Cary's *Mariam*?" Unpublished manuscript.

Smidt, Kristian. *Iniurious Impostors and "Richard III."* New York: Humanities Press, 1964.

Smith, Hilda L., and Susan Cardinale. *Women and the Literature of the Seventeenth Century*. Westport, Conn.: Greenwood Press, 1990.

Smith, Joshua Toulmin, and Lucy Toulmin Smith, eds. *English Gilds*. Early English Text Society, no. 40. London: Oxford University Press, 1870.

Snyder, Susan. "*Macbeth:* A Modern Perspective." In *Macbeth,* edited by Barbara A. Mowat and Paul Werstine, 197–207. New York: Washington Square Press, 1992.

———. "Naming Names in *All's Well that Ends Well.*" *SQ* 43 (1992): 265–79.

———. "*Othello:* A Modern Perspective." In *Othello,* edited by Barbara A. Mowat and Paul Werstine, 287–98. New York: Washington Square Press, 1993.

Somerset, Alan. "'How chances it they travel?': Provincial Touring, Playing Places, and the King's Men." *Shakespeare Survey* 47 (1994): 45–60.

Stallybrass, Peter. "Patriarchal Territories: The Body Enclosed." In *Rewriting the Renaissance: The Discourses of Sexual Difference in Early Modern Europe,* edited by Margaret W. Ferguson, Maureen Quilligan, and Nancy J. Vickers, 123–42. Chicago: University of Chicago Press, 1986.

The Statutes of the Realm. Vol. 2. 1816. Reprint, London: Dawsons, 1963.

Steen, Sara Jayne. "Behind the Arras: Editing Renaissance Women's Letters." In *New Ways of Looking at Old Texts,* ed. W. Speed Hill, 229–38. Binghamton, N.Y.: MRTS, 1993.

[Stephens, John.] *Cynthia's Revenge.* 1613.

Stone, Lawrence. *The Family, Sex, and Marriage in England, 1500–1800.* New York: Harper and Row, 1977.

Stow, John. *Annales of England.* 1592.

Strype, John. *Annals of the Reformation.* Oxford: Clarendon Press, 1824.

Styan, J. L. *The Elements of Drama.* Cambridge: Cambridge University Press, 1960.

T., P. "Observations on Shakespeare's Falstaff." *Gentleman's Magazine* 22 (October 1752), 459–61.

Tanner, J. R. *Tudor Constitutional Documents.* 1922. Reprint, Cambridge: Cambridge University Press, 1951.

Tanselle, G. Thomas. "The Editorial Problem of Final Authorial Intention." *SB* 32 (1979): 309–54.

———. "External Fact as an Editorial Problem." *SB* 32 (1979), 1–47.

———. "Historicism and Critical Editing." *SB* 39 (1986): 1–46.

———. *A Rationale of Textual Criticism.* Philadelphia: University of Pennsylvania Press, 1989.

Taylor, Gary. "The Fortunes of Oldcastle." *Shakespeare Survey* 38 (1985): 85–100.

———. "Proximities." Introduction to *Thomas Middleton and Early Modern Textual Culture.* Forthcoming.

———. *Reinventing Shakespeare.* New York: Weidenfeld & Nicolson, 1989.

———. "The Renaissance and the End of Editing." In *Palimpsest,* edited by George Bornstein and Ralph G. Williams, 121–49. Ann Arbor: University of Michigan Press, 1993.

———. "The Rhetoric of Textual Criticism." *TEXT* 4 (1988): 39–57.

———. "Textual and Sexual Criticism: A Crux in *The Comedy of Errors.*" *RD* 19 (1988): 195–225.

———. "William Shakespeare, Richard James and the House of Cobham." *RES,* n.s., 38 (1987): 334–54.

Taylor, Gary, and John Jowett. *Shakespeare Reshaped: 1606–1623.* Oxford: Clarendon Press, 1993.

Taylor, Gary, and Michael Warren, eds. *The Division of the Kingdoms.* Oxford: Oxford University Press, 1983.

Thaler, Alwin. "The Travelling Players in Shakspere's England." *Modern Philology* 17 (1920): 129–46.

Theobald, Lewis, ed. *The Works of Shakespeare.* 1733.

Thompson, Ann, and Sasha Roberts, eds. *Women Reading Shakespeare.* Manchester: Manchester University Press, 1997.

Thorne, Samuel E., trans. *Bracton on the Laws and Customs of England.* Vol. 2. Cambridge: Belknap Press of Harvard University Press, 1968.

Thorpe, James. "The Aesthetics of Textual Criticism." *PMLA* 80 (1965): 465–82.

Tilney, Edward. *The Flower of Friendship: A Renaissance Dialogue Contesting Marriage.* Edited by Valerie Wayne. Ithaca: Cornell University Press, 1992.

Tilney-Bassett, J. G. "Edmund Tilney's *The Flower of Friendshippe.*" *The Library,* 4th ser., 26 (1946): 175–81.

Tolman, Alfred. "Shakespeare's Part in *The Taming of the Shrew.*" *PMLA* 5 (1890): 201–78.

Tricomi, Albert H. *Anticourt Drama in England, 1603–42.* Charlottesville: University Press of Virginia, 1989.

A True and Historical Relation of the Poysoning of Sir Thomas Overbury. 1651.

Ure, Peter. "A Pointer to the Date of Ford's Perkin Warbeck." *N&Q* 215 (1970): 215–17.

Urkowitz, Steven. "'Well–sayd olde Mole': Burying Three *Hamlet*s in Modern Editions." In *Shakespeare Study Today: The Horace Howard Furness Memorial Lectures 1982,* edited by Georgianna Ziegler, 37–70. New York: AMS Press, 1986.

van Dam, B. A. P. "Alleyn's Player's Part of Greene's *Orlando Furioso,* and the Text of Q of 1594." *English Studies* 11 (1929): 182–203, 209–20.

———. *"The Taming of the Shrew."* *English Studies* 10 (1928): 97–106.

Vickers, Brian. "Hamlet by Dogberry." *TLS,* 24 December 1993, 5–6.

Warburton, William. *The Works of Shakespear.* 8 vols. 1747.

Ward, A. W., and A. R. Waller, eds. *Cambridge History of English Literature.* Vol. 5. Cambridge: Cambridge University Press, 1918.

Waugh, W. T. "Sir John Oldcastle." *English Historical Review* 20 (1905): 434–56, 637–58.

Webster, John. *The White Devil.* 1612.

———. *The White Devil.* Edited by John Russell Brown. 2d ed. London: Methuen, 1966.

Weller, Barry, and Margaret W. Ferguson, eds. *The Tragedy of Mariam, The Fair Queen of Jewry* with *The Lady Falkland: Her Life by One of her Daughters.* Berkeley: University of California Press, 1994.

Wells, Stanley. *Editing Shakespeare for the Modern Reader.* Oxford: Oxford University Press, 1984.

———. "Revision in Shakespeare's Plays." In *Editing and Editors: A Retrospect,* edited by Richard Landon, 67–79. New York: AMS Press, 1988.

Wells, Stanley, and Gary Taylor. *Modernizing Shakespeare's Spelling (with Three Studies in the Text of "Henry V").* Oxford: Clarendon Press, 1979.

Wells, Stanley, and Gary Taylor, with John Jowett, and William Montgomery. *William Shakespeare: A Textual Companion.* Oxford: Clarendon Press, 1987.

Wells, Stanley, and Gary Taylor, with John Jowett, and William Montgomery, eds. *William Shakespeare: The Complete Works.* Oxford: Clarendon Press, 1986 [Modern Spelling]; 1988 ["Original" Spelling].

Werstine, Paul. "'Foul Papers' and 'Prompt–books': Printer's Copy of Shakespeare's *Comedy of Errors.*" *SB* 41 (1988): 232–46.

———. "McKerrow's 'Suggestion' and Twentieth–Century Shakespeare Textual Criticism." *RD*, n.s., 19 (1989): 149–73.

———. "Narratives about Printed Shakespeare Texts: 'Foul Papers' and 'Bad' Quartos." *SQ* 41 (1990): 65–86.

———. "The Textual Mystery of Hamlet." *SQ* 39 (1988): 1–26.

White, Beatrice. *Cast of Ravens: The Strange Case of Sir Thomas Overbury.* London: Murray, 1965.

Williams, George Walton, "On Editing Shakespeare: *Annus Mirabilis.*" *Medieval and Renaissance Studies* 5 (1971): 61–79.

———, ed. *The Changeling.* Lincoln: University of Nebraska Press, 1966.

Williams, George Walton, and G. Blakemore Evans, eds. *The History of King Henry the Fourth, as revised by Sir Edward Dering.* Charlottesville: University Press of Virginia, 1974.

Willis, James. *Latin Textual Criticism.* Urbana: University of Illinois Press, 1972.

Wilson, F. P. *Shakespeare and the New Bibliography.* Revised and edited by Helen Gardner. Oxford: Clarendon Press, 1970.

———. "Shakespeare and the New Bibliography." In *The Bibliographical Society, 1892–1942,* edited by F. C. Francis, 76–135. London: The Bibliographical Society, 1945.

Wilson, John Dover. "Alfred William Pollard." *PBA* 31 (1945): 257–306.

———. "The Origin and Development of Shakespeare's *Henry IV.*" *The Library,* 4th ser., 26 (1945–46): 1–16.

———, ed. *The Merchant of Venice.* Cambridge University Press, 1926.

Wither, George. *Abuses Stript and Whipt.* London, 1613.

Wolf, Edwin, II, with John F. Fleming. *Rosenbach: A Biography.* Cleveland and New York: World Publishing, 1960.

Woolf, D. R. *The Idea of History in Early Stuart England.* Toronto: University of Toronto Press, 1990.

Contributors

THOMAS L. BERGER teaches at St. Lawrence University. He has prepared facsimile editions of the first quartos of *2 Henry IV* and *A Midsummer Night's Dream* for the Malone Society and edited (with Suzanne Gossett) academic plays of the early seventeenth century for the Society. He is co-editing (with George W. Williams) *Henry V* for the New Variorum Shakespeare.

A. R. BRAUNMULLER teaches early modern British and Continental drama at the University of California, Los Angeles. He is associate general editor of the New Cambridge Shakespeare, in which series he has published an edition of *Macbeth;* he is currently editing *Measure for Measure* for the Arden Shakespeare.

RALPH ALAN COHEN is professor of English at James Madison University and executive director of the Shenandoah Shakespeare Express. His productions of Shakespeare's plays have appeared in Canada, the U.K., France, Germany, and throughout the United States. He has published articles on Ben Jonson and on the staging and teaching of Shakespeare's works and has served as guest editor for two *Shakespeare Quarterly* special issues on teaching.

TOM DAVIS teaches bibliography and paleography at the University of Birmingham (U.K.). He has edited Goldsmith and written on the theory of textual criticism, but his main interest is forensic handwriting identification.

DAVID SCOTT KASTAN is professor of English and comparative literature at Columbia University. He is the author of *Shakespeare and the Shapes of Time,* editor (with Peter Stallybrass) of *Staging the Renaissance,* and, most recently, editor (with John Cox) of *A New History of Early English Drama.*

He is also a general editor of the Arden Shakespeare and is preparing *1 Henry IV* for that series.

JOSEPH LOEWENSTEIN is an associate professor at Washington University. He is currently completing a book on the ownership of ideas in the English Renaissance, to be entitled *The Authorial Response.*

CHUCK LOWER has taught at the University of Georgia since 1964, currently with a Sandy Beaver teaching professorship. He continues to explore problems involving stage directions, with special attention to *Romeo and Juliet, Coriolanus,* and *Antony and Cleopatra.*

LAURIE MAGUIRE is associate professor at the University of Ottawa. She is the author of *Shakespearean Suspect Texts* and several articles on early modern English drama.

STEPHEN MILLER works in the Archives Office at King's College, University of London. He has edited *The Taming of a Shrew* for the Malone Society reprints and for Cambridge University Press.

BARBARA MOWAT is director of academic programs at the Folger Shakespeare Library and coeditor, with Paul Werstine, of the New Folger edition of Shakespeare. Now senior editor of *Shakespeare Quarterly,* she served as editor of that journal from 1985 to 1998. She has written widely on Shakespeare and editing.

RICHARD PROUDFOOT is professor of English literature at King's College London, where he has taught since 1966. He is general editor of the Arden Shakespeare and from 1971 to 1983 was general editor of the Malone Society, for which he edited *A Knack to Know a Knave, Tom o' Lincoln,* and other texts. He has published articles in *Shakespeare Survey, Essays and Studies, The Library,* and other periodicals.

JEANNE ROBERTS is the author of *The Shakespearean Wild: Geography, Genus, and Gender* and of "Margaret Cavendish Plays with Shakespeare," forthcoming in *Renaissance Papers 1997.*

MICHAEL WARREN is professor of English literature at the University of California, Santa Cruz. He has published *The Division of the Kingdoms: Shakespeare's Two Versions of "King Lear"* (coedited with Gary Taylor), *The Complete "King Lear," 1608–1623* and *The Parallel "King Lear," 1608–1623,* and numerous articles on the texts of English drama.

VALERIE WAYNE is professor of English at the University of Hawaii at Manoa. She has edited a collection of essays called *The Matter of Difference: Materialist Feminist Criticism of Shakespeare* (1991), an old-spelling edition of Edmund Tilney's *The Flower of Friendship: A Renaissance Dialogue Contesting Marriage* (1992), and Thomas Middleton's *A Trick to Catch the Old One* in *The Collected Works of Thomas Middleton,* for which she is an associate general editor. Her work in progress includes a cultural edition of *The Winter's Tale* in the Bedford Shakespeare series and an edition of *Cymbeline* for the Arden Shakespeare, third series.

PAUL WERSTINE is professor of English at King's College and the Graduate School of the University of Western Ontario. He has written widely about editorial issues and is editor, with Barbara Mowat, of the New Folger Shakespeare and general editor, with Richard Knowles, of the New Variorum Shakespeare, to which he is contributing an edition of *Romeo and Juliet.*

Index

302